# SHORTCAKE CAKE

STORY AND ART BY

## suu Morishita

8

# Characters

## 3F

### TEN

NEKO-CHIYA HIGH

**Calls her "Ugly"!** →

Protagonist. Ageha invites her to move into the boardinghouse. She has pluck and is as emotional as a rock, except when it comes to love...

### AGEHA

NEKO-CHIYA HIGH

Ten's childhood friend. She's never seen without makeup.

**Best friends** ↔

Now dating. ↓    He likes her. ↑

## 2F

**Did something happen in their past?** ↓

### RIKU

SHOGYO HIGH

First-year. Gives the impression of being a player. He lives in the boardinghouse, but he's from Nekochiya.

### CHIAKI

NEKO-CHIYA HIGH

First-year. He's a gorgeous guy who loves books. He's a bit spacey sometimes. He likes Ten.

### YUTO

NEKO-CHIYA HIGH

Second-year. He tutors Ten and the other first-years.

## M2F

### AOI

SHOGYO HIGH

Third-year. She's the oldest in the house and likes talking about relationships.

## 1F

### RAN

House mom. She's tough but kind. She likes cooking and cars.

WE'RE HERE!

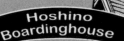

Hoshino Boardinghouse

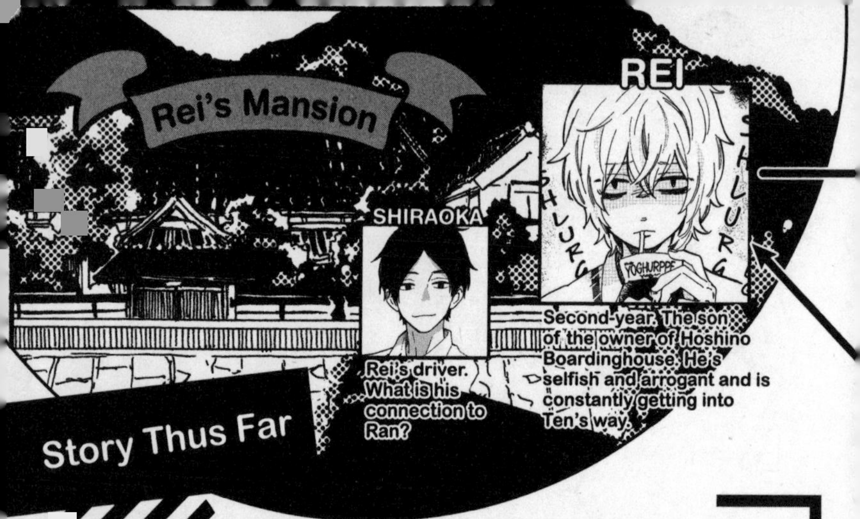
Rei's Mansion
REI
SHLURG
SHLURG
YOGHURPPE
Second-year. The son of the owner of Hoshino Boardinghouse. He's selfish and arrogant and is constantly getting into Ten's way.
SHIRAOKA
Rei's driver. What is his connection to Ran?

# Story Thus Far

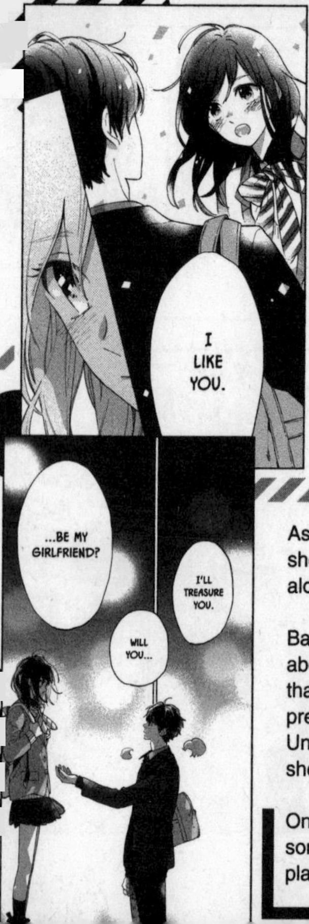
I LIKE YOU.
WILL YOU...
...BE MY GIRLFRIEND?
I'LL TREASURE YOU.

Ten was commuting two hours each way to school by bus until her friend Ageha invited her to move into the Hoshino Boardinghouse. The place is full of characters, and it's there that she meets Riku and Chiaki.

Early on Riku tells Ten that he likes her, but she doesn't take him seriously. She rejects him out of hand. It's only after they spend more time together that Ten realizes she has feelings for him.

With Chiaki's support, Ten tells Riku how she feels, but she stops him before he can respond in turn. Ten wants to work on herself first. She believes she owes that to Riku after having rejected him once before, and to Chiaki for his encouraging words.

As fall turns to winter, Ten tells Riku once more that she likes him. Riku replies that he has liked her all along. The two decide to start dating.

Back at the boardinghouse, Ran voices her concerns about their new relationship. Ten and Riku decide that when they're at the boardinghouse, it's best to pretend like nothing has changed between them. Unfortunately, Ten isn't adept at hiding secrets, and she struggles to act as before.

On Christmas Eve, the new couple decides to go somewhere on a real date, and Ten has a special place in mind...

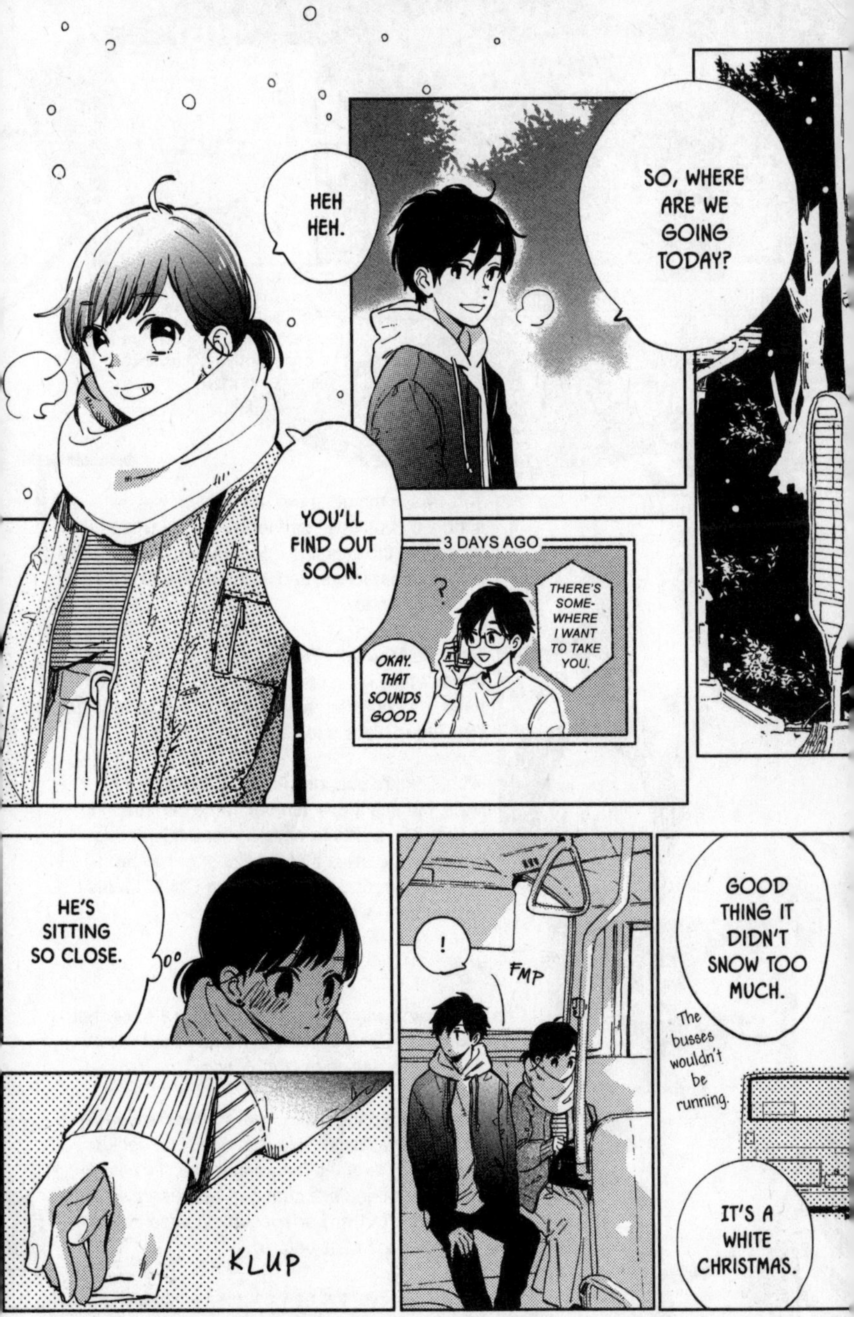
SO, WHERE ARE WE GOING TODAY?
HEH HEH.
YOU'LL FIND OUT SOON.
3 DAYS AGO
THERE'S SOME-WHERE I WANT TO TAKE YOU.
?
OKAY. THAT SOUNDS GOOD.
GOOD THING IT DIDN'T SNOW TOO MUCH.
The busses wouldn't be running.
IT'S A WHITE CHRISTMAS.
!
FMP
HE'S SITTING SO CLOSE.
KLUP

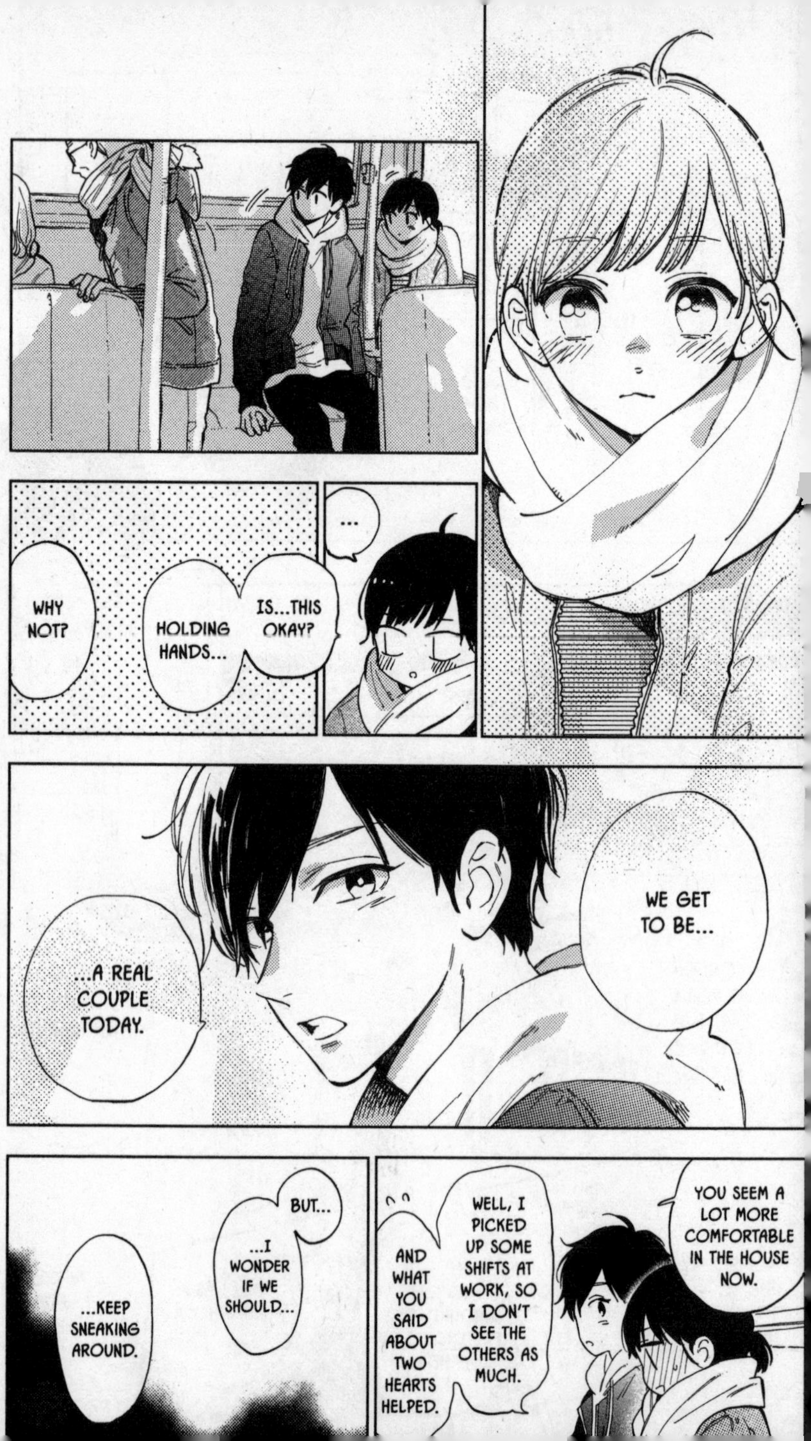
...
IS...THIS OKAY?
HOLDING HANDS...
WHY NOT?
WE GET TO BE...
...A REAL COUPLE TODAY.
YOU SEEM A LOT MORE COMFORTABLE IN THE HOUSE NOW.
WELL, I PICKED UP SOME SHIFTS AT WORK, SO I DON'T SEE THE OTHERS AS MUCH.
AND WHAT YOU SAID ABOUT TWO HEARTS HELPED.
BUT...
...I WONDER IF WE SHOULD...
...KEEP SNEAKING AROUND.

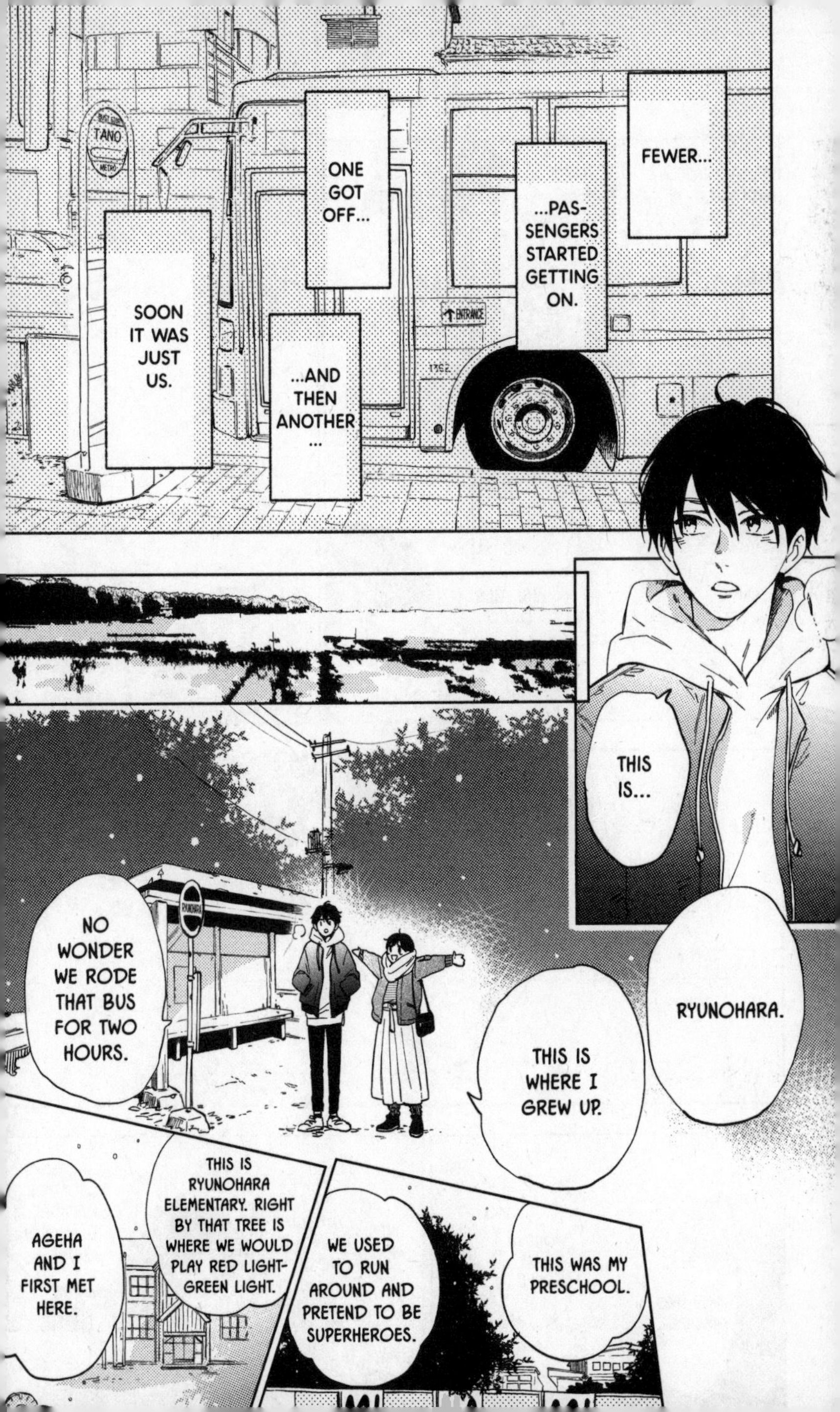
FEWER...
...PAS-SENGERS STARTED GETTING ON.
ONE GOT OFF...
...AND THEN ANOTHER...
TANO
SOON IT WAS JUST US.
THIS IS...
RYUNOHARA.
THIS IS WHERE I GREW UP.
NO WONDER WE RODE THAT BUS FOR TWO HOURS.
THIS WAS MY PRESCHOOL.
WE USED TO RUN AROUND AND PRETEND TO BE SUPERHEROES.
THIS IS RYUNOHARA ELEMENTARY. RIGHT BY THAT TREE IS WHERE WE WOULD PLAY RED LIGHT-GREEN LIGHT.
AGEHA AND I FIRST MET HERE.

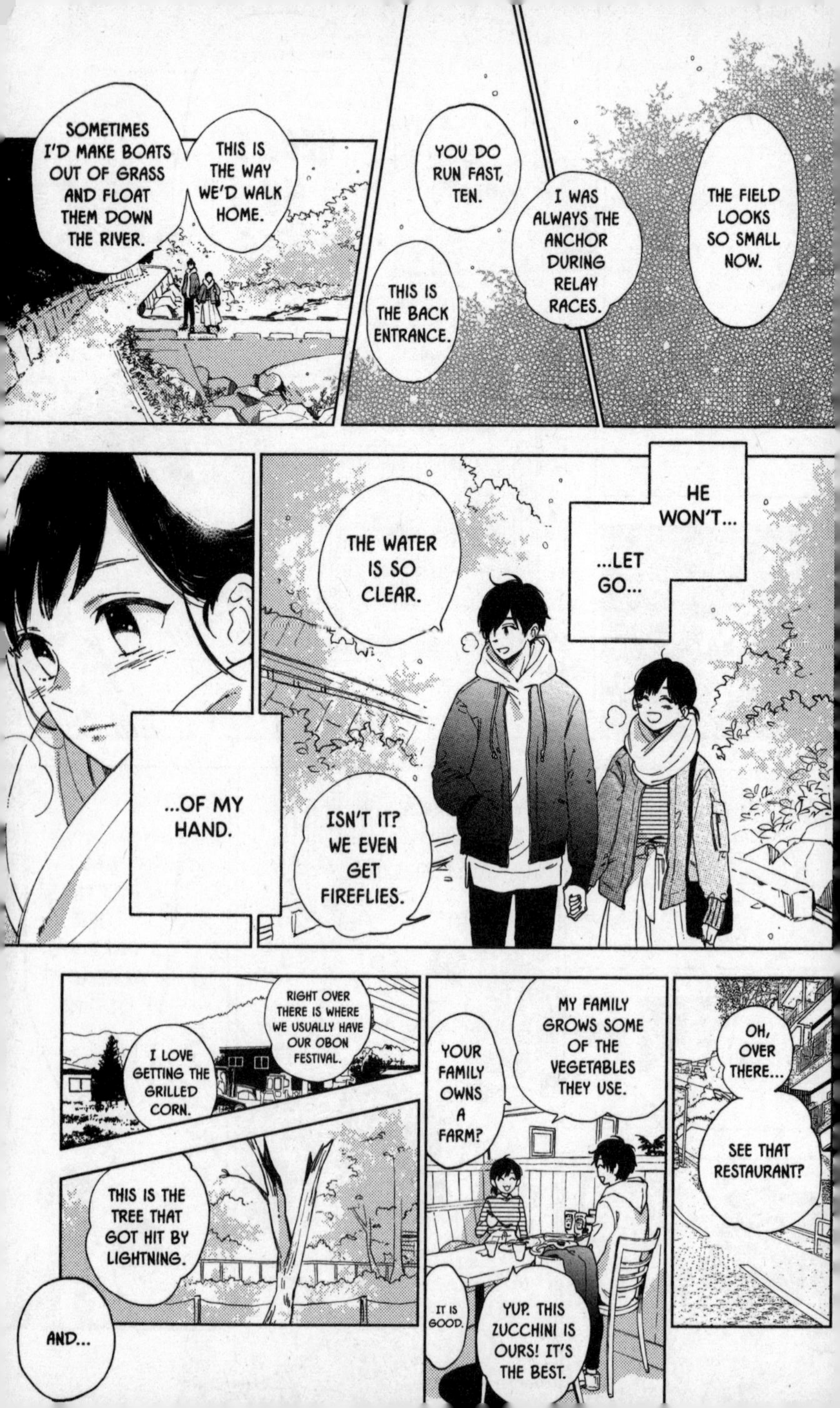
THE FIELD LOOKS SO SMALL NOW.
I WAS ALWAYS THE ANCHOR DURING RELAY RACES.
YOU DO RUN FAST, TEN.
THIS IS THE BACK ENTRANCE.
THIS IS THE WAY WE'D WALK HOME.
SOMETIMES I'D MAKE BOATS OUT OF GRASS AND FLOAT THEM DOWN THE RIVER.
HE WON'T...
...LET GO...
THE WATER IS SO CLEAR.
ISN'T IT? WE EVEN GET FIREFLIES.
...OF MY HAND.
OH, OVER THERE...
SEE THAT RESTAURANT?
MY FAMILY GROWS SOME OF THE VEGETABLES THEY USE.
YOUR FAMILY OWNS A FARM?
YUP. THIS ZUCCHINI IS OURS! IT'S THE BEST.
IT IS GOOD.
RIGHT OVER THERE IS WHERE WE USUALLY HAVE OUR OBON FESTIVAL.
I LOVE GETTING THE GRILLED CORN.
THIS IS THE TREE THAT GOT HIT BY LIGHTNING.
AND...

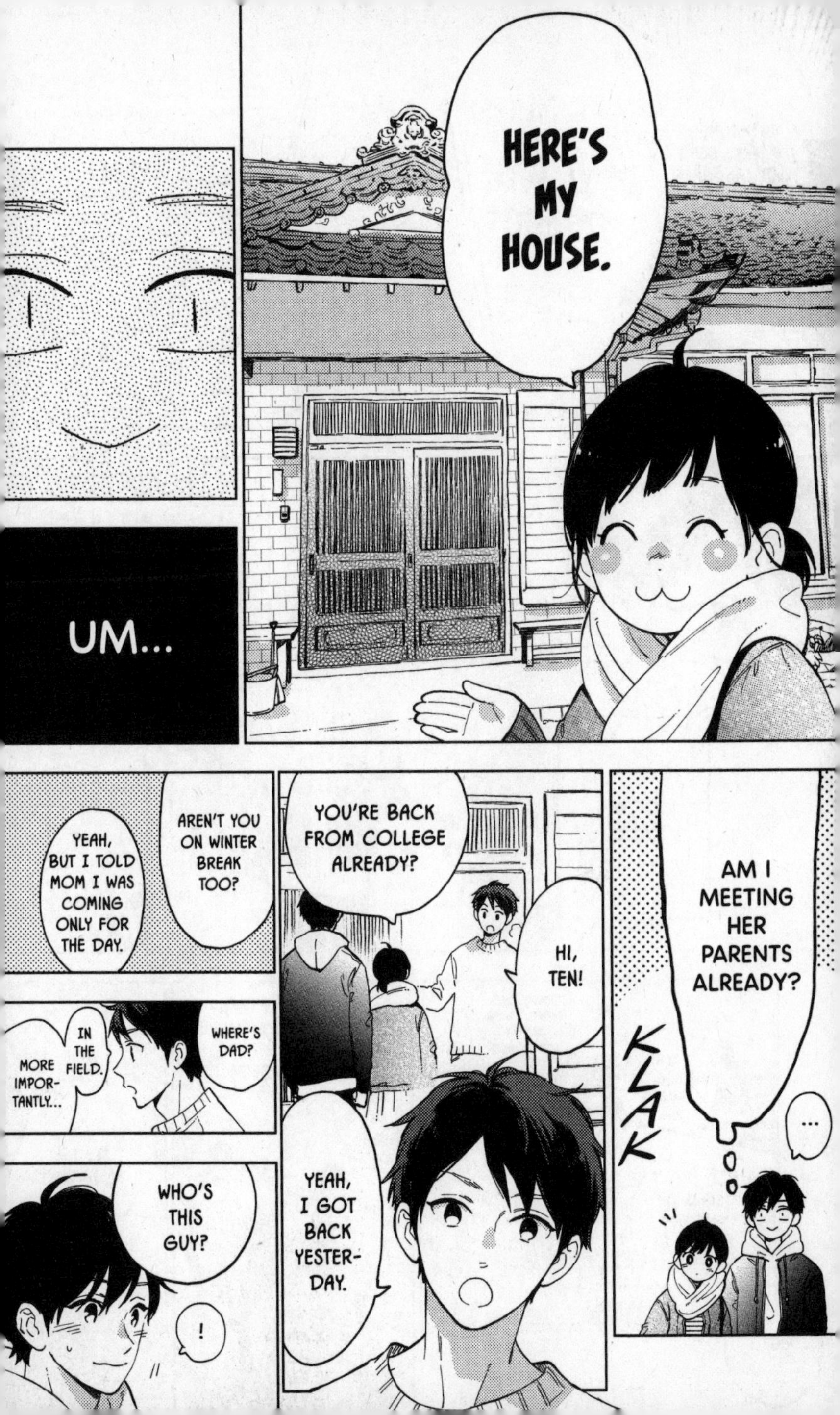
HERE'S MY HOUSE.
UM...
AM I MEETING HER PARENTS ALREADY?
KLAK
...
HI, TEN!
YOU'RE BACK FROM COLLEGE ALREADY?
YEAH, I GOT BACK YESTERDAY.
AREN'T YOU ON WINTER BREAK TOO?
YEAH, BUT I TOLD MOM I WAS COMING ONLY FOR THE DAY.
WHERE'S DAD?
IN THE FIELD.
MORE IMPORTANTLY...
WHO'S THIS GUY?
!

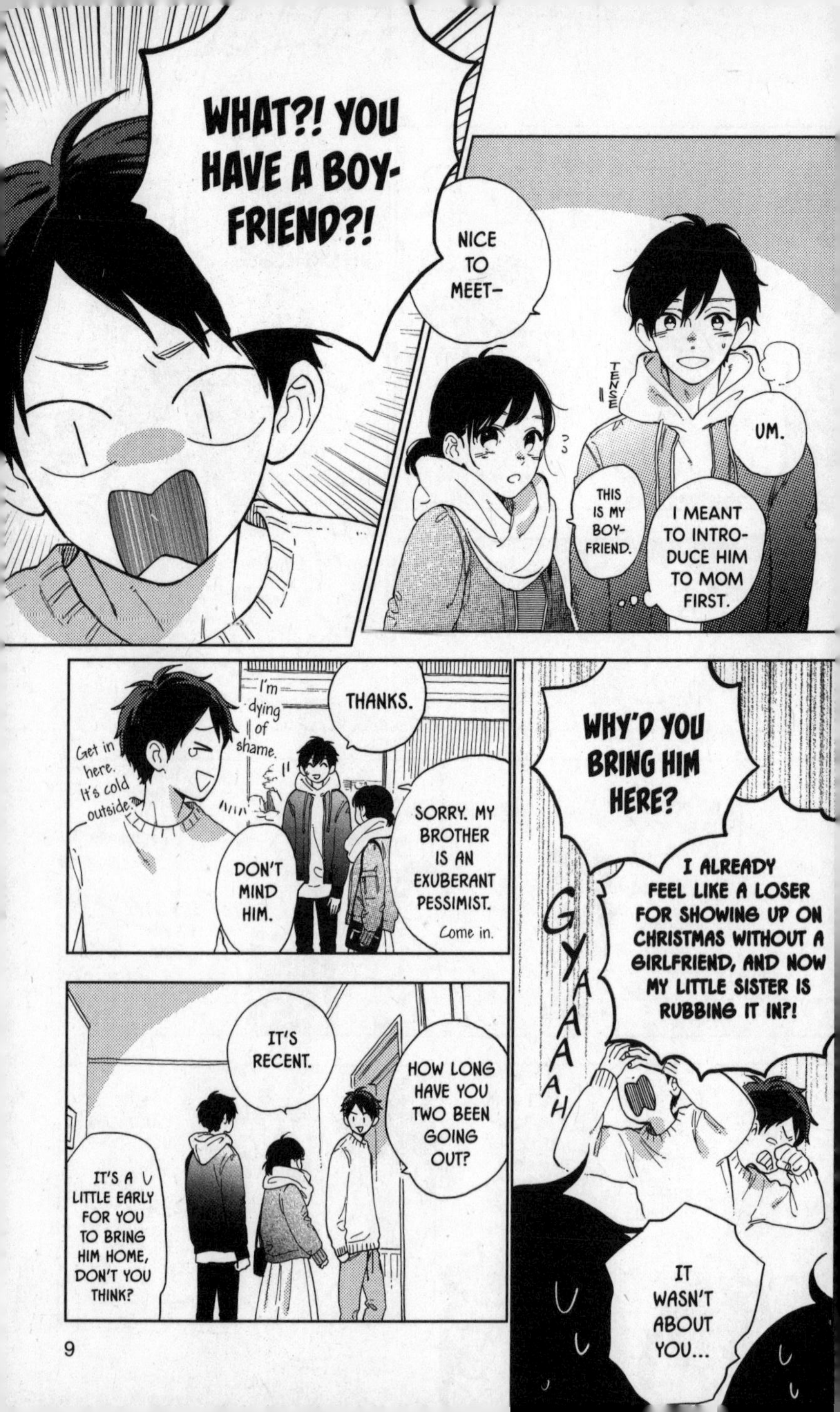
NICE TO MEET–
TENSE
UM.
I MEANT TO INTRODUCE HIM TO MOM FIRST.
THIS IS MY BOYFRIEND.
WHAT?! YOU HAVE A BOYFRIEND?!
WHY'D YOU BRING HIM HERE?
I ALREADY FEEL LIKE A LOSER FOR SHOWING UP ON CHRISTMAS WITHOUT A GIRLFRIEND, AND NOW MY LITTLE SISTER IS RUBBING IT IN?!
GYAAAAH
IT WASN'T ABOUT YOU...
THANKS.
I'm dying of shame.
SORRY. MY BROTHER IS AN EXUBERANT PESSIMIST.
Come in.
DON'T MIND HIM.
Get in here. It's cold outside.
HOW LONG HAVE YOU TWO BEEN GOING OUT?
IT'S RECENT.
IT'S A LITTLE EARLY FOR YOU TO BRING HIM HOME, DON'T YOU THINK?

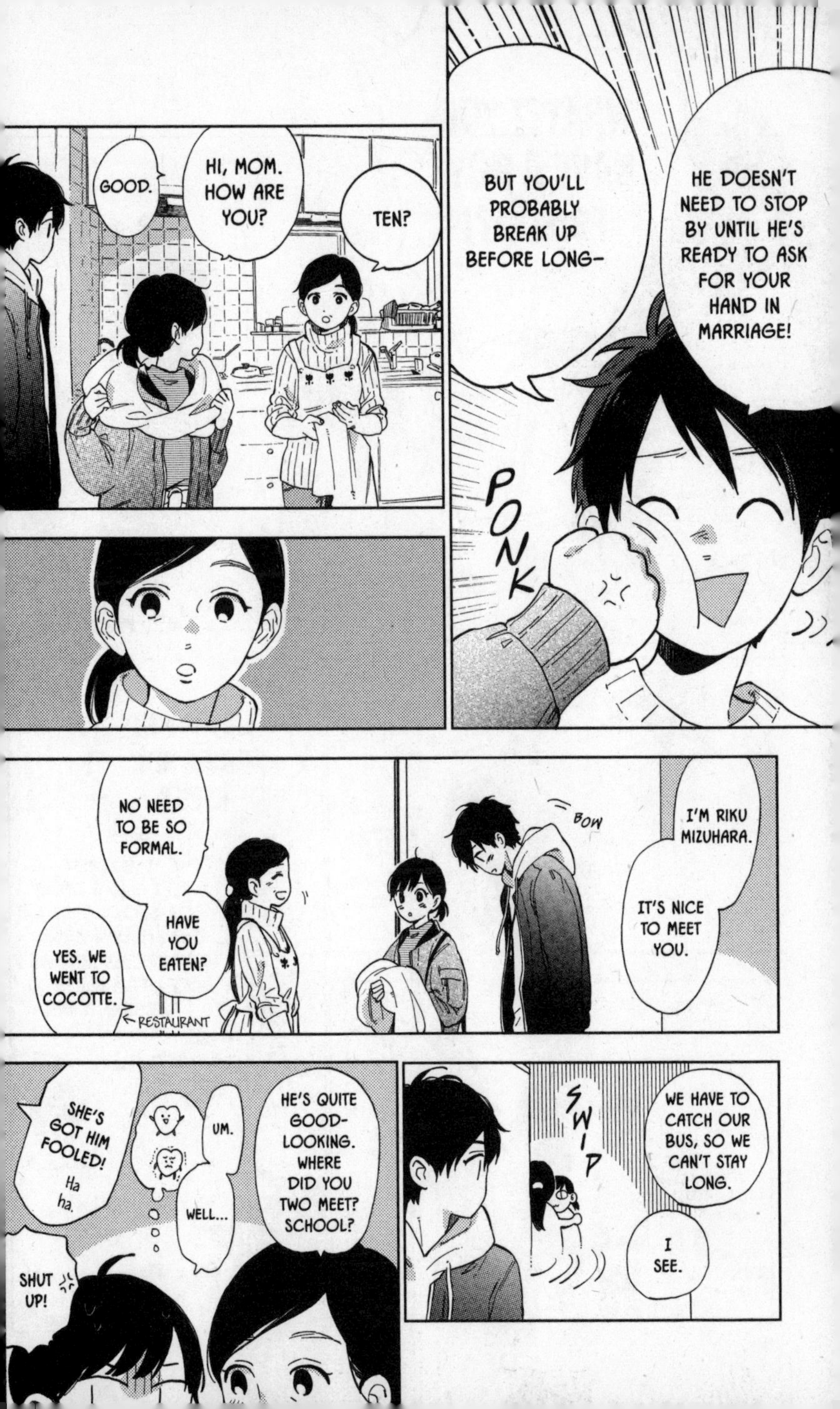
HE DOESN'T NEED TO STOP BY UNTIL HE'S READY TO ASK FOR YOUR HAND IN MARRIAGE!
BUT YOU'LL PROBABLY BREAK UP BEFORE LONG–
PONK
TEN?
HI, MOM. HOW ARE YOU?
GOOD.
BOW
I'M RIKU MIZUHARA.
IT'S NICE TO MEET YOU.
NO NEED TO BE SO FORMAL.
HAVE YOU EATEN?
YES. WE WENT TO COCOTTE.
← RESTAURANT
WE HAVE TO CATCH OUR BUS, SO WE CAN'T STAY LONG.
SWIP
I SEE.
HE'S QUITE GOOD-LOOKING. WHERE DID YOU TWO MEET? SCHOOL?
UM.
WELL...
SHE'S GOT HIM FOOLED!
Ha ha.
SHUT UP!

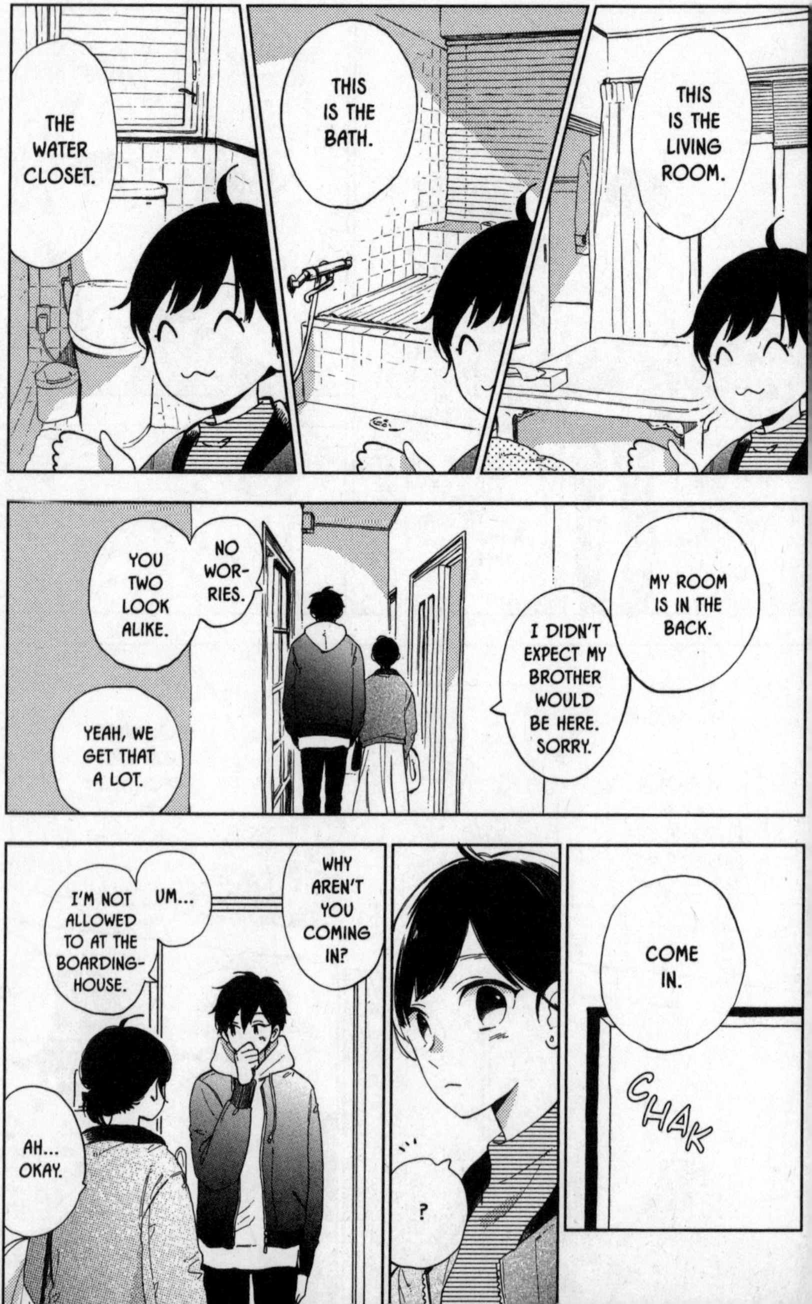
THIS IS THE LIVING ROOM.
THIS IS THE BATH.
THE WATER CLOSET.
MY ROOM IS IN THE BACK.
I DIDN'T EXPECT MY BROTHER WOULD BE HERE. SORRY.
NO WOR-RIES.
YOU TWO LOOK ALIKE.
YEAH, WE GET THAT A LOT.
COME IN.
CHAK
?
WHY AREN'T YOU COMING IN?
UM...
I'M NOT ALLOWED TO AT THE BOARDING-HOUSE.
AH... OKAY.

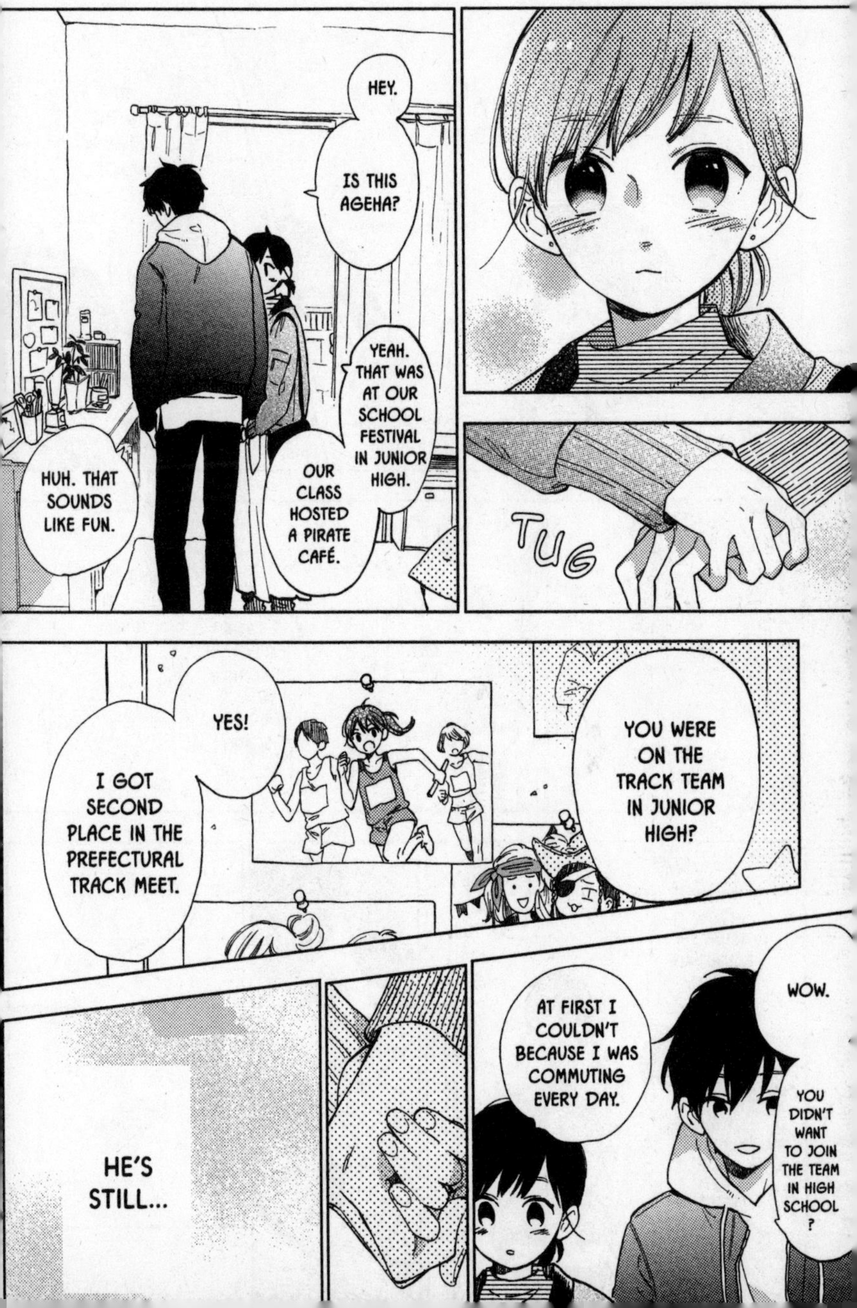
TUG
HEY.
IS THIS AGEHA?
YEAH. THAT WAS AT OUR SCHOOL FESTIVAL IN JUNIOR HIGH.
OUR CLASS HOSTED A PIRATE CAFÉ.
HUH. THAT SOUNDS LIKE FUN.
YOU WERE ON THE TRACK TEAM IN JUNIOR HIGH?
YES!
I GOT SECOND PLACE IN THE PREFECTURAL TRACK MEET.
WOW.
YOU DIDN'T WANT TO JOIN THE TEAM IN HIGH SCHOOL?
AT FIRST I COULDN'T BECAUSE I WAS COMMUTING EVERY DAY.
HE'S STILL...

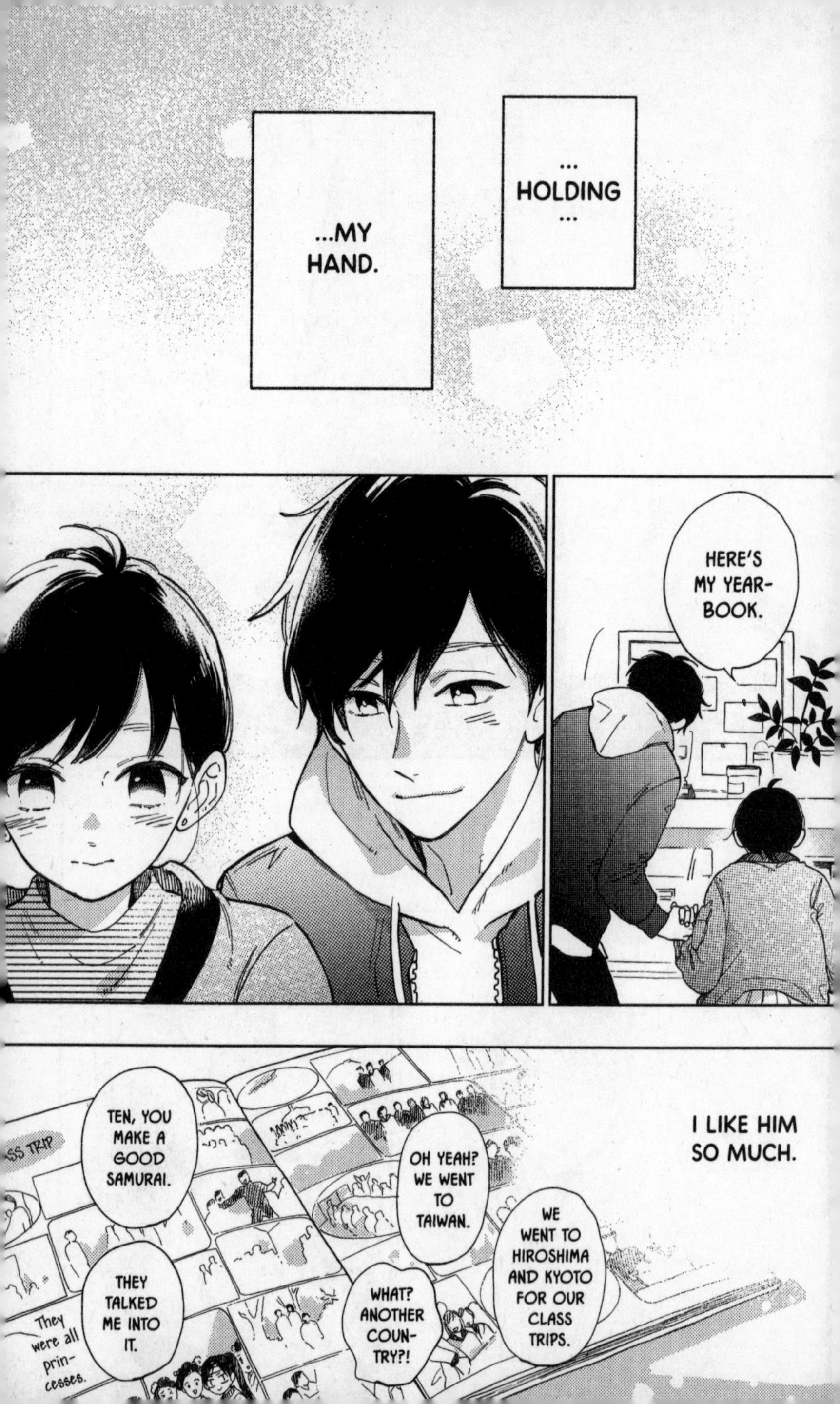
...
HOLDING
...
...MY HAND.
HERE'S MY YEAR-BOOK.
I LIKE HIM SO MUCH.
WE WENT TO HIROSHIMA AND KYOTO FOR OUR CLASS TRIPS.
OH YEAH? WE WENT TO TAIWAN.
WHAT? ANOTHER COUN-TRY?!
TEN, YOU MAKE A GOOD SAMURAI.
THEY TALKED ME INTO IT.
They were all prin-cesses.

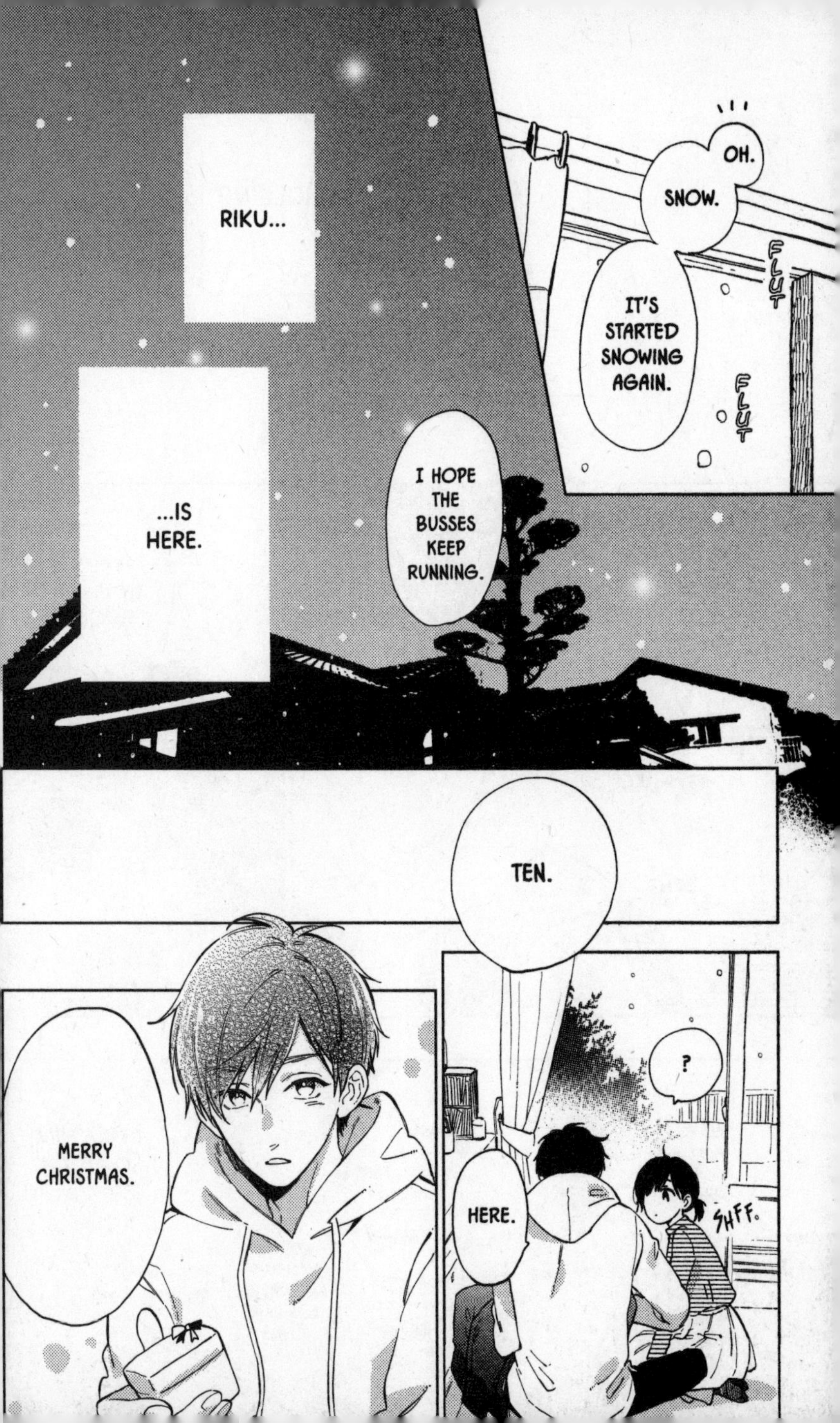
OH.
SNOW.
IT'S STARTED SNOWING AGAIN.
FLUT
FLUT
I HOPE THE BUSSES KEEP RUNNING.
RIKU...
...IS HERE.
TEN.
?
HERE.
SHFF.
MERRY CHRISTMAS.

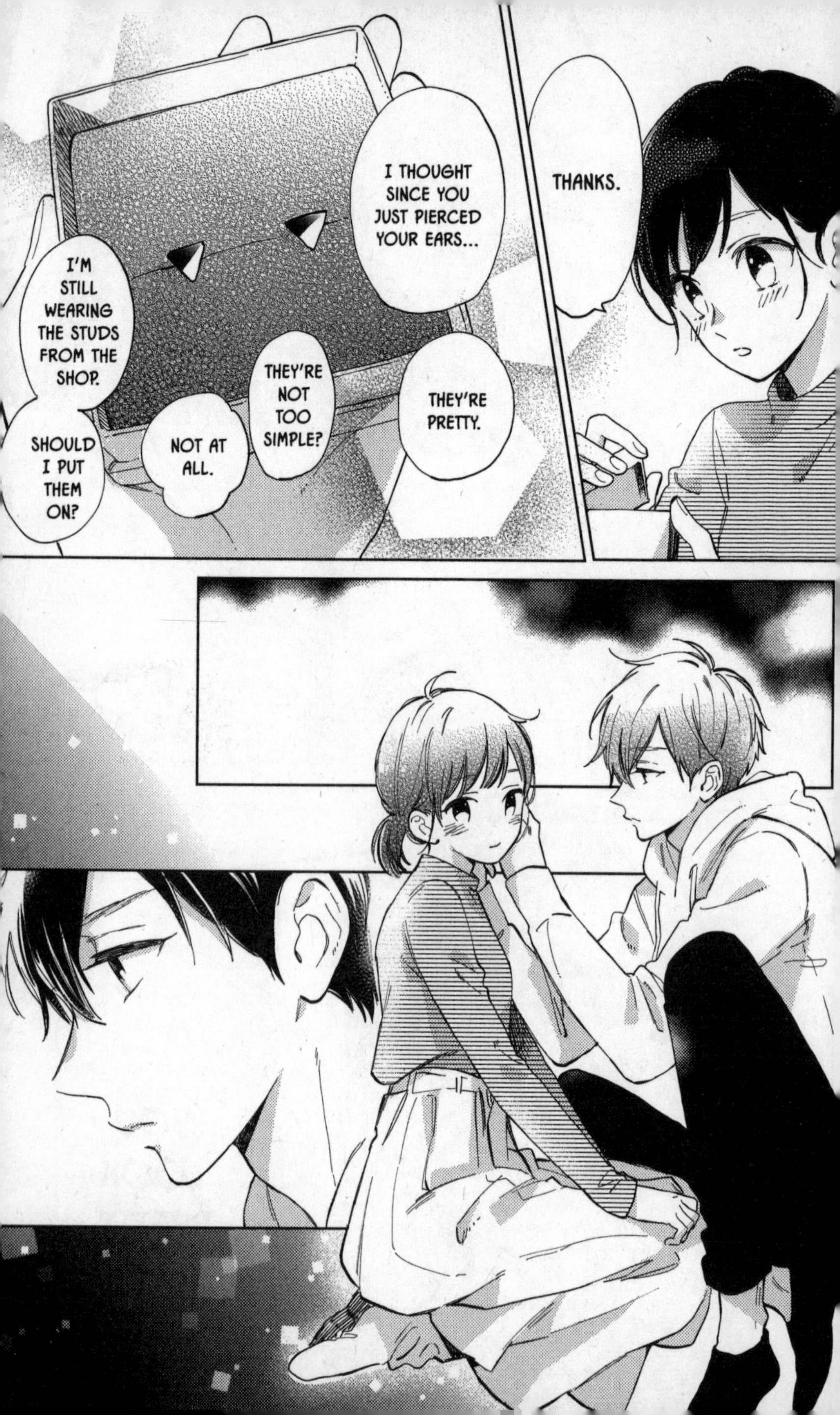
THANKS.
I THOUGHT SINCE YOU JUST PIERCED YOUR EARS...
THEY'RE PRETTY.
THEY'RE NOT TOO SIMPLE?
NOT AT ALL.
I'M STILL WEARING THE STUDS FROM THE SHOP.
SHOULD I PUT THEM ON?

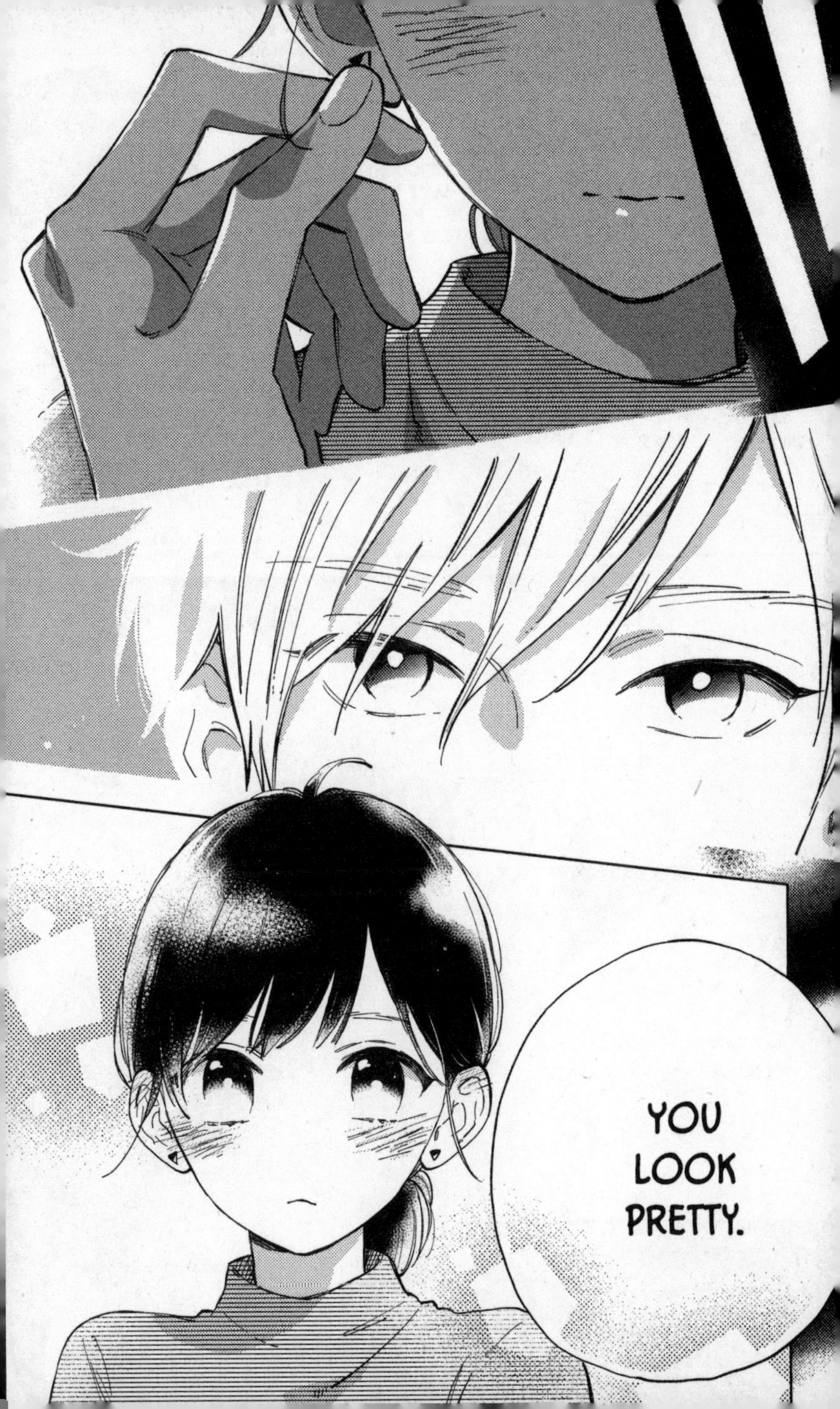
YOU LOOK PRETTY.

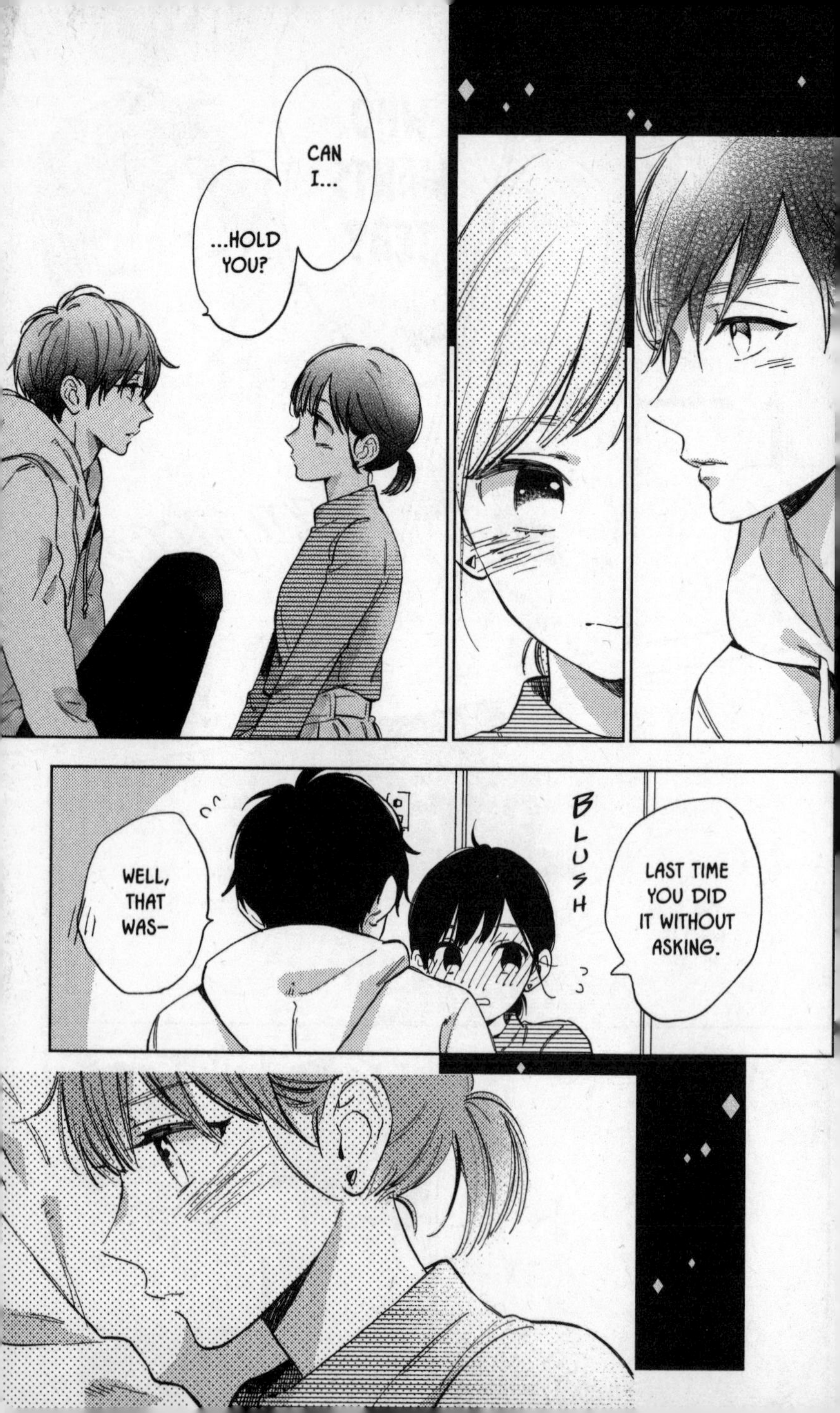
CAN I...
...HOLD YOU?
LAST TIME YOU DID IT WITHOUT ASKING.
BLUSH
WELL, THAT WAS-

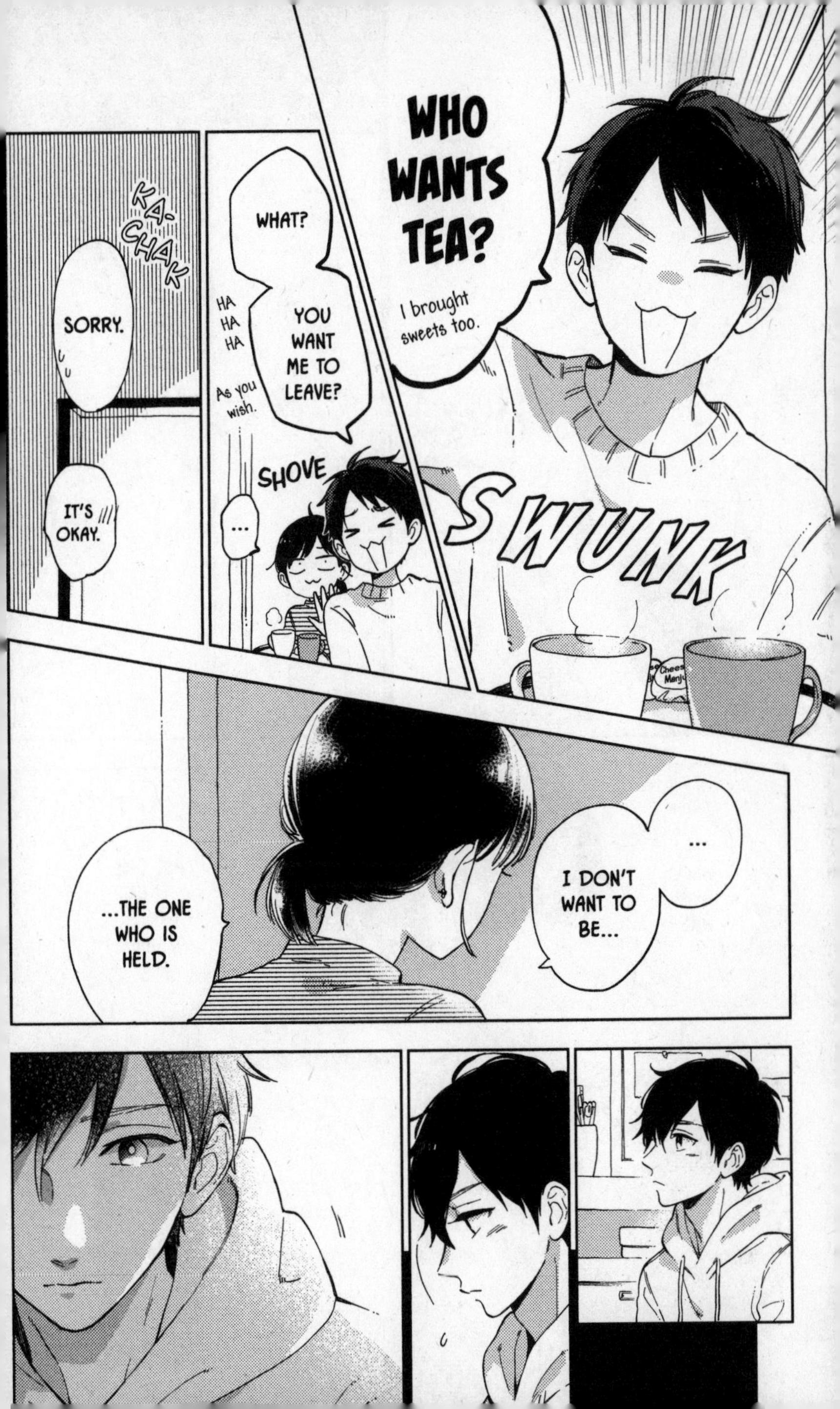
WHO WANTS TEA?
I brought sweets too.
SWUNK
WHAT?
YOU WANT ME TO LEAVE?
HA HA HA
As you wish.
SHOVE
...
KA-CHAK
SORRY.
IT'S OKAY.
...
I DON'T WANT TO BE...
...THE ONE WHO IS HELD.

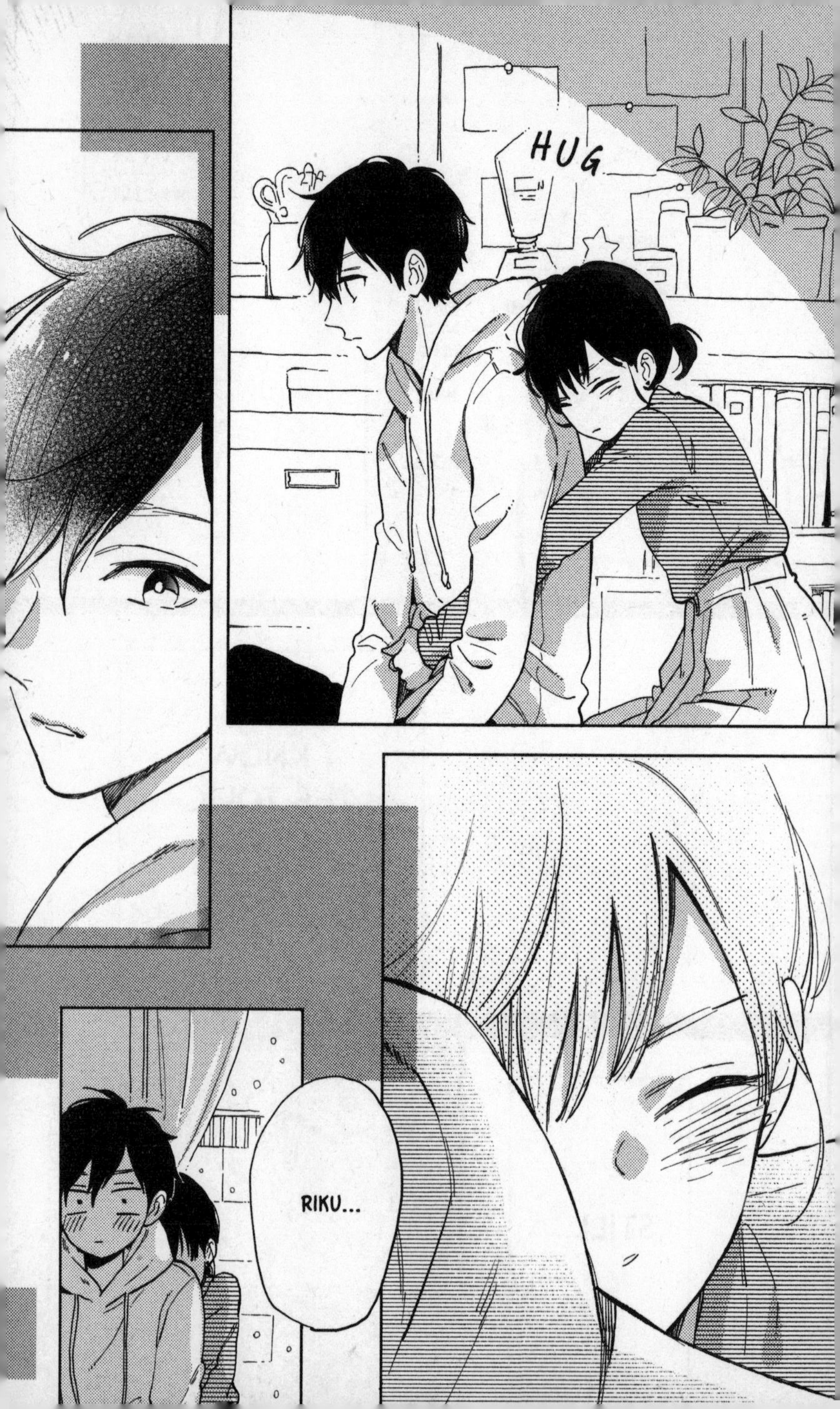
HUG
RIKU...

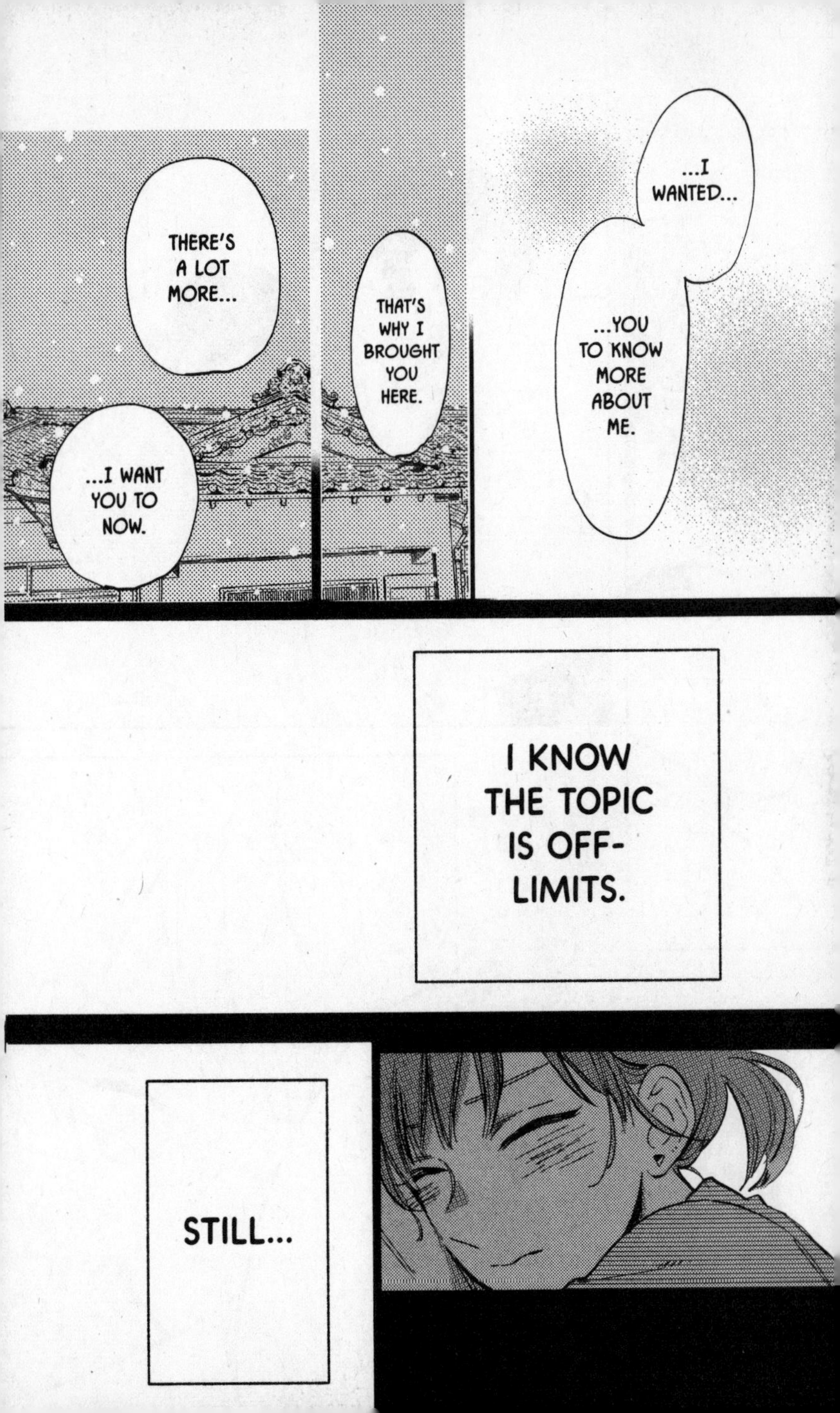
...I WANTED...
...YOU TO KNOW MORE ABOUT ME.
THAT'S WHY I BROUGHT YOU HERE.
THERE'S A LOT MORE...
...I WANT YOU TO NOW.
I KNOW THE TOPIC IS OFF-LIMITS.
STILL...

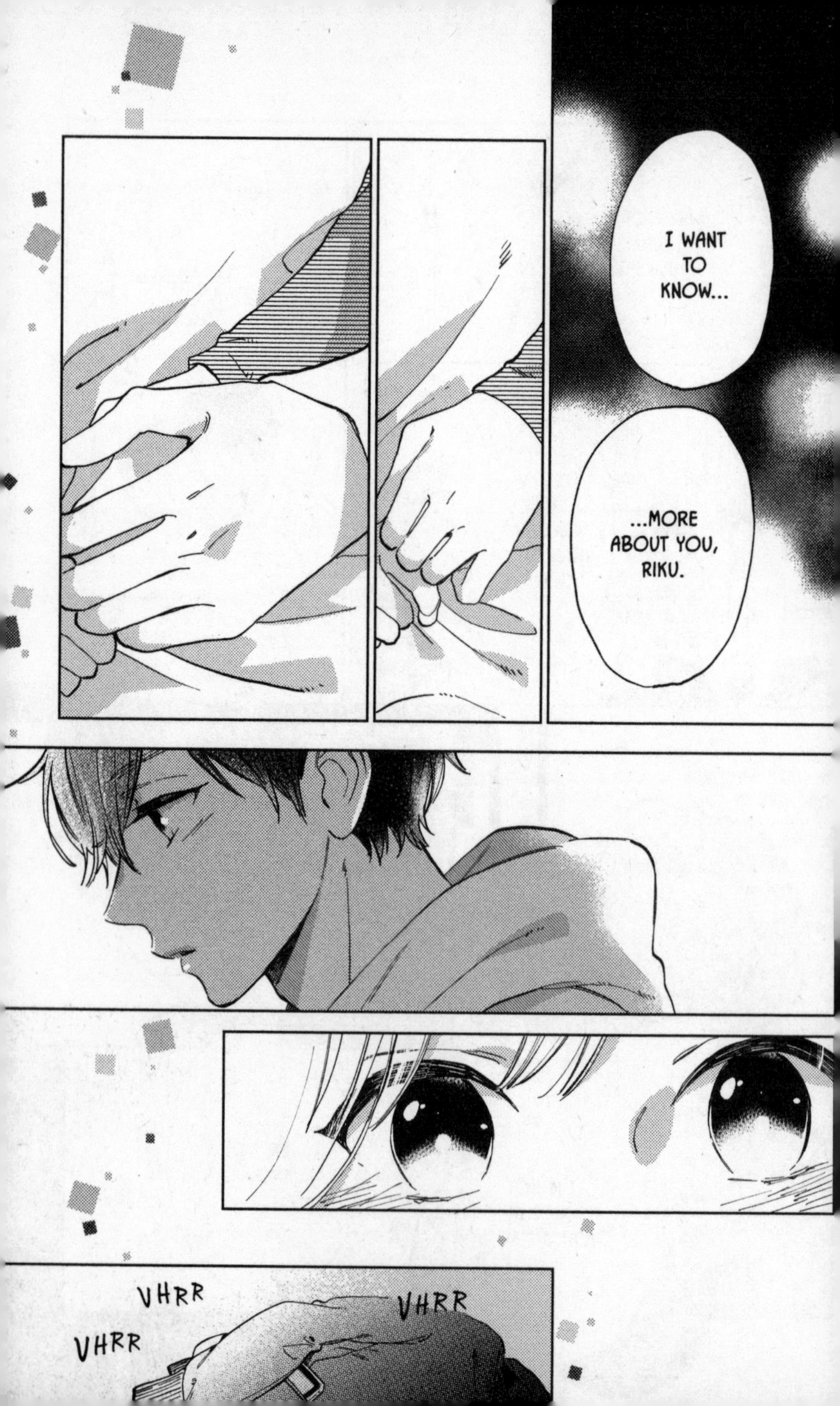
I WANT TO KNOW...
...MORE ABOUT YOU, RIKU.
VHRR
VHRR
VHRR

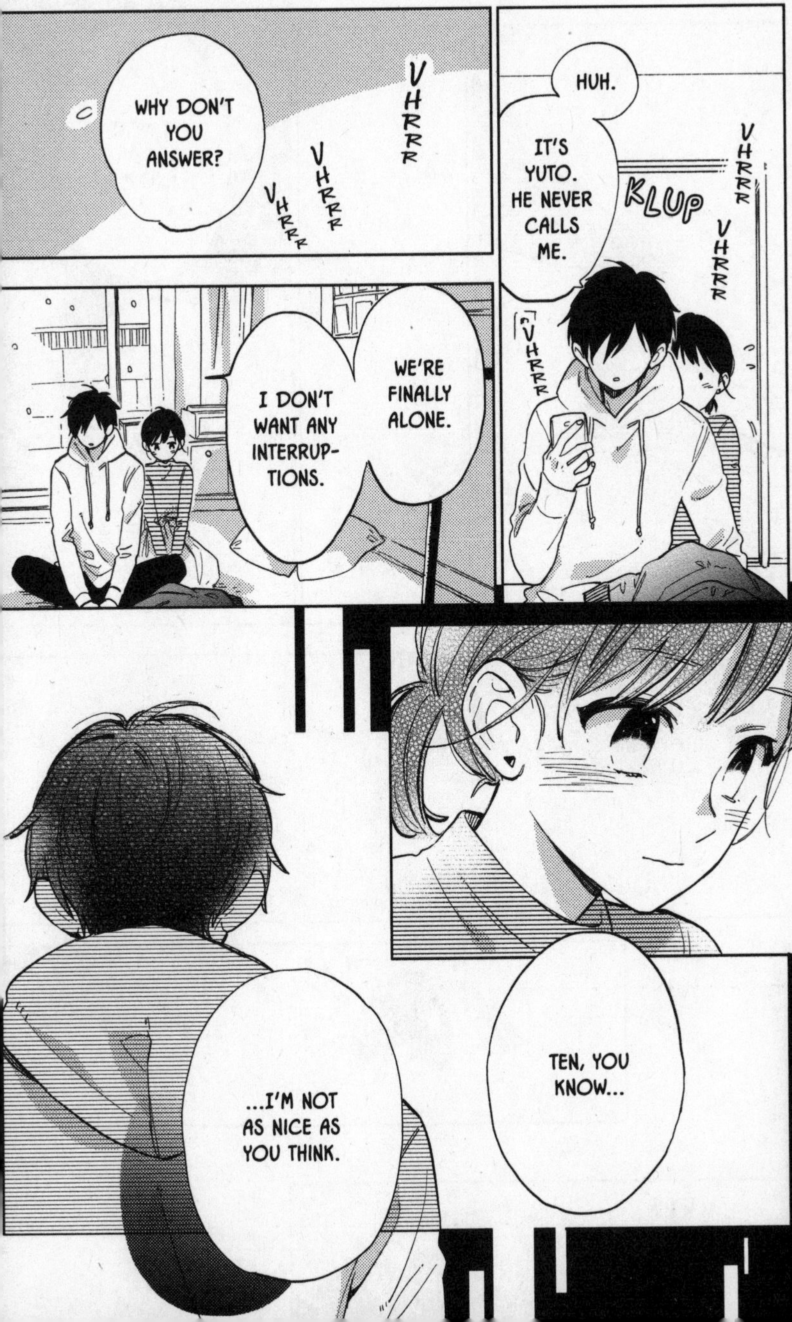
HUH.
IT'S YUTO. HE NEVER CALLS ME.
VHRRR
KLUP
VHRRR
VHRRR
WHY DON'T YOU ANSWER?
VHRRR
VHRRR
VHRRR
WE'RE FINALLY ALONE.
I DON'T WANT ANY INTERRUP-TIONS.
TEN, YOU KNOW...
...I'M NOT AS NICE AS YOU THINK.

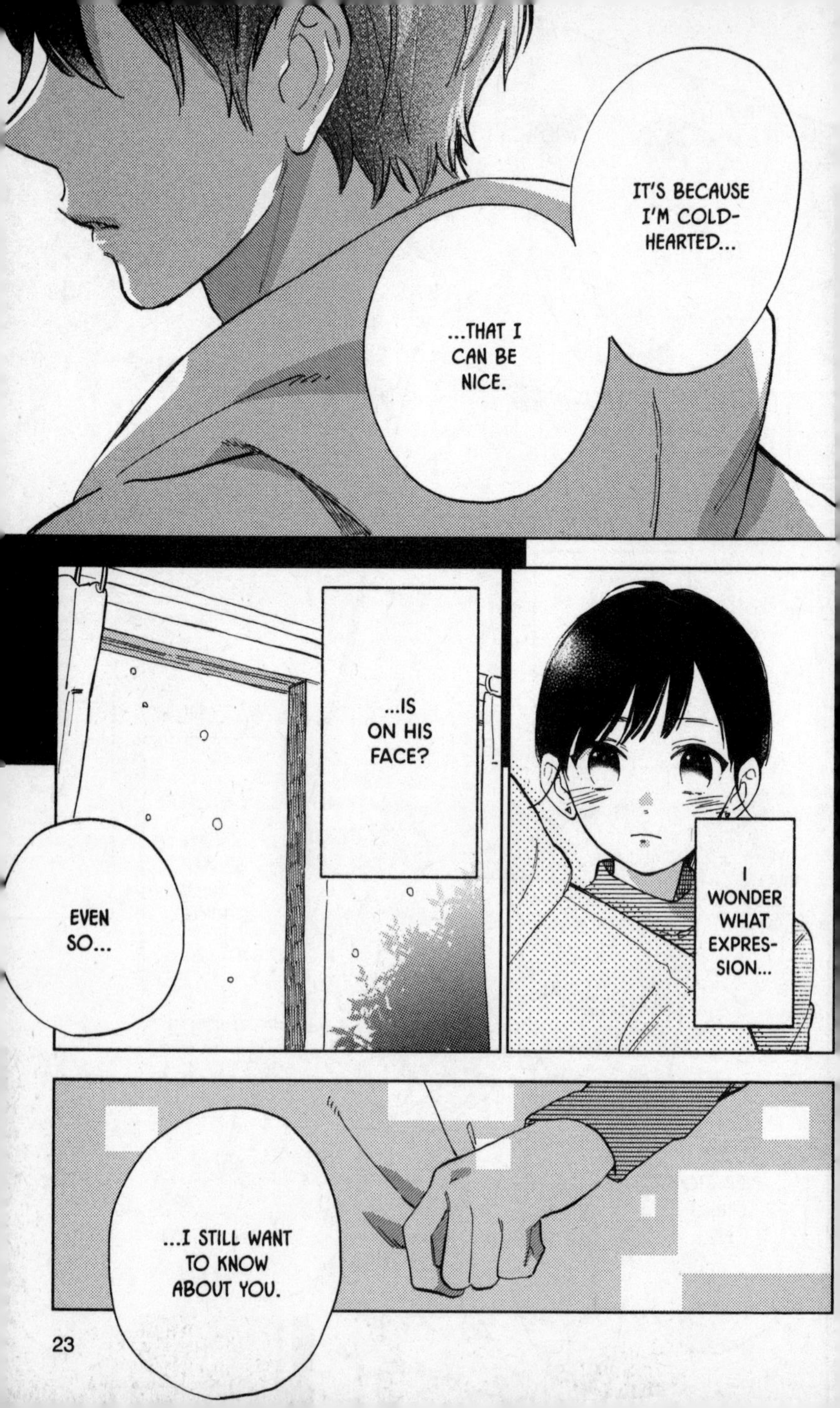
IT'S BECAUSE I'M COLD-HEARTED...
...THAT I CAN BE NICE.
I WONDER WHAT EXPRESSION...
...IS ON HIS FACE?
EVEN SO...
...I STILL WANT TO KNOW ABOUT YOU.

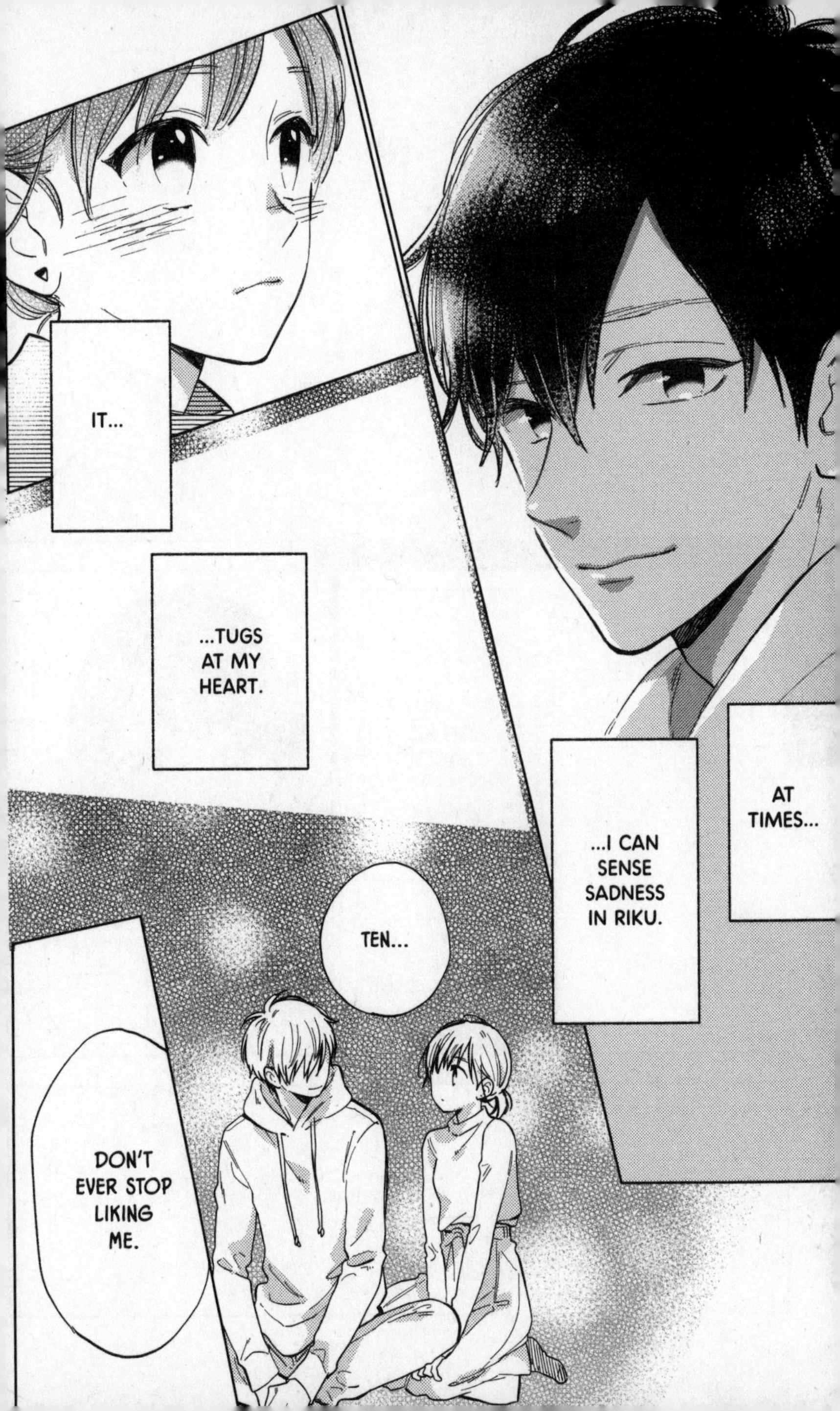
AT TIMES...
...I CAN SENSE SADNESS IN RIKU.
IT...
...TUGS AT MY HEART.
TEN...
DON'T EVER STOP LIKING ME.

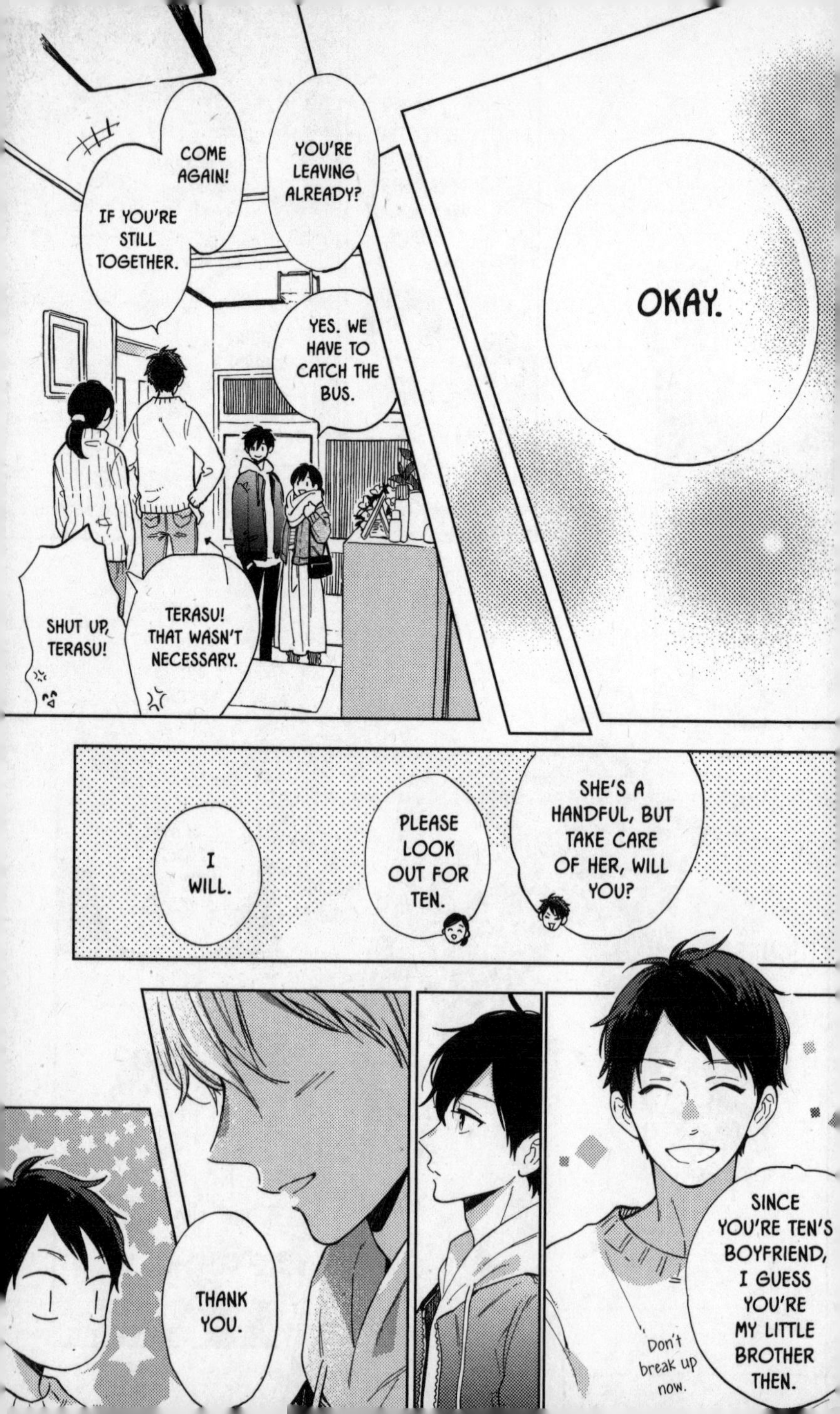
OKAY.
YOU'RE LEAVING ALREADY?
COME AGAIN!
IF YOU'RE STILL TOGETHER.
YES. WE HAVE TO CATCH THE BUS.
TERASU! THAT WASN'T NECESSARY.
SHUT UP, TERASU!
SHE'S A HANDFUL, BUT TAKE CARE OF HER, WILL YOU?
PLEASE LOOK OUT FOR TEN.
I WILL.
SINCE YOU'RE TEN'S BOYFRIEND, I GUESS YOU'RE MY LITTLE BROTHER THEN.
Don't break up now.
THANK YOU.

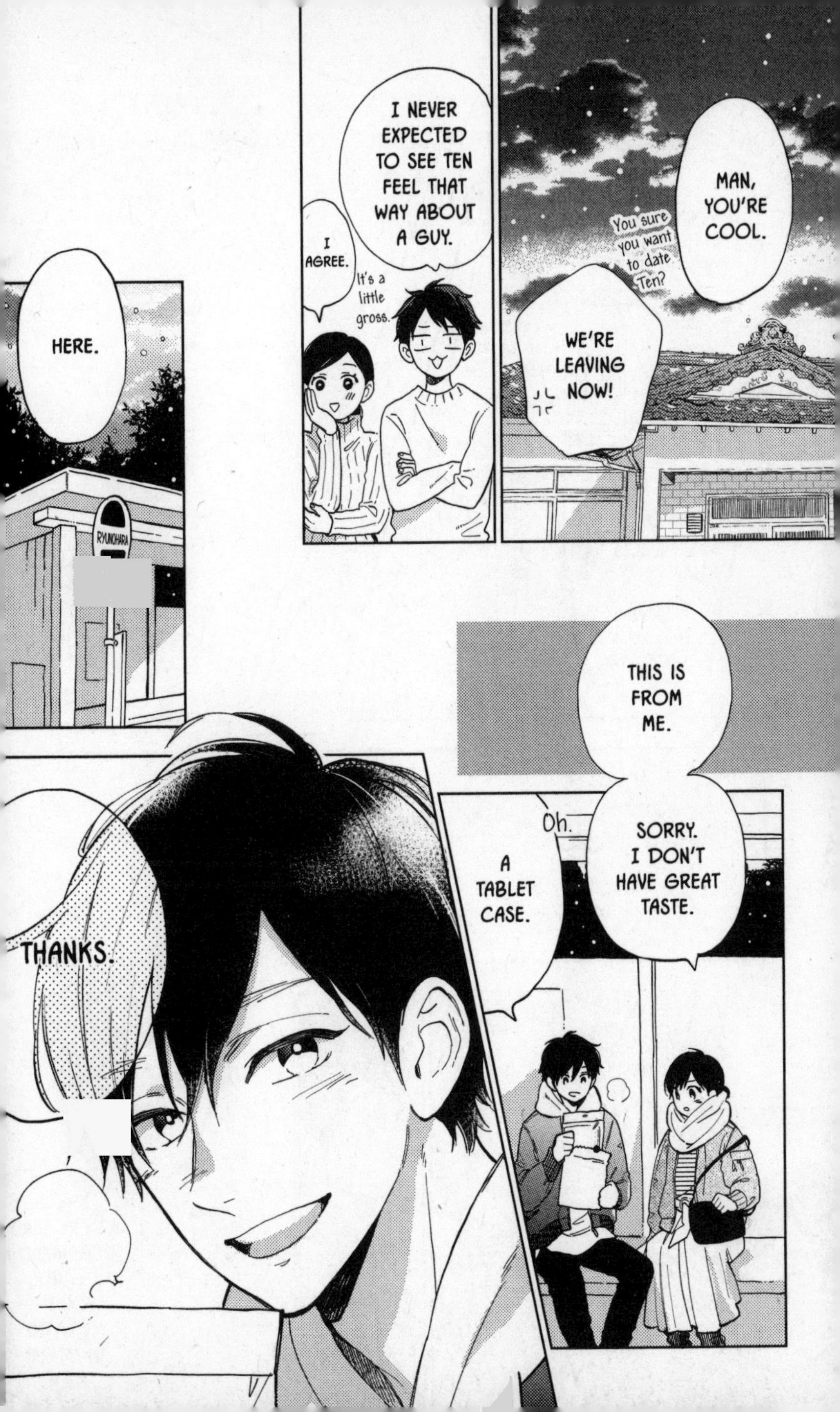
MAN, YOU'RE COOL.
You sure you want to date Ten?
WE'RE LEAVING NOW!
I NEVER EXPECTED TO SEE TEN FEEL THAT WAY ABOUT A GUY.
I AGREE.
It's a little gross.
HERE.
RYUNOHARA
THIS IS FROM ME.
SORRY. I DON'T HAVE GREAT TASTE.
Oh.
A TABLET CASE.
THANKS.

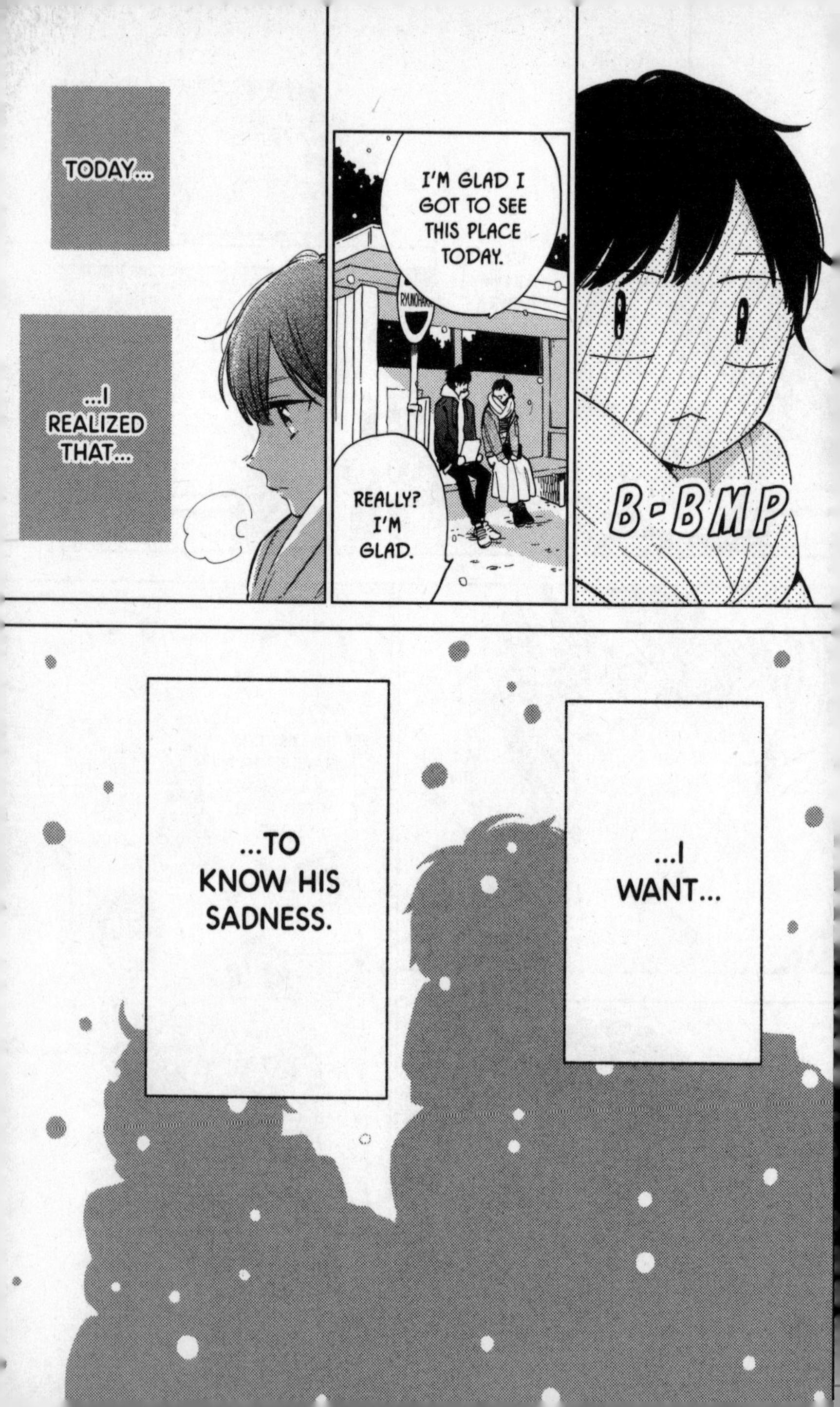
B-BMP
I'M GLAD I GOT TO SEE THIS PLACE TODAY.
REALLY? I'M GLAD.
TODAY...
...I REALIZED THAT...
...I WANT...
...TO KNOW HIS SADNESS.

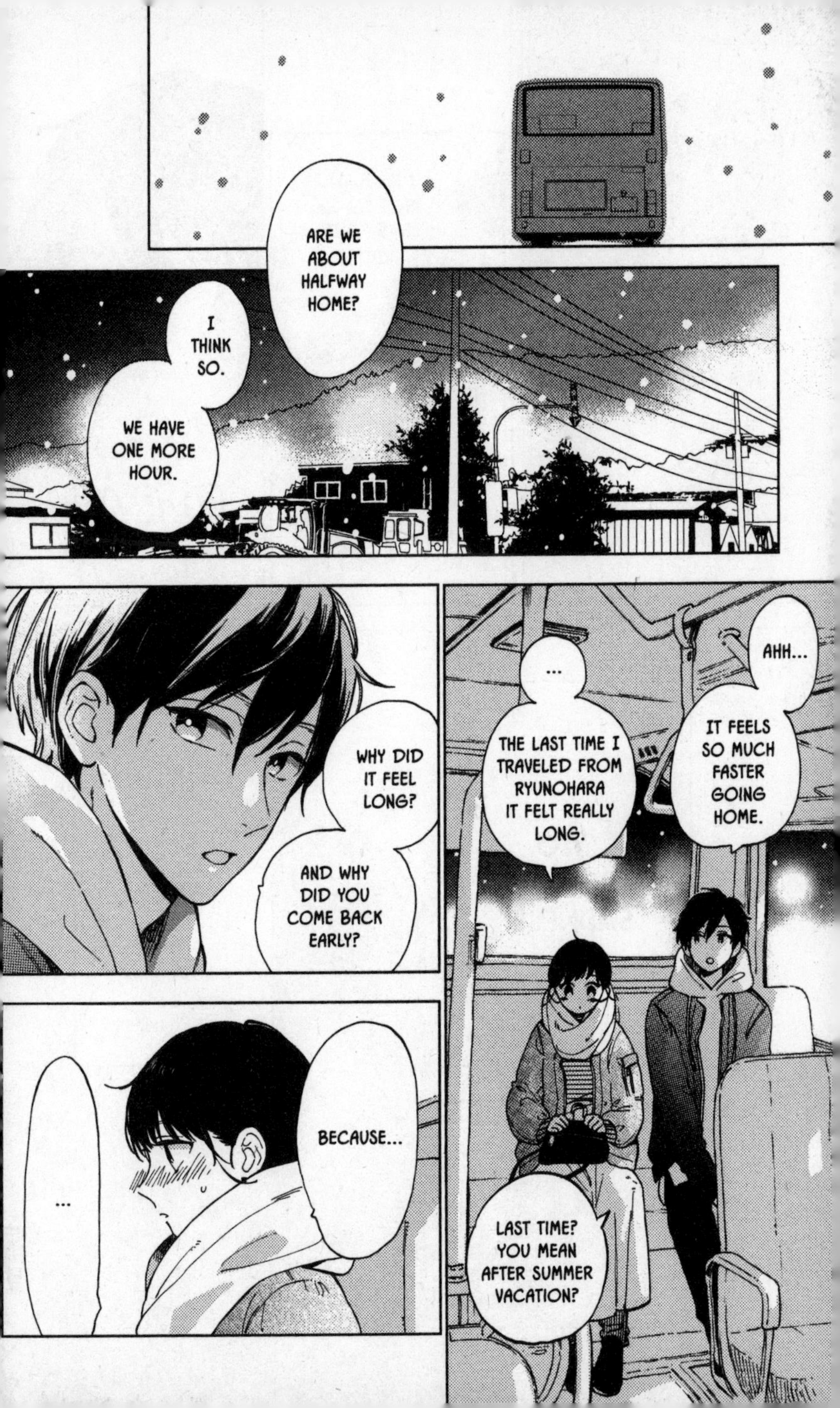
ARE WE ABOUT HALFWAY HOME?
I THINK SO.
WE HAVE ONE MORE HOUR.
AHH...
IT FEELS SO MUCH FASTER GOING HOME.
...
THE LAST TIME I TRAVELED FROM RYUNOHARA IT FELT REALLY LONG.
LAST TIME? YOU MEAN AFTER SUMMER VACATION?
WHY DID IT FEEL LONG?
AND WHY DID YOU COME BACK EARLY?
BECAUSE...
...

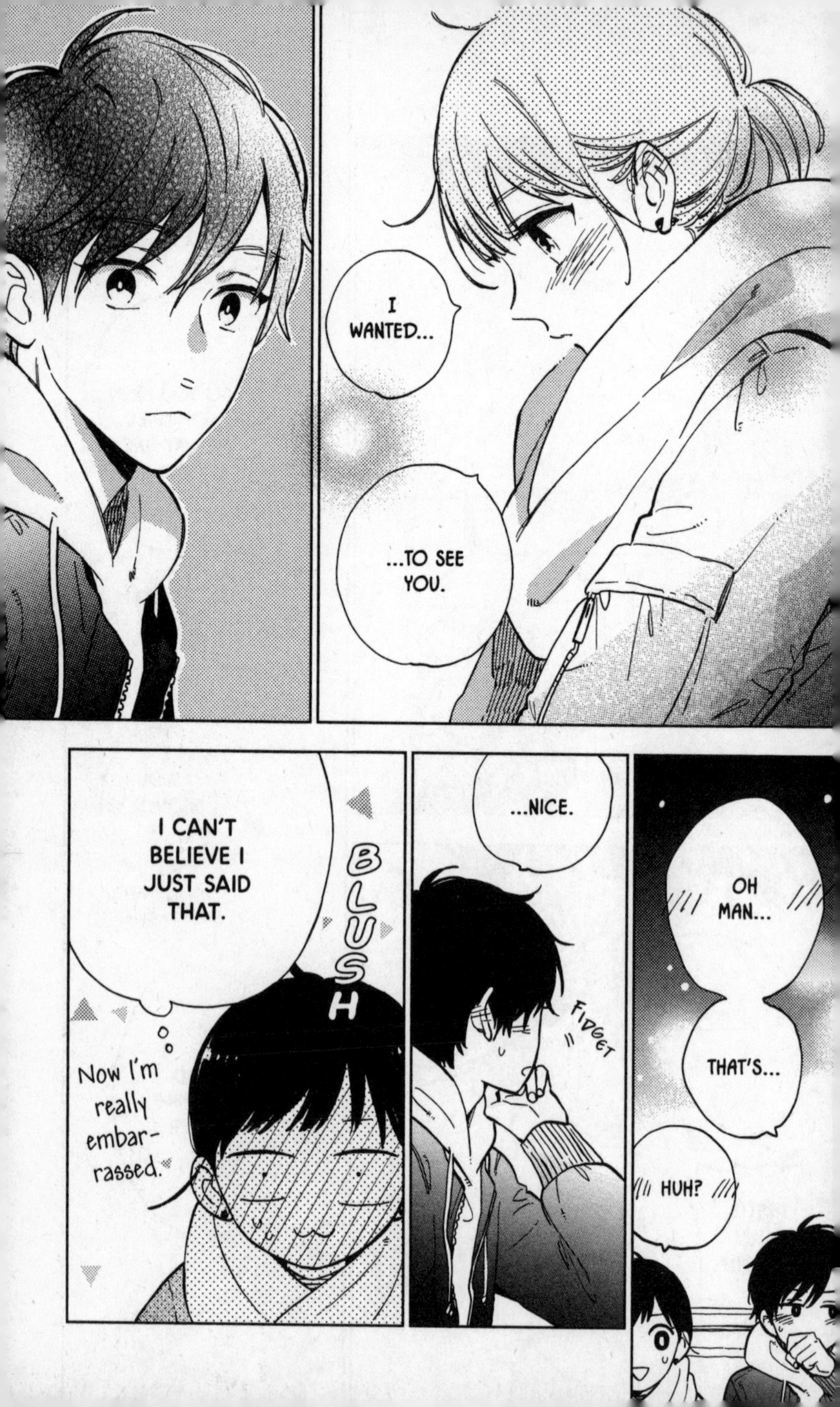

I WANTED...
...TO SEE YOU.
OH MAN...
THAT'S...
HUH?
...NICE.
FIDGET
I CAN'T BELIEVE I JUST SAID THAT.
BLUSH
Now I'm really embarrassed.

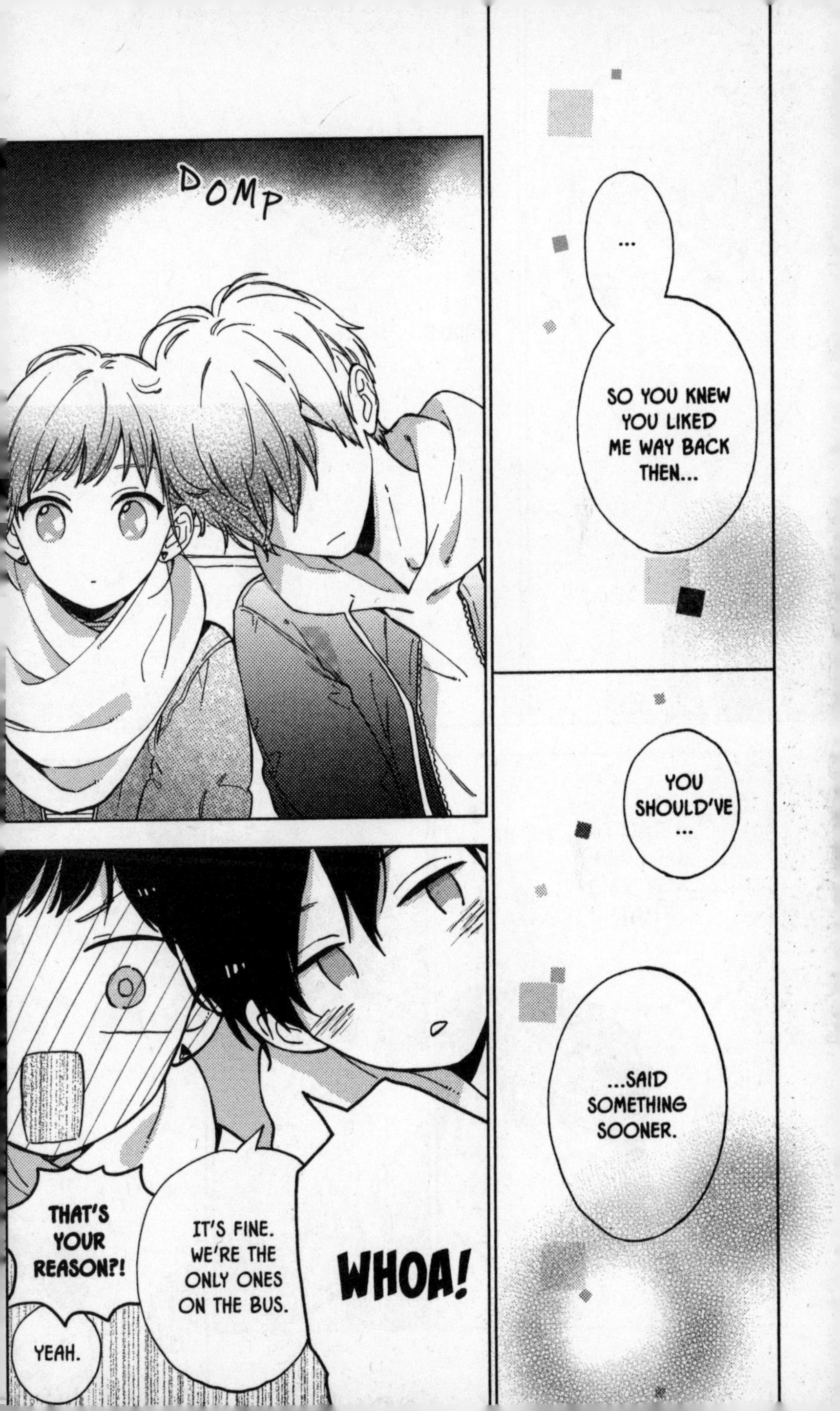
...
SO YOU KNEW YOU LIKED ME WAY BACK THEN...
YOU SHOULD'VE ...
...SAID SOMETHING SOONER.
DOMP
WHOA!
IT'S FINE. WE'RE THE ONLY ONES ON THE BUS.
THAT'S YOUR REASON?!
YEAH.

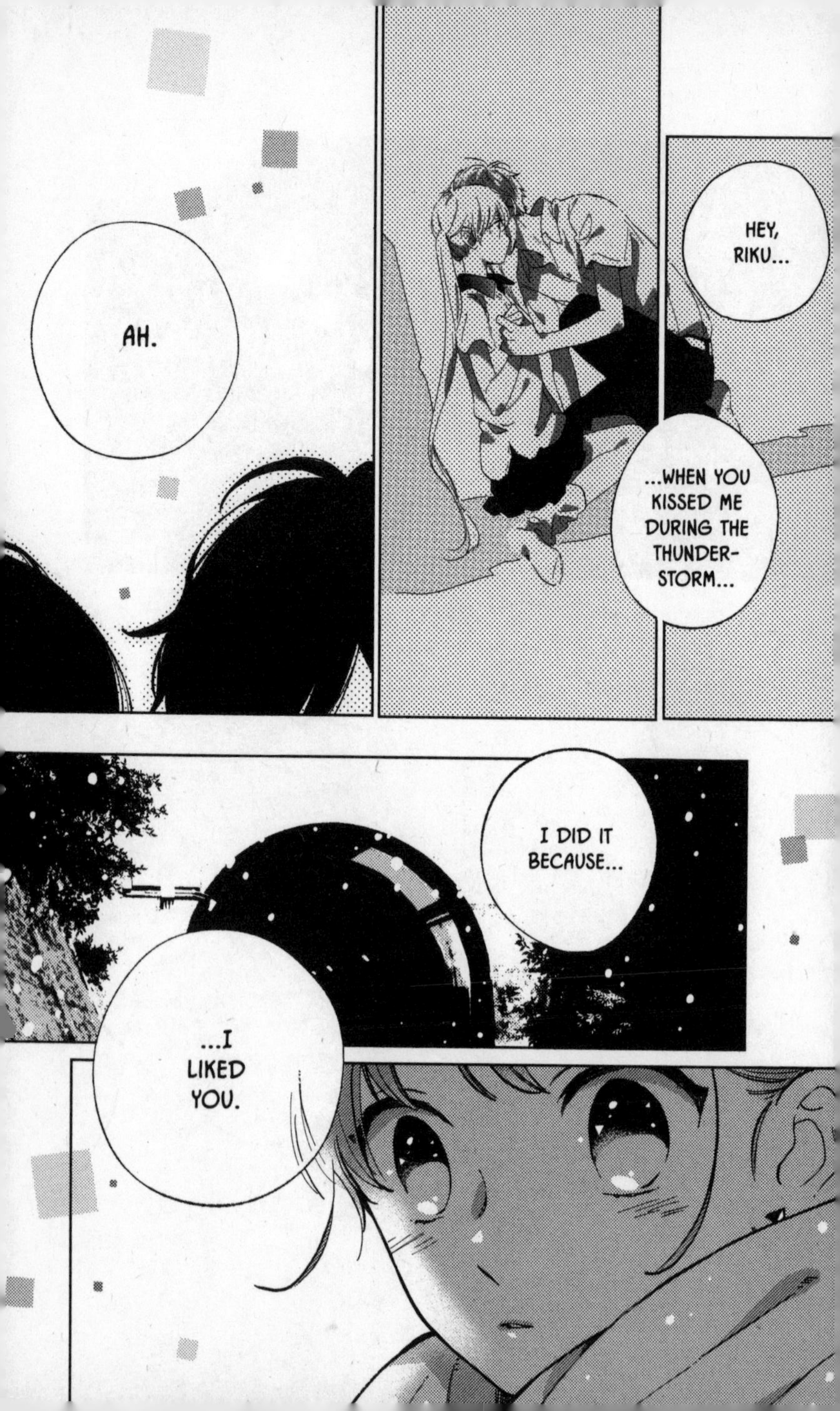
HEY, RIKU...
...WHEN YOU KISSED ME DURING THE THUNDER-STORM...
AH.
I DID IT BECAUSE...
...I LIKED YOU.

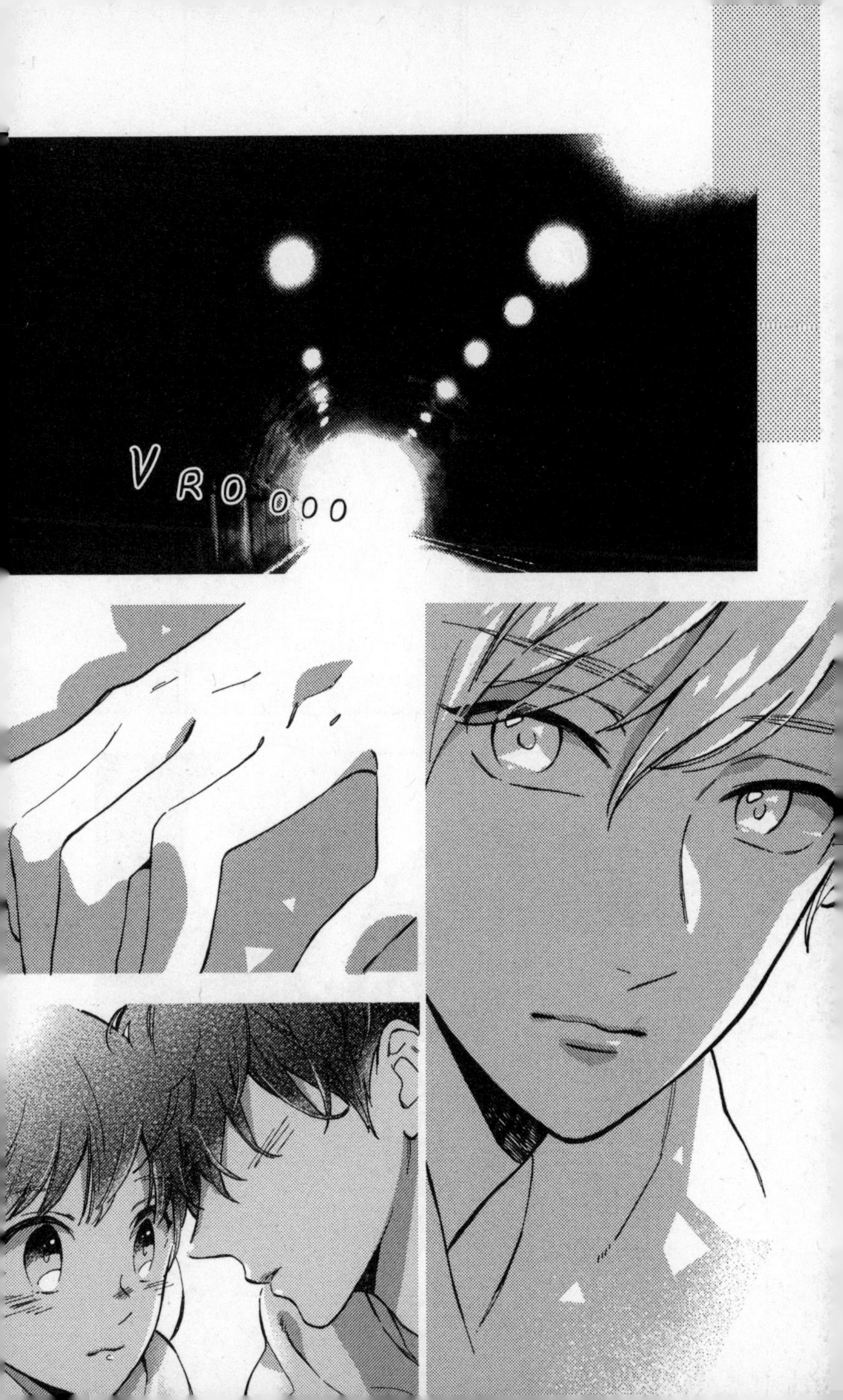
VROOOOO

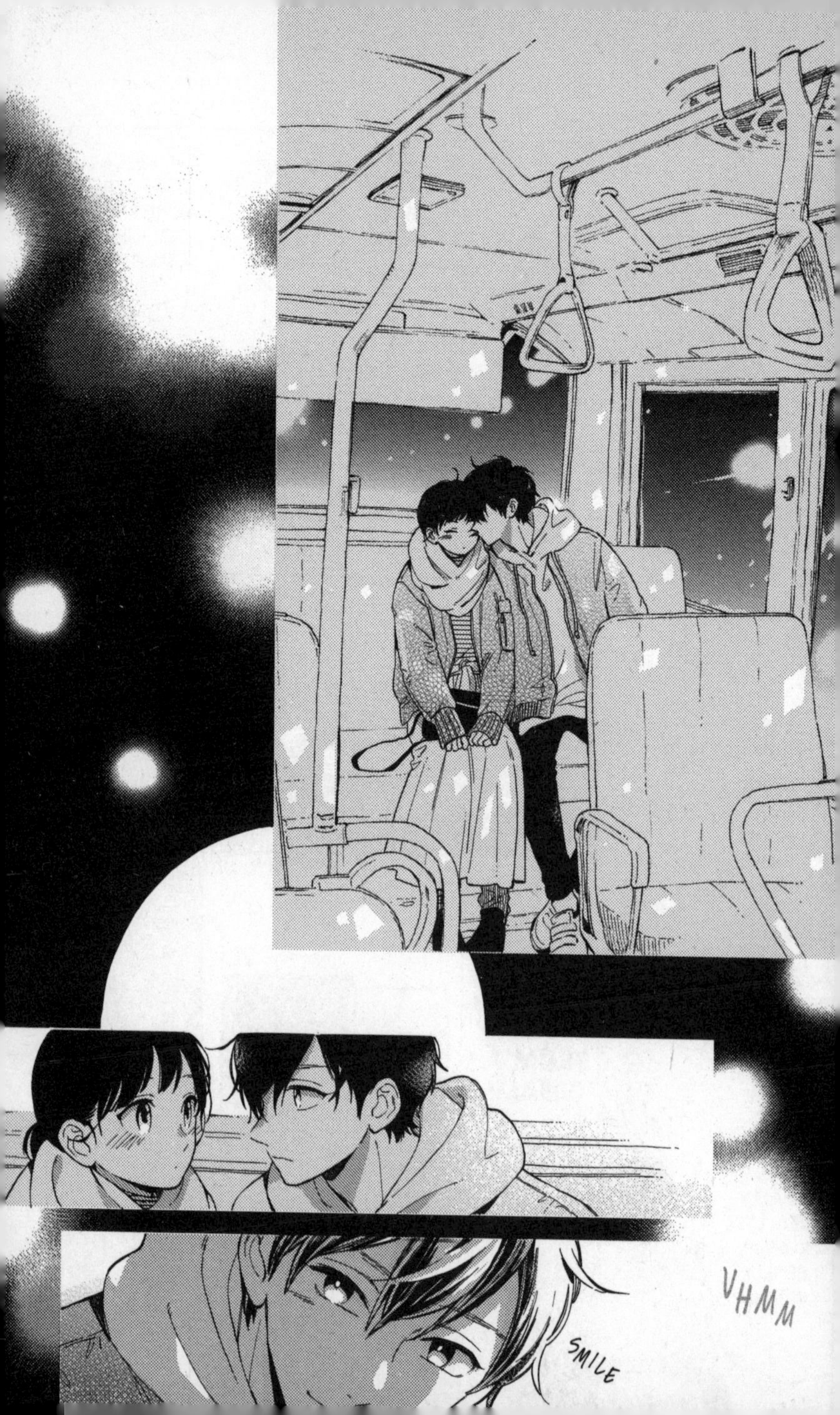
VHMM
SMILE

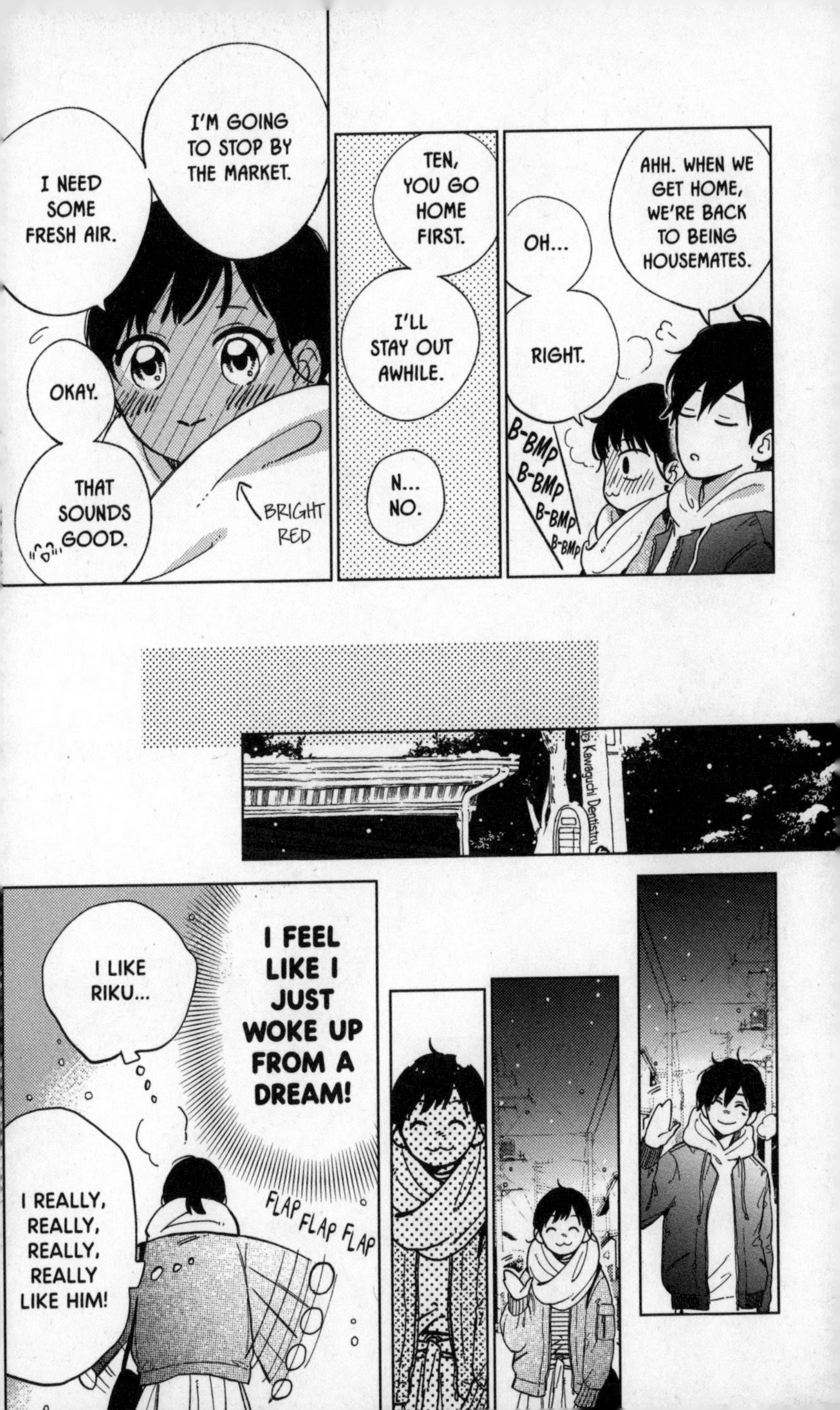
AHH. WHEN WE GET HOME, WE'RE BACK TO BEING HOUSEMATES.
OH...
RIGHT.
B-BMP B-BMP B-BMP B-BMP
TEN, YOU GO HOME FIRST.
I'LL STAY OUT AWHILE.
N... NO.
I'M GOING TO STOP BY THE MARKET.
I NEED SOME FRESH AIR.
OKAY.
THAT SOUNDS GOOD.
BRIGHT RED
Kawaguchi Dentistry
I FEEL LIKE I JUST WOKE UP FROM A DREAM!
I LIKE RIKU...
I REALLY, REALLY, REALLY, REALLY LIKE HIM!
FLAP FLAP FLAP

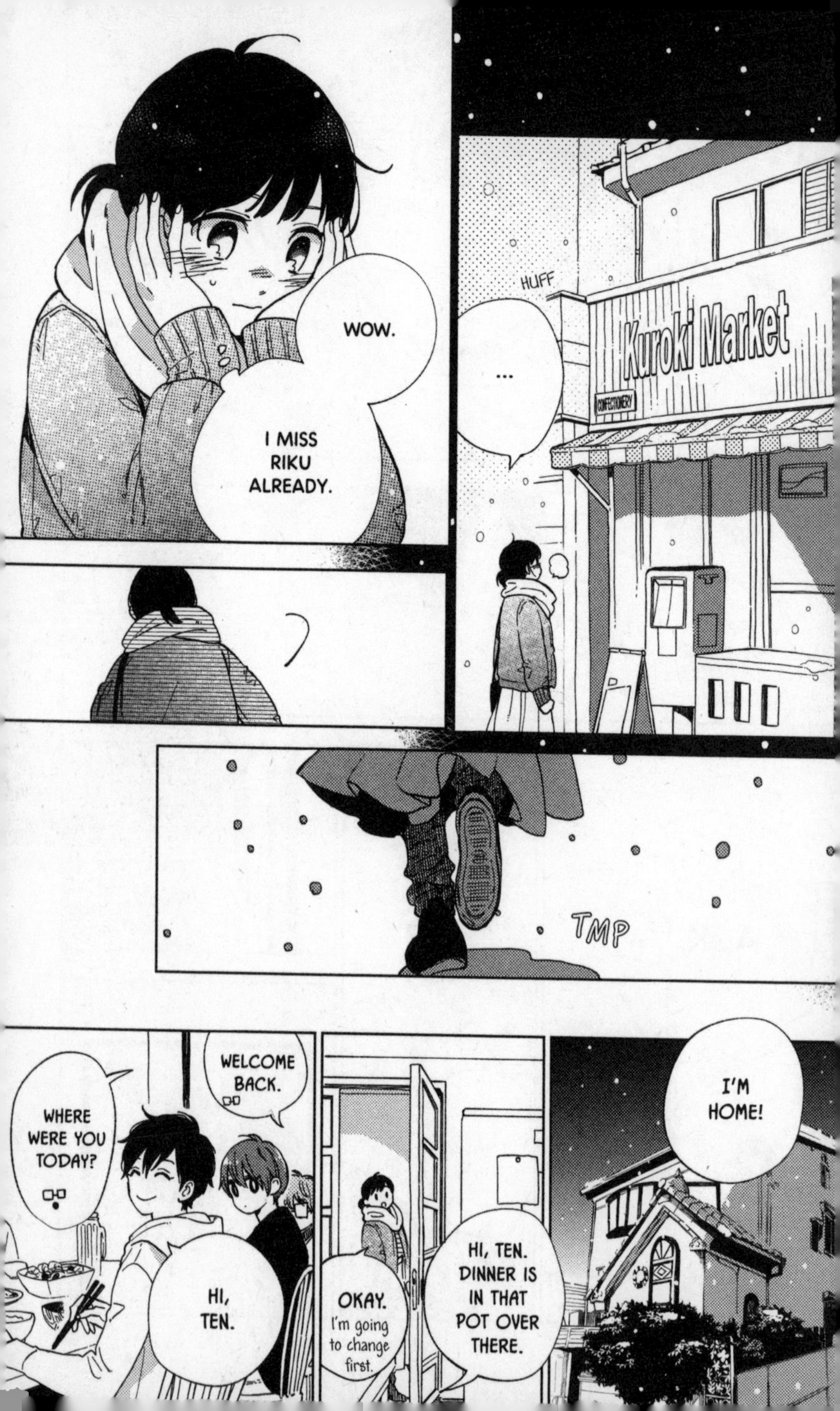
HUFF
...
WOW.
I MISS RIKU ALREADY.
TMP
I'M HOME!
HI, TEN. DINNER IS IN THAT POT OVER THERE.
OKAY. I'm going to change first.
WELCOME BACK.
WHERE WERE YOU TODAY?
HI, TEN.

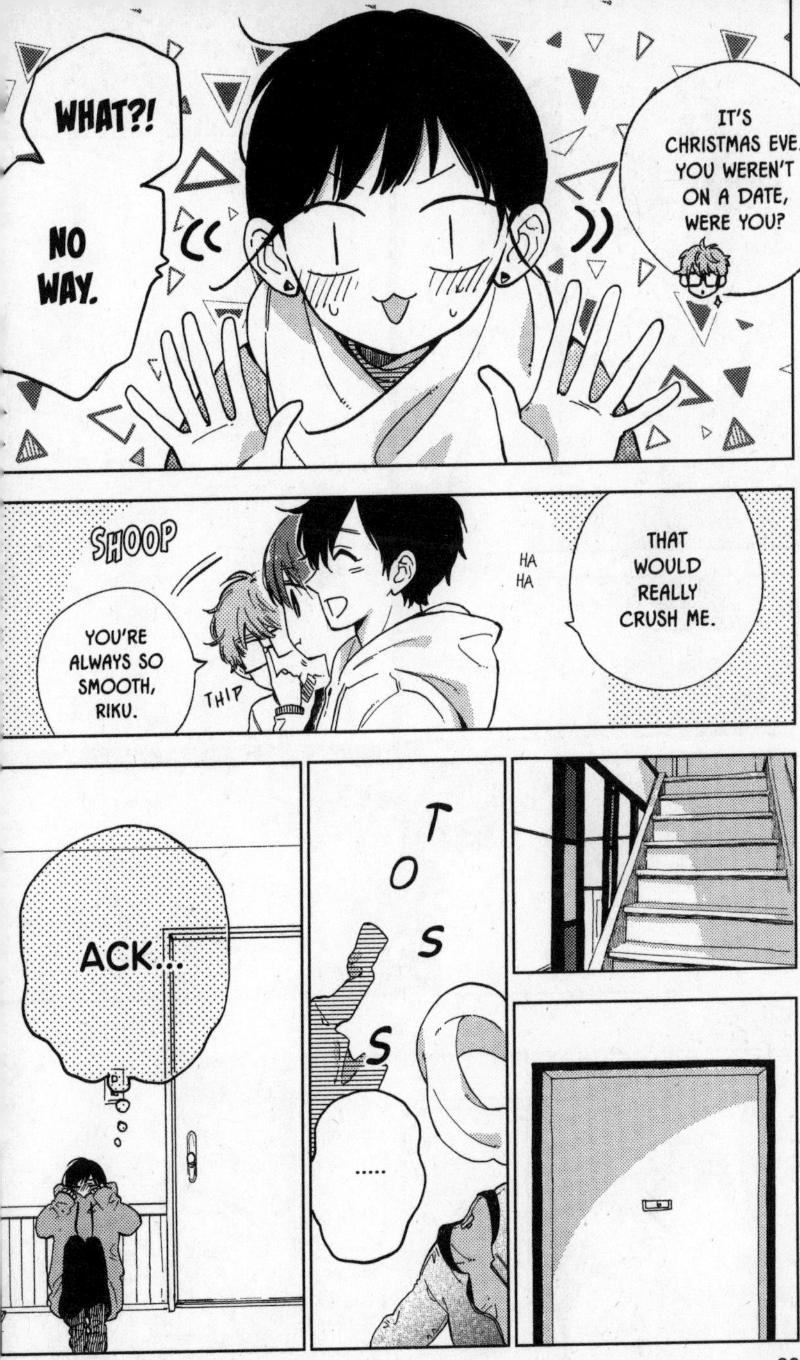
IT'S CHRISTMAS EVE. YOU WEREN'T ON A DATE, WERE YOU?
WHAT?!
NO WAY.
THAT WOULD REALLY CRUSH ME.
HA HA
SHOOP
THIP
YOU'RE ALWAYS SO SMOOTH, RIKU.
TOSS
......
ACK...

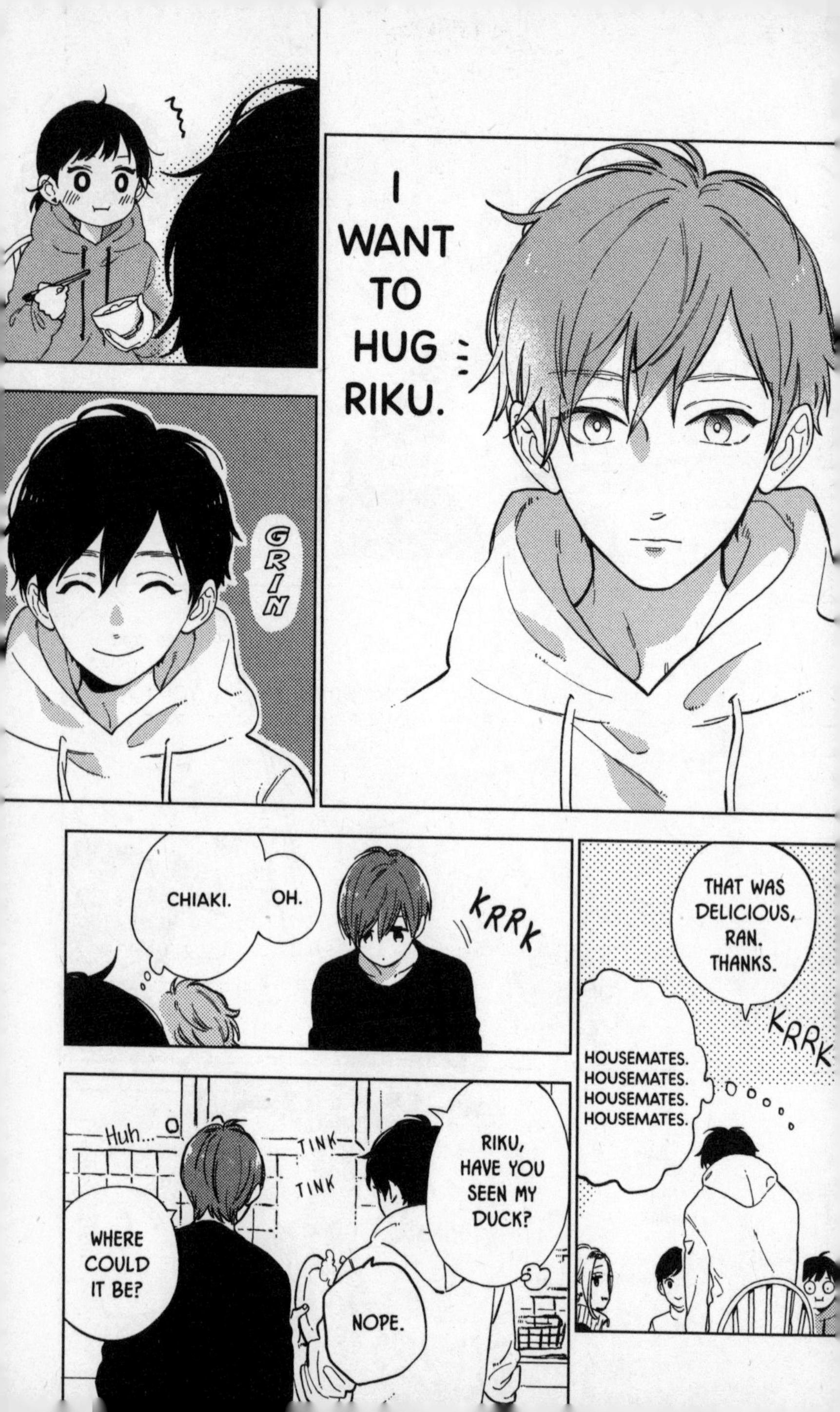
I WANT TO HUG RIKU.
GRIN
THAT WAS DELICIOUS, RAN. THANKS.
KRRK
HOUSEMATES. HOUSEMATES. HOUSEMATES. HOUSEMATES.
KRRK
OH.
CHIAKI.
RIKU, HAVE YOU SEEN MY DUCK?
NOPE.
TINK
TINK
Huh...
WHERE COULD IT BE?

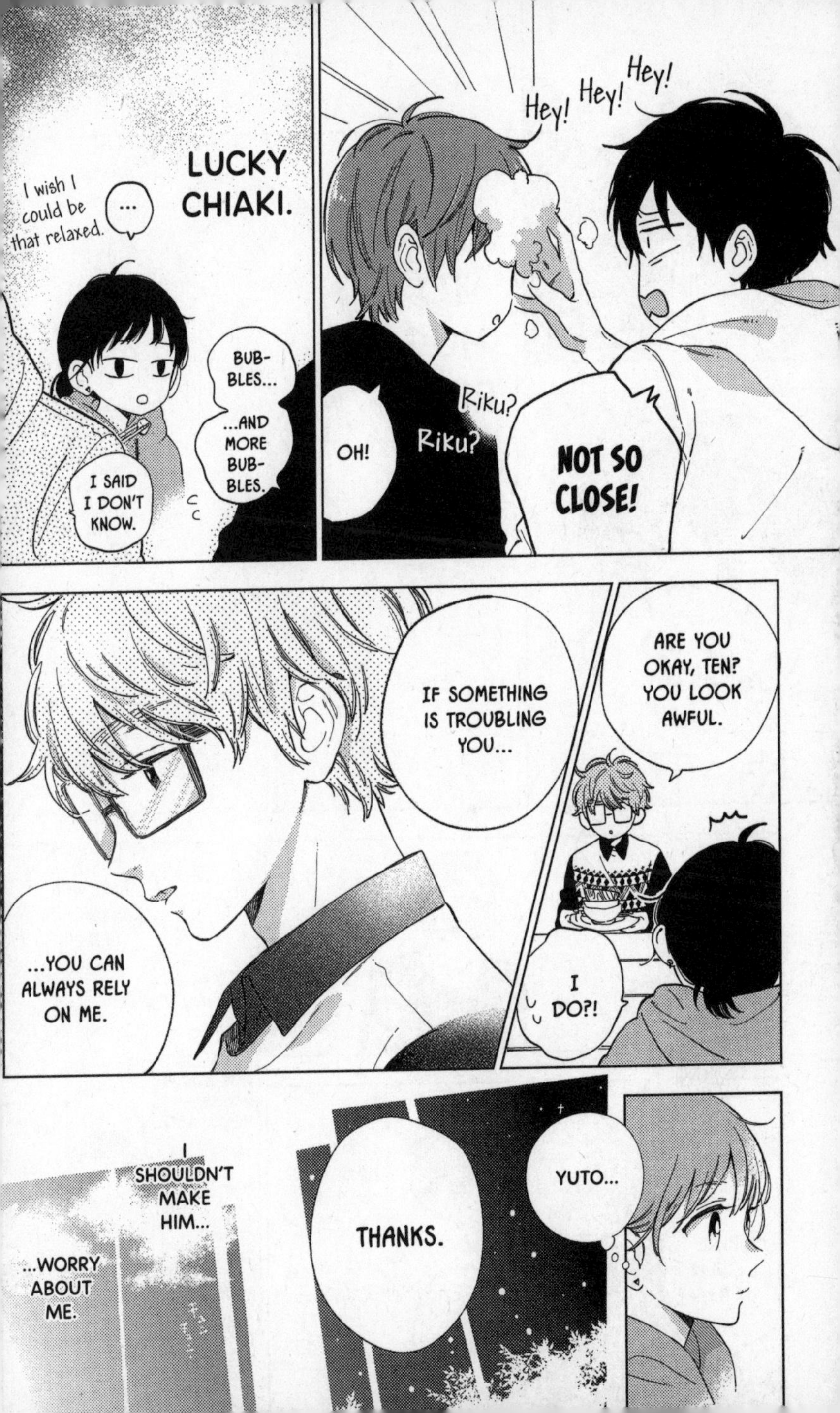
Hey!
Hey!
Hey!
NOT SO CLOSE!
OH!
Riku?
Riku?
LUCKY CHIAKI.
...
I wish I could be that relaxed.
BUB-BLES...
...AND MORE BUB-BLES.
I SAID I DON'T KNOW.
ARE YOU OKAY, TEN? YOU LOOK AWFUL.
I DO?!
IF SOMETHING IS TROUBLING YOU...
...YOU CAN ALWAYS RELY ON ME.
YUTO...
THANKS.
I SHOULDN'T MAKE HIM...
...WORRY ABOUT ME.

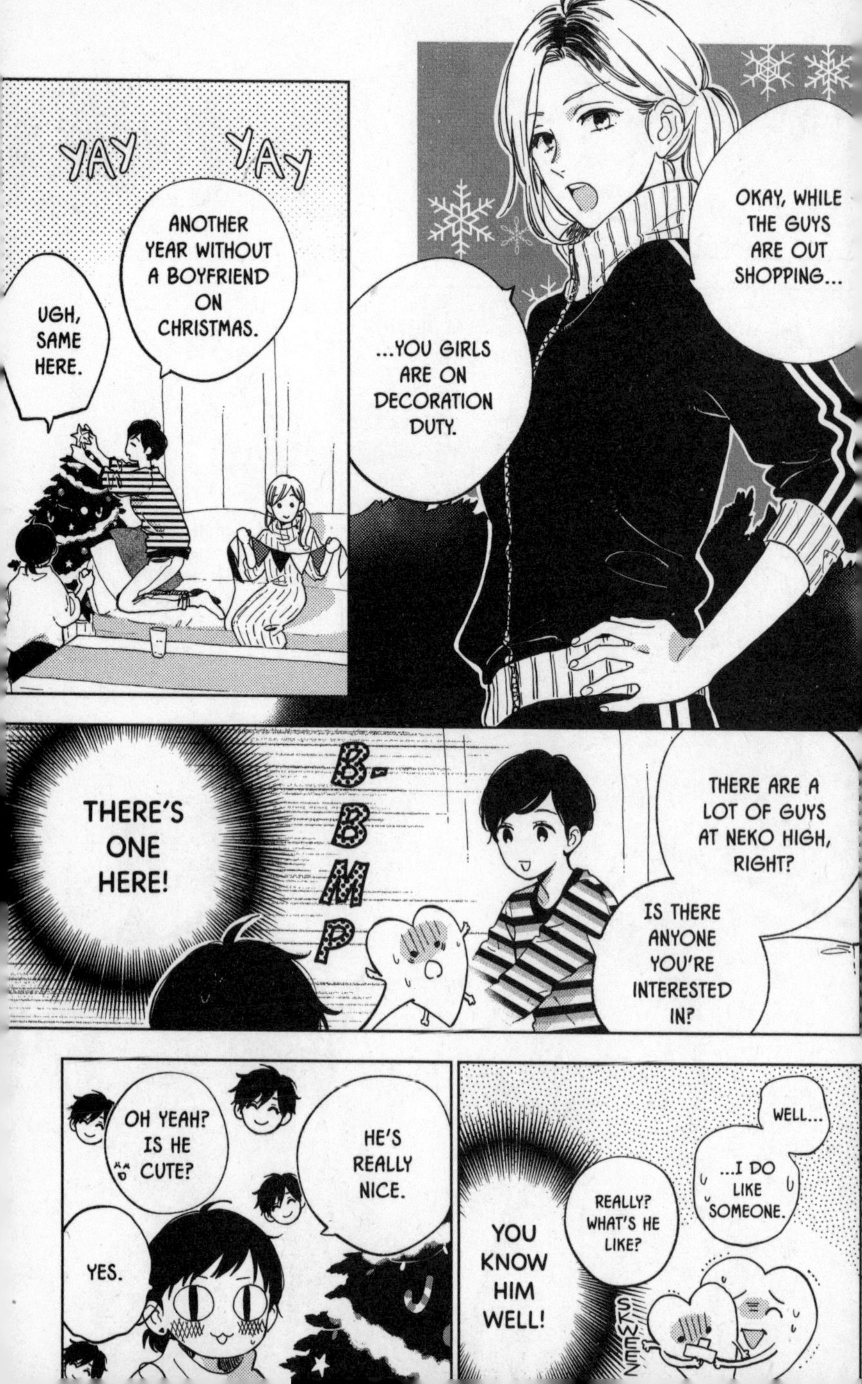
OKAY, WHILE THE GUYS ARE OUT SHOPPING...
...YOU GIRLS ARE ON DECORATION DUTY.
YAY
YAY
ANOTHER YEAR WITHOUT A BOYFRIEND ON CHRISTMAS.
UGH, SAME HERE.
THERE ARE A LOT OF GUYS AT NEKO HIGH, RIGHT?
IS THERE ANYONE YOU'RE INTERESTED IN?
B-BMP
THERE'S ONE HERE!
WELL...
...I DO LIKE SOMEONE.
REALLY? WHAT'S HE LIKE?
YOU KNOW HIM WELL!
HE'S REALLY NICE.
OH YEAH? IS HE CUTE?
YES.

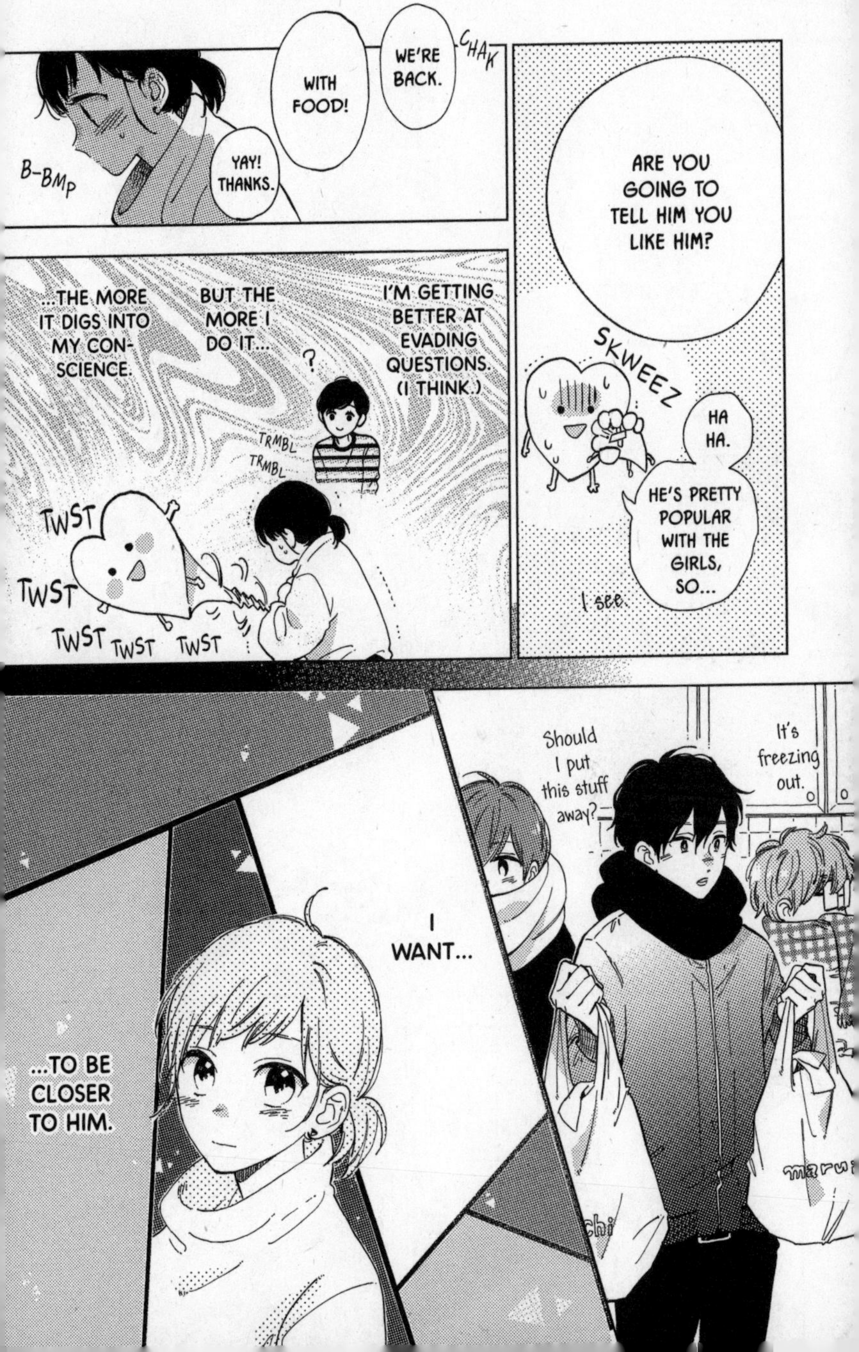
ARE YOU GOING TO TELL HIM YOU LIKE HIM?
SKWEEZ
HA HA.
HE'S PRETTY POPULAR WITH THE GIRLS, SO...
I see.
CHAK
WE'RE BACK.
WITH FOOD!
YAY! THANKS.
B-BMP
I'M GETTING BETTER AT EVADING QUESTIONS. (I THINK.)
BUT THE MORE I DO IT...
...THE MORE IT DIGS INTO MY CON-SCIENCE.
?
TRMBL
TRMBL
TWST
TWST
TWST
TWST
TWST
It's freezing out.
Should I put this stuff away?
I WANT...
...TO BE CLOSER TO HIM.

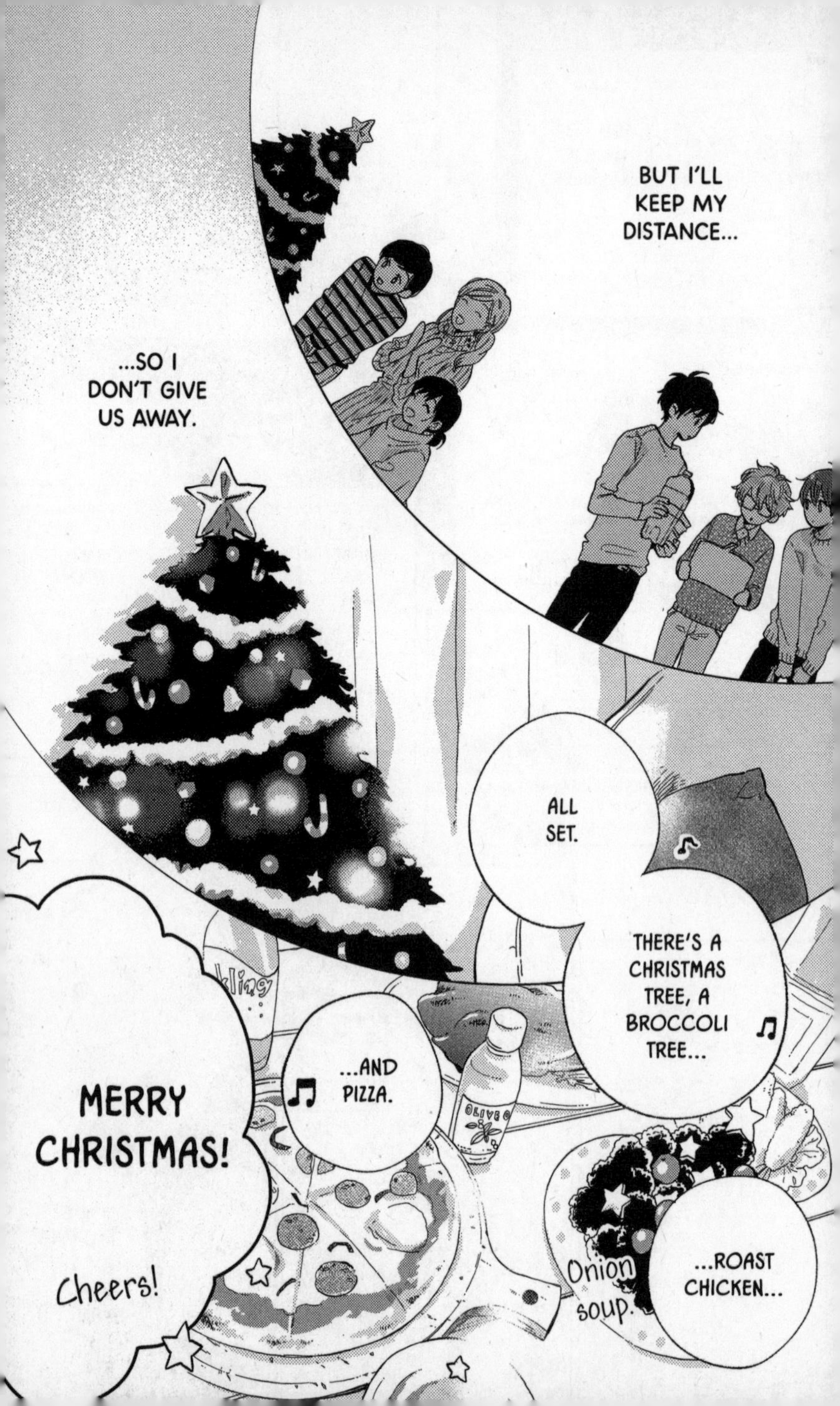
BUT I'LL KEEP MY DISTANCE...
...SO I DON'T GIVE US AWAY.
ALL SET.
THERE'S A CHRISTMAS TREE, A BROCCOLI TREE...
...ROAST CHICKEN...
Onion soup.
...AND PIZZA.
MERRY CHRISTMAS!
Cheers!

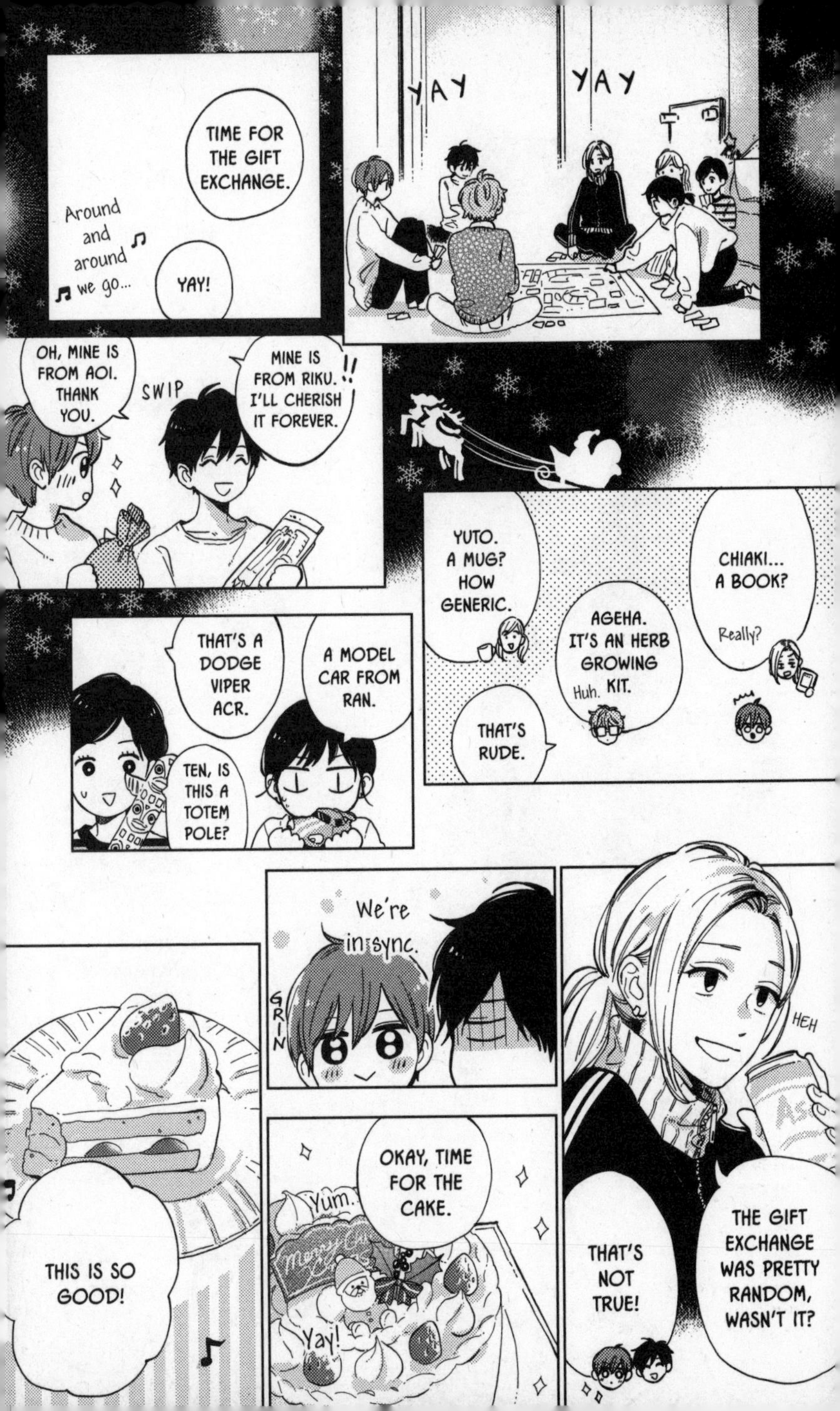

YAY
YAY
TIME FOR THE GIFT EXCHANGE.
Around and around ♫ we go...
YAY!
MINE IS FROM RIKU. I'LL CHERISH IT FOREVER.
SWIP
OH, MINE IS FROM AOI. THANK YOU.
CHIAKI... A BOOK?
Really?
AGEHA. IT'S AN HERB GROWING KIT.
Huh.
YUTO. A MUG? HOW GENERIC.
THAT'S RUDE.
A MODEL CAR FROM RAN.
THAT'S A DODGE VIPER ACR.
TEN, IS THIS A TOTEM POLE?
HEH
THE GIFT EXCHANGE WAS PRETTY RANDOM, WASN'T IT?
THAT'S NOT TRUE!
We're in sync.
GRIN
OKAY, TIME FOR THE CAKE.
Yum.
Yay!
THIS IS SO GOOD!

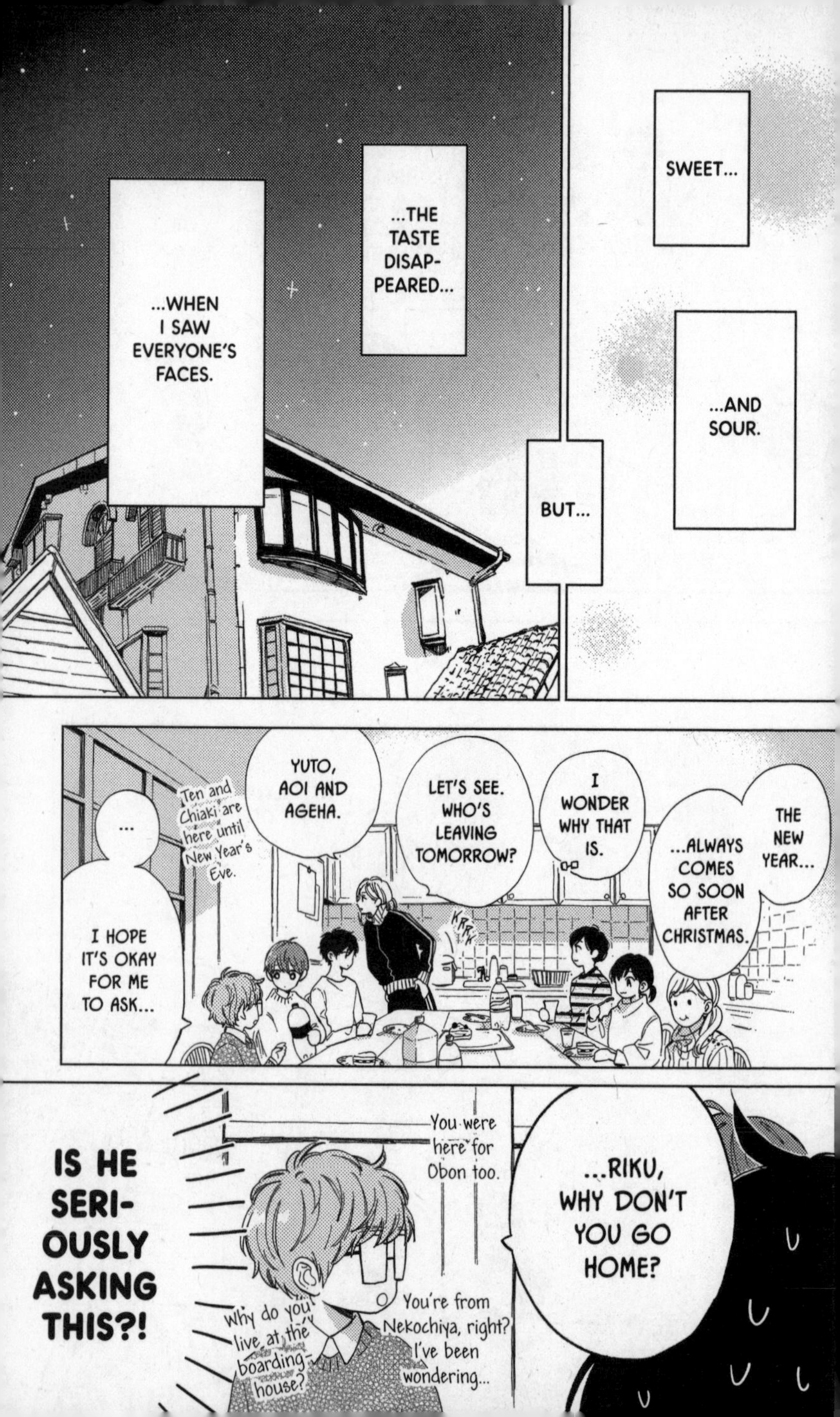
SWEET...
...AND SOUR.
BUT...
...THE TASTE DISAPPEARED...
...WHEN I SAW EVERYONE'S FACES.
THE NEW YEAR...
...ALWAYS COMES SO SOON AFTER CHRISTMAS.
I WONDER WHY THAT IS.
LET'S SEE. WHO'S LEAVING TOMORROW?
YUTO, AOI AND AGEHA.
KRRK
Ten and Chiaki are here until New Year's Eve.
...
I HOPE IT'S OKAY FOR ME TO ASK...
...RIKU, WHY DON'T YOU GO HOME?
You were here for Obon too.
IS HE SERIOUSLY ASKING THIS?!
You're from Nekochiya, right? I've been wondering...
Why do you live at the boardinghouse?

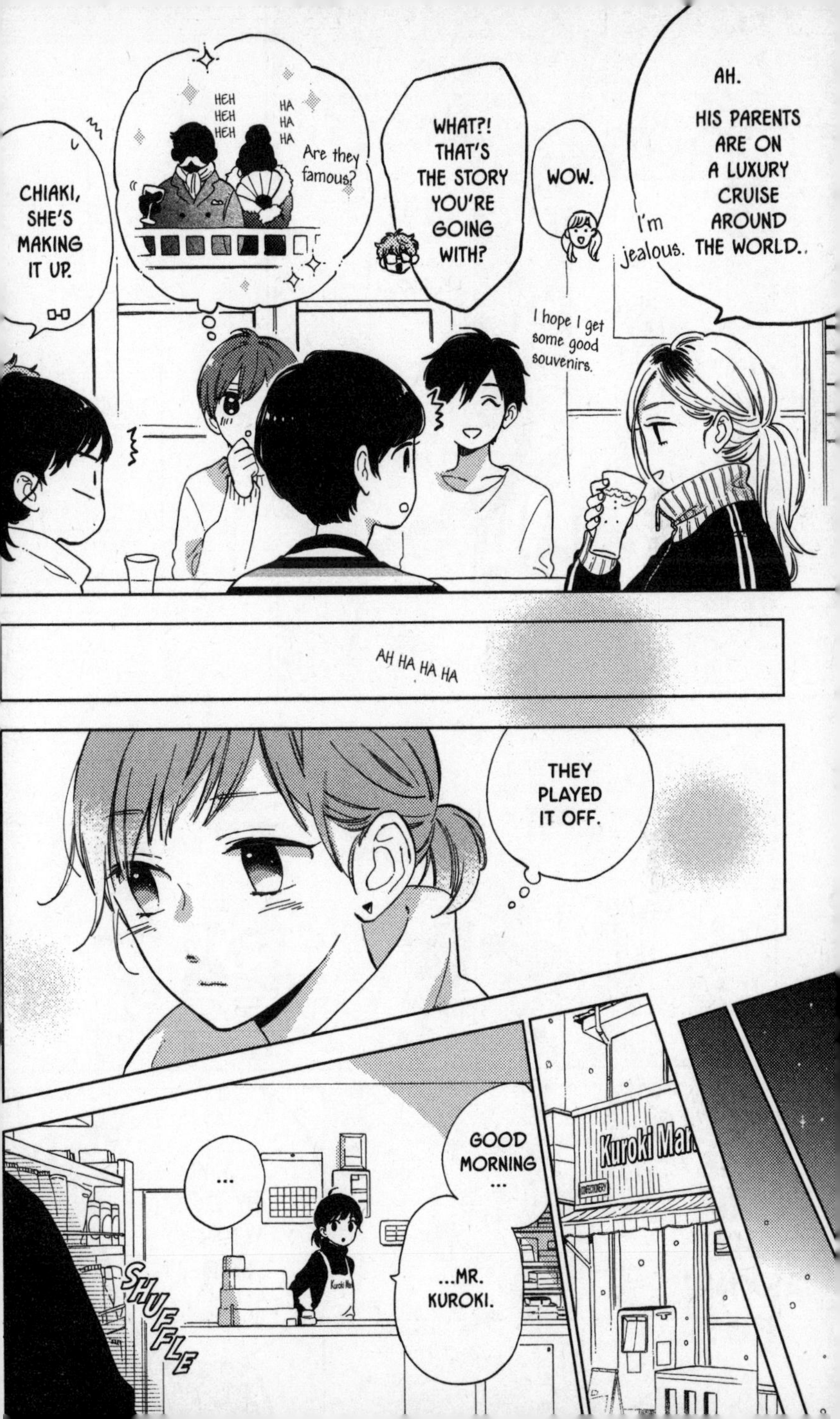

AH. HIS PARENTS ARE ON A LUXURY CRUISE AROUND THE WORLD..
I'm jealous.
I hope I get some good souvenirs.
WOW.
WHAT?! THAT'S THE STORY YOU'RE GOING WITH?
HEH HEH HEH
HA HA HA
Are they famous?
CHIAKI, SHE'S MAKING IT UP.
AH HA HA HA
THEY PLAYED IT OFF.
GOOD MORNING ...
...MR. KUROKI.
...
SHUFFLE

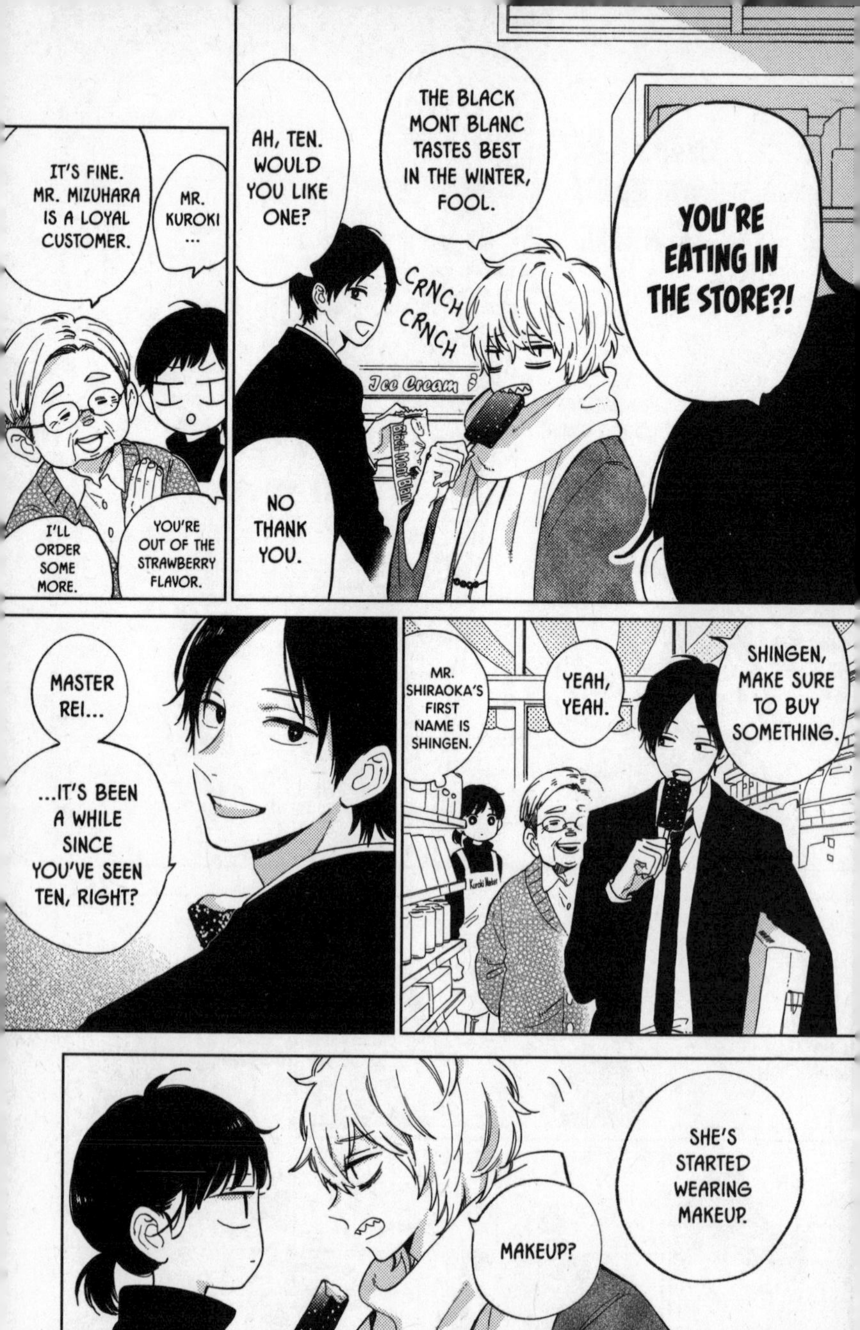
YOU'RE EATING IN THE STORE?!
THE BLACK MONT BLANC TASTES BEST IN THE WINTER, FOOL.
CRNCH CRNCH
Ice Cream
AH, TEN. WOULD YOU LIKE ONE?
Black Mont Blanc
NO THANK YOU.
MR. KUROKI ...
IT'S FINE. MR. MIZUHARA IS A LOYAL CUSTOMER.
YOU'RE OUT OF THE STRAWBERRY FLAVOR.
I'LL ORDER SOME MORE.
SHINGEN, MAKE SURE TO BUY SOMETHING.
YEAH, YEAH.
MR. SHIRAOKA'S FIRST NAME IS SHINGEN.
MASTER REI...
...IT'S BEEN A WHILE SINCE YOU'VE SEEN TEN, RIGHT?
SHE'S STARTED WEARING MAKEUP.
MAKEUP?

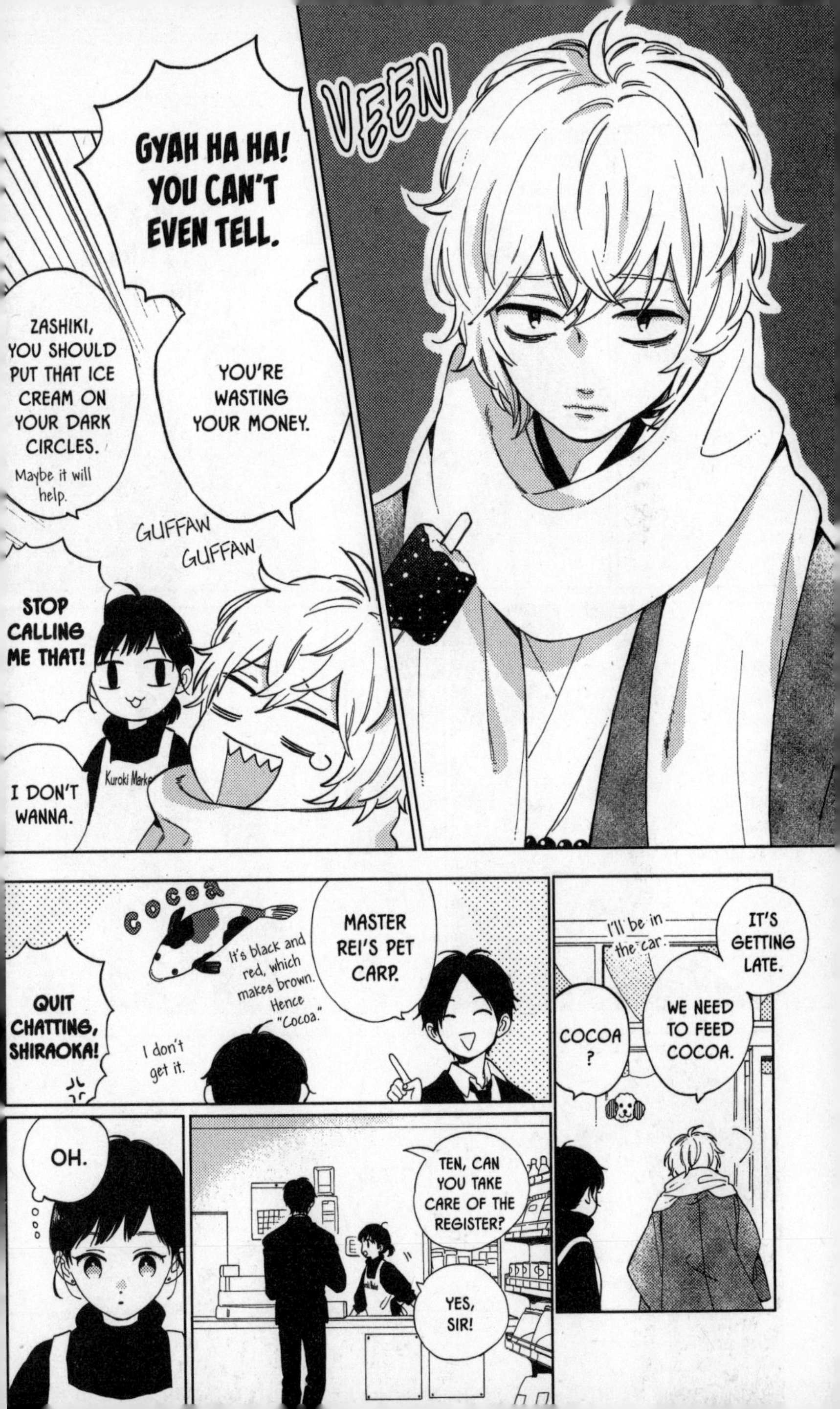
VEEN
GYAH HA HA! YOU CAN'T EVEN TELL.
YOU'RE WASTING YOUR MONEY.
ZASHIKI, YOU SHOULD PUT THAT ICE CREAM ON YOUR DARK CIRCLES.
Maybe it will help.
GUFFAW GUFFAW
STOP CALLING ME THAT!
Kuroki Market
I DON'T WANNA.
IT'S GETTING LATE.
I'll be in the car.
WE NEED TO FEED COCOA.
COCOA ?
MASTER REI'S PET CARP.
It's black and red, which makes brown. Hence "Cocoa."
COCOA
I don't get it.
QUIT CHATTING, SHIRAOKA!
TEN, CAN YOU TAKE CARE OF THE REGISTER?
YES, SIR!
OH.

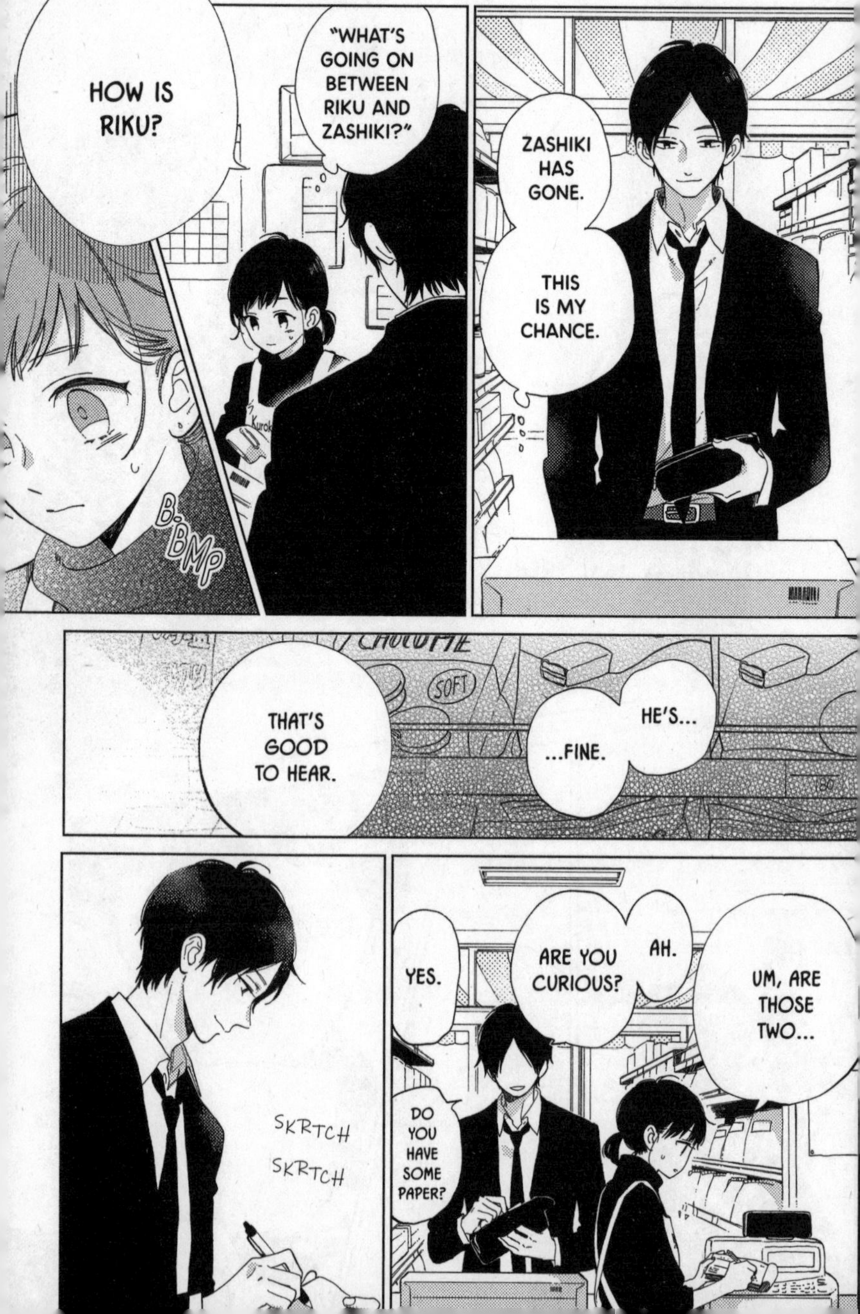
ZASHIKI HAS GONE.
THIS IS MY CHANCE.
"WHAT'S GOING ON BETWEEN RIKU AND ZASHIKI?"
HOW IS RIKU?
B-BMP
HE'S...
...FINE.
SOFT
THAT'S GOOD TO HEAR.
UM, ARE THOSE TWO...
AH.
ARE YOU CURIOUS?
YES.
DO YOU HAVE SOME PAPER?
SKRTCH
SKRTCH

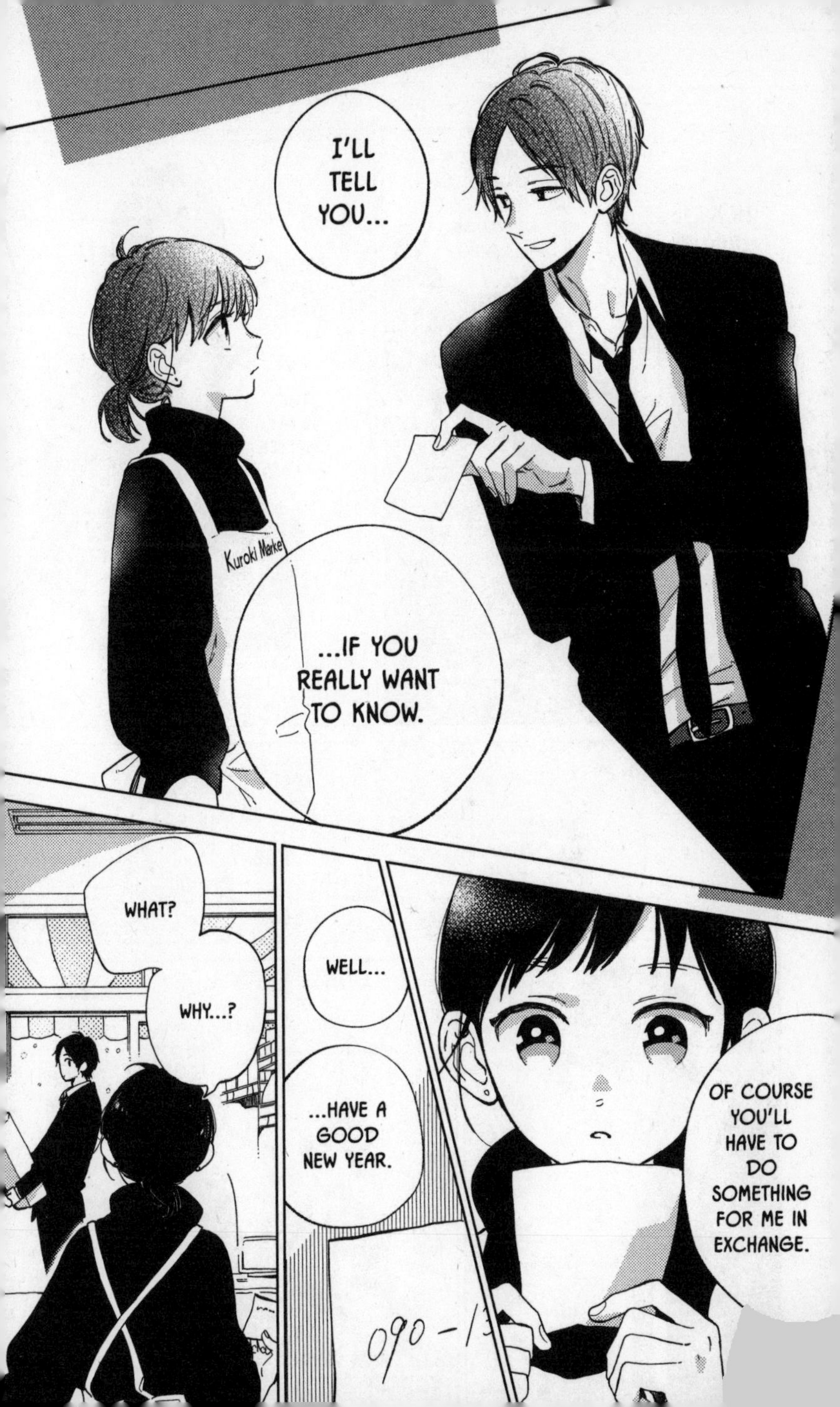
I'LL TELL YOU...
...IF YOU REALLY WANT TO KNOW.
OF COURSE YOU'LL HAVE TO DO SOMETHING FOR ME IN EXCHANGE.
WELL...
...HAVE A GOOD NEW YEAR.
WHAT?
WHY...?

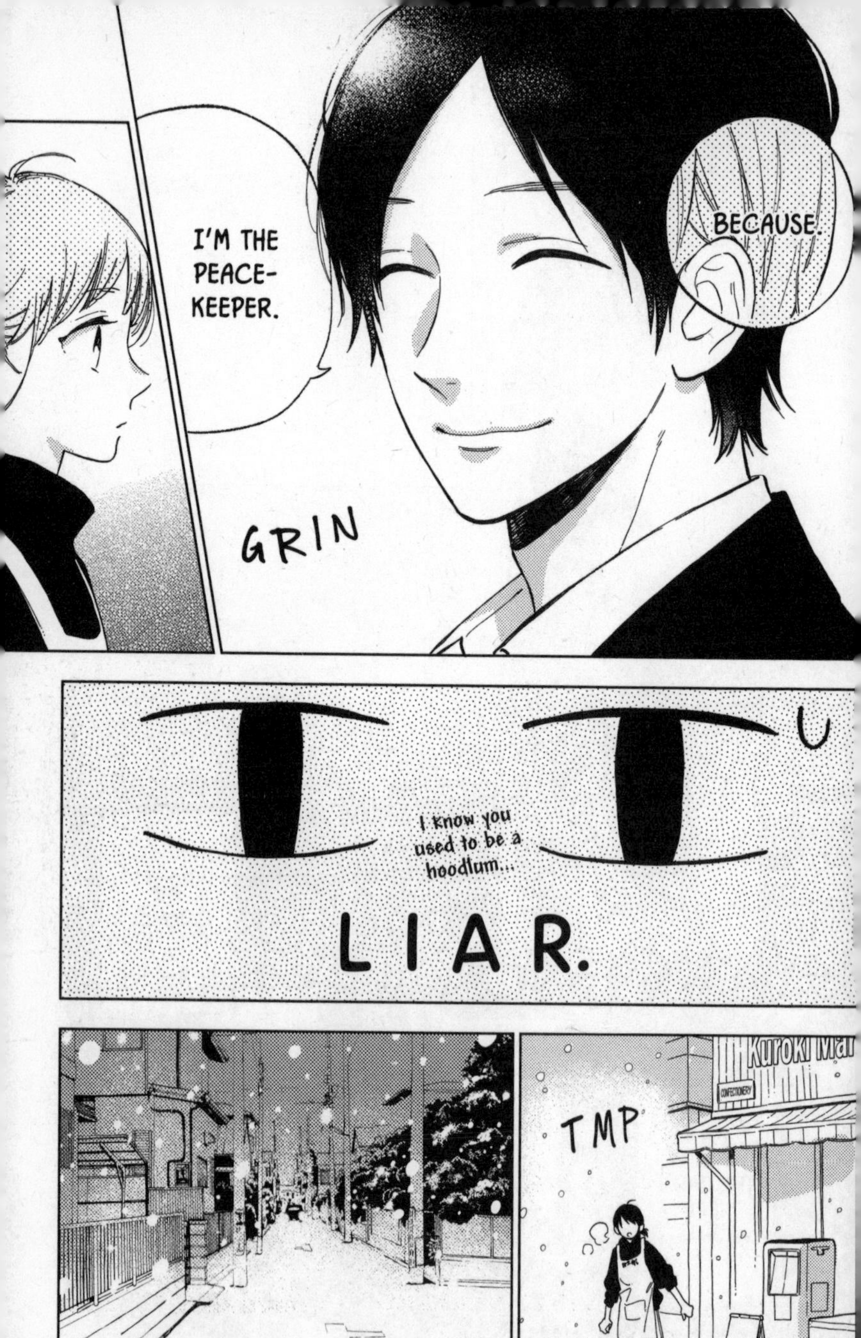
BECAUSE.
I'M THE PEACE-KEEPER.
GRIN
I know you used to be a hoodlum...
LIAR.
Kuroki Ma
CONFECTIONERY
TMP

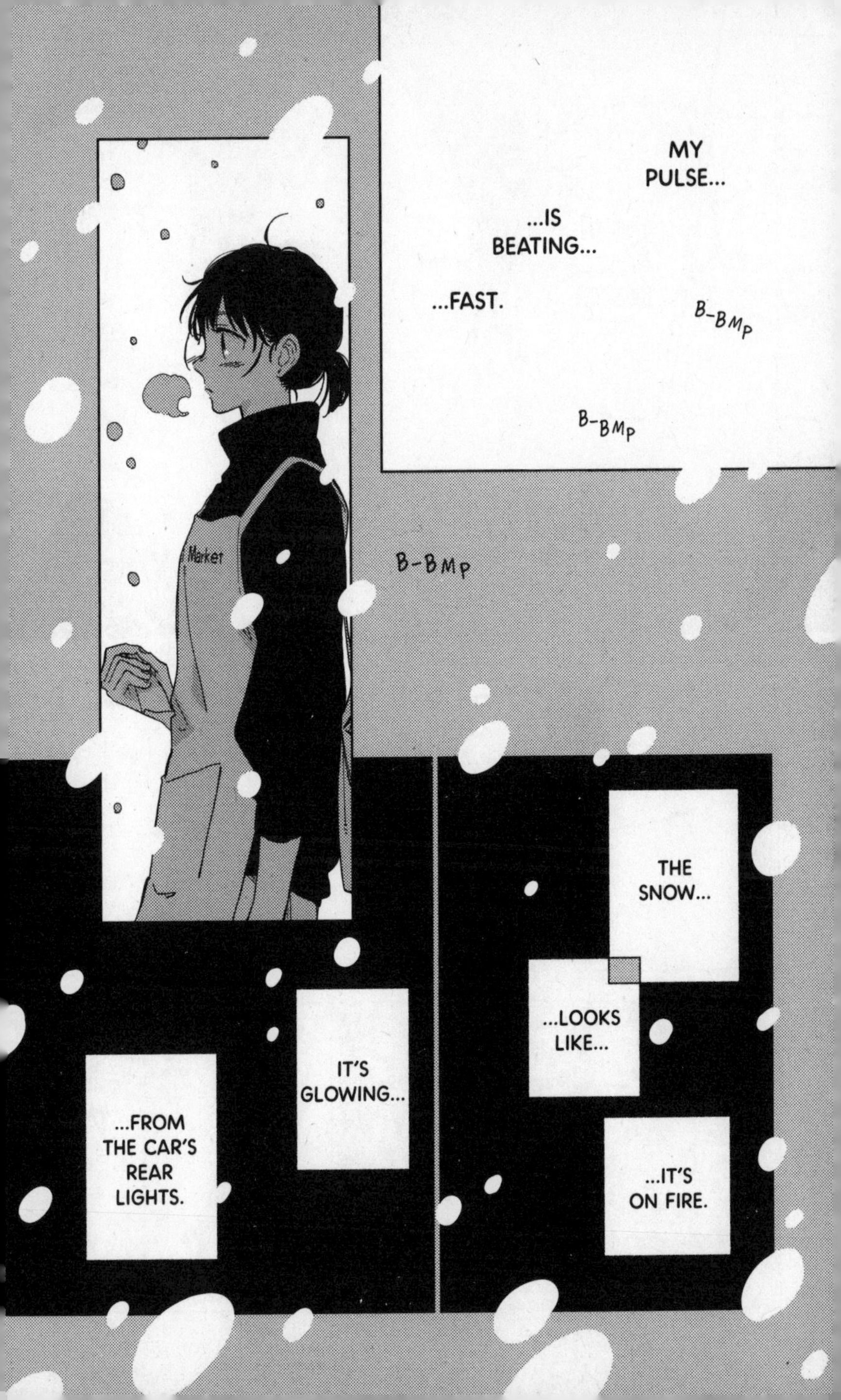
MY PULSE...
...IS BEATING...
...FAST.
B-BMP
B-BMP
B-BMP
Market
THE SNOW...
...LOOKS LIKE...
...IT'S ON FIRE.
IT'S GLOWING...
...FROM THE CAR'S REAR LIGHTS.

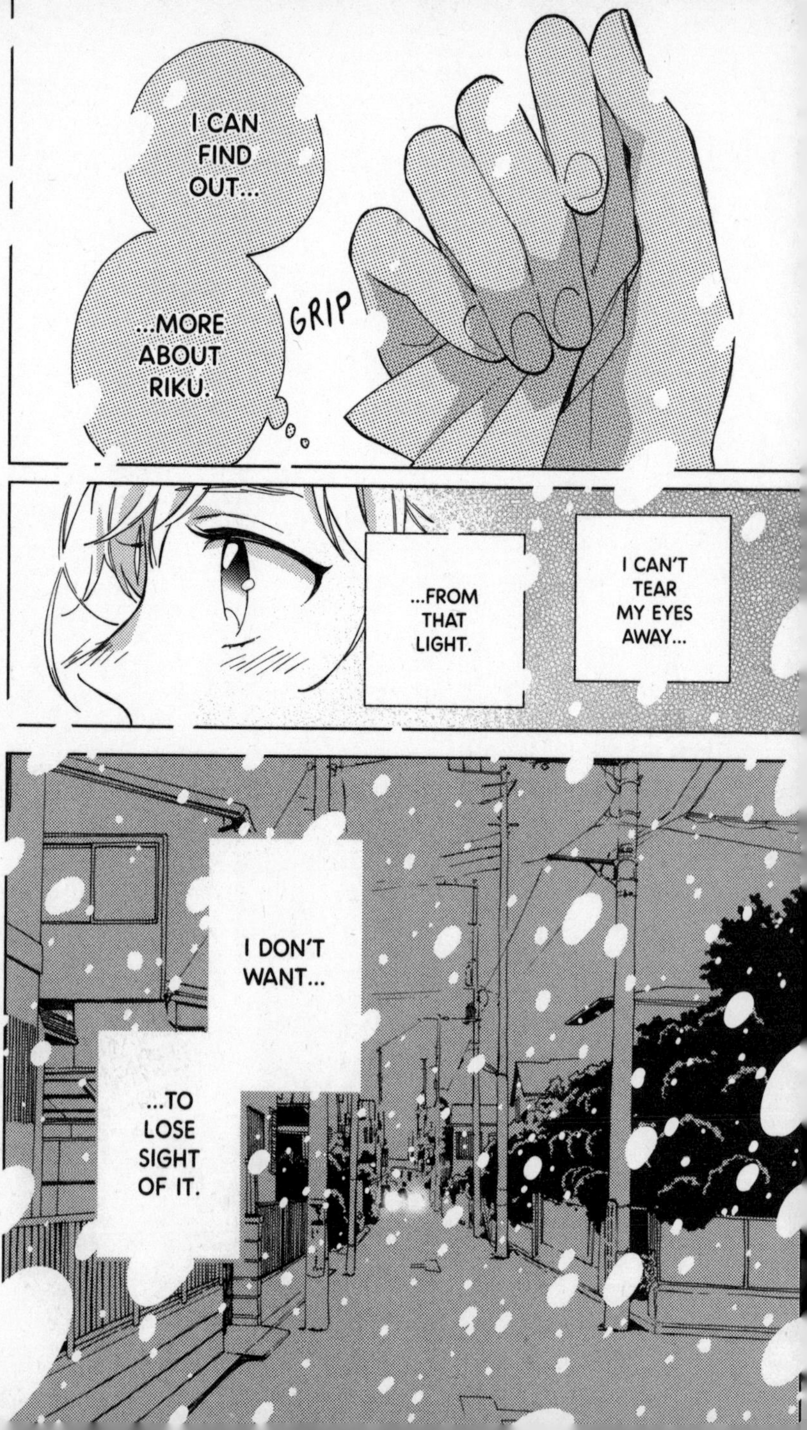
I CAN FIND OUT...
...MORE ABOUT RIKU.
GRIP
I CAN'T TEAR MY EYES AWAY...
...FROM THAT LIGHT.
I DON'T WANT...
...TO LOSE SIGHT OF IT.

SHORTCAKE
CAKE

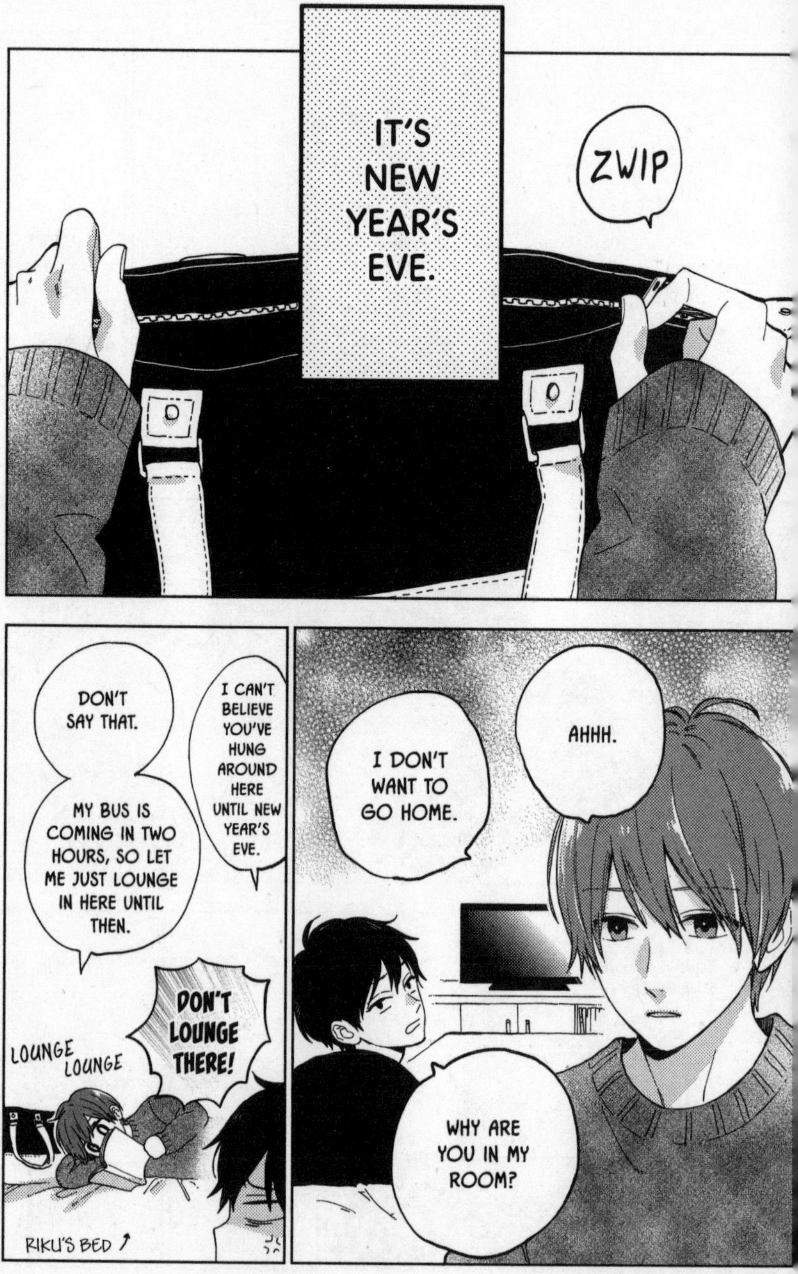
ZWIP
IT'S NEW YEAR'S EVE.
AHHH.
I DON'T WANT TO GO HOME.
WHY ARE YOU IN MY ROOM?
I CAN'T BELIEVE YOU'VE HUNG AROUND HERE UNTIL NEW YEAR'S EVE.
DON'T SAY THAT.
MY BUS IS COMING IN TWO HOURS, SO LET ME JUST LOUNGE IN HERE UNTIL THEN.
DON'T LOUNGE THERE!
LOUNGE LOUNGE
RIKU'S BED

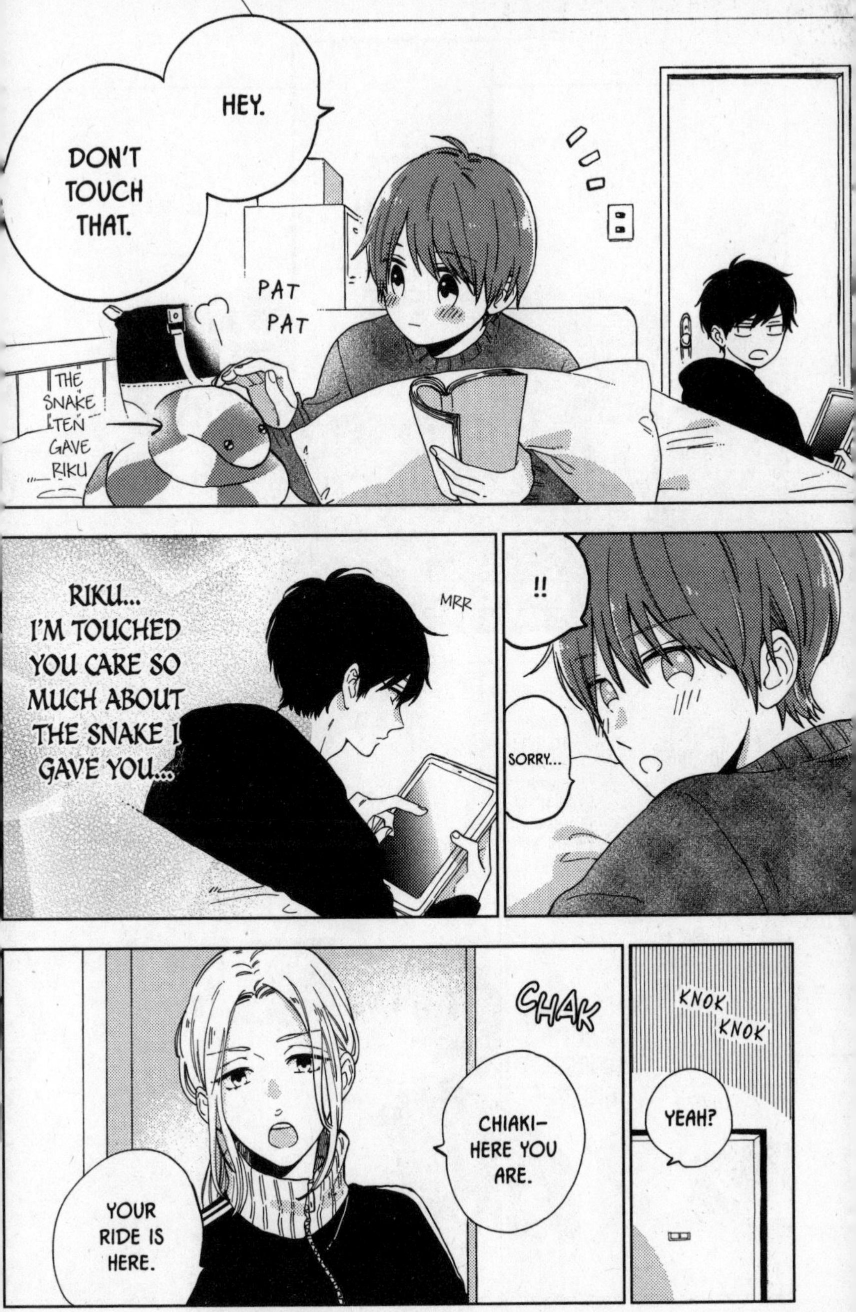
HEY.
DON'T TOUCH THAT.
PAT PAT
THE SNAKE TEN GAVE RIKU
!!
SORRY...
MRR
RIKU... I'M TOUCHED YOU CARE SO MUCH ABOUT THE SNAKE I GAVE YOU...
KNOK KNOK
YEAH?
CHAK
CHIAKI—HERE YOU ARE.
YOUR RIDE IS HERE.

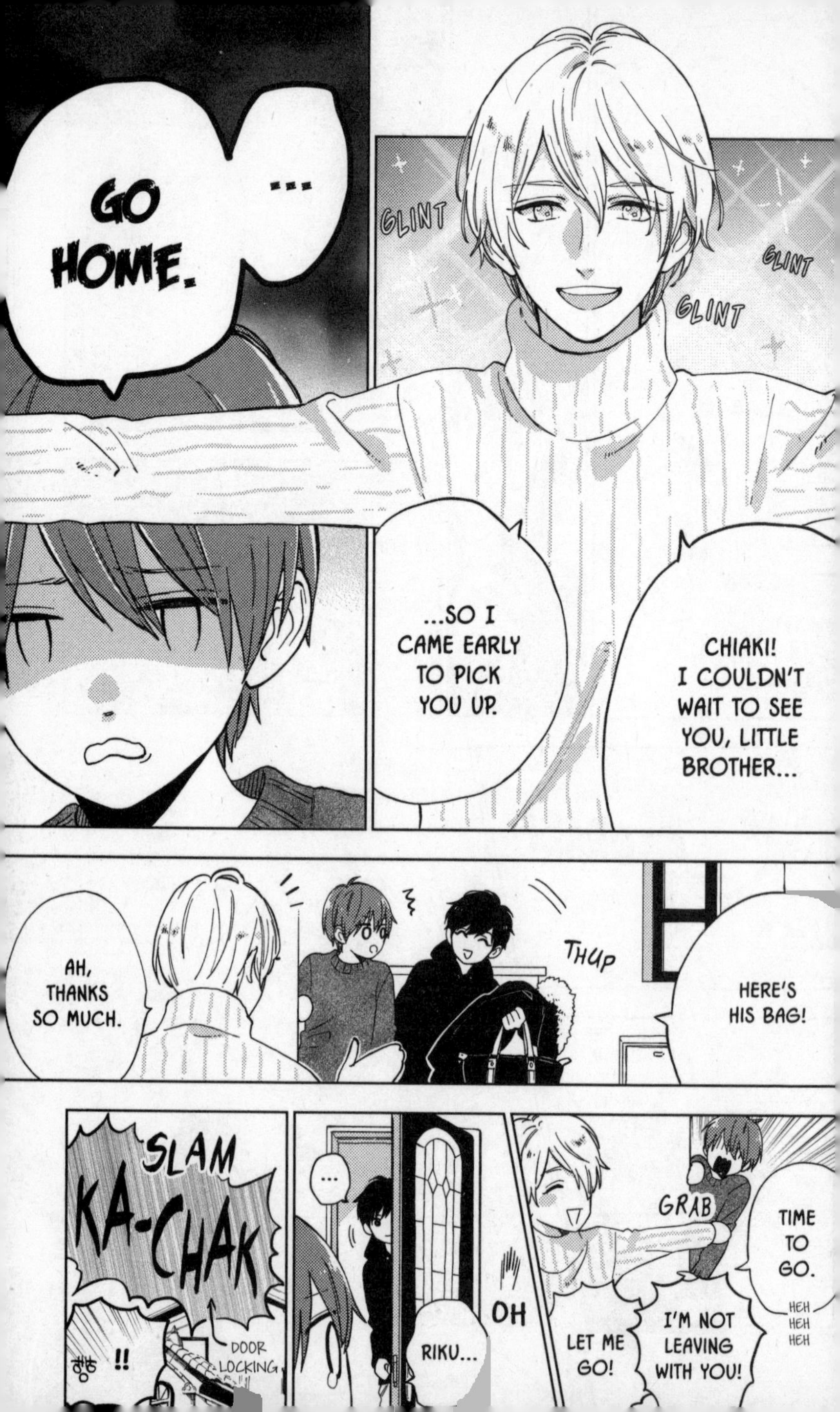
GLINT
GLINT
GLINT
CHIAKI! I COULDN'T WAIT TO SEE YOU, LITTLE BROTHER...
...SO I CAME EARLY TO PICK YOU UP.
...
GO HOME.
HERE'S HIS BAG!
THUP
AH, THANKS SO MUCH.
TIME TO GO.
HEH HEH HEH
GRAB
I'M NOT LEAVING WITH YOU!
LET ME GO!
OH
...
RIKU...
SLAM
KA-CHAK
DOOR LOCKING
!!

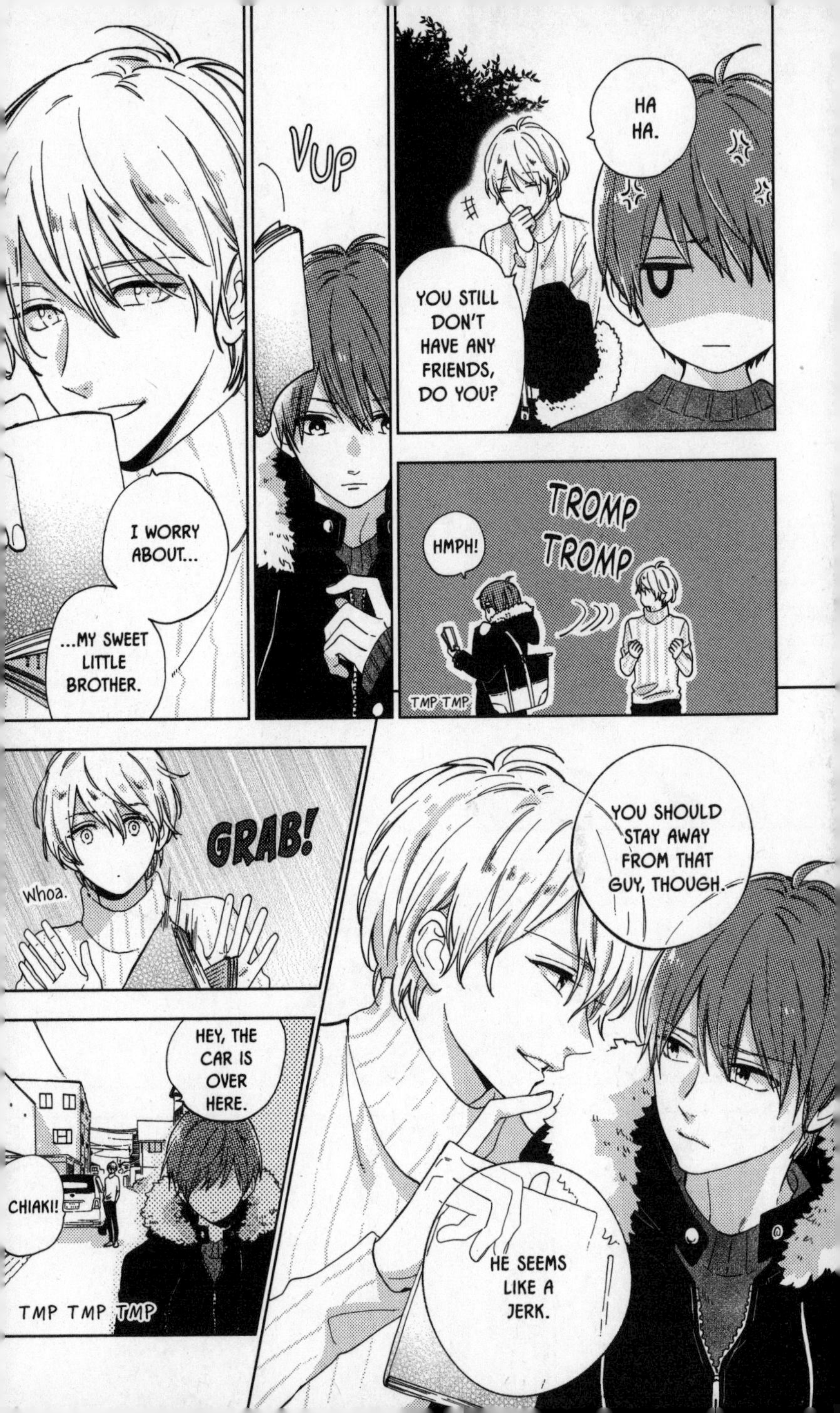
HA HA.
YOU STILL DON'T HAVE ANY FRIENDS, DO YOU?
TROMP TROMP
HMPH!
TMP TMP
VUP
I WORRY ABOUT...
...MY SWEET LITTLE BROTHER.
YOU SHOULD STAY AWAY FROM THAT GUY, THOUGH.
HE SEEMS LIKE A JERK.
GRAB!
Whoa.
HEY, THE CAR IS OVER HERE.
CHIAKI!
TMP TMP TMP

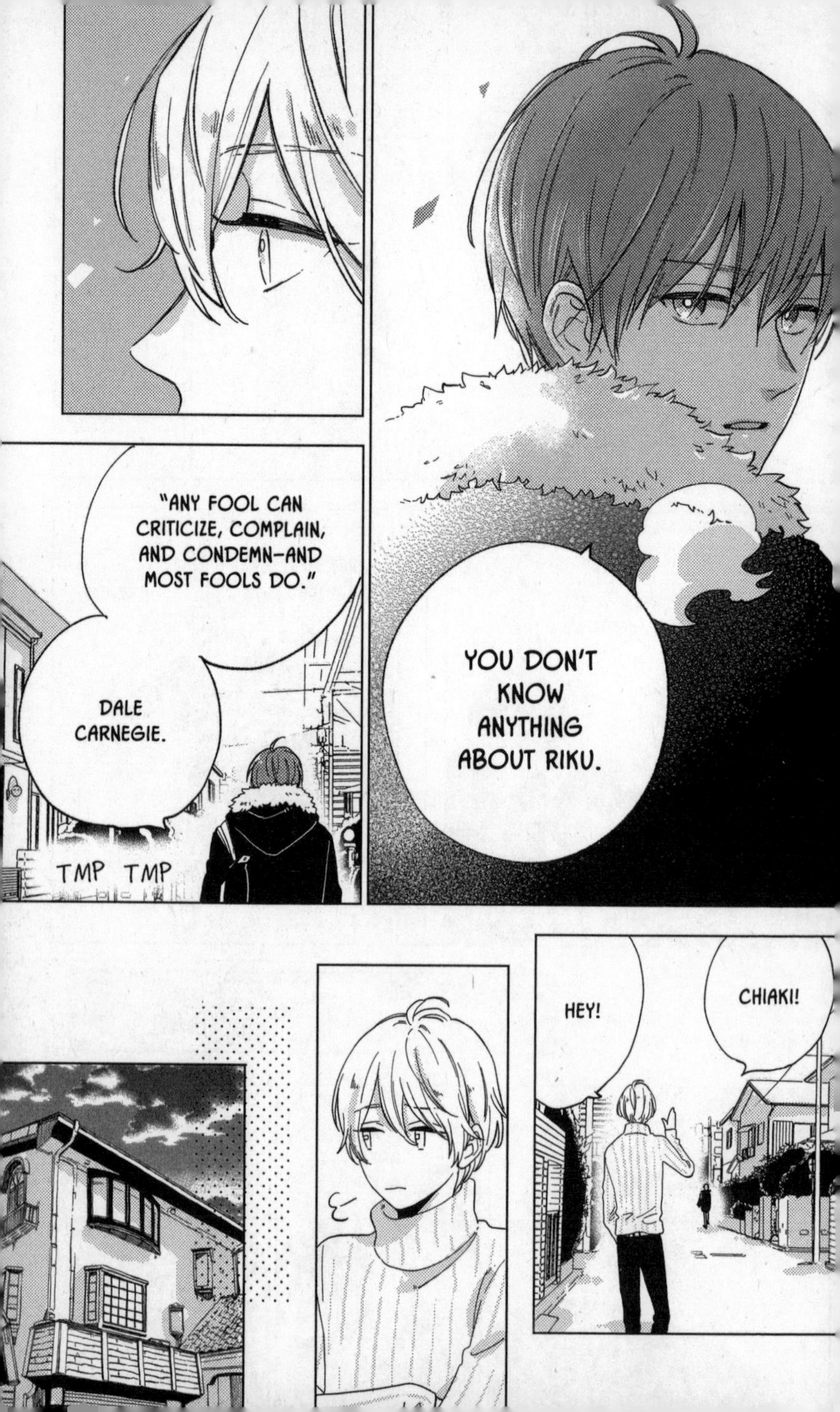
YOU DON'T KNOW ANYTHING ABOUT RIKU.
"ANY FOOL CAN CRITICIZE, COMPLAIN, AND CONDEMN—AND MOST FOOLS DO."
DALE CARNEGIE.
TMP TMP
CHIAKI!
HEY!

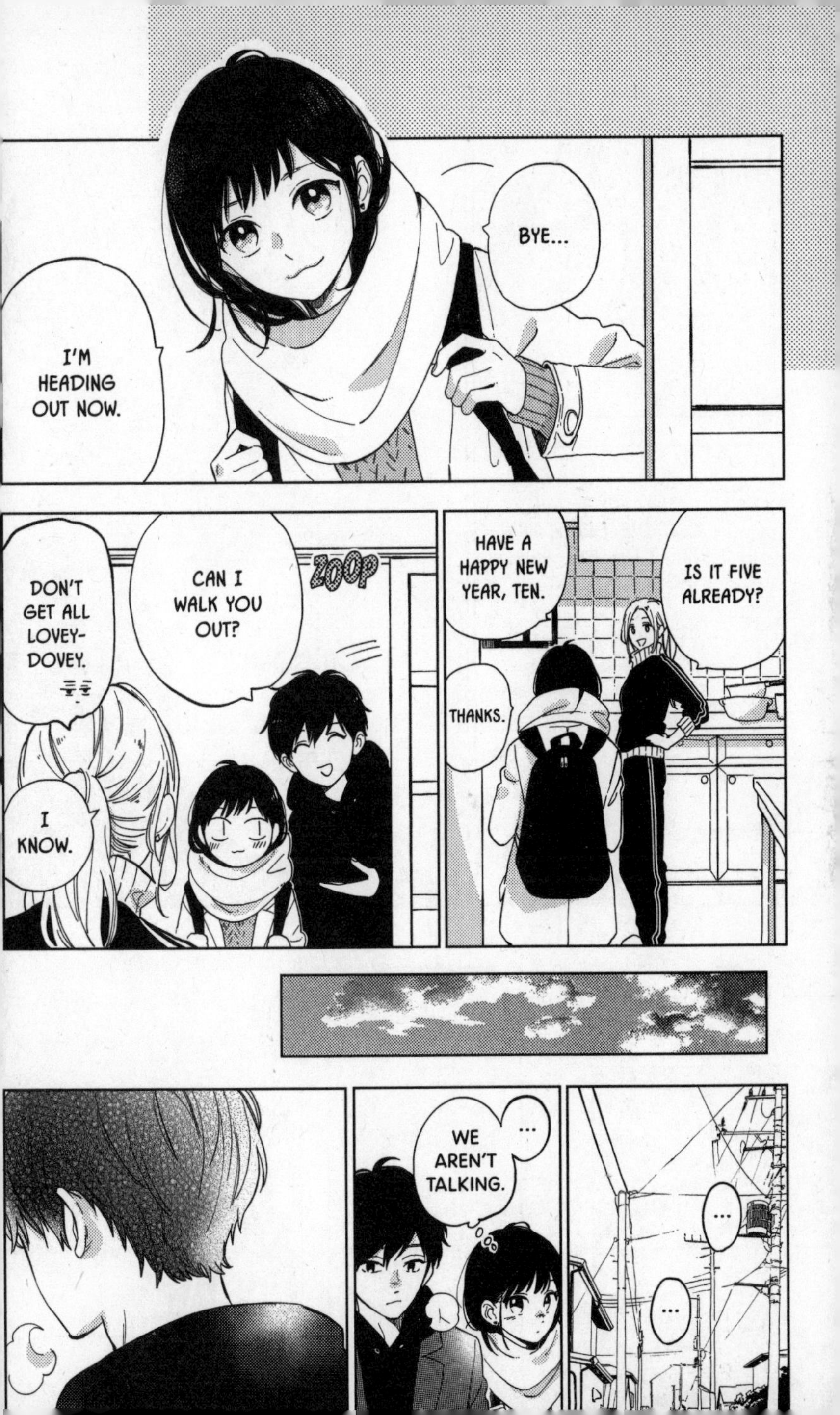
BYE...
I'M HEADING OUT NOW.
IS IT FIVE ALREADY?
HAVE A HAPPY NEW YEAR, TEN.
THANKS.
ZOOP
CAN I WALK YOU OUT?
DON'T GET ALL LOVEY-DOVEY.
I KNOW.
...
...
...
WE AREN'T TALKING.

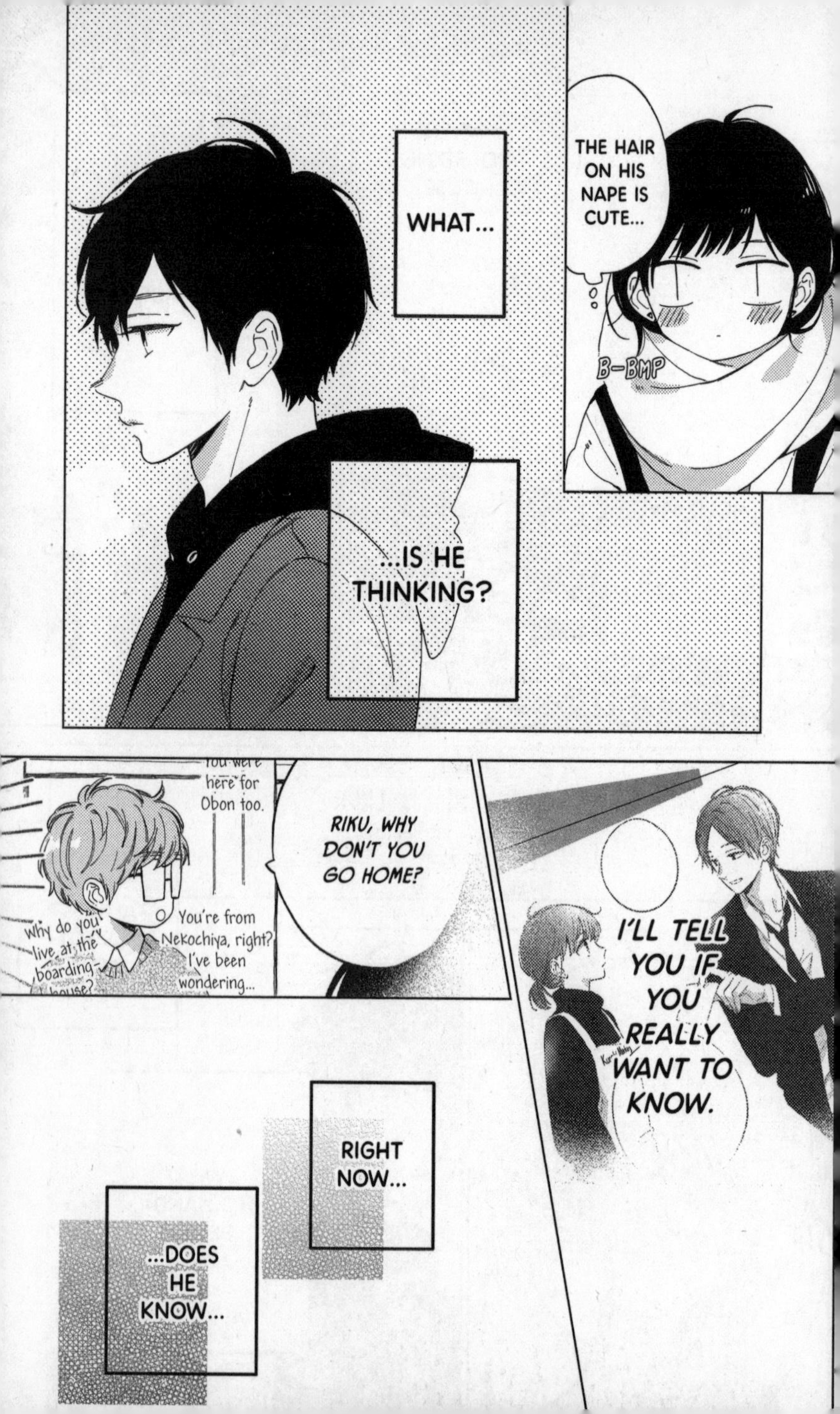
THE HAIR ON HIS NAPE IS CUTE...
B-BMP
WHAT...
...IS HE THINKING?
I'LL TELL YOU IF YOU REALLY WANT TO KNOW.
RIKU, WHY DON'T YOU GO HOME?
here for Obon too.
You're from Nekochiya, right? I've been wondering...
Why do you live at the boarding-house?
RIGHT NOW...
...DOES HE KNOW...

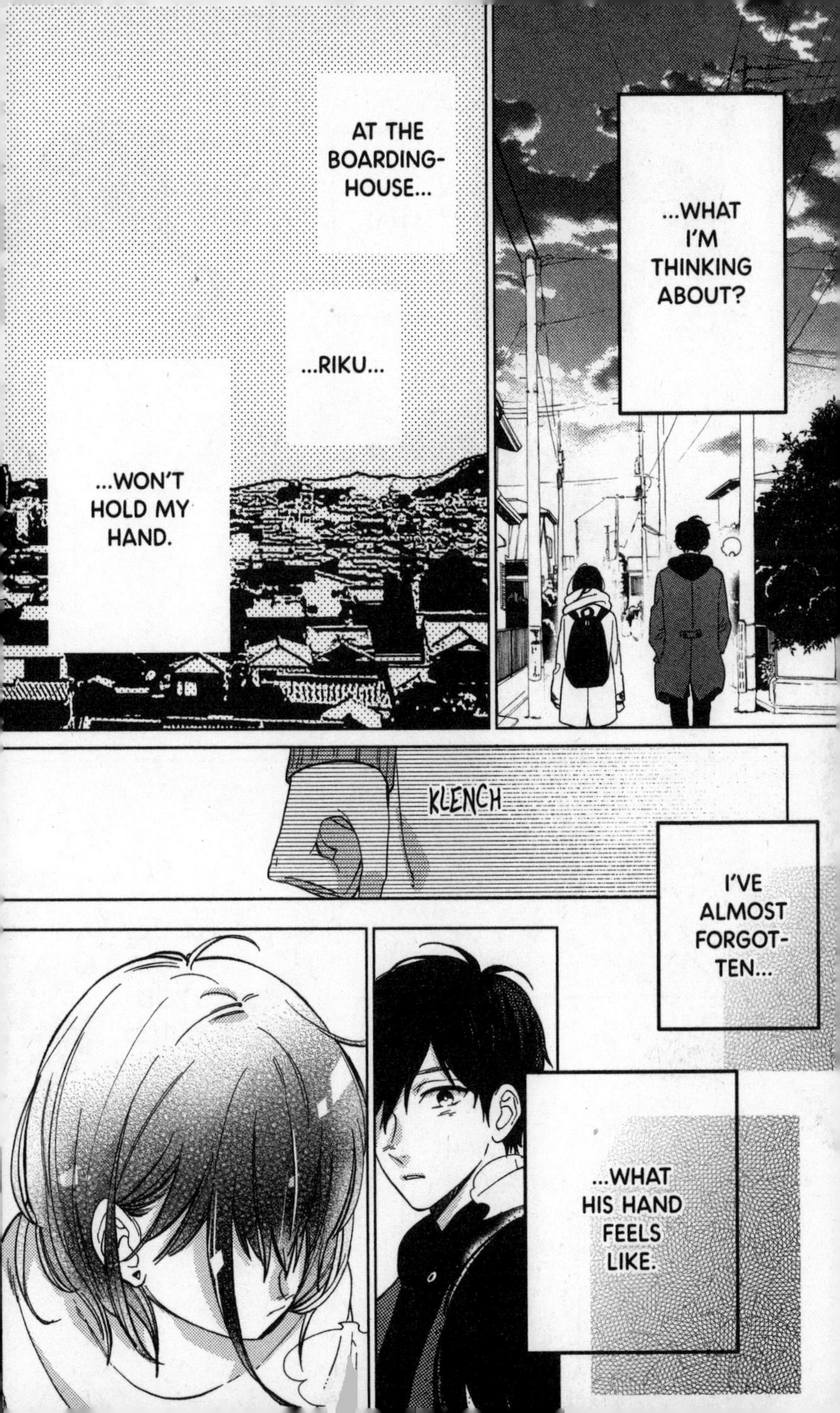
...WHAT I'M THINKING ABOUT?
AT THE BOARDING-HOUSE...
...RIKU...
...WON'T HOLD MY HAND.
KLENCH
I'VE ALMOST FORGOT-TEN...
...WHAT HIS HAND FEELS LIKE.

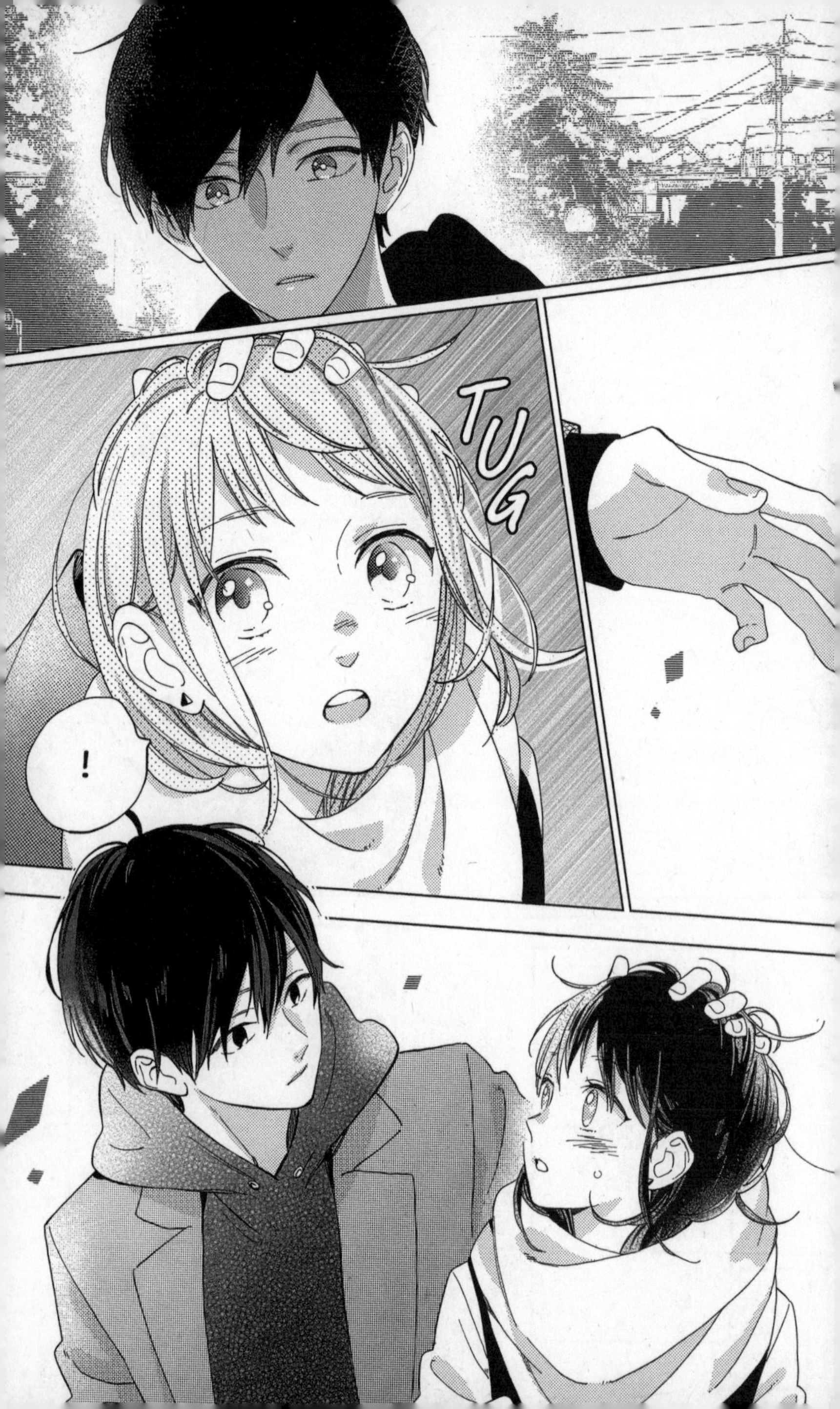
TUG
!

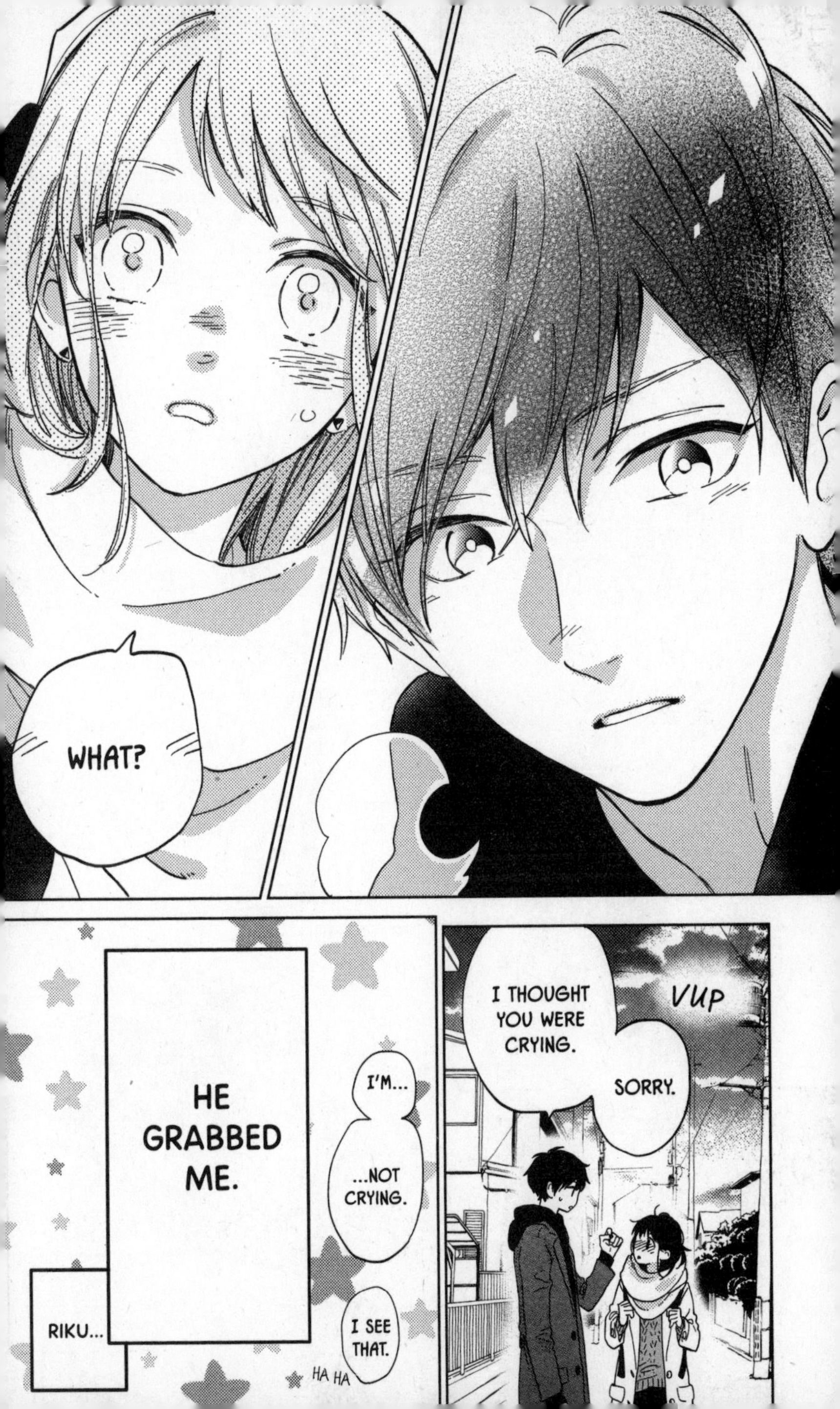
WHAT?
I THOUGHT YOU WERE CRYING.
VUP
SORRY.
I'M...
...NOT CRYING.
I SEE THAT.
HA HA
HE GRABBED ME.
RIKU...

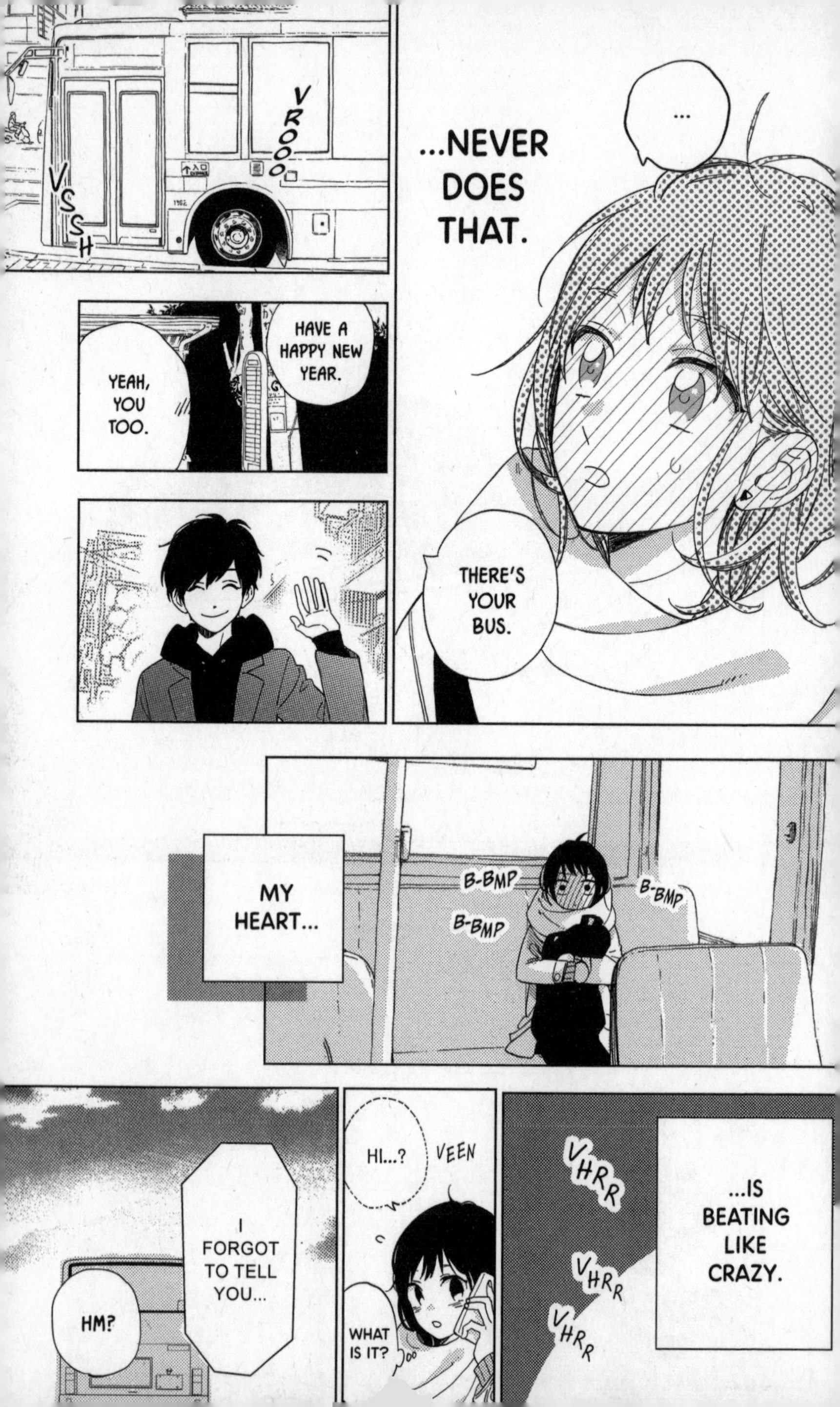
...
...NEVER DOES THAT.
THERE'S YOUR BUS.
VROOOO
VSSH
HAVE A HAPPY NEW YEAR.
YEAH, YOU TOO.
B-BMP
B-BMP
MY HEART...
B-BMP
...IS BEATING LIKE CRAZY.
VHRR
VHRR
VHRR
VEEN
HI...?
WHAT IS IT?
I FORGOT TO TELL YOU...
HM?

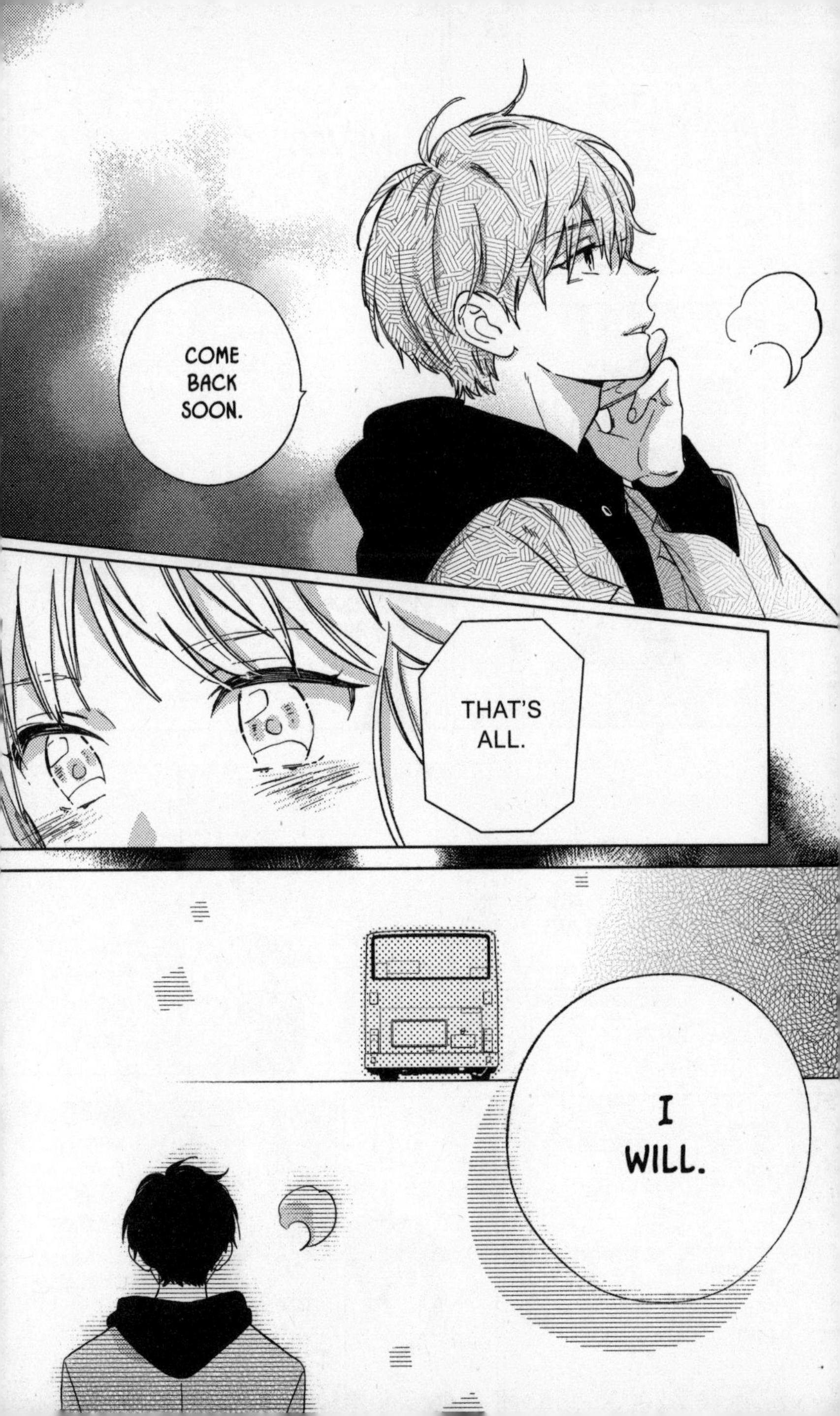
COME BACK SOON.
THAT'S ALL.
I WILL.

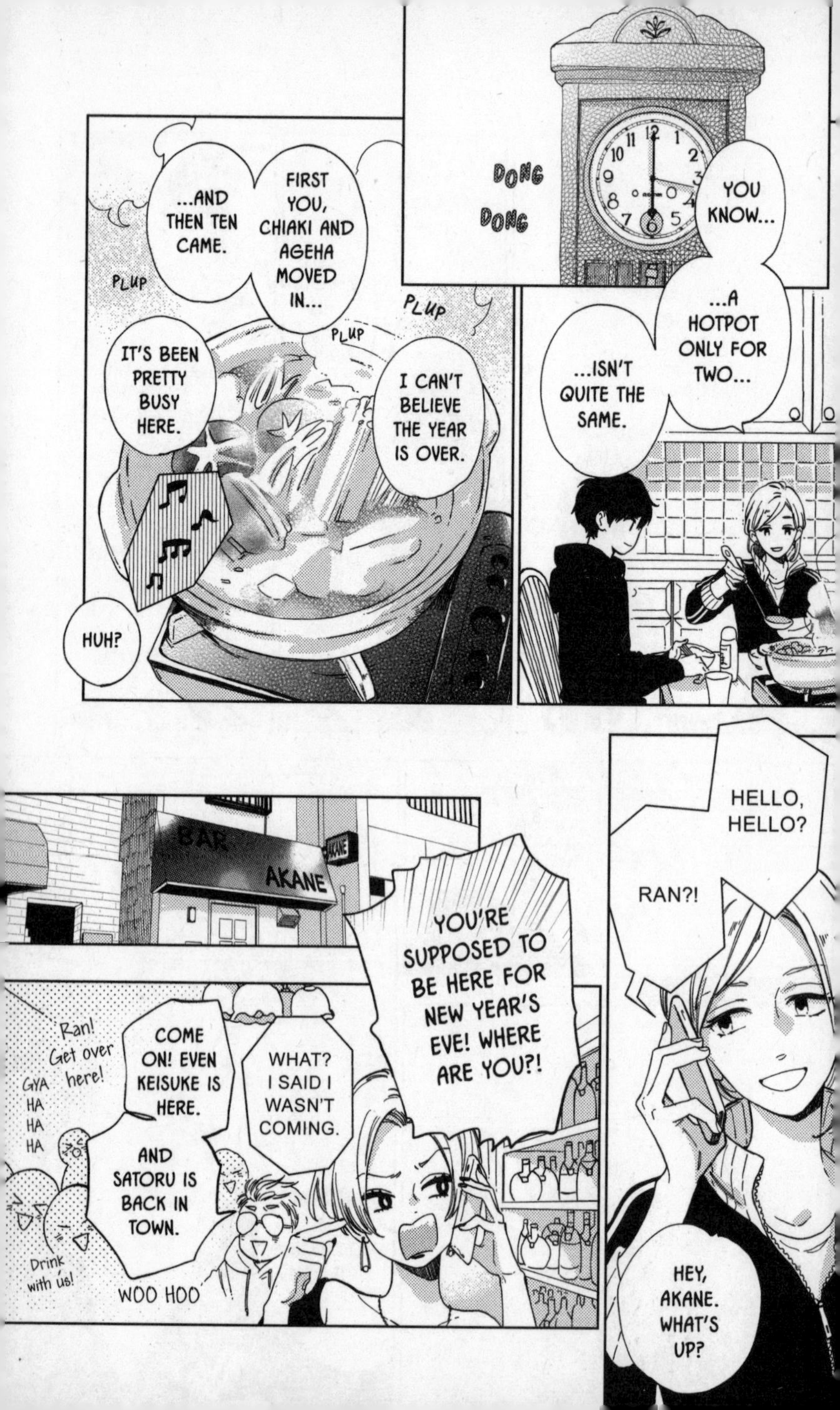
DONG
DONG
YOU KNOW...
...A HOTPOT ONLY FOR TWO...
...ISN'T QUITE THE SAME.
FIRST YOU, CHIAKI AND AGEHA MOVED IN...
...AND THEN TEN CAME.
PLUP
PLUP
PLUP
I CAN'T BELIEVE THE YEAR IS OVER.
IT'S BEEN PRETTY BUSY HERE.
HUH?
HELLO, HELLO?
RAN?!
HEY, AKANE. WHAT'S UP?
BAR
AKANE
AKANE
YOU'RE SUPPOSED TO BE HERE FOR NEW YEAR'S EVE! WHERE ARE YOU?!
WHAT? I SAID I WASN'T COMING.
COME ON! EVEN KEISUKE IS HERE.
AND SATORU IS BACK IN TOWN.
Ran! Get over here!
GYA HA HA HA
Drink with us!
WOO HOO

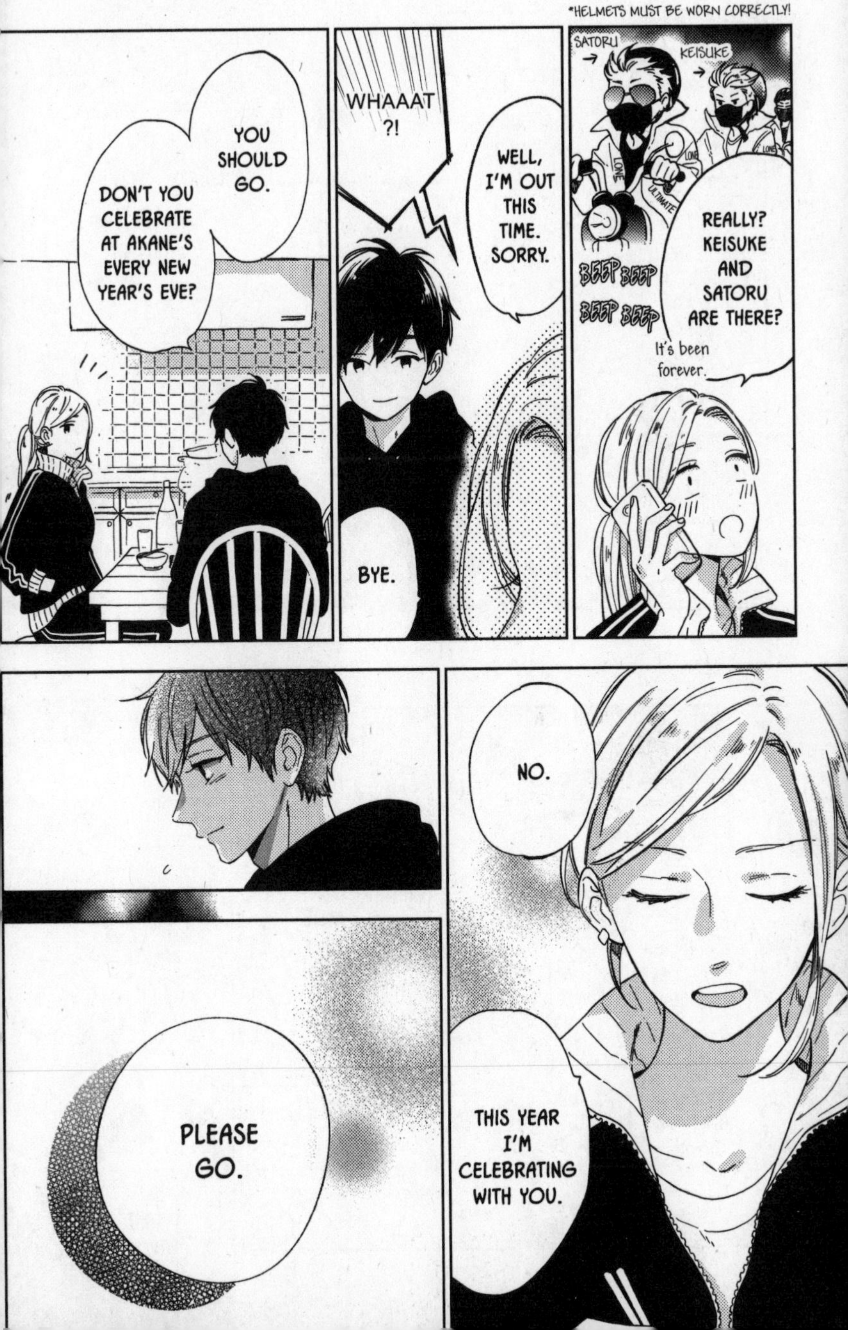
*HELMETS MUST BE WORN CORRECTLY!
SATORU
KEISUKE
LONE
ULTIMATE
BEEP BEEP
BEEP BEEP
REALLY? KEISUKE AND SATORU ARE THERE?
It's been forever.
WELL, I'M OUT THIS TIME. SORRY.
WHAAAT?!
BYE.
YOU SHOULD GO.
DON'T YOU CELEBRATE AT AKANE'S EVERY NEW YEAR'S EVE?
NO.
THIS YEAR I'M CELEBRATING WITH YOU.
PLEASE GO.

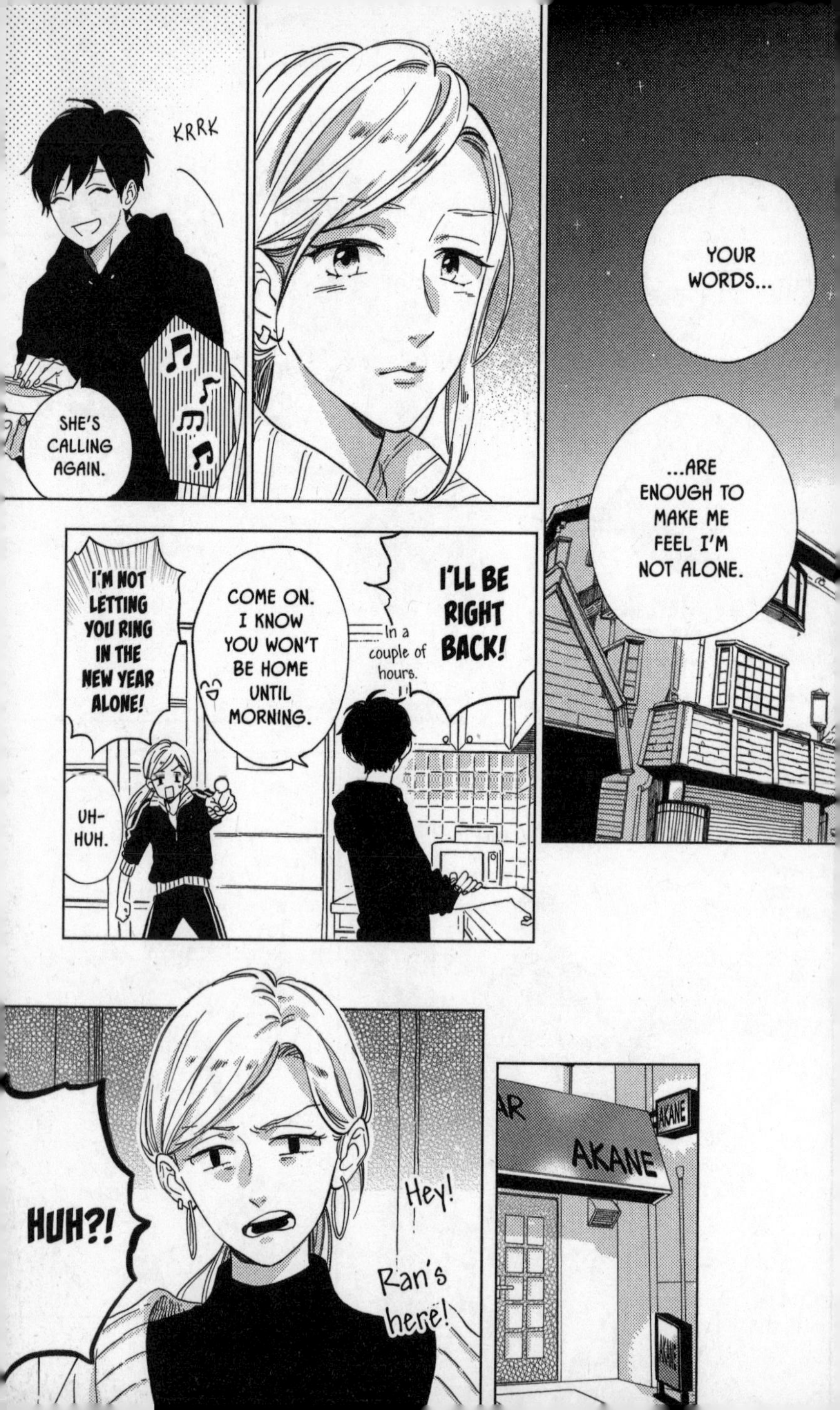
YOUR WORDS...
...ARE ENOUGH TO MAKE ME FEEL I'M NOT ALONE.
KRRK
SHE'S CALLING AGAIN.
I'LL BE RIGHT BACK!
In a couple of hours.
COME ON. I KNOW YOU WON'T BE HOME UNTIL MORNING.
I'M NOT LETTING YOU RING IN THE NEW YEAR ALONE!
UH-HUH.
AKANE
AR
AKANE
Hey!
Ran's here!
HUH?!

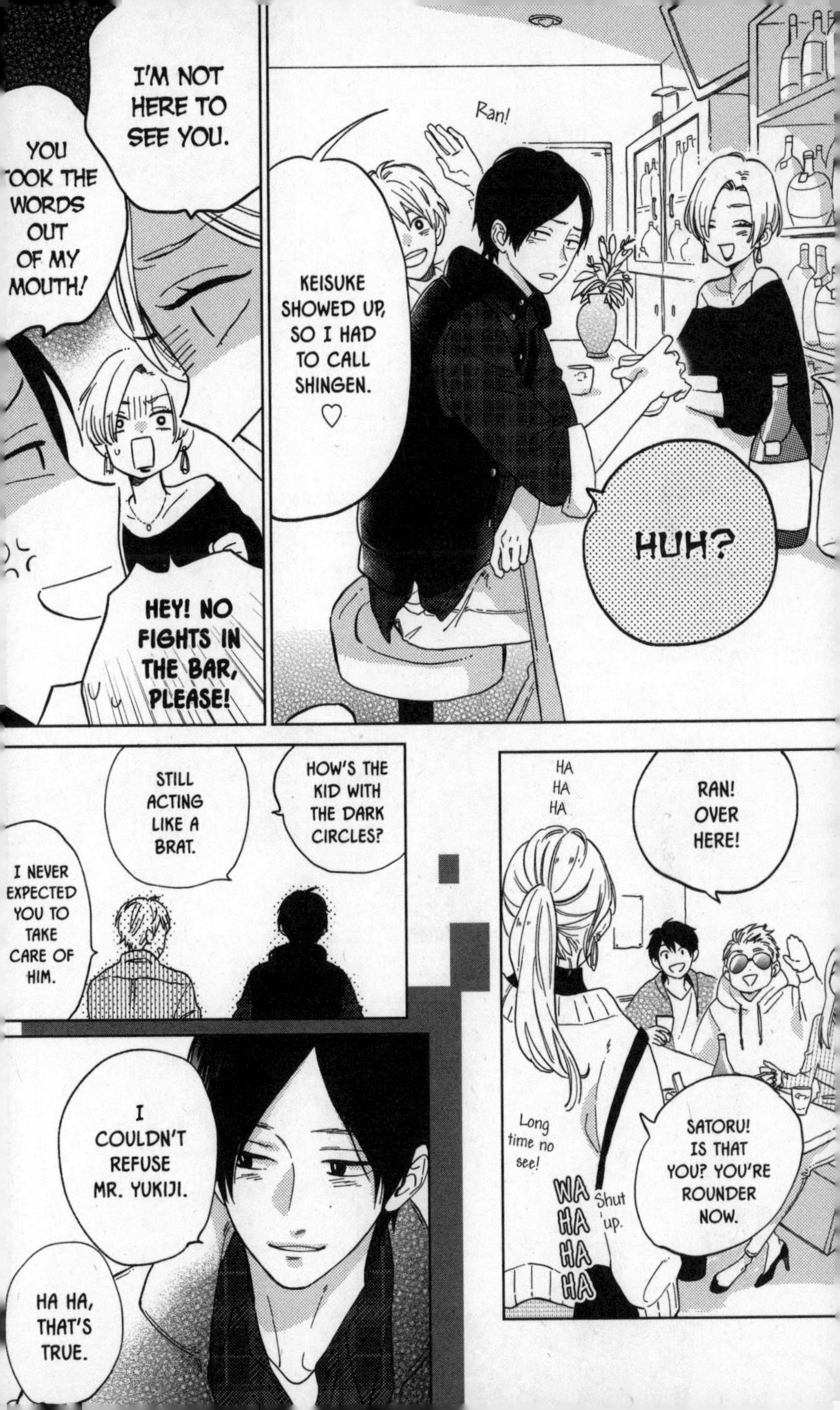
Ran!
KEISUKE SHOWED UP, SO I HAD TO CALL SHINGEN. ♡
HUH?
I'M NOT HERE TO SEE YOU.
YOU TOOK THE WORDS OUT OF MY MOUTH!
HEY! NO FIGHTS IN THE BAR, PLEASE!
HA HA HA
RAN! OVER HERE!
SATORU! IS THAT YOU? YOU'RE ROUNDER NOW.
Long time no see!
WA HA HA HA HA
Shut up.
HOW'S THE KID WITH THE DARK CIRCLES?
STILL ACTING LIKE A BRAT.
I NEVER EXPECTED YOU TO TAKE CARE OF HIM.
I COULDN'T REFUSE MR. YUKIJI.
HA HA, THAT'S TRUE.

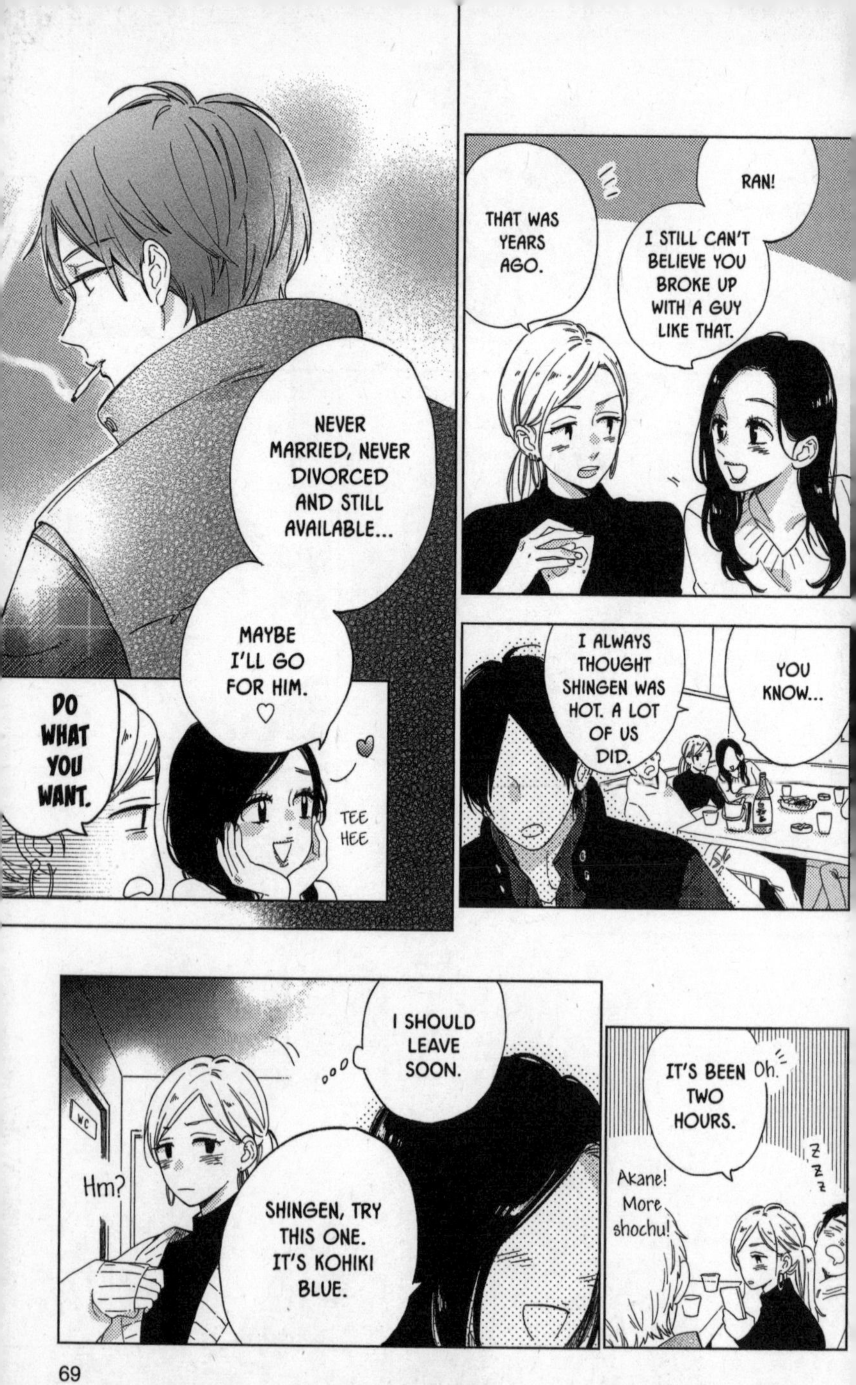
RAN!
I STILL CAN'T BELIEVE YOU BROKE UP WITH A GUY LIKE THAT.
THAT WAS YEARS AGO.
YOU KNOW...
I ALWAYS THOUGHT SHINGEN WAS HOT. A LOT OF US DID.
NEVER MARRIED, NEVER DIVORCED AND STILL AVAILABLE...
MAYBE I'LL GO FOR HIM. ♡
TEE HEE
DO WHAT YOU WANT.
Oh.
IT'S BEEN TWO HOURS.
Akane! More shochu!
I SHOULD LEAVE SOON.
Hm?
SHINGEN, TRY THIS ONE. IT'S KOHIKI BLUE.

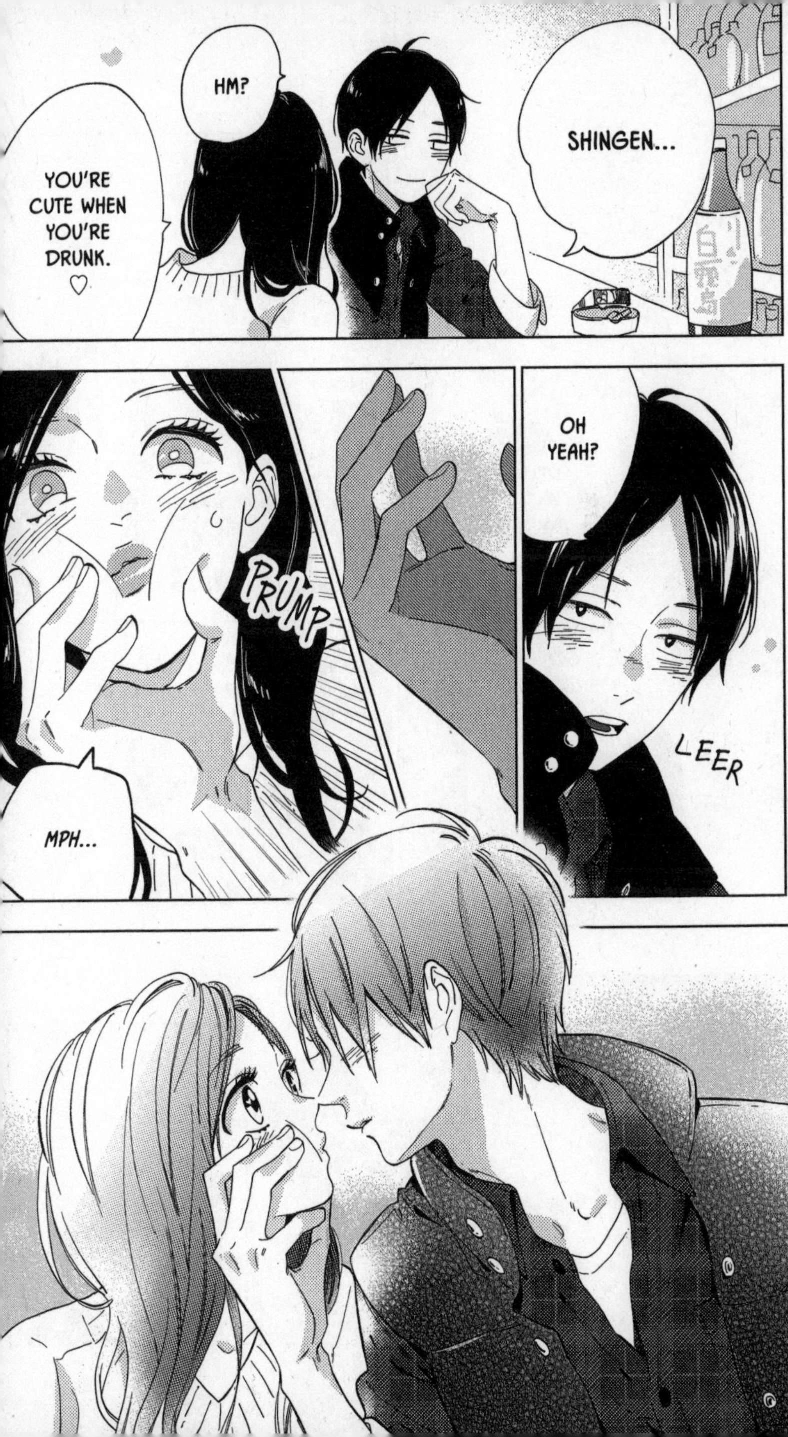
SHINGEN...
HM?
YOU'RE CUTE WHEN YOU'RE DRUNK. ♡
OH YEAH?
LEER
PRUMP
MPH...

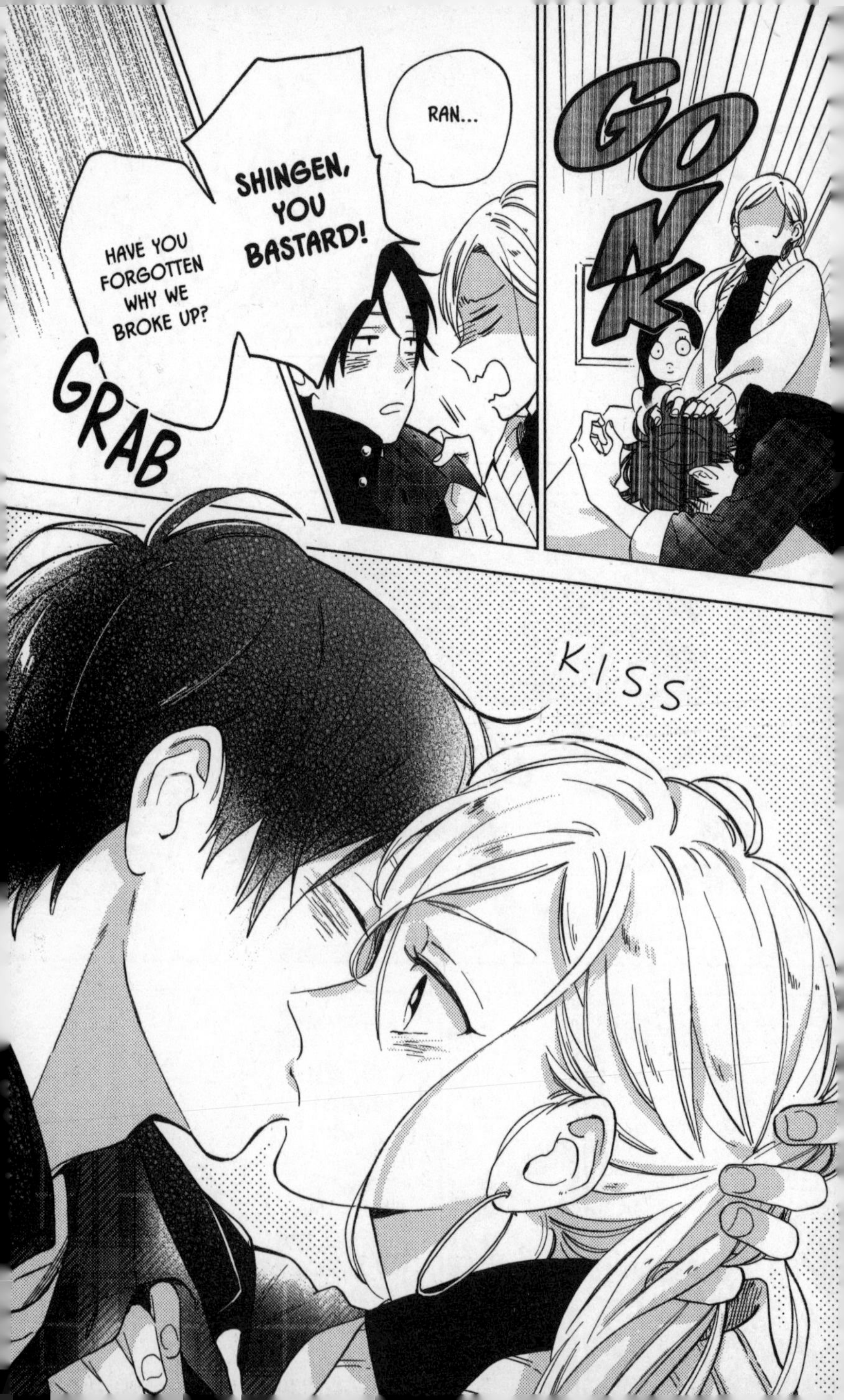
GONK
RAN...
SHINGEN, YOU BASTARD!
HAVE YOU FORGOTTEN WHY WE BROKE UP?
GRAB
KISS

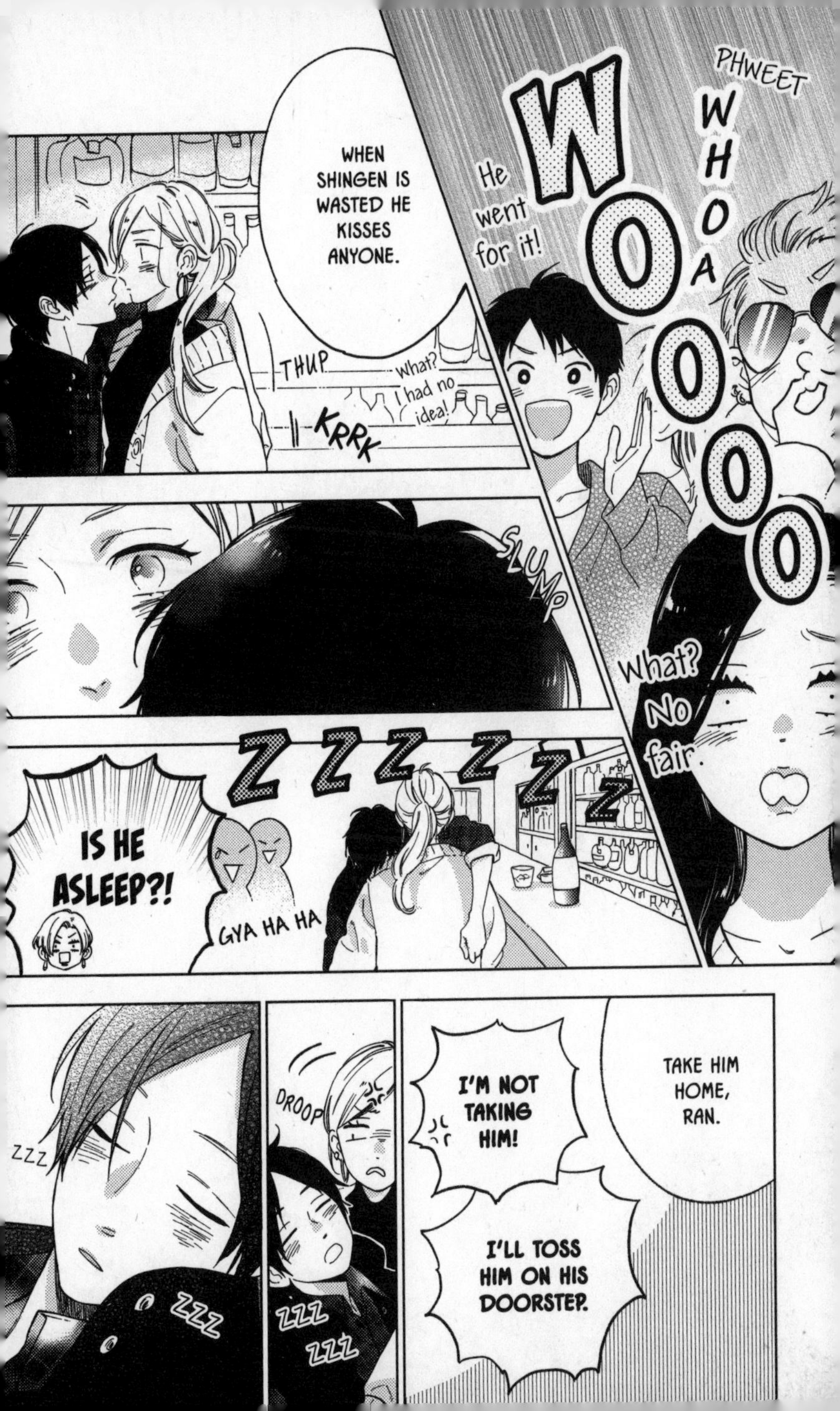
PHWEET
WHOA
WOOOOO
He went for it!
What? No fair.
WHEN SHINGEN IS WASTED HE KISSES ANYONE.
THUP
What? I had no idea!
KRRK
SLUMP
ZZZZZZ
IS HE ASLEEP?!
GYA HA HA
TAKE HIM HOME, RAN.
I'M NOT TAKING HIM!
I'LL TOSS HIM ON HIS DOORSTEP.
DROOP
ZZZ
ZZZ
ZZZ
ZZZ

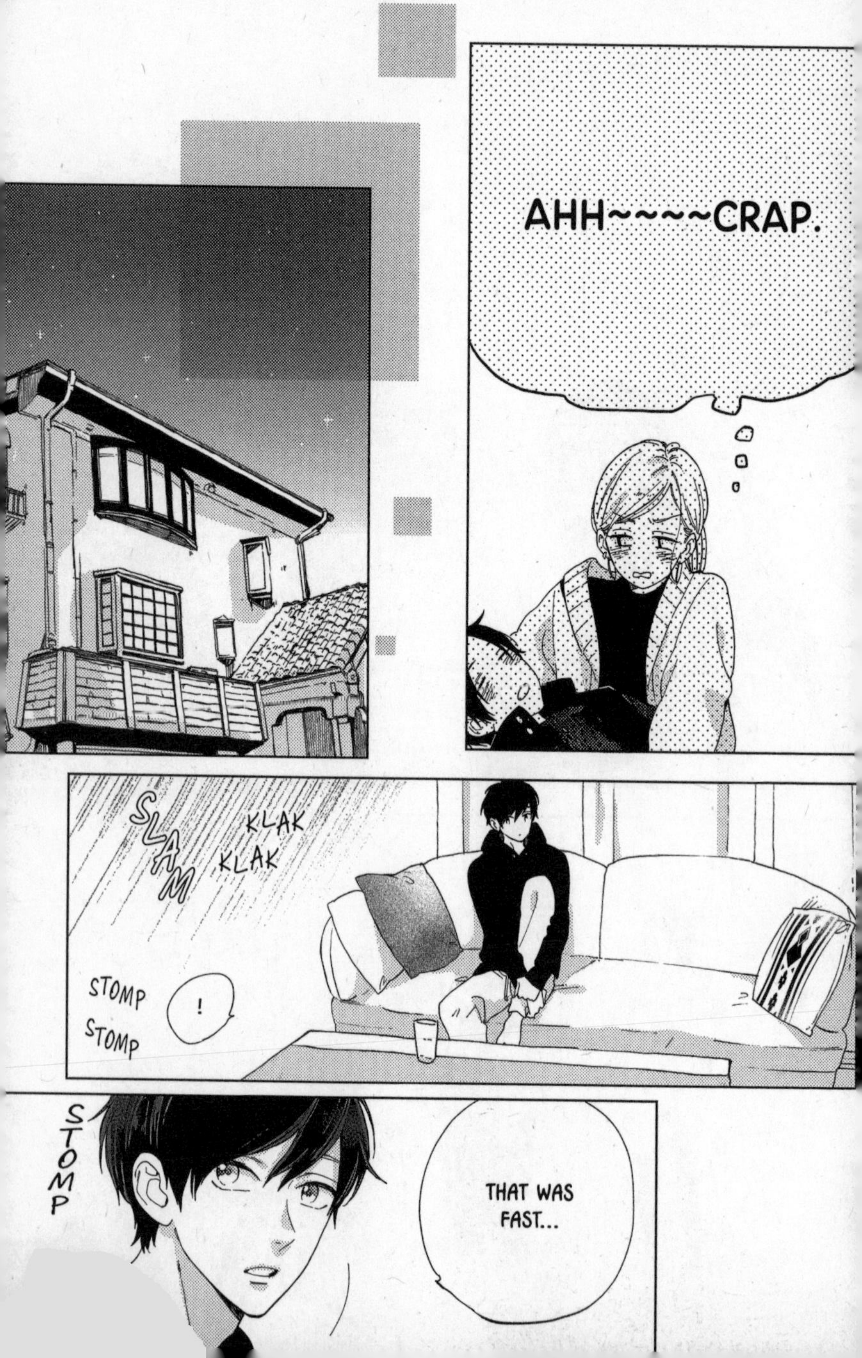
AHH~~~~CRAP.
SLAM
KLAK
KLAK
STOMP
STOMP
!
THAT WAS FAST...
STOMP

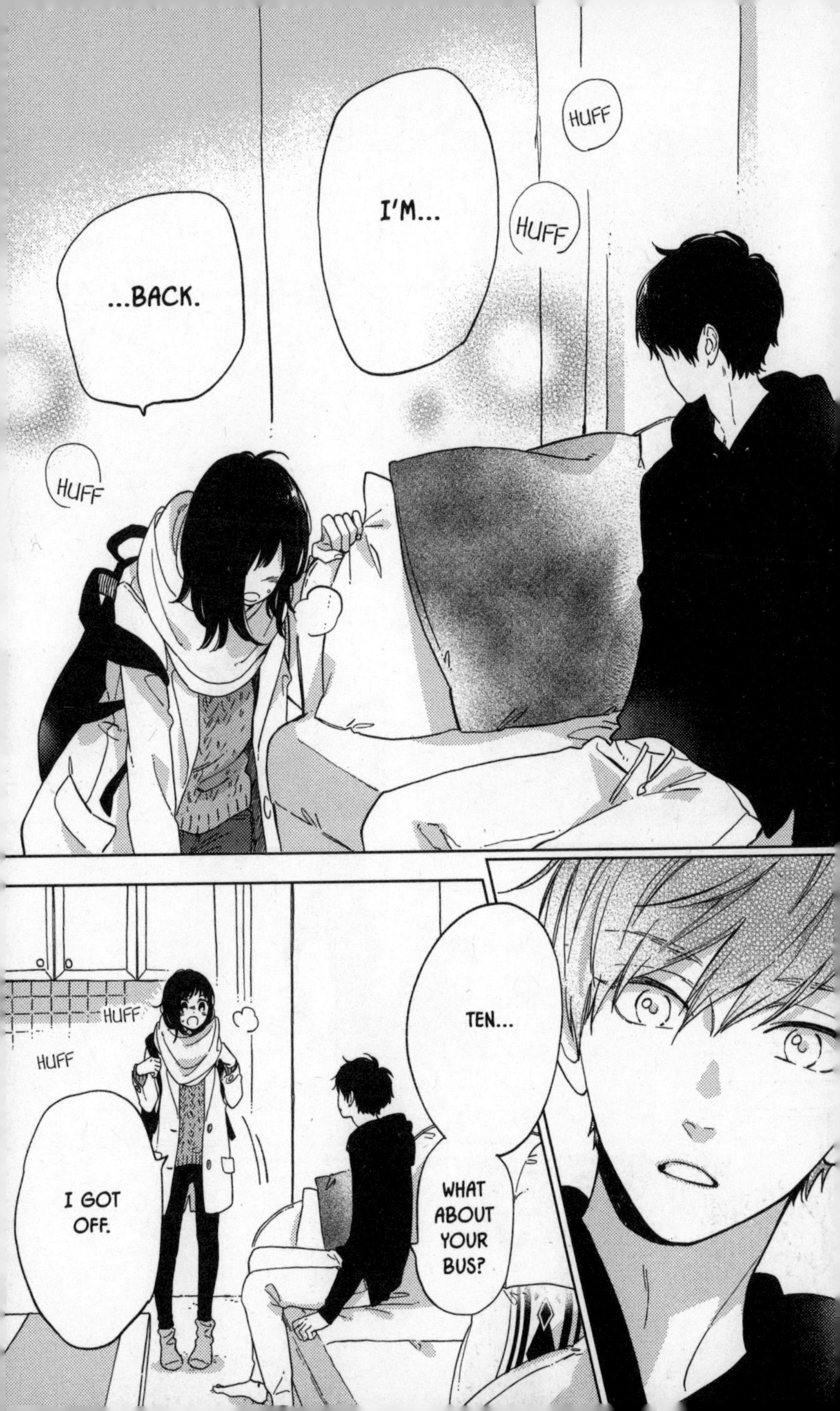
HUFF
HUFF
I'M...
...BACK.
HUFF
TEN...
WHAT ABOUT YOUR BUS?
HUFF
HUFF
I GOT OFF.

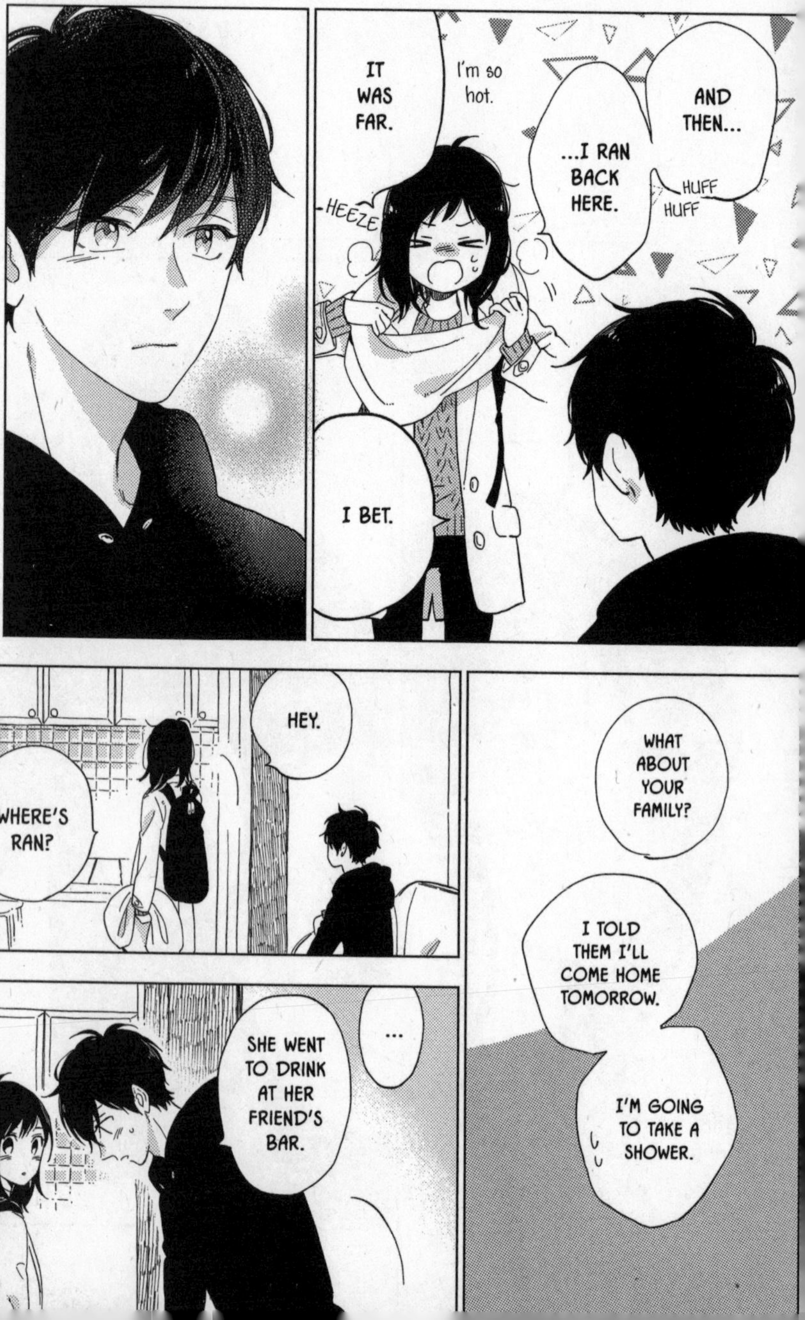
AND THEN...
...I RAN BACK HERE.
HUFF HUFF
I'm so hot.
IT WAS FAR.
HEEZE
I BET.
WHAT ABOUT YOUR FAMILY?
I TOLD THEM I'LL COME HOME TOMORROW.
I'M GOING TO TAKE A SHOWER.
HEY.
WHERE'S RAN?
...
SHE WENT TO DRINK AT HER FRIEND'S BAR.

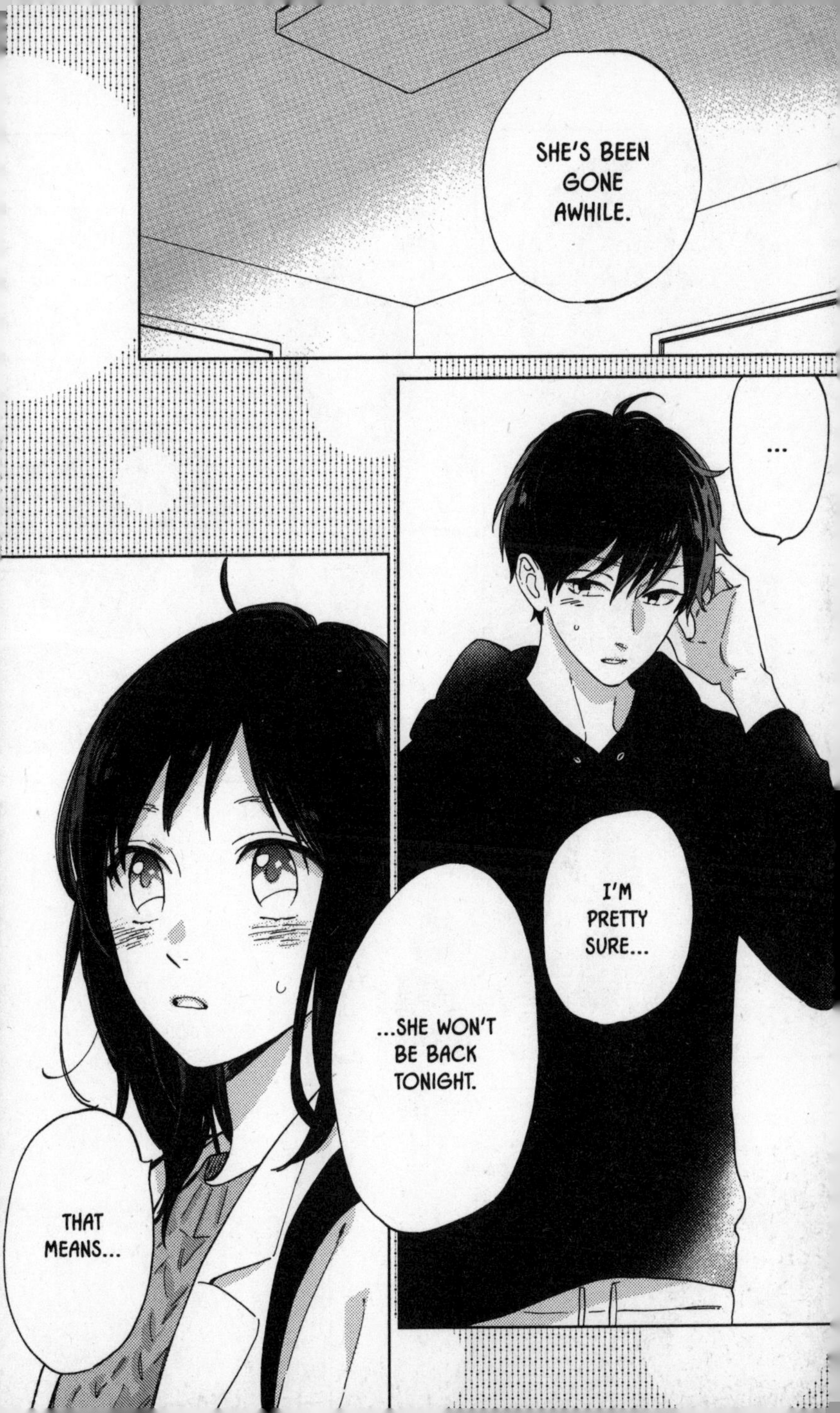
SHE'S BEEN GONE AWHILE.
...
I'M PRETTY SURE...
...SHE WON'T BE BACK TONIGHT.
THAT MEANS...

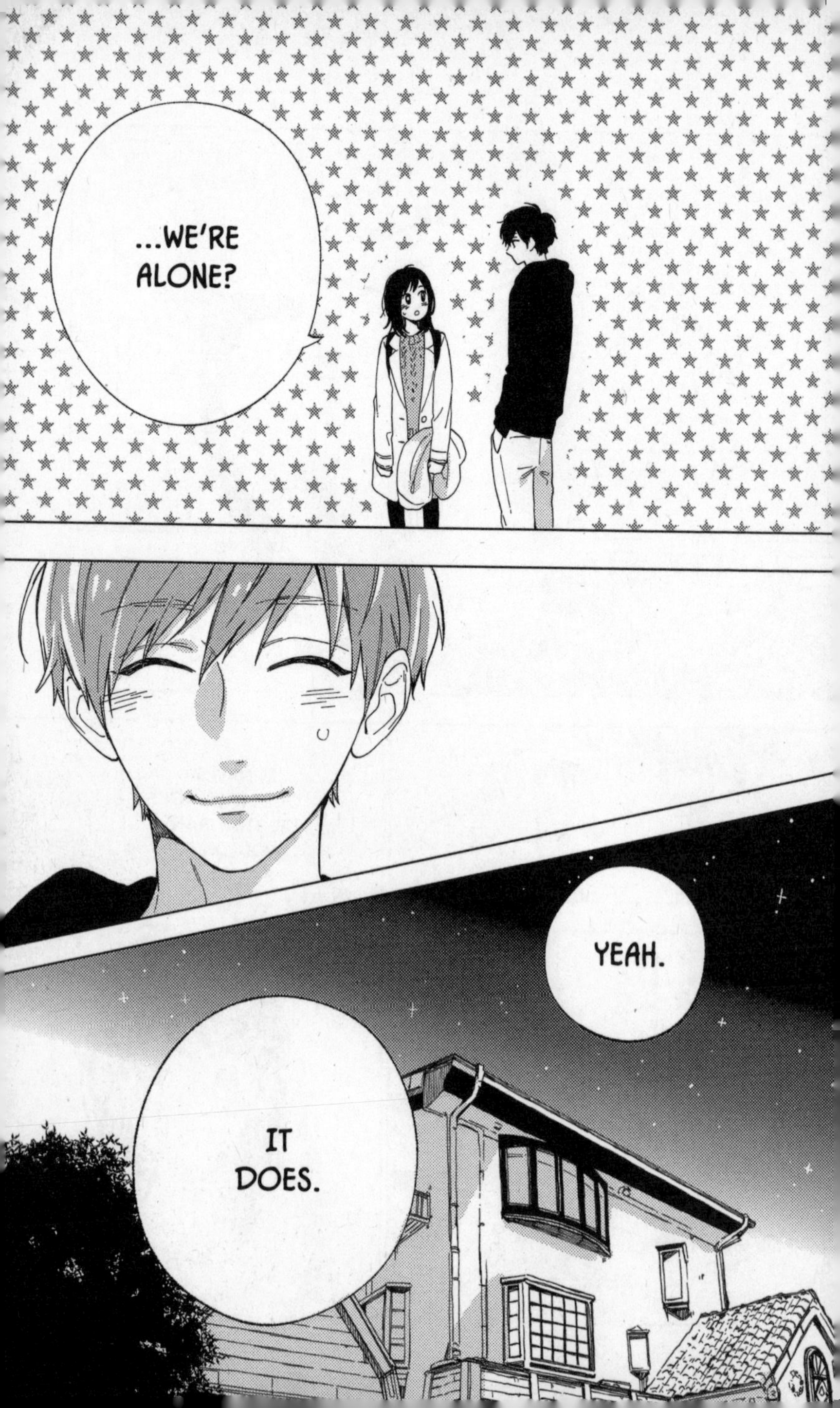
...WE'RE ALONE?
YEAH.
IT DOES.

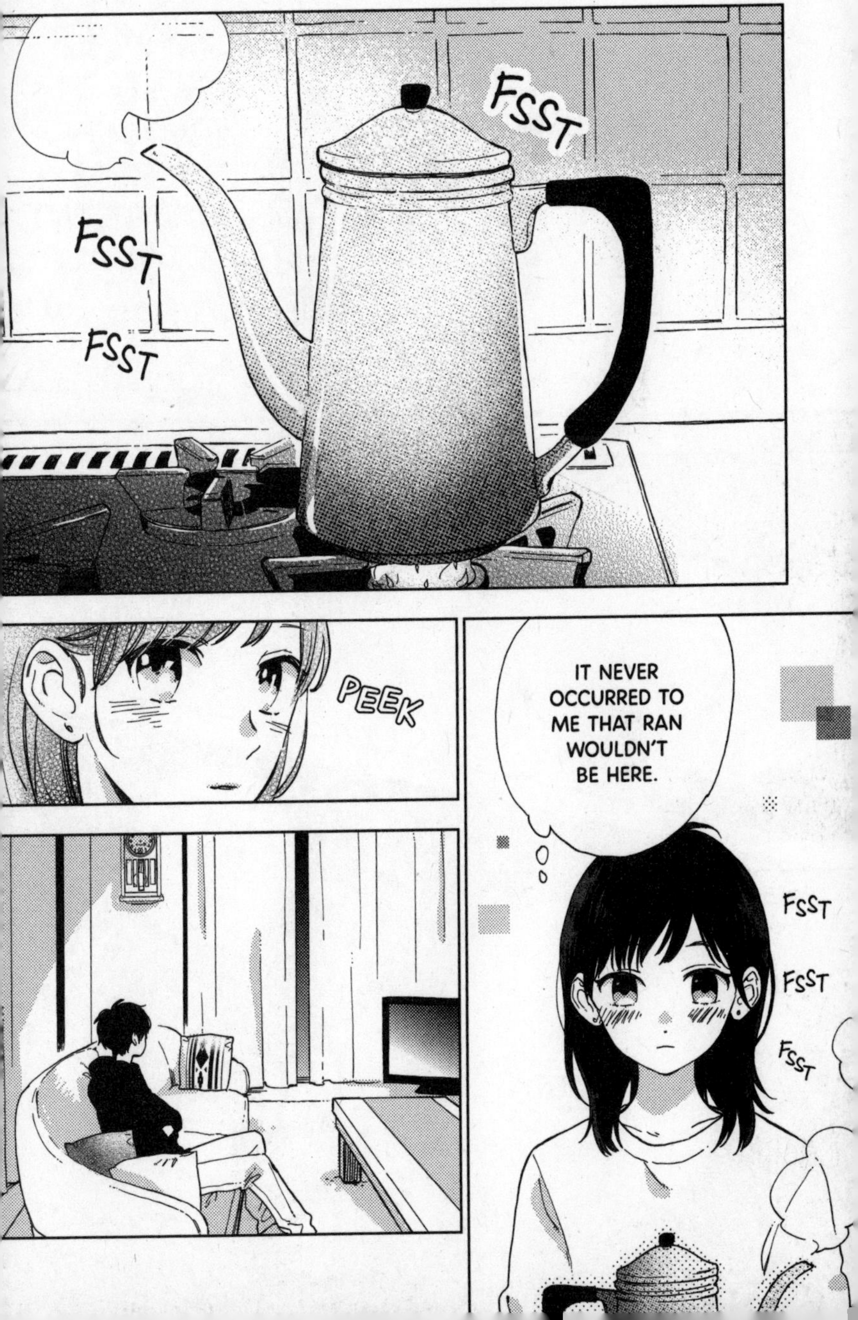
FSST
FSST
FSST
IT NEVER OCCURRED TO ME THAT RAN WOULDN'T BE HERE.
FSST
FSST
FSST
PEEK

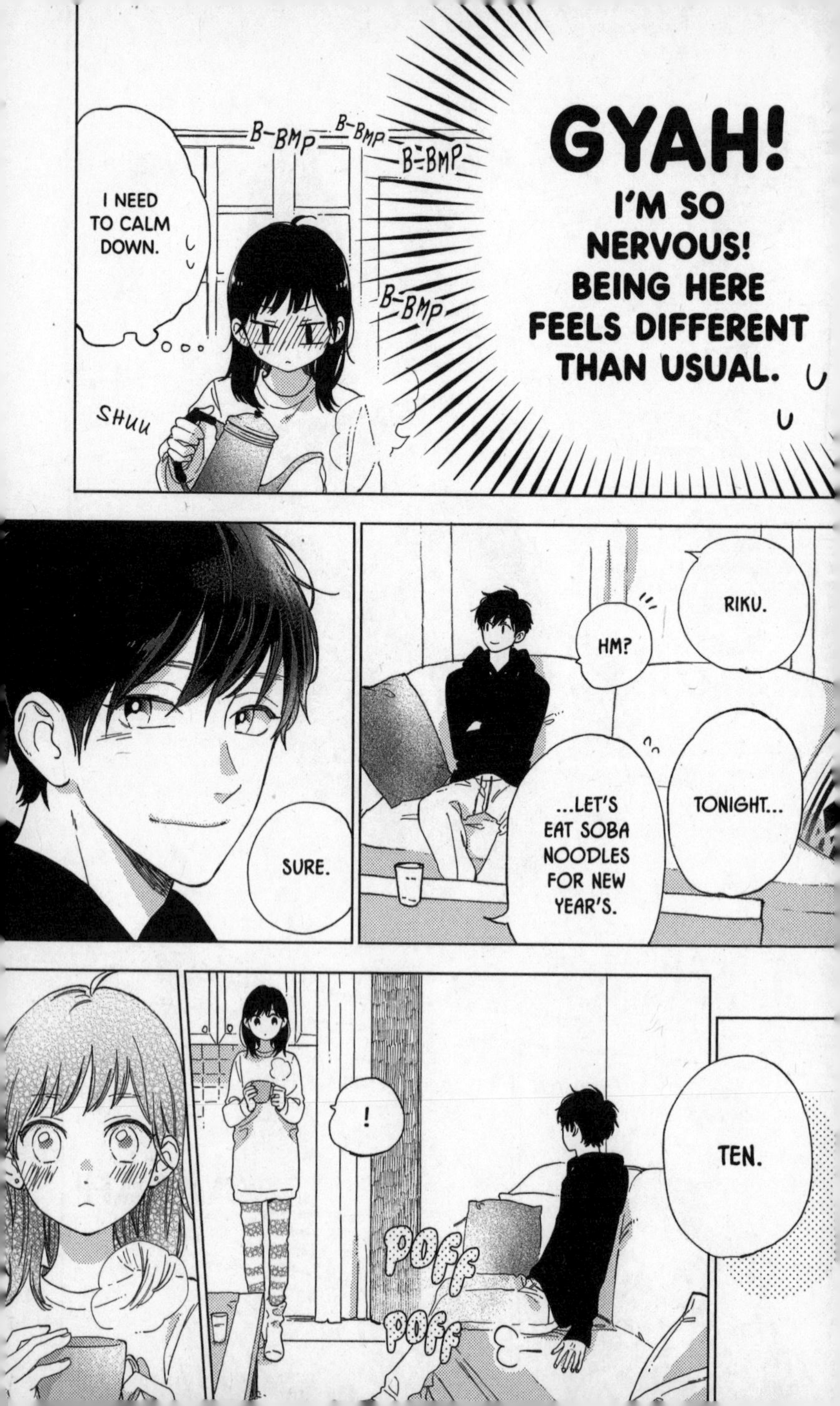
GYAH!
I'M SO NERVOUS! BEING HERE FEELS DIFFERENT THAN USUAL.
B-BMP B-BMP B-BMP B-BMP
I NEED TO CALM DOWN.
SHUU
RIKU.
HM?
TONIGHT...
...LET'S EAT SOBA NOODLES FOR NEW YEAR'S.
SURE.
TEN.
POFF
POFF
!

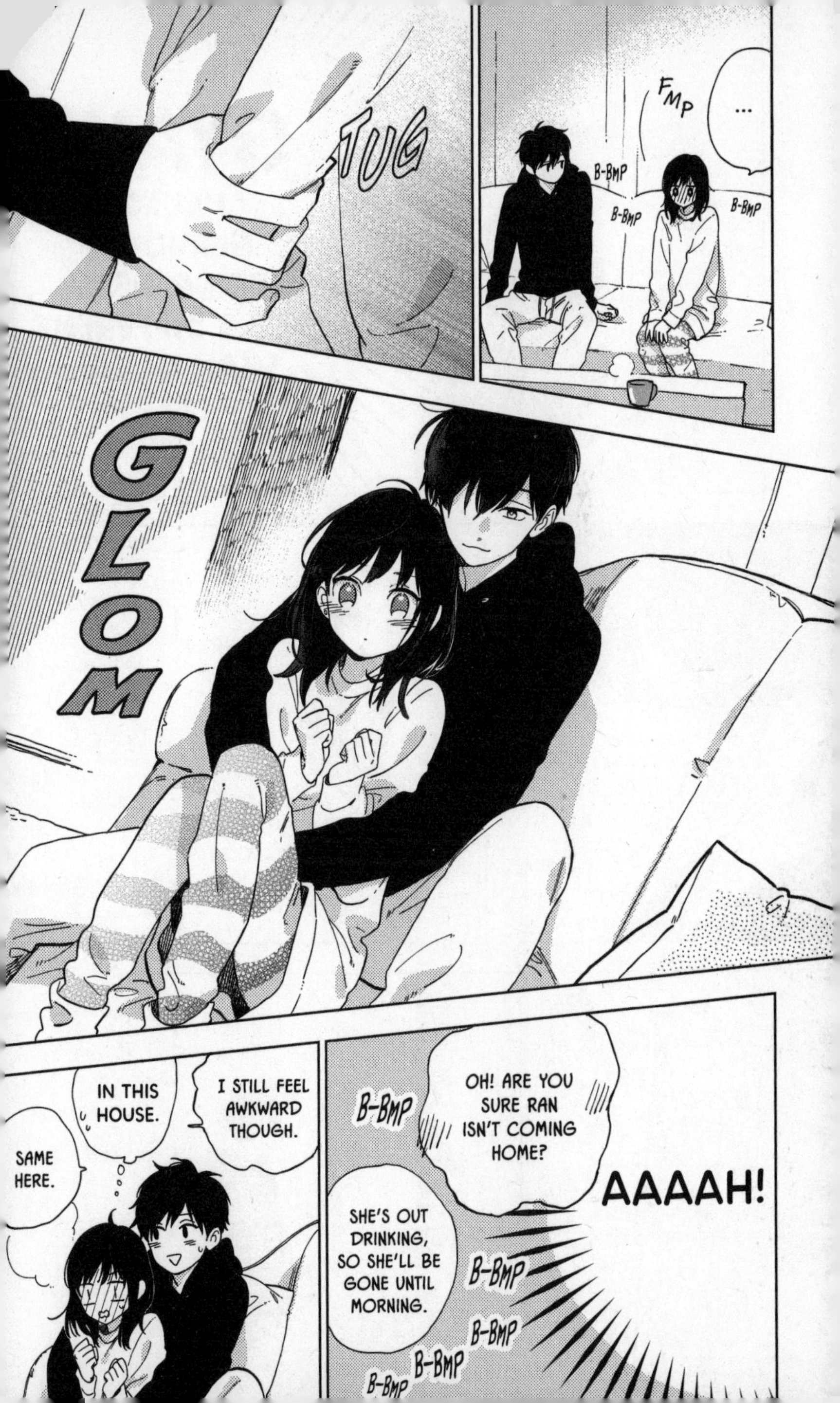
...
FMP
B-BMP
B-BMP
B-BMP
TUG
GLOM
OH! ARE YOU SURE RAN ISN'T COMING HOME?
B-BMP
AAAAH!
SHE'S OUT DRINKING, SO SHE'LL BE GONE UNTIL MORNING.
B-BMP
B-BMP
B-BMP
B-BMP
I STILL FEEL AWKWARD THOUGH.
IN THIS HOUSE.
SAME HERE.

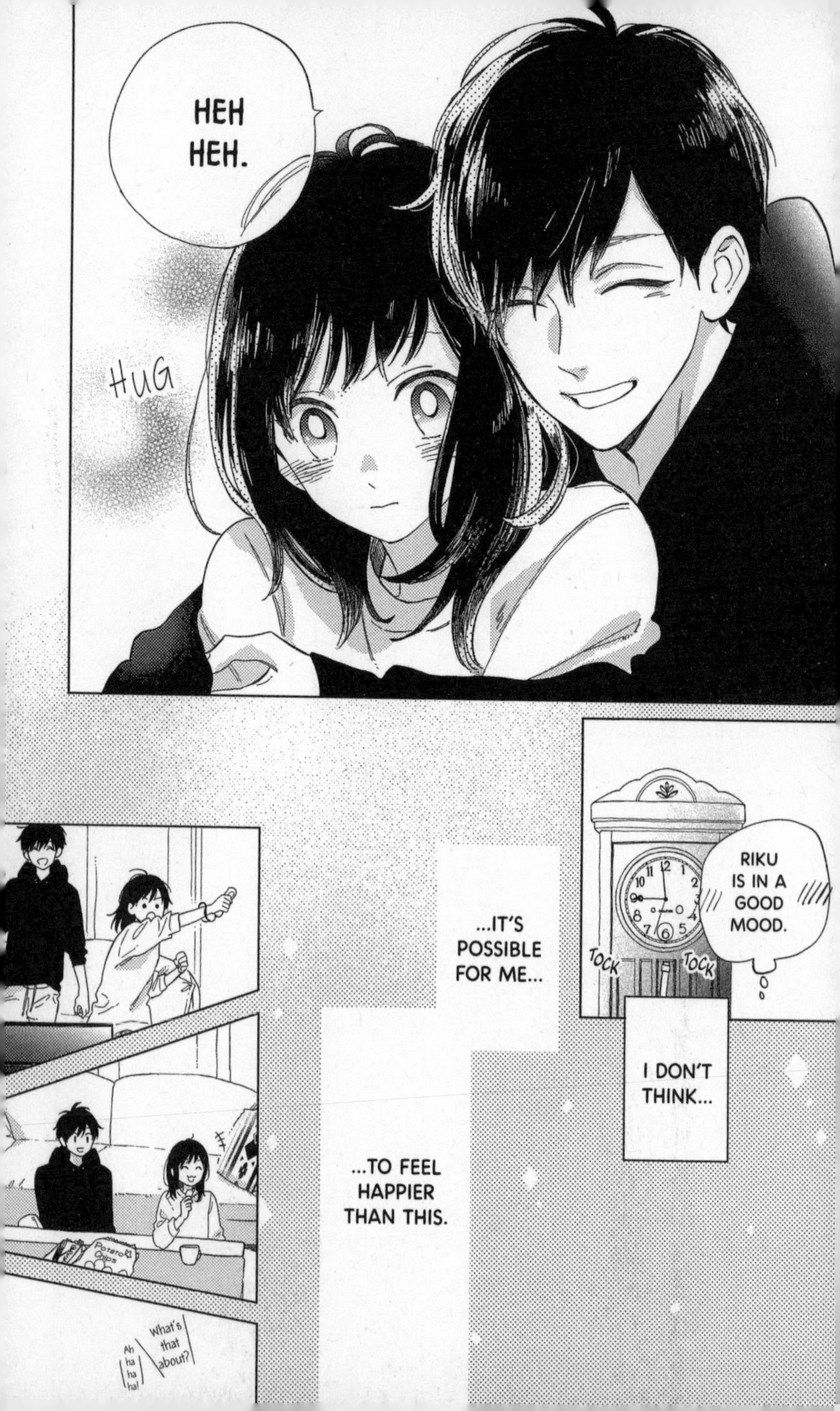
HEH HEH.
HUG
TOCK
TOCK
RIKU IS IN A GOOD MOOD.
I DON'T THINK...
...IT'S POSSIBLE FOR ME...
...TO FEEL HAPPIER THAN THIS.
Potato Chips
What's that about?
Ah ha ha ha!

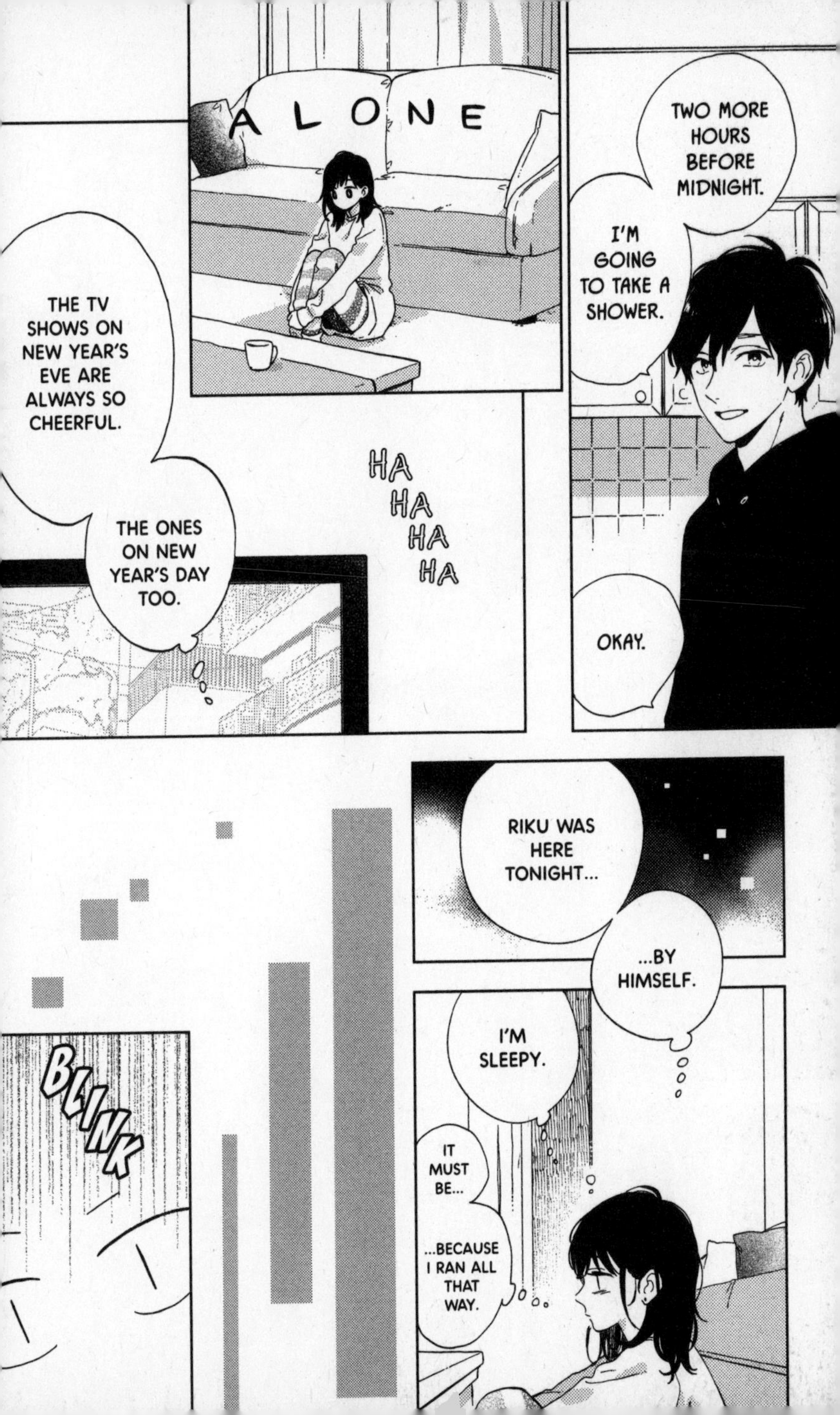
TWO MORE HOURS BEFORE MIDNIGHT.
I'M GOING TO TAKE A SHOWER.
OKAY.
ALONE
THE TV SHOWS ON NEW YEAR'S EVE ARE ALWAYS SO CHEERFUL.
THE ONES ON NEW YEAR'S DAY TOO.
HA HA HA HA
RIKU WAS HERE TONIGHT...
...BY HIMSELF.
I'M SLEEPY.
IT MUST BE...
...BECAUSE I RAN ALL THAT WAY.
BLINK

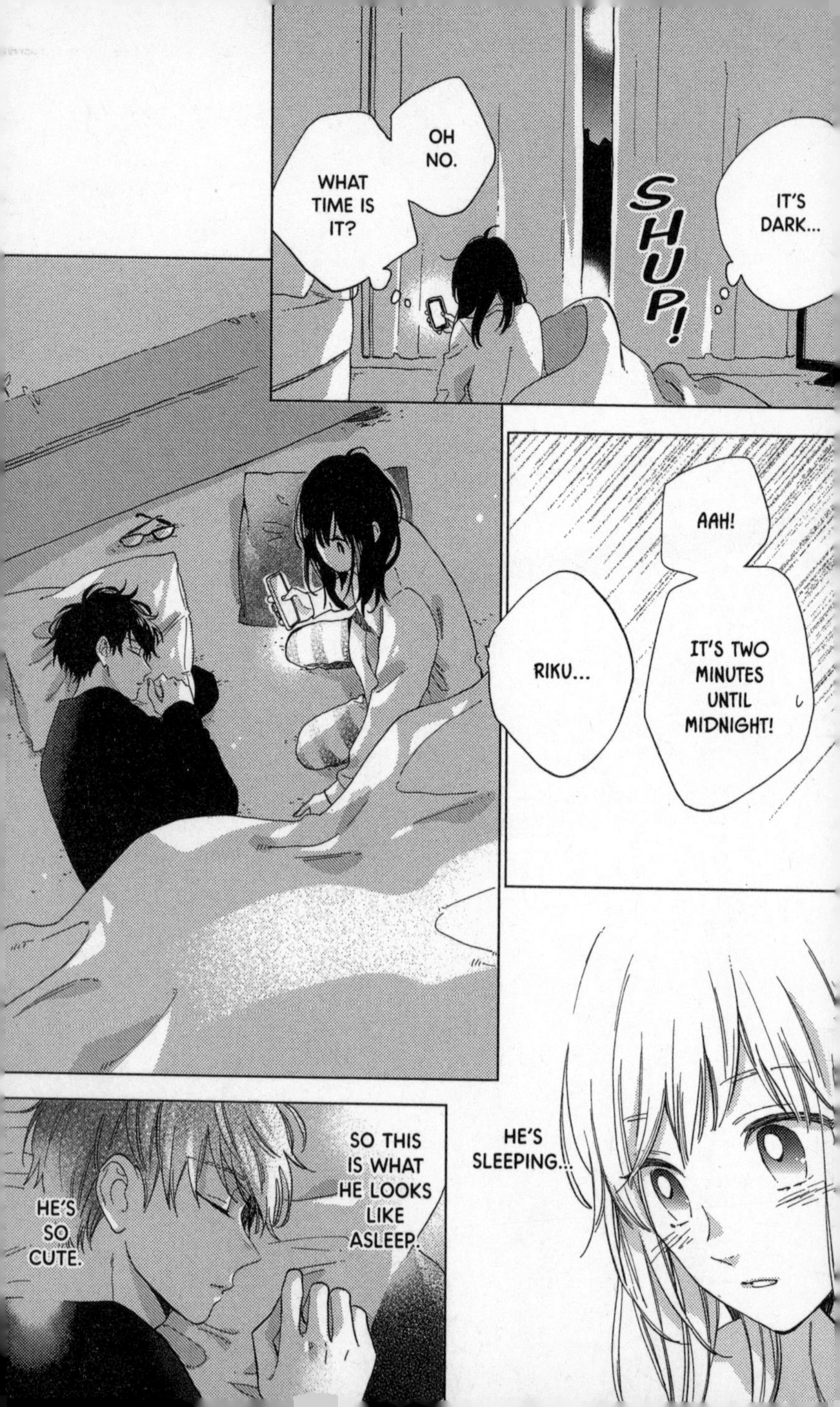
IT'S DARK...
SHUP!
OH NO.
WHAT TIME IS IT?
AAH!
IT'S TWO MINUTES UNTIL MIDNIGHT!
RIKU...
HE'S SLEEPING...
SO THIS IS WHAT HE LOOKS LIKE ASLEEP.
HE'S SO CUTE.

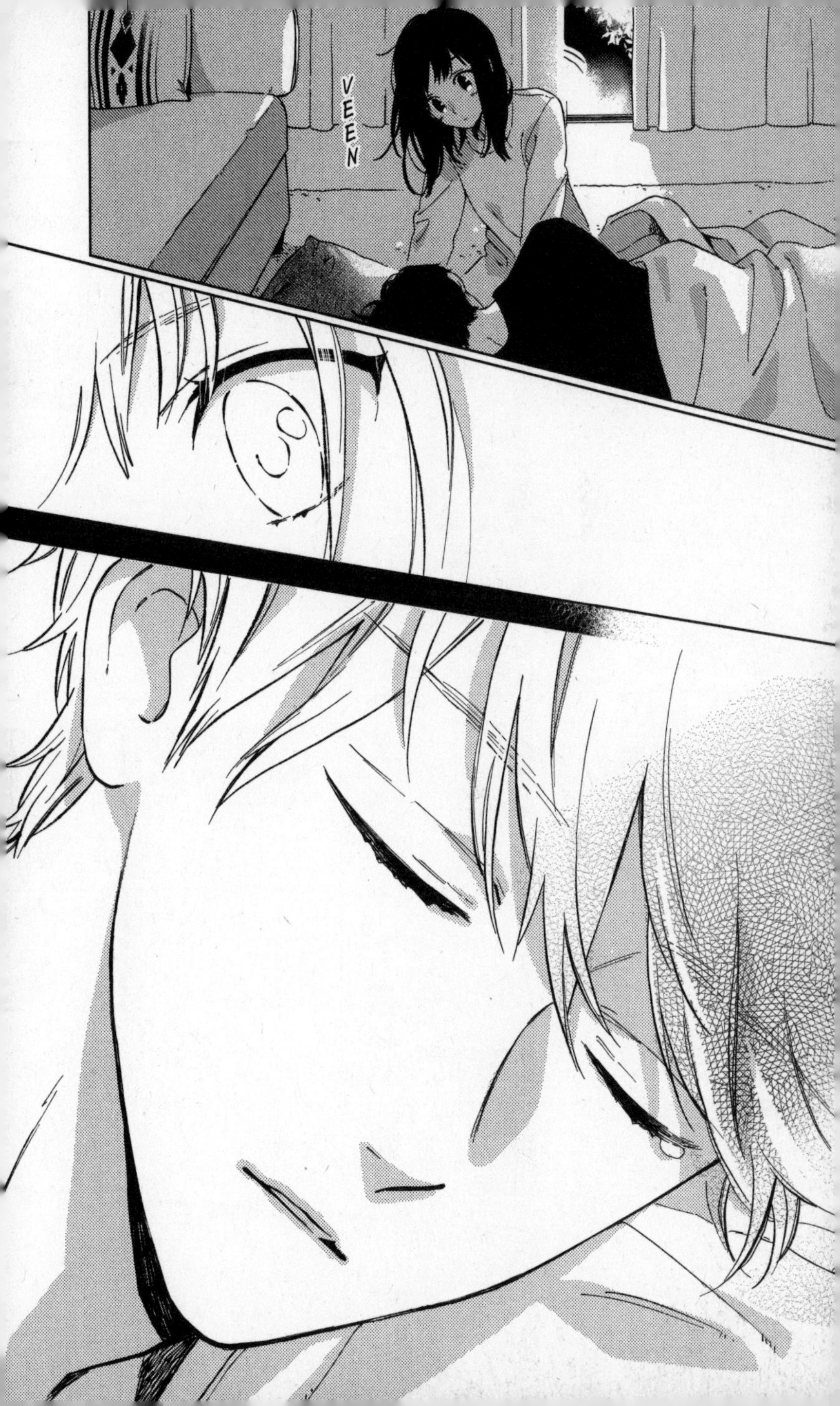
VEEN

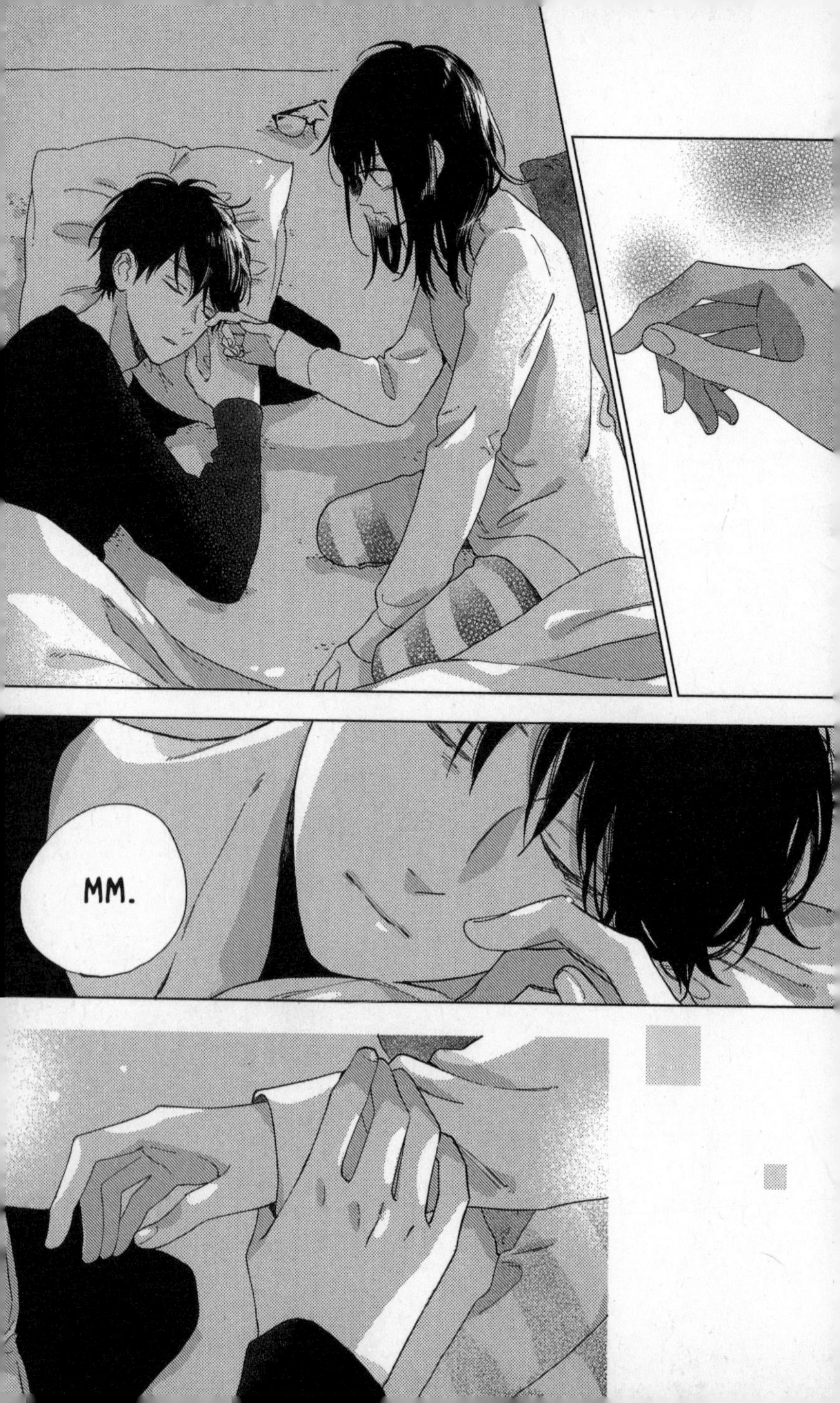
MM.

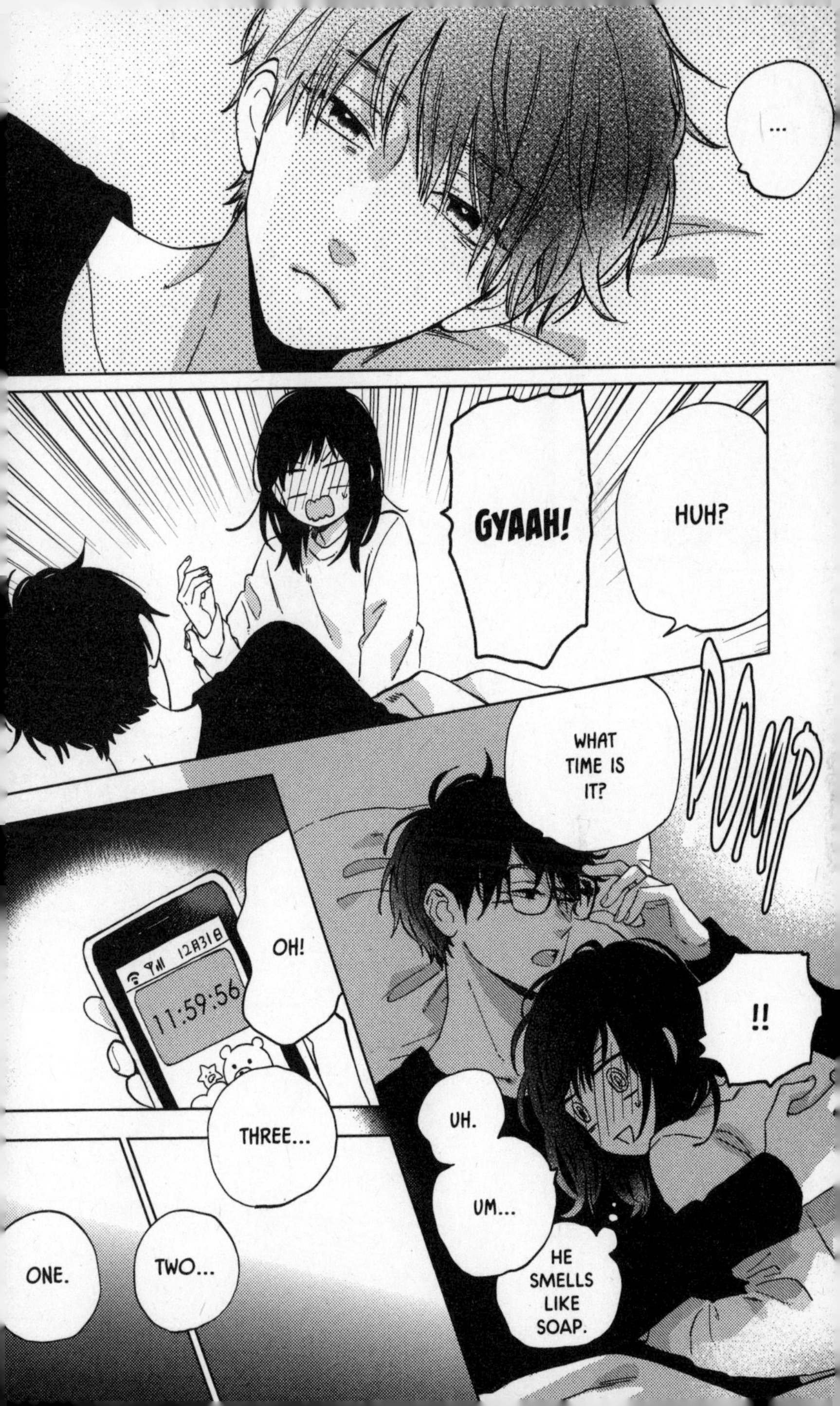
...
HUH?
GYAAH!
DOMP
WHAT TIME IS IT?
!!
UH.
UM...
HE SMELLS LIKE SOAP.
OH!
12月31日
11:59:56
THREE...
TWO...
ONE.

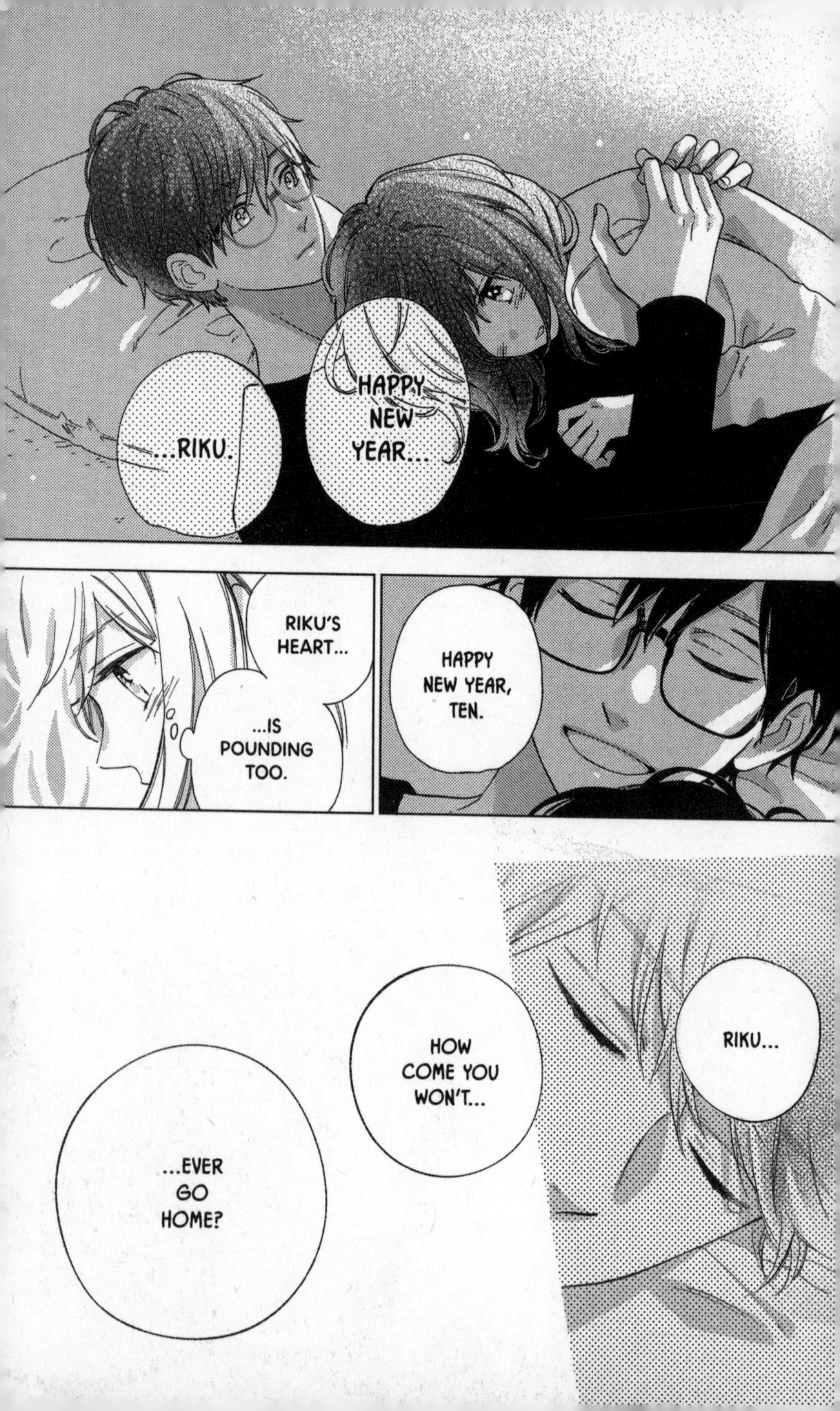
HAPPY NEW YEAR...
...RIKU.
HAPPY NEW YEAR, TEN.
RIKU'S HEART...
...IS POUNDING TOO.
RIKU...
HOW COME YOU WON'T...
...EVER GO HOME?

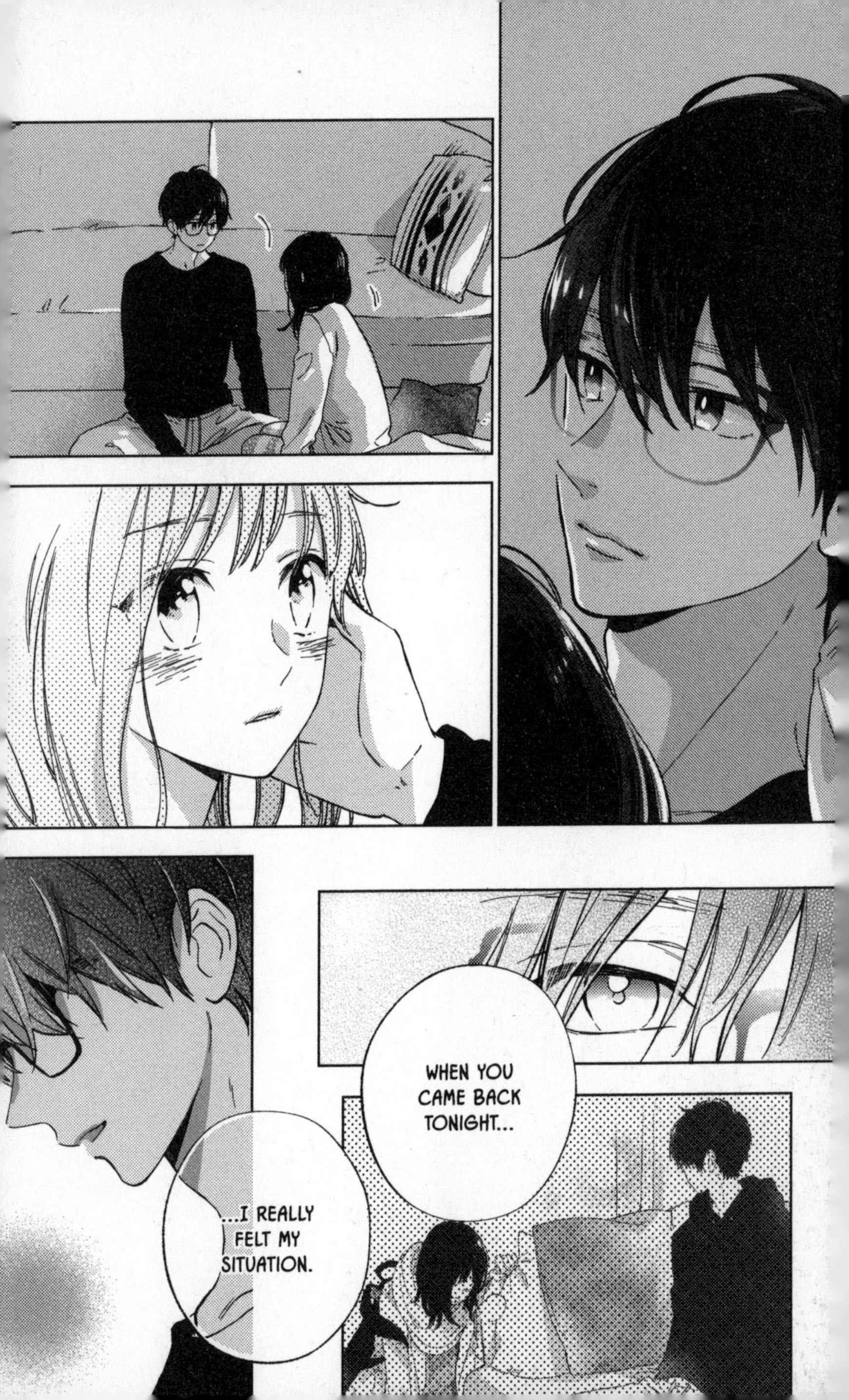
WHEN YOU CAME BACK TONIGHT...
...I REALLY FELT MY SITUATION.

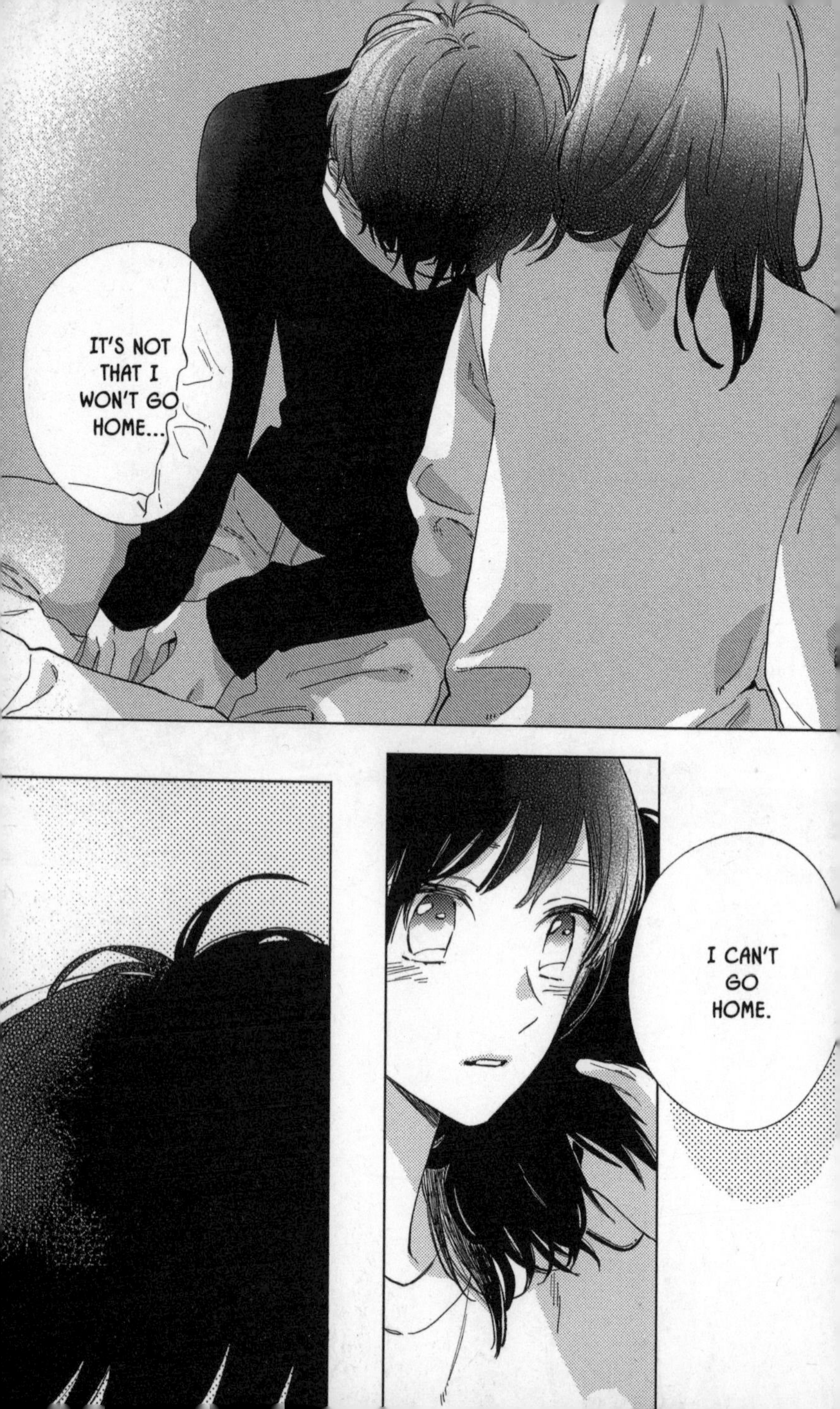
IT'S NOT THAT I WON'T GO HOME...
I CAN'T GO HOME.

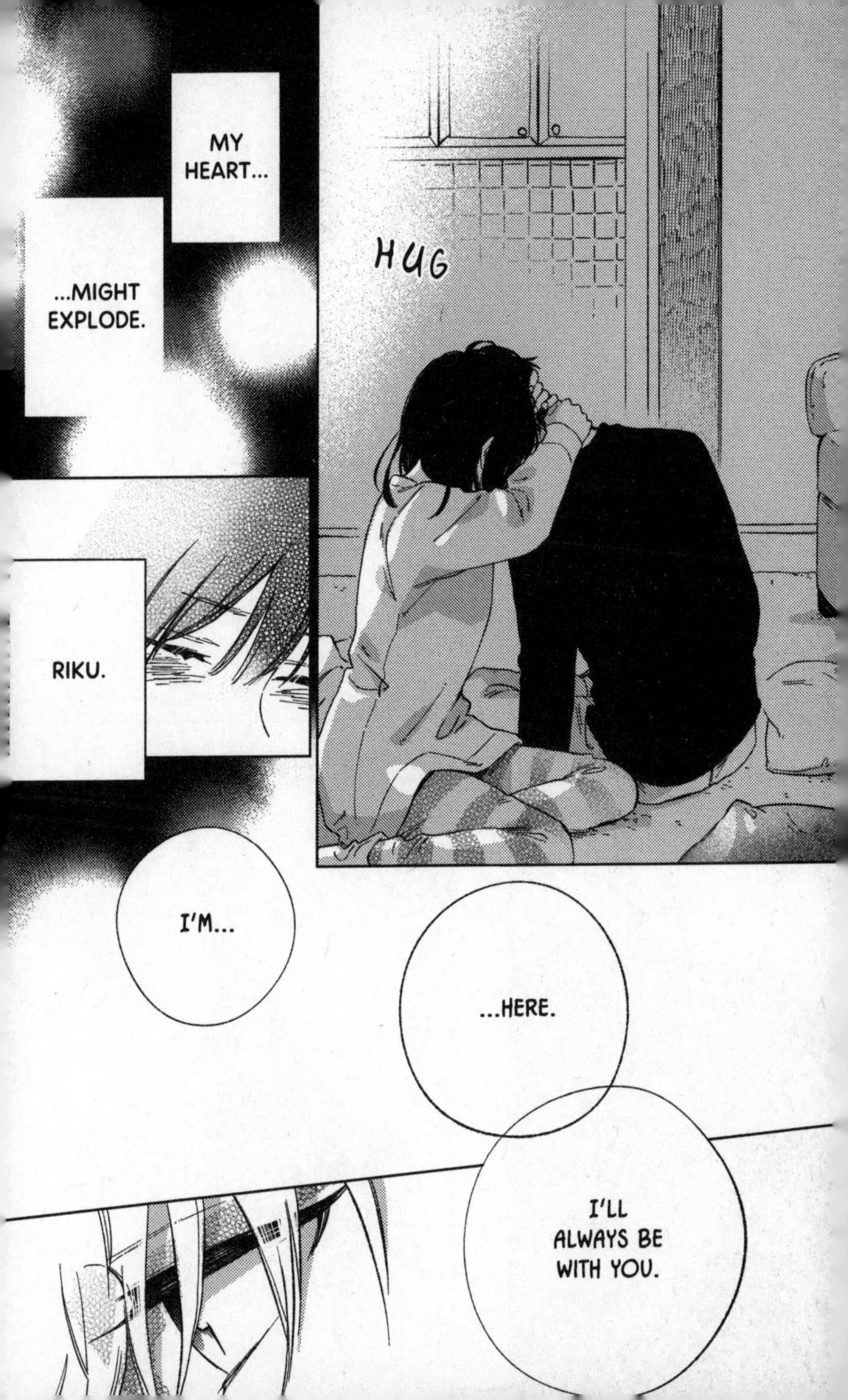
HUG
MY HEART...
...MIGHT EXPLODE.
RIKU.
I'M...
...HERE.
I'LL ALWAYS BE WITH YOU.

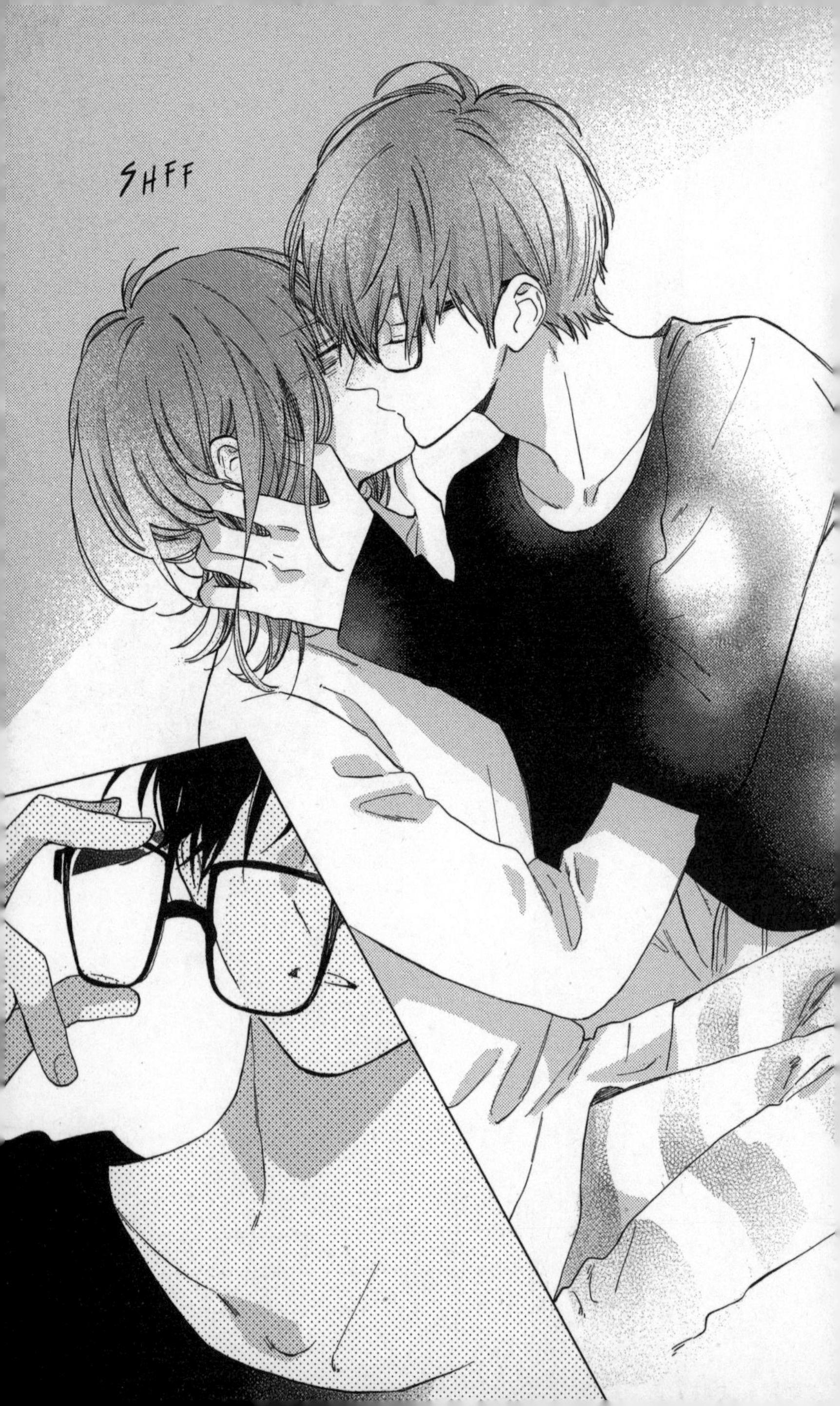
SHFF

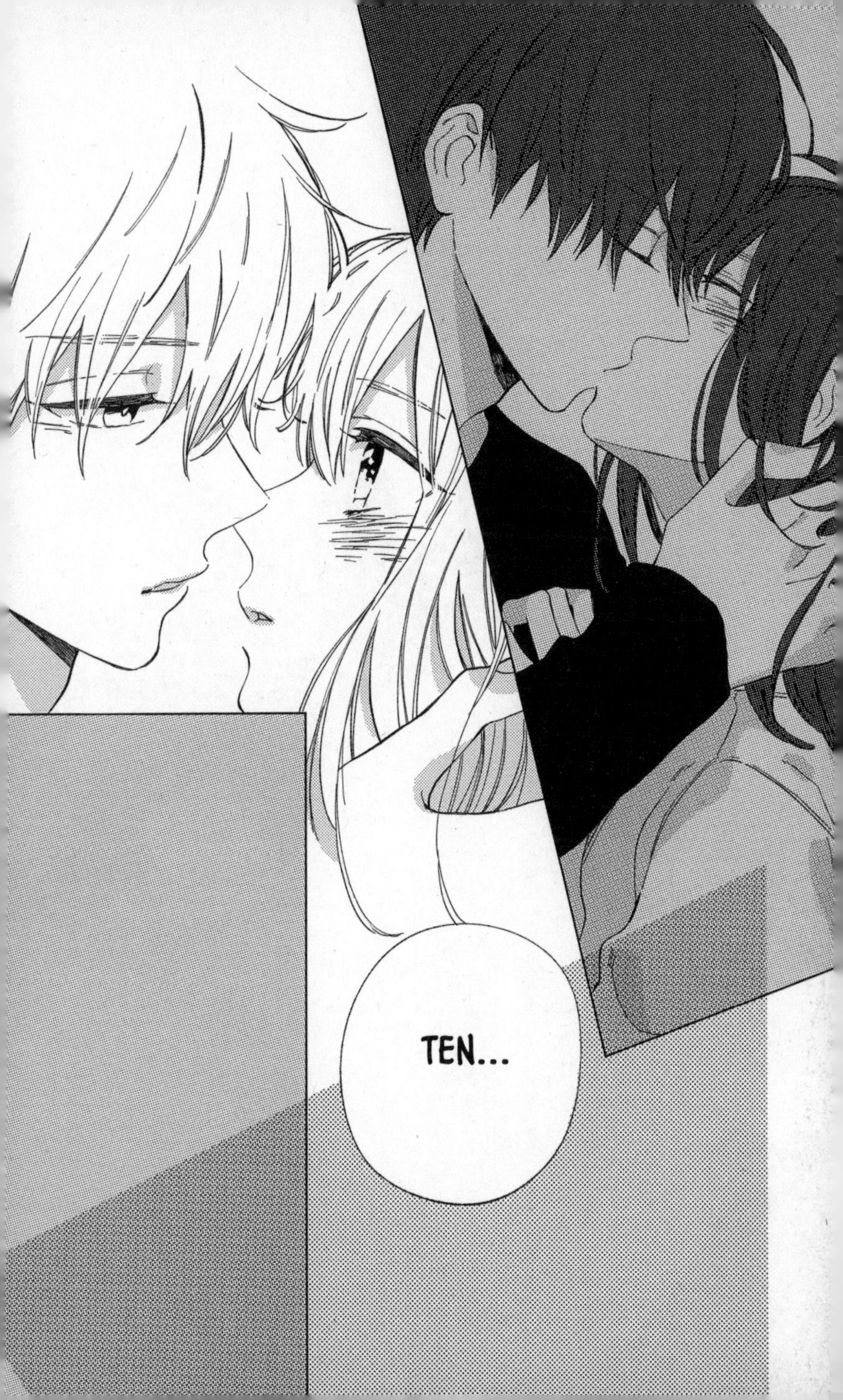
TEN...

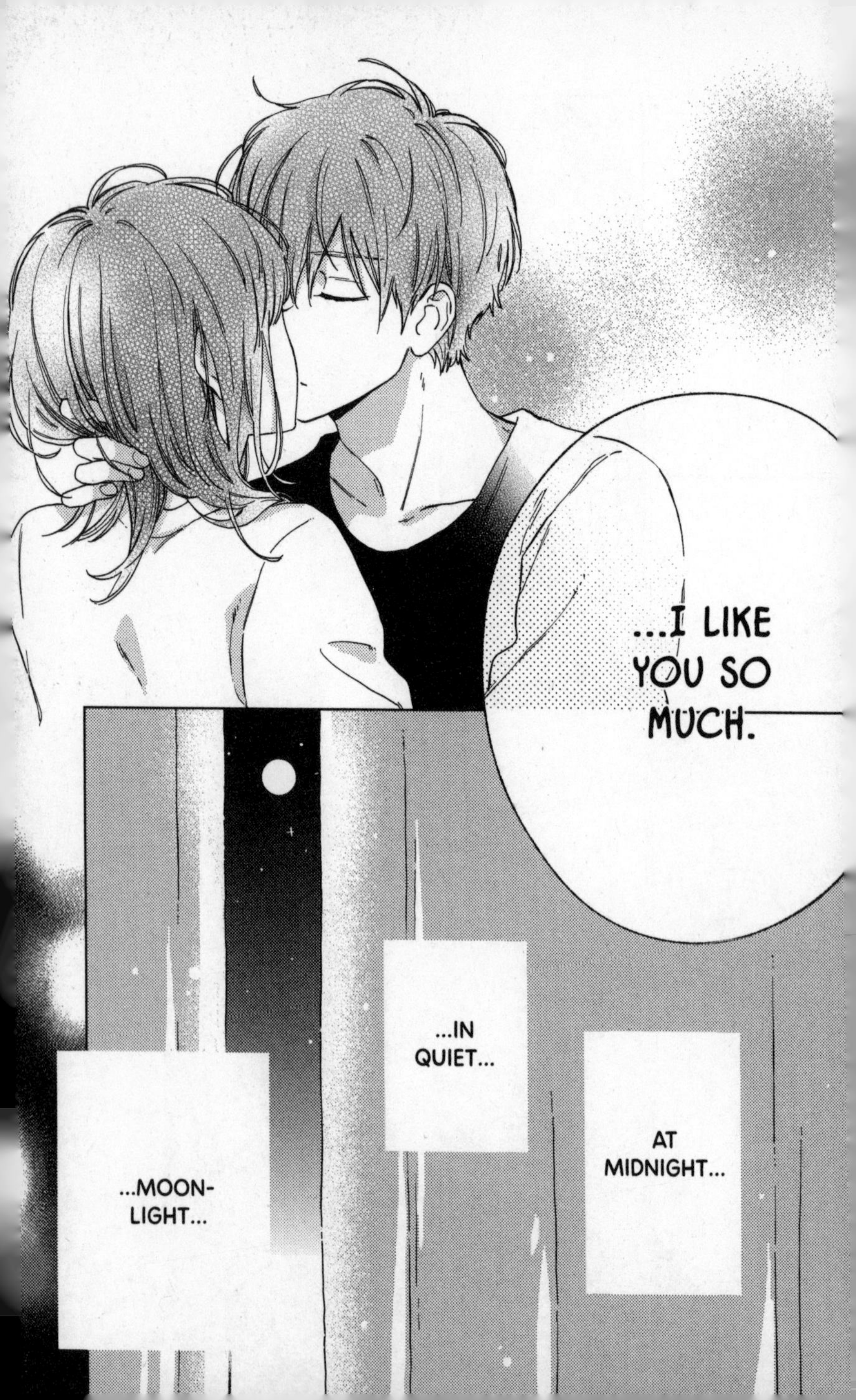
...I LIKE YOU SO MUCH.
AT MIDNIGHT...
...IN QUIET...
...MOON-LIGHT...

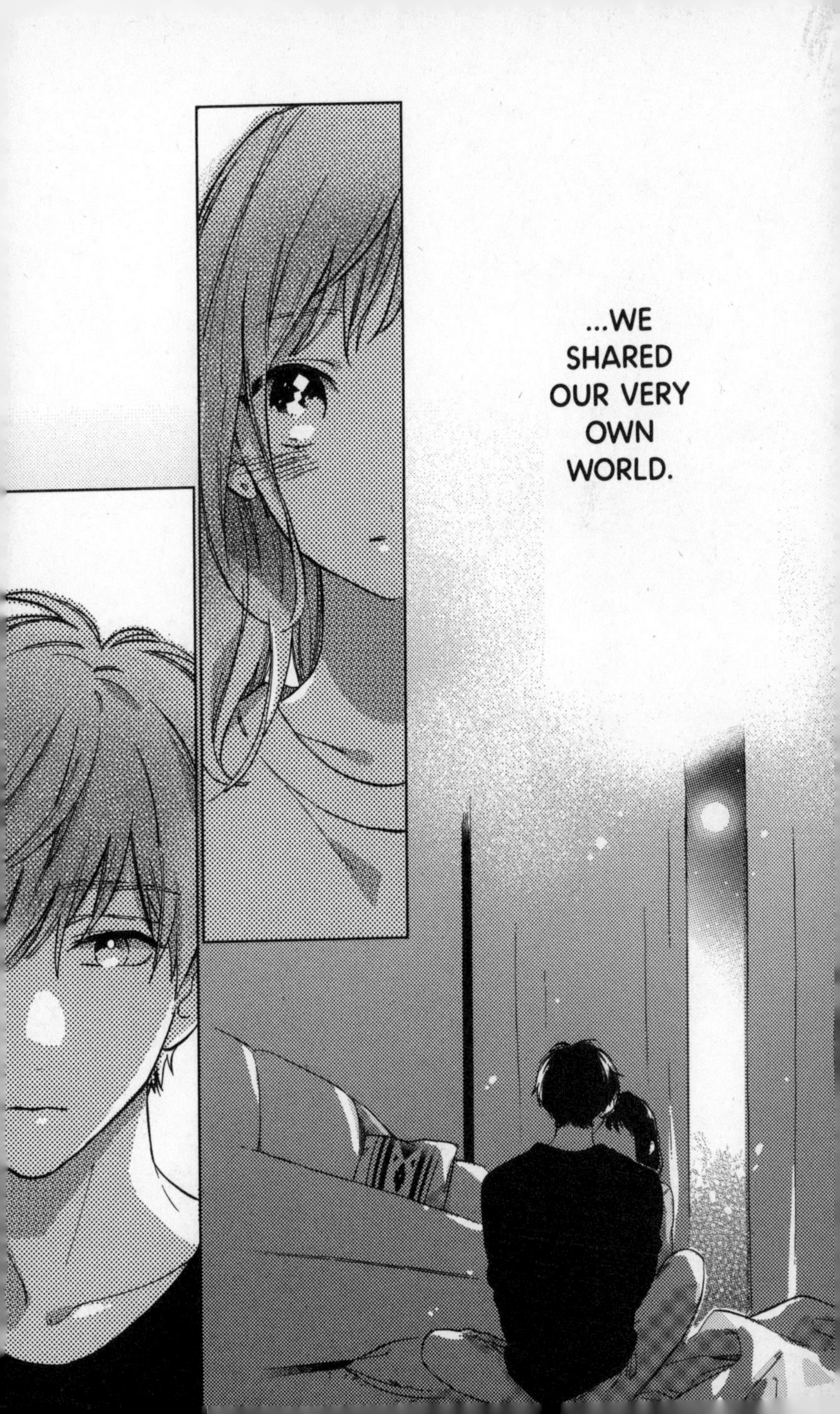
...WE SHARED OUR VERY OWN WORLD.

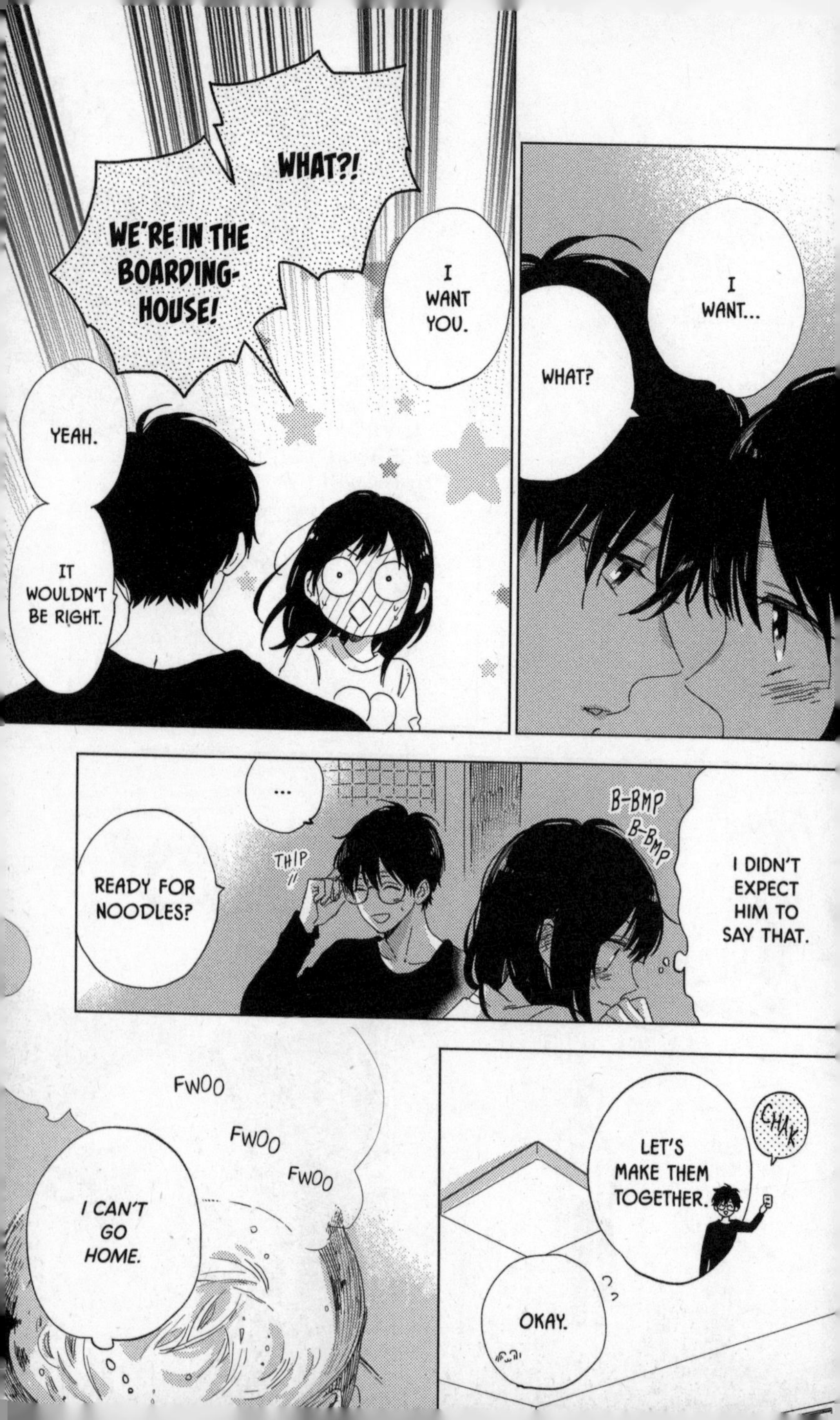
I WANT...
WHAT?
I WANT YOU.
WHAT?!
WE'RE IN THE BOARDING-HOUSE!
YEAH.
IT WOULDN'T BE RIGHT.
B-BMP
B-BMP
I DIDN'T EXPECT HIM TO SAY THAT.
...
THIP
READY FOR NOODLES?
CHAK
LET'S MAKE THEM TOGETHER.
OKAY.
FWOO
FWOO
FWOO
I CAN'T GO HOME.

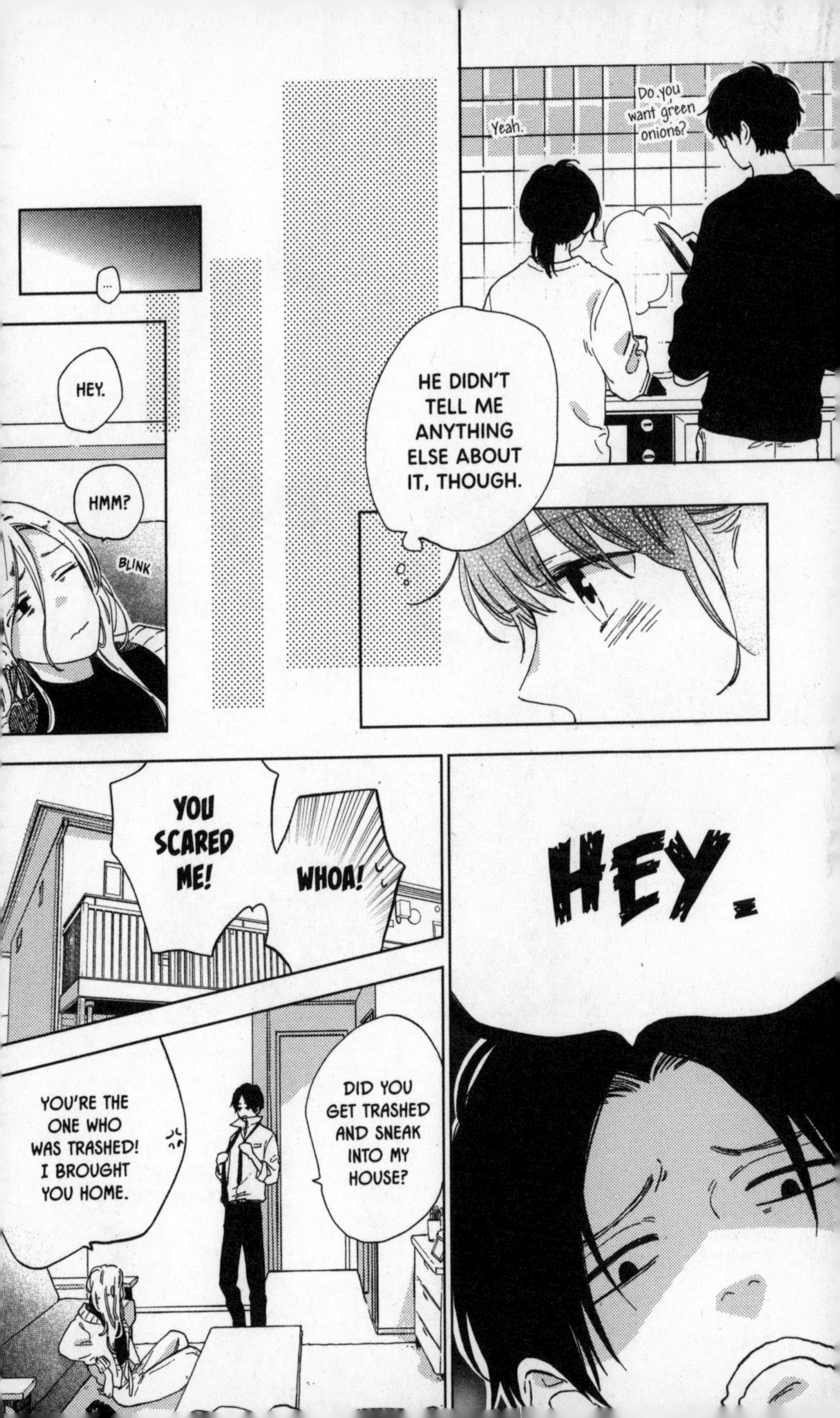
Do you want green onions?
Yeah.
HE DIDN'T TELL ME ANYTHING ELSE ABOUT IT, THOUGH.
...
HEY.
HMM?
BLINK
HEY.
WHOA!
YOU SCARED ME!
DID YOU GET TRASHED AND SNEAK INTO MY HOUSE?
YOU'RE THE ONE WHO WAS TRASHED! I BROUGHT YOU HOME.

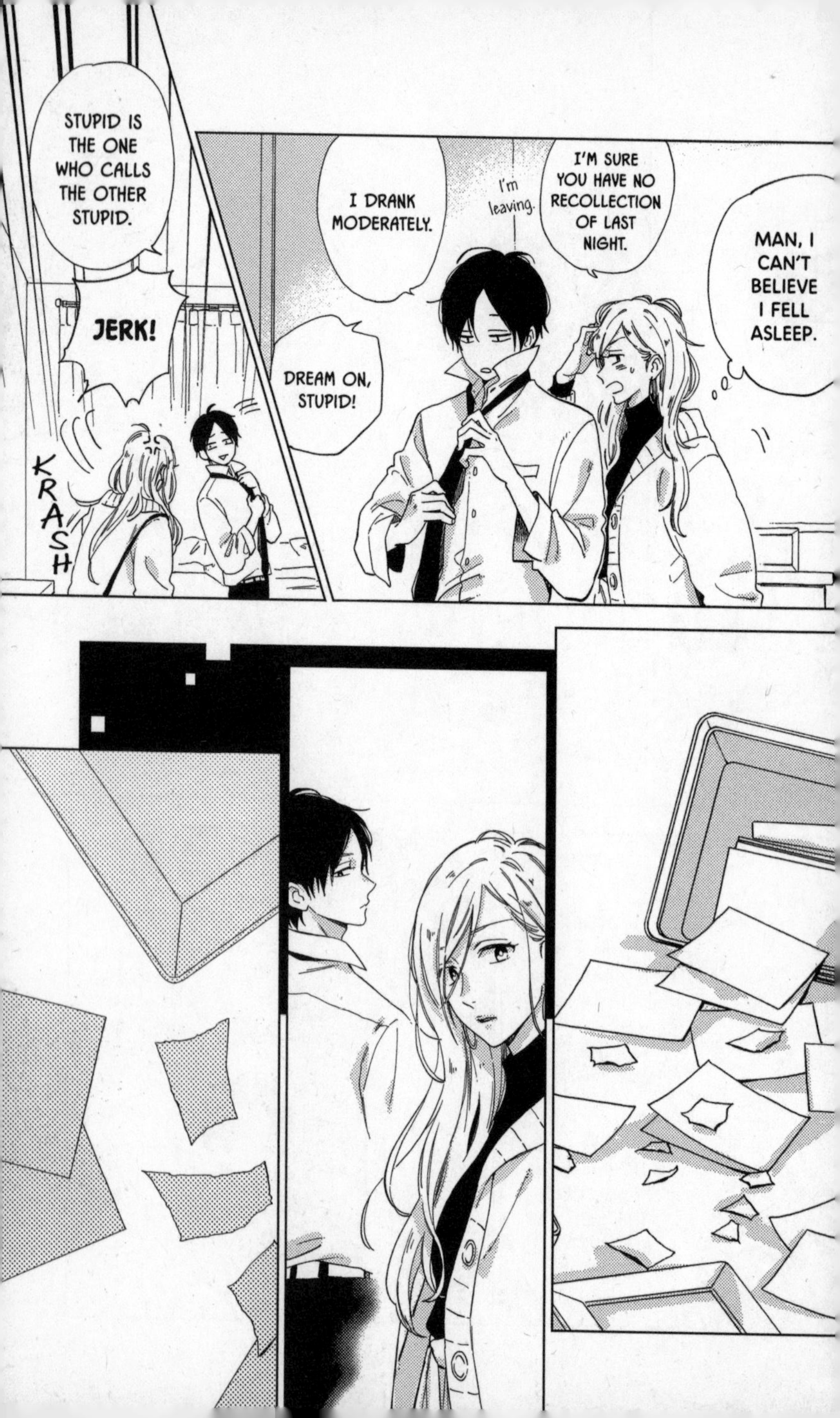
MAN, I CAN'T BELIEVE I FELL ASLEEP.
I'M SURE YOU HAVE NO RECOLLECTION OF LAST NIGHT.
I'm leaving.
I DRANK MODERATELY.
DREAM ON, STUPID!
STUPID IS THE ONE WHO CALLS THE OTHER STUPID.
JERK!
KRASH

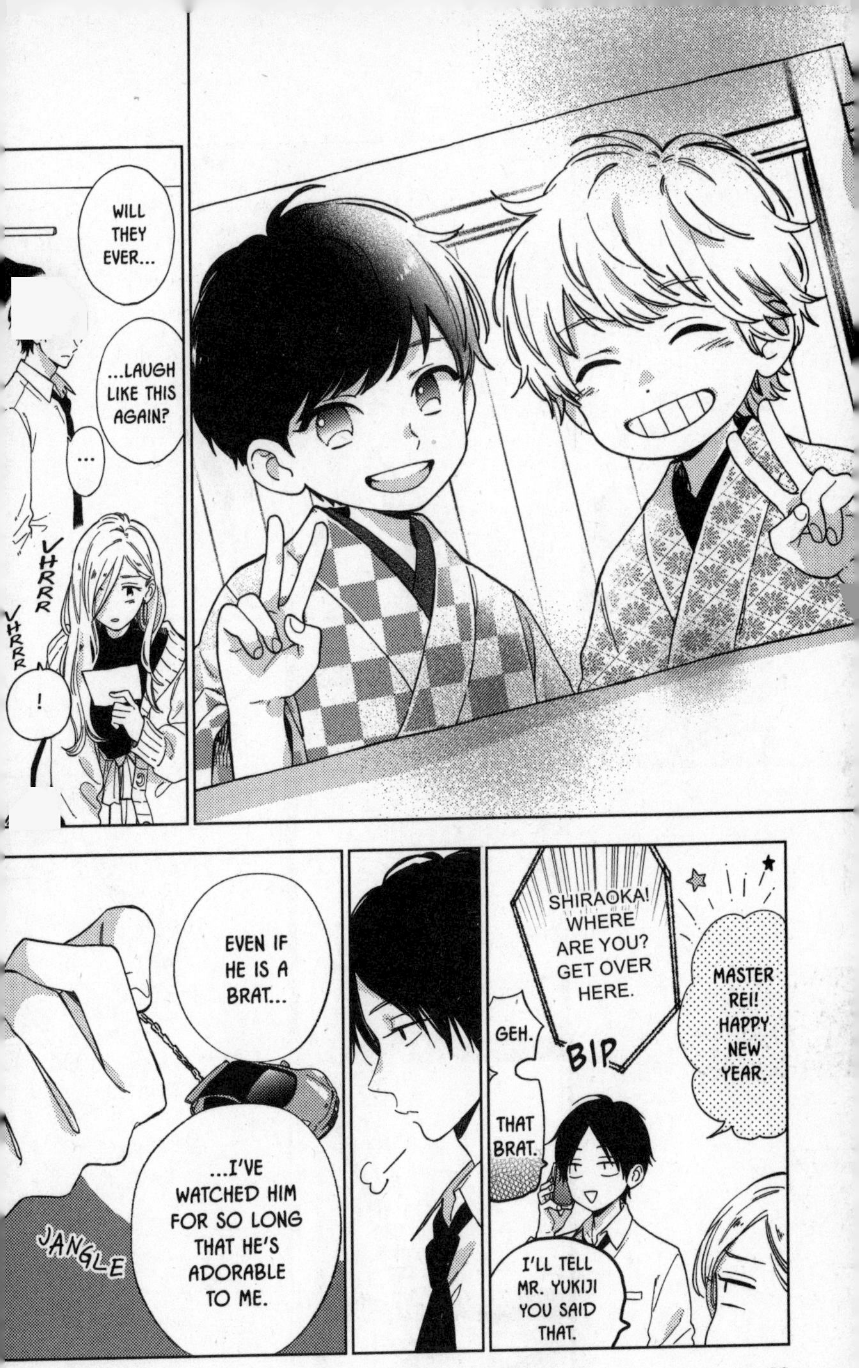
WILL THEY EVER...
...LAUGH LIKE THIS AGAIN?
...
VHRRR
VHRRR
!
MASTER REI! HAPPY NEW YEAR.
SHIRAOKA! WHERE ARE YOU? GET OVER HERE.
BIP
GEH.
THAT BRAT.
I'LL TELL MR. YUKIJI YOU SAID THAT.
EVEN IF HE IS A BRAT...
...I'VE WATCHED HIM FOR SO LONG THAT HE'S ADORABLE TO ME.
JANGLE

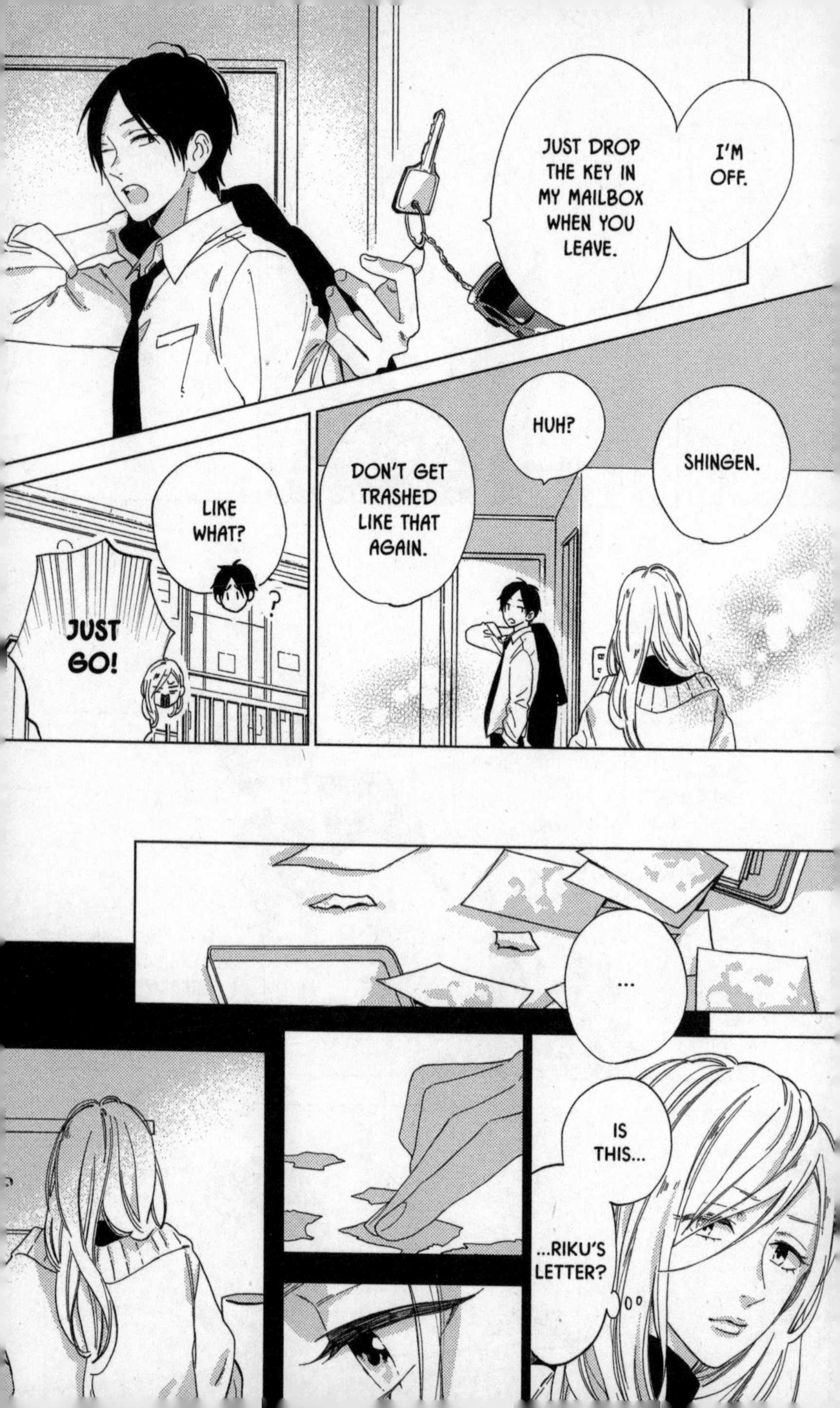
I'M OFF.
JUST DROP THE KEY IN MY MAILBOX WHEN YOU LEAVE.
SHINGEN.
HUH?
DON'T GET TRASHED LIKE THAT AGAIN.
LIKE WHAT?
?
JUST GO!
...
IS THIS...
...RIKU'S LETTER?

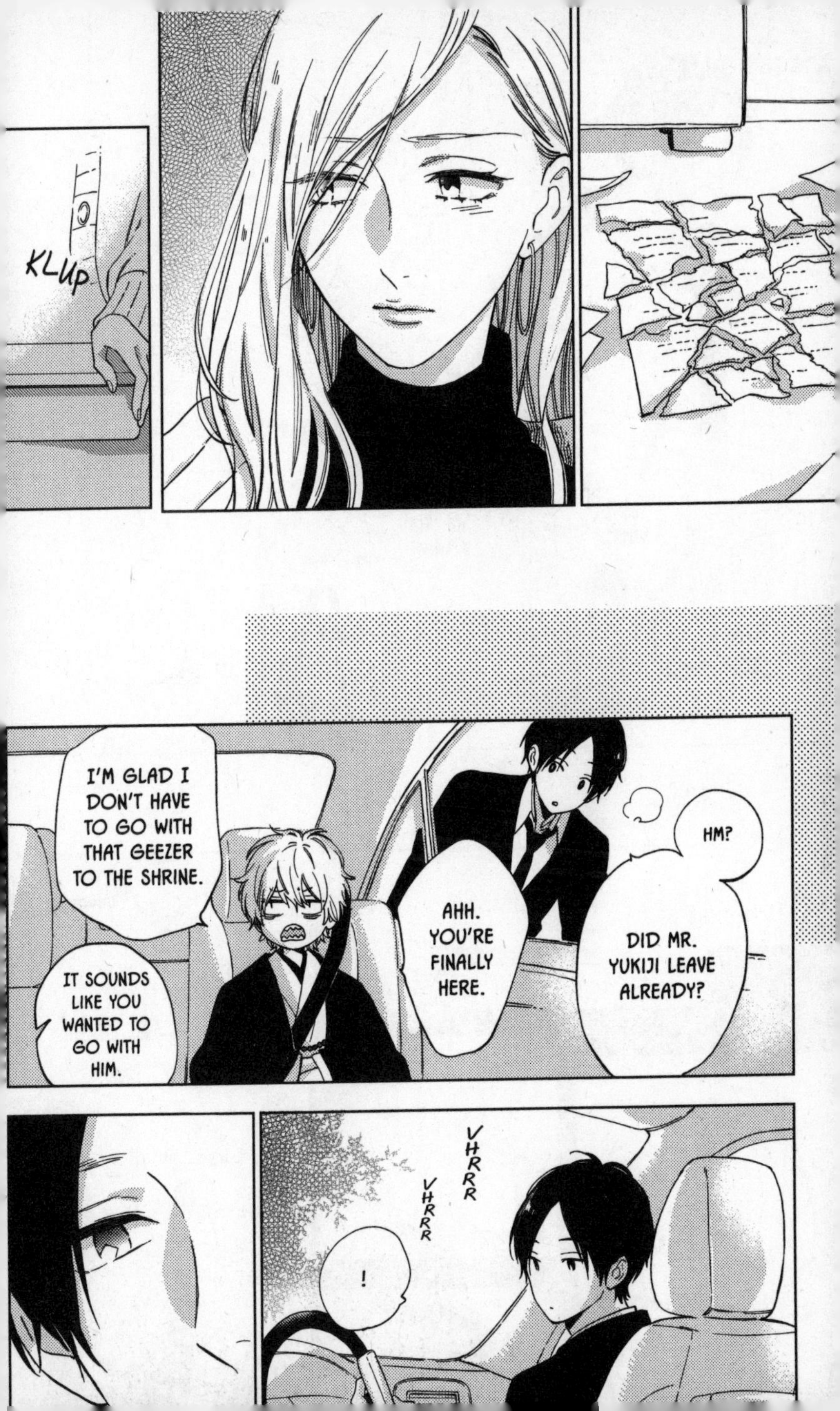
KLUP
HM?
DID MR. YUKIJI LEAVE ALREADY?
AHH. YOU'RE FINALLY HERE.
I'M GLAD I DON'T HAVE TO GO WITH THAT GEEZER TO THE SHRINE.
IT SOUNDS LIKE YOU WANTED TO GO WITH HIM.
VHRRR
VHRRR
!

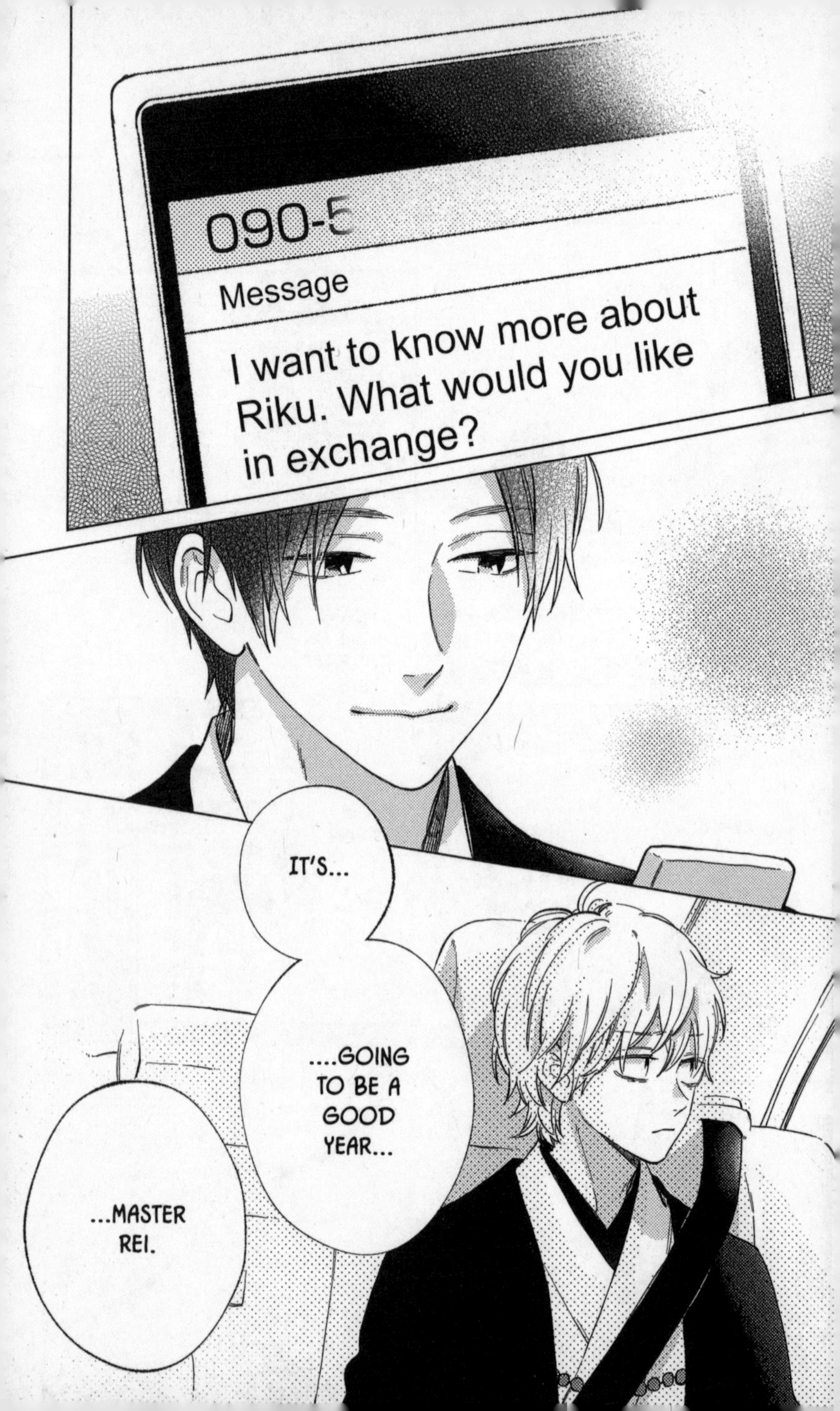
090-5
Message
I want to know more about Riku. What would you like in exchange?
IT'S...
....GOING TO BE A GOOD YEAR...
...MASTER REI.

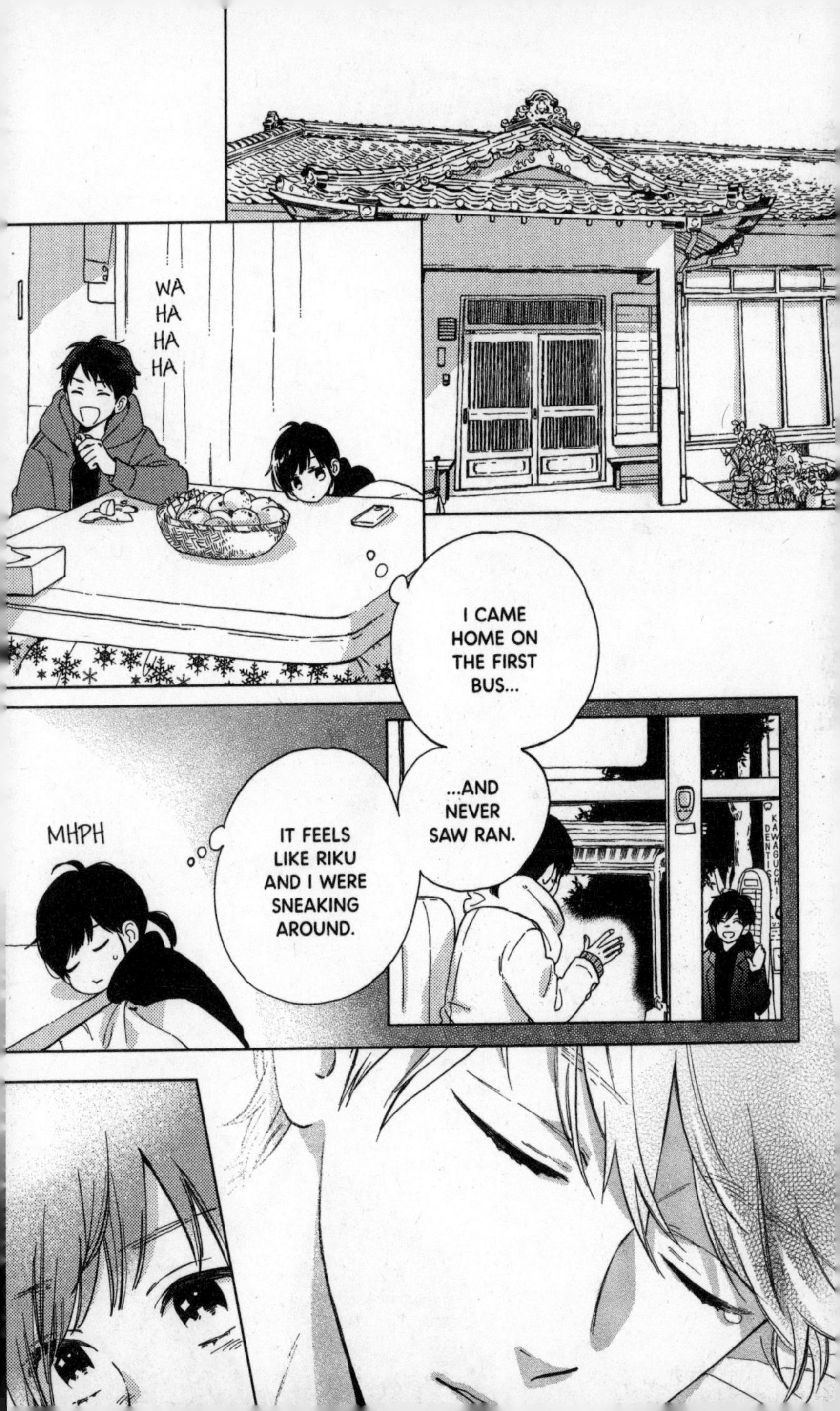
WA HA HA HA
I CAME HOME ON THE FIRST BUS...
...AND NEVER SAW RAN.
IT FEELS LIKE RIKU AND I WERE SNEAKING AROUND.
MHPH

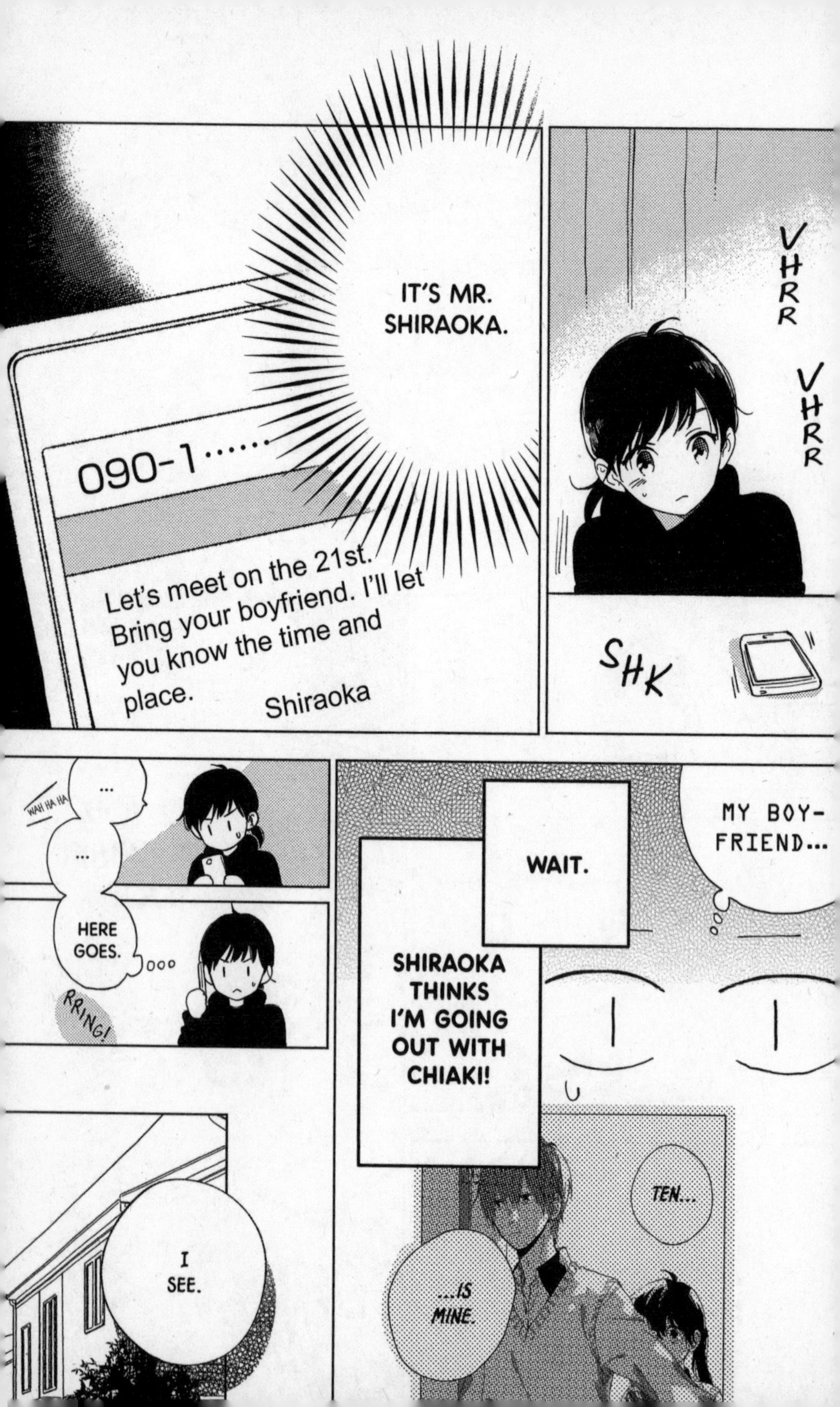
VHRR
VHRR
SHK
IT'S MR. SHIRAOKA.
090-1......
Let's meet on the 21st. Bring your boyfriend. I'll let you know the time and place. Shiraoka
MY BOY-FRIEND...
WAIT.
SHIRAOKA THINKS I'M GOING OUT WITH CHIAKI!
TEN...
...IS MINE.
...
WAH HA HA
...
HERE GOES.
RRING!
I SEE.

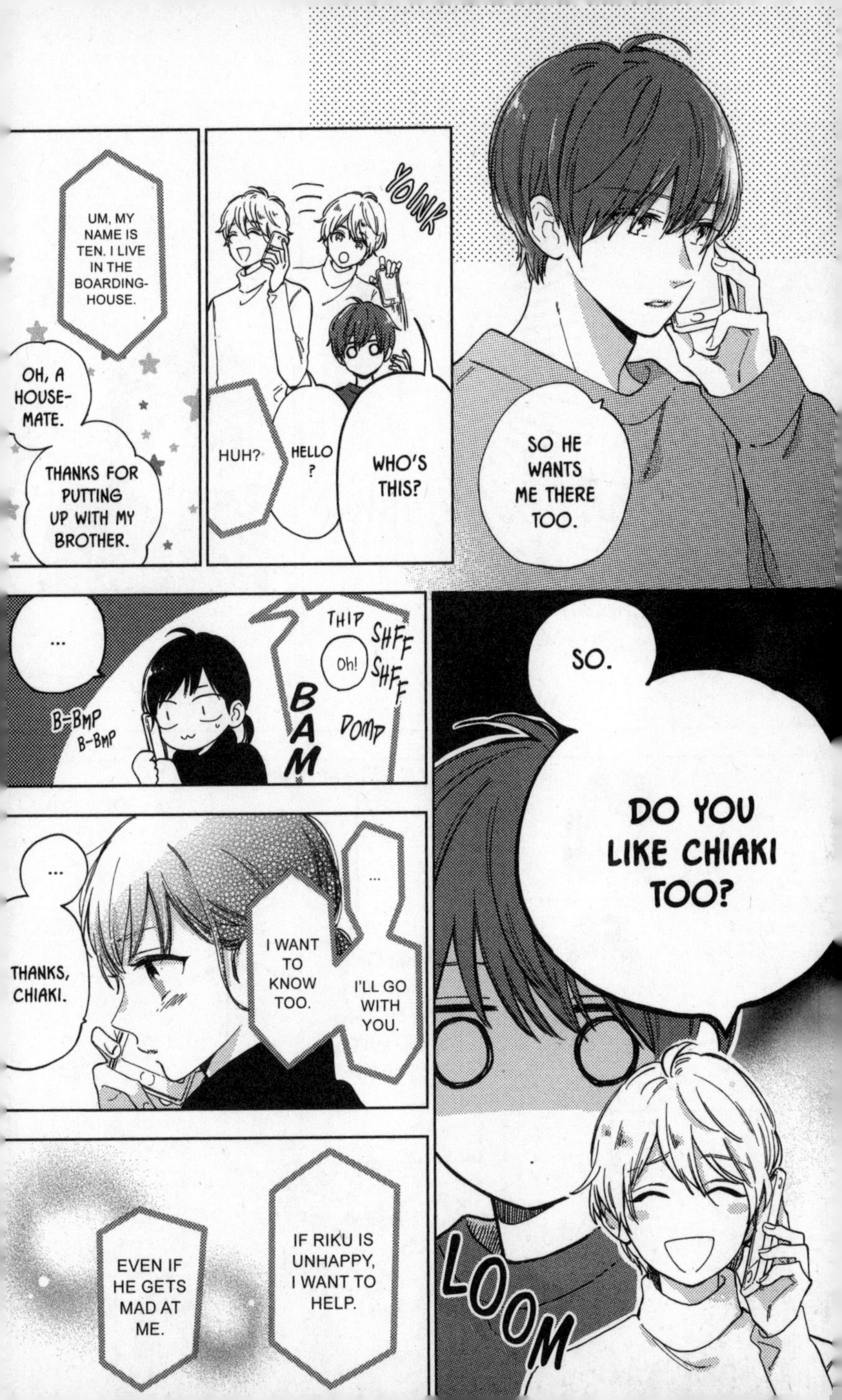
SO HE WANTS ME THERE TOO.
YOINK
WHO'S THIS?
HELLO ?
HUH?
UM, MY NAME IS TEN. I LIVE IN THE BOARDING-HOUSE.
OH, A HOUSE-MATE.
THANKS FOR PUTTING UP WITH MY BROTHER.
SO.
DO YOU LIKE CHIAKI TOO?
LOOM
THIP
SHFF SHFF
Oh!
BAM
DOMP
...
B-BMP B-BMP
...
I'LL GO WITH YOU.
I WANT TO KNOW TOO.
...
THANKS, CHIAKI.
IF RIKU IS UNHAPPY, I WANT TO HELP.
EVEN IF HE GETS MAD AT ME.

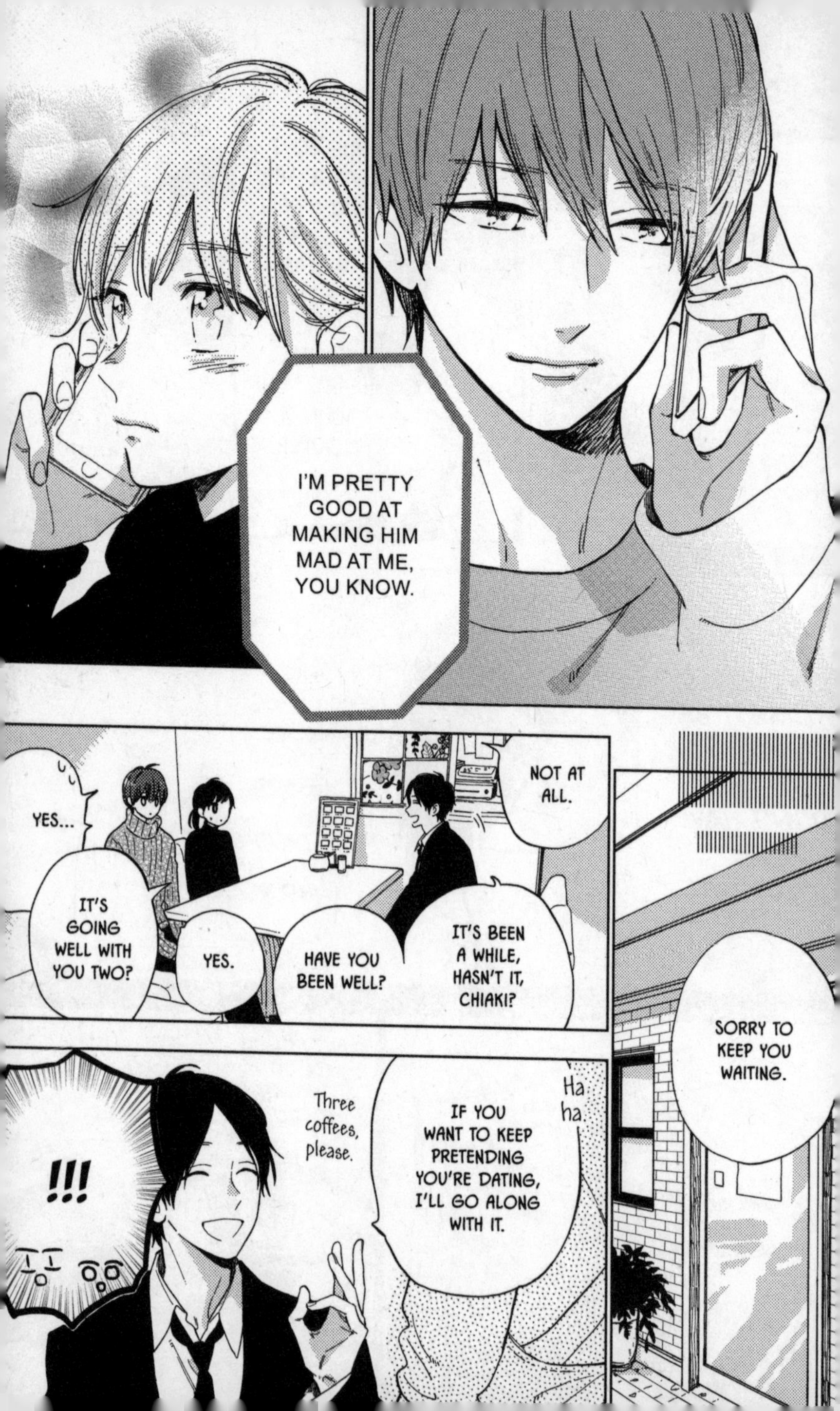
I'M PRETTY GOOD AT MAKING HIM MAD AT ME, YOU KNOW.
SORRY TO KEEP YOU WAITING.
NOT AT ALL.
IT'S BEEN A WHILE, HASN'T IT, CHIAKI?
HAVE YOU BEEN WELL?
YES.
IT'S GOING WELL WITH YOU TWO?
YES...
Ha ha.
IF YOU WANT TO KEEP PRETENDING YOU'RE DATING, I'LL GO ALONG WITH IT.
Three coffees, please.
!!!

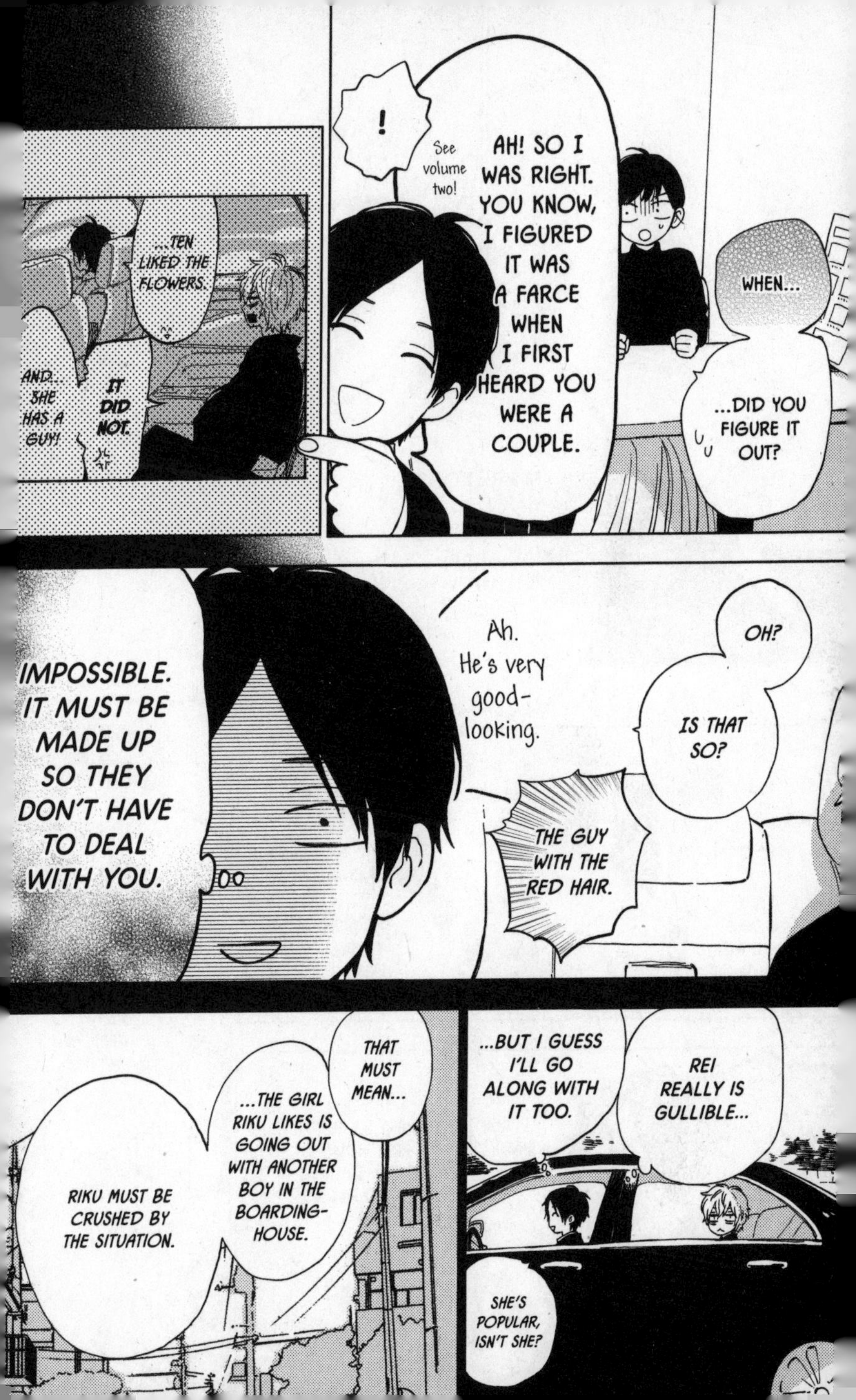
WHEN...
...DID YOU FIGURE IT OUT?
!
See volume two!
AH! SO I WAS RIGHT. YOU KNOW, I FIGURED IT WAS A FARCE WHEN I FIRST HEARD YOU WERE A COUPLE.
...TEN LIKED THE FLOWERS.
IT DID NOT.
AND... SHE HAS A GUY!
OH?
IS THAT SO?
THE GUY WITH THE RED HAIR.
Ah. He's very good-looking.
IMPOSSIBLE. IT MUST BE MADE UP SO THEY DON'T HAVE TO DEAL WITH YOU.
REI REALLY IS GULLIBLE...
...BUT I GUESS I'LL GO ALONG WITH IT TOO.
SHE'S POPULAR, ISN'T SHE?
THAT MUST MEAN...
...THE GIRL RIKU LIKES IS GOING OUT WITH ANOTHER BOY IN THE BOARDING-HOUSE.
RIKU MUST BE CRUSHED BY THE SITUATION.

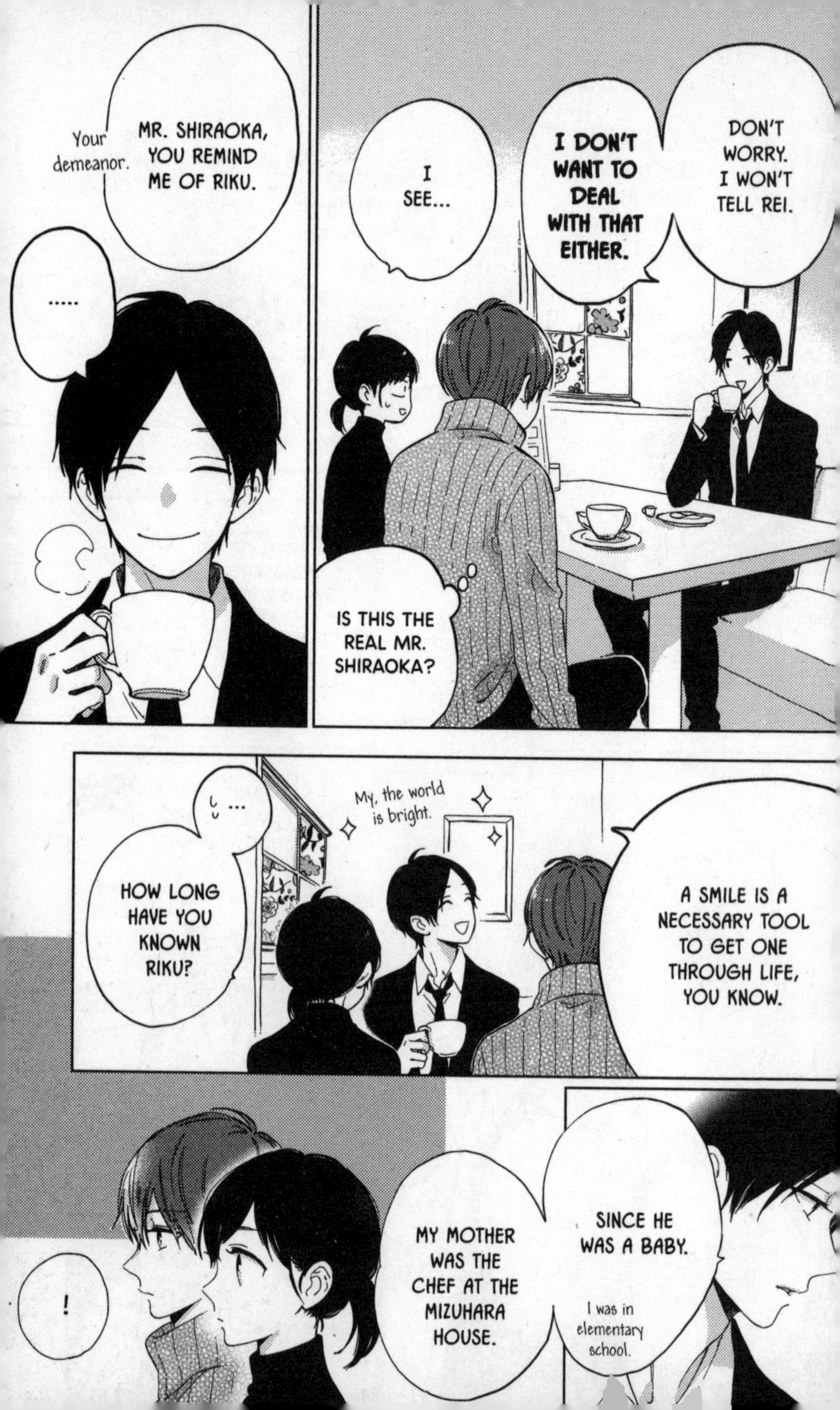
DON'T WORRY. I WON'T TELL REI.
I DON'T WANT TO DEAL WITH THAT EITHER.
I SEE...
IS THIS THE REAL MR. SHIRAOKA?
MR. SHIRAOKA, YOU REMIND ME OF RIKU.
Your demeanor.
.....
A SMILE IS A NECESSARY TOOL TO GET ONE THROUGH LIFE, YOU KNOW.
My, the world is bright.
...
HOW LONG HAVE YOU KNOWN RIKU?
SINCE HE WAS A BABY.
I was in elementary school.
MY MOTHER WAS THE CHEF AT THE MIZUHARA HOUSE.
!

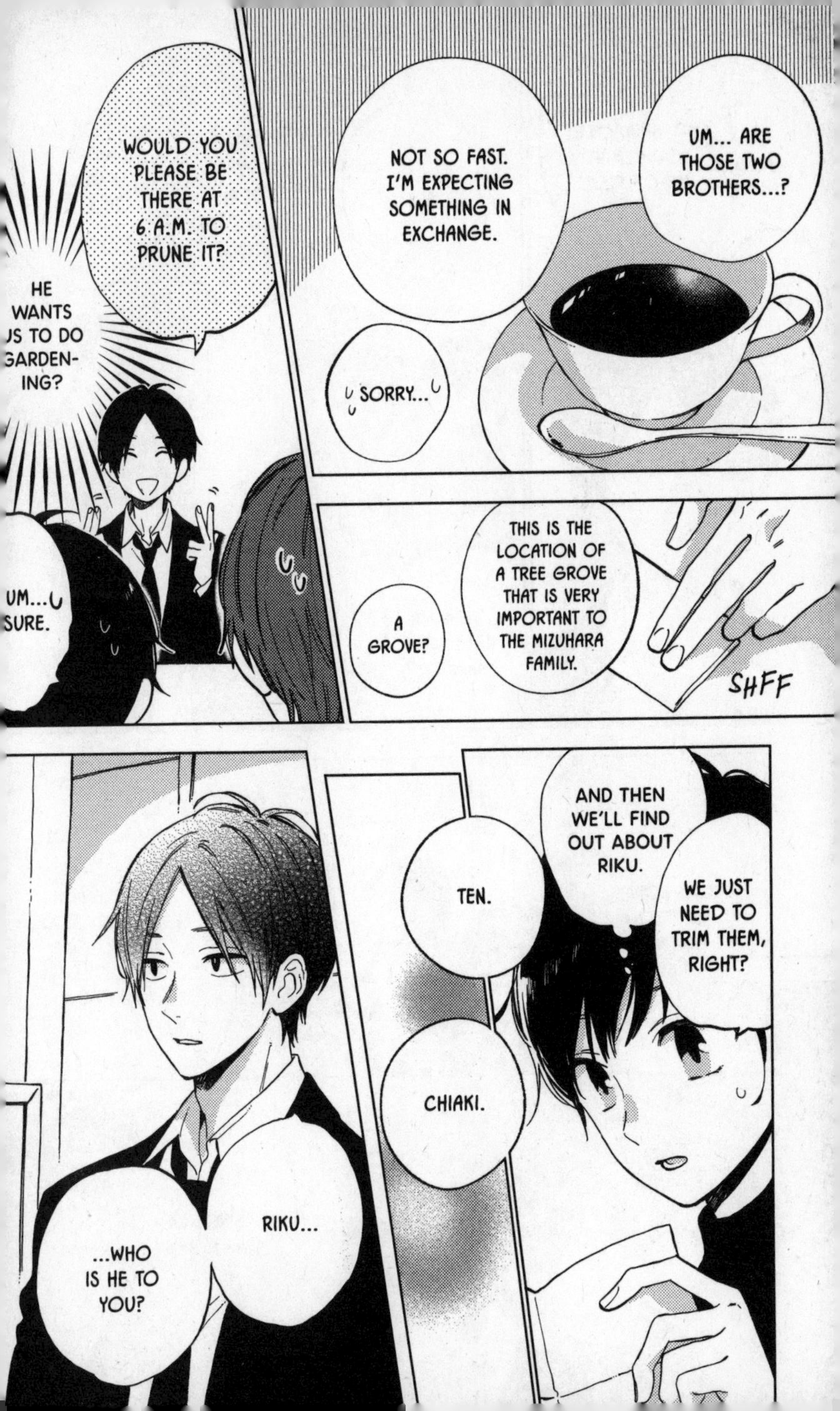
UM... ARE THOSE TWO BROTHERS...?
NOT SO FAST. I'M EXPECTING SOMETHING IN EXCHANGE.
SORRY...
THIS IS THE LOCATION OF A TREE GROVE THAT IS VERY IMPORTANT TO THE MIZUHARA FAMILY.
A GROVE?
SHFF
WOULD YOU PLEASE BE THERE AT 6 A.M. TO PRUNE IT?
HE WANTS US TO DO GARDEN- ING?
UM... SURE.
WE JUST NEED TO TRIM THEM, RIGHT?
AND THEN WE'LL FIND OUT ABOUT RIKU.
TEN.
CHIAKI.
RIKU...
...WHO IS HE TO YOU?

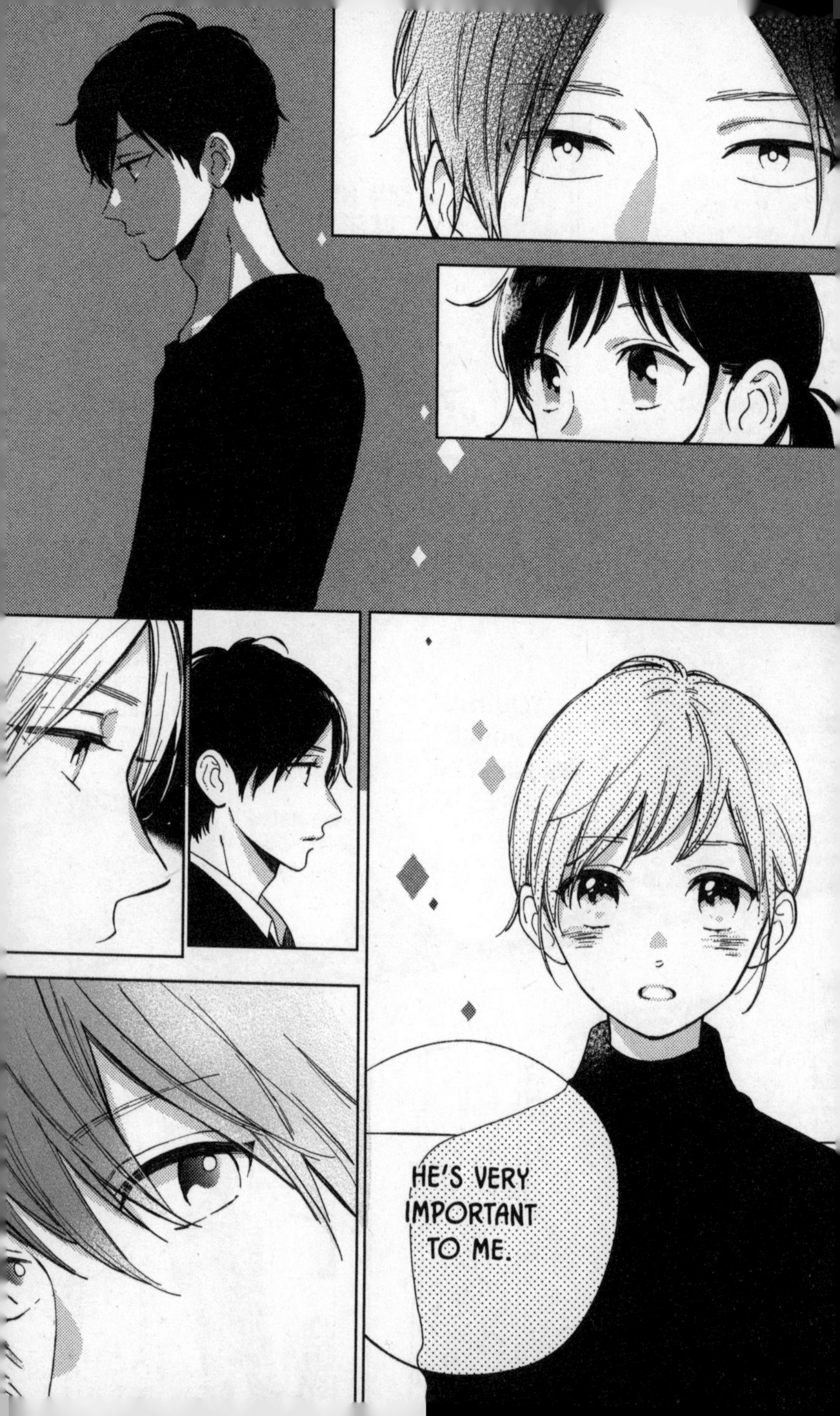
HE'S VERY IMPORTANT TO ME.

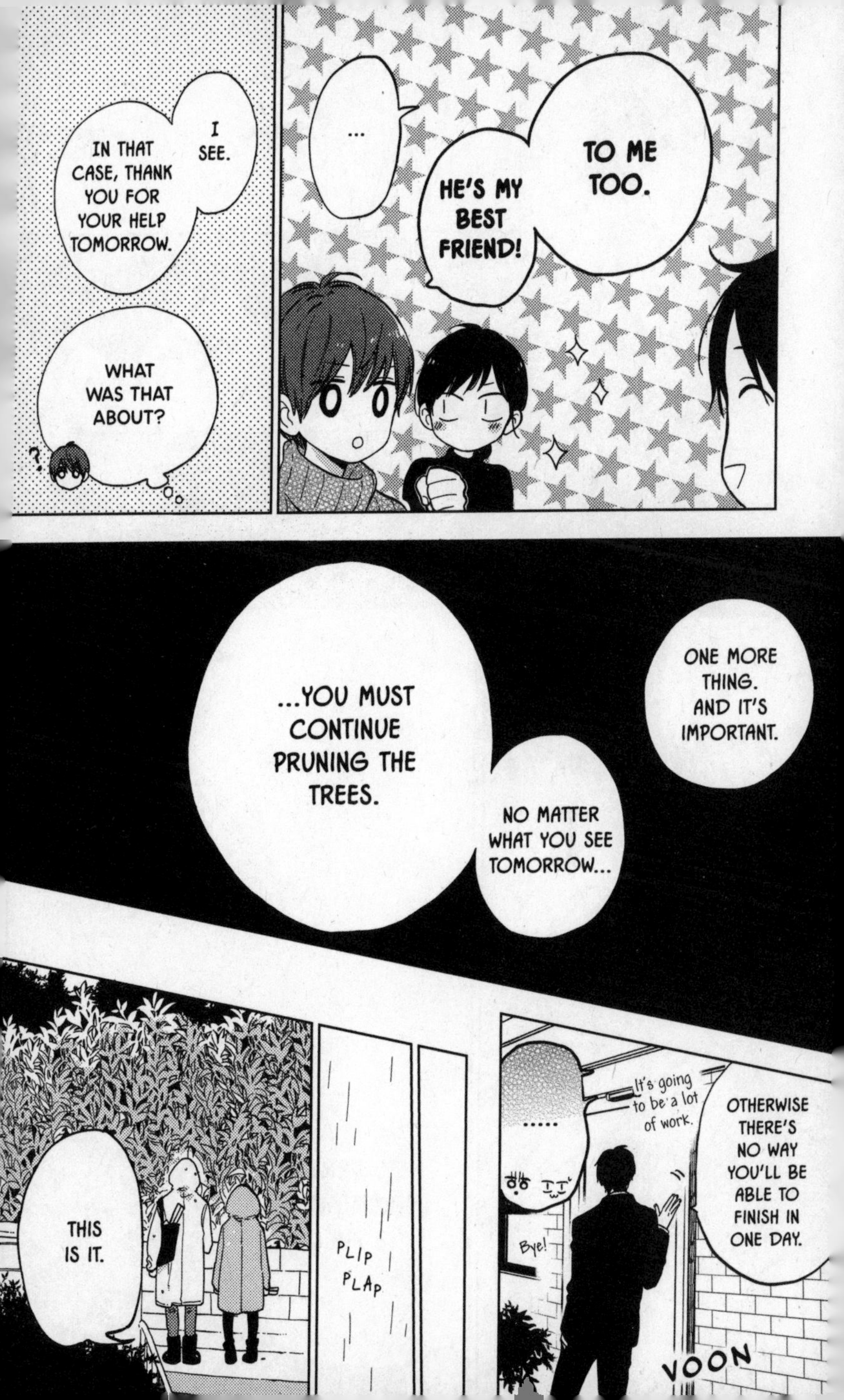
TO ME TOO.
HE'S MY BEST FRIEND!
...
I SEE.
IN THAT CASE, THANK YOU FOR YOUR HELP TOMORROW.
WHAT WAS THAT ABOUT?
?
ONE MORE THING. AND IT'S IMPORTANT.
NO MATTER WHAT YOU SEE TOMORROW...
...YOU MUST CONTINUE PRUNING THE TREES.
OTHERWISE THERE'S NO WAY YOU'LL BE ABLE TO FINISH IN ONE DAY.
It's going to be a lot of work.
.....
Bye!
VOON
PLIP PLAP
THIS IS IT.

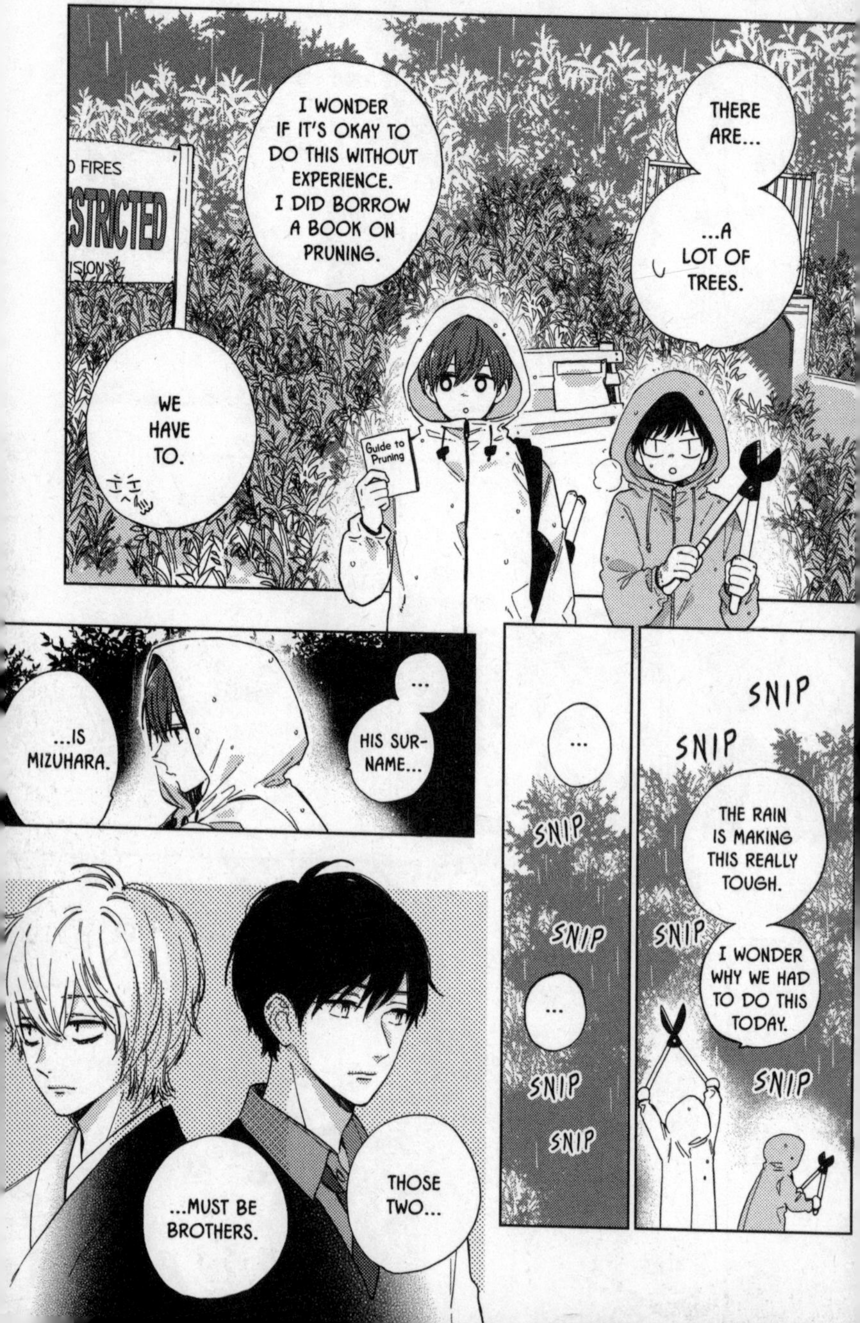
THERE ARE...
...A LOT OF TREES.
I WONDER IF IT'S OKAY TO DO THIS WITHOUT EXPERIENCE. I DID BORROW A BOOK ON PRUNING.
Guide to Pruning
WE HAVE TO.
SNIP
SNIP
THE RAIN IS MAKING THIS REALLY TOUGH.
SNIP
I WONDER WHY WE HAD TO DO THIS TODAY.
SNIP
...
SNIP
SNIP
...
SNIP
SNIP
...
HIS SUR-NAME...
...IS MIZUHARA.
THOSE TWO...
...MUST BE BROTHERS.

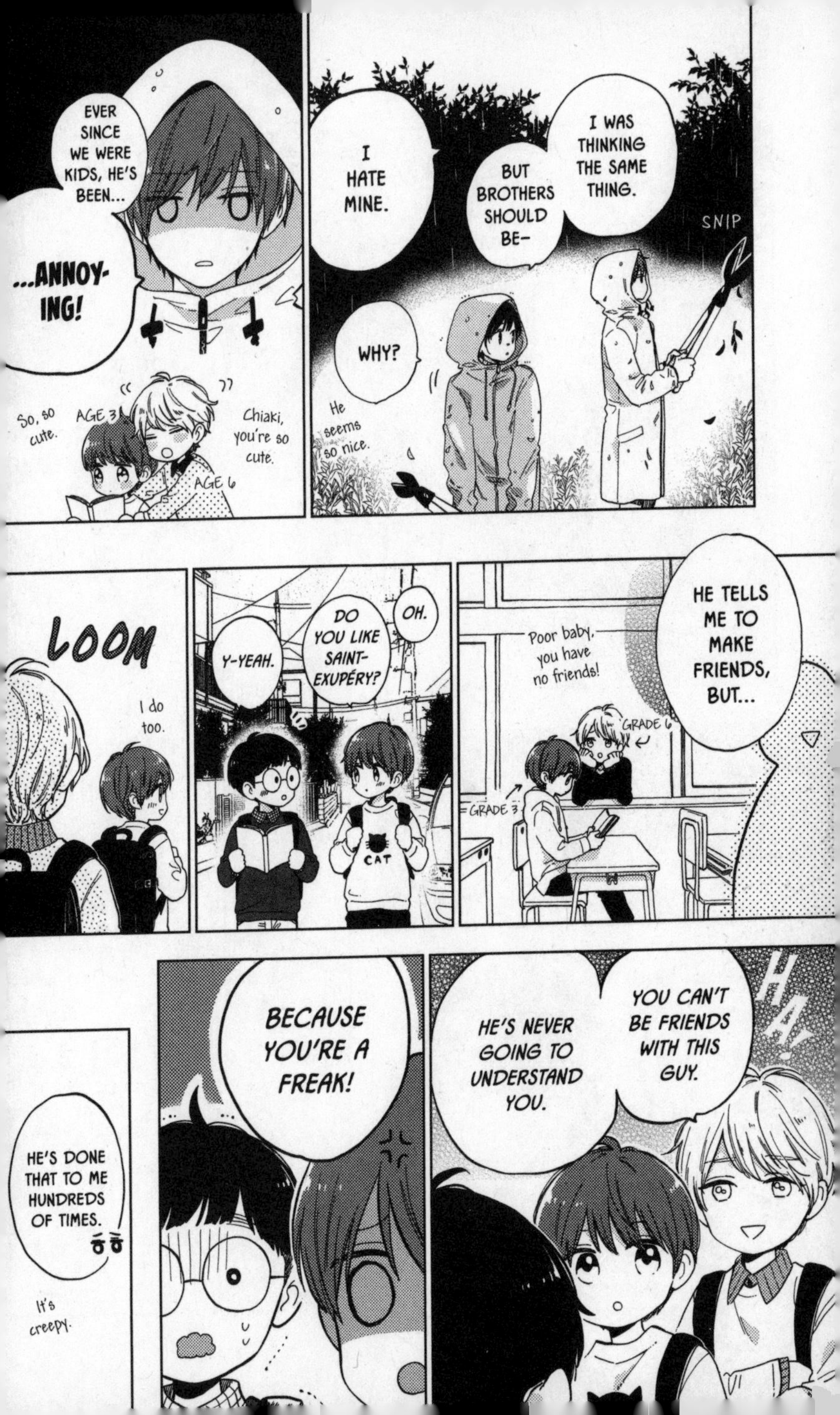
I WAS THINKING THE SAME THING.
BUT BROTHERS SHOULD BE–
I HATE MINE.
SNIP
WHY?
He seems so nice.
EVER SINCE WE WERE KIDS, HE'S BEEN...
...ANNOYING!
Chiaki, you're so cute.
AGE 6
AGE 3
So, so cute.
HE TELLS ME TO MAKE FRIENDS, BUT...
GRADE 6
Poor baby, you have no friends!
GRADE 3
OH.
DO YOU LIKE SAINT-EXUPÉRY?
Y-YEAH.
LOOM
I do too.
HA!
YOU CAN'T BE FRIENDS WITH THIS GUY.
HE'S NEVER GOING TO UNDERSTAND YOU.
BECAUSE YOU'RE A FREAK!
HE'S DONE THAT TO ME HUNDREDS OF TIMES.
It's creepy.

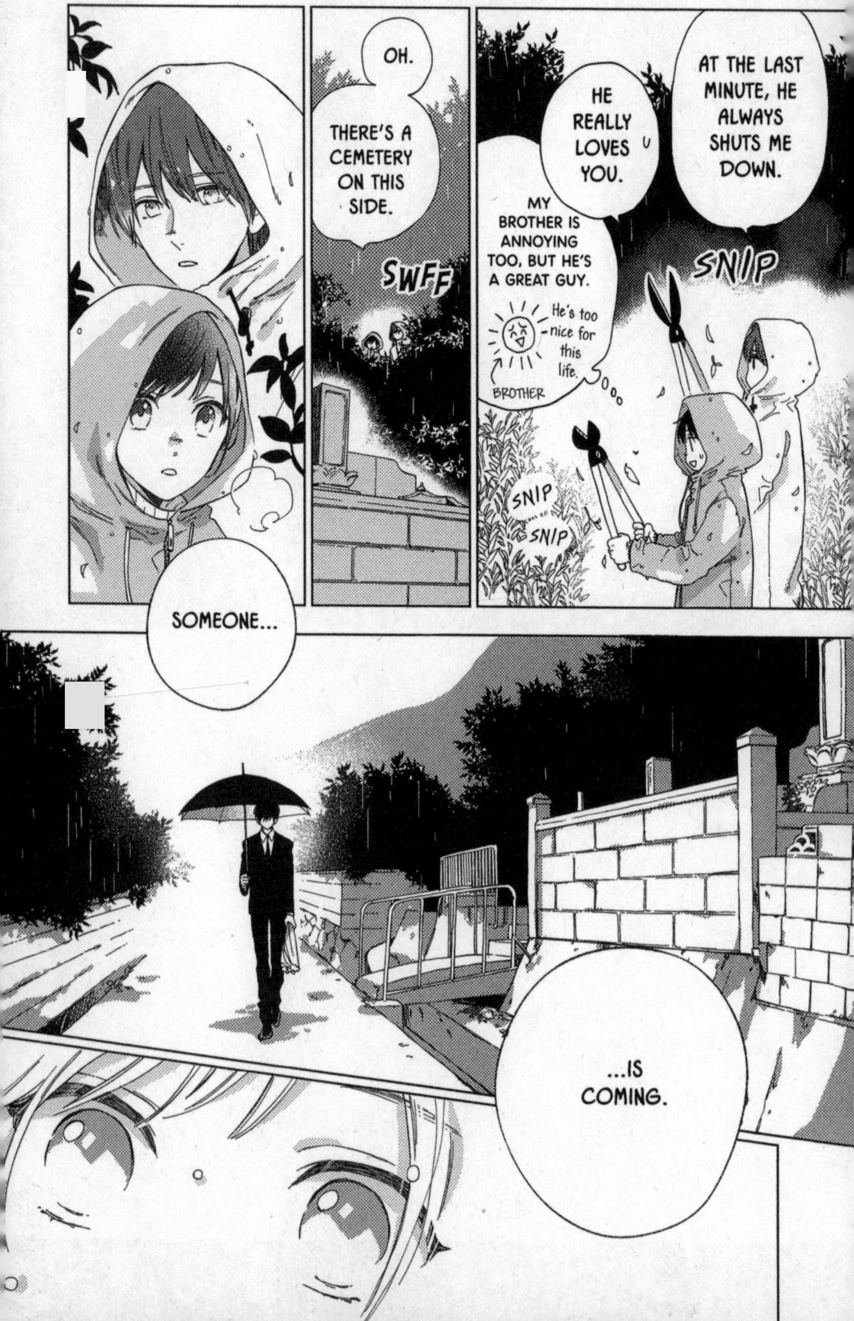
AT THE LAST MINUTE, HE ALWAYS SHUTS ME DOWN.
SNIP
HE REALLY LOVES YOU.
MY BROTHER IS ANNOYING TOO, BUT HE'S A GREAT GUY.
He's too nice for this life.
BROTHER
SNIP
SNIP
OH.
THERE'S A CEMETERY ON THIS SIDE.
SWFF
SOMEONE...
...IS COMING.

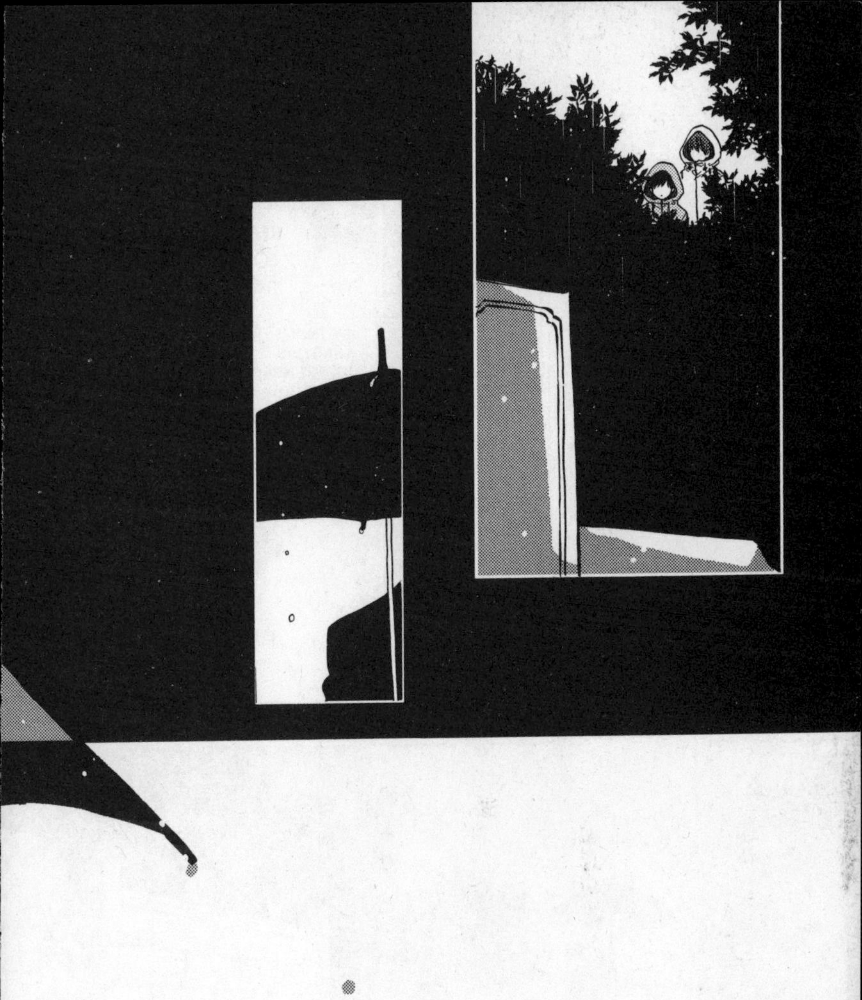

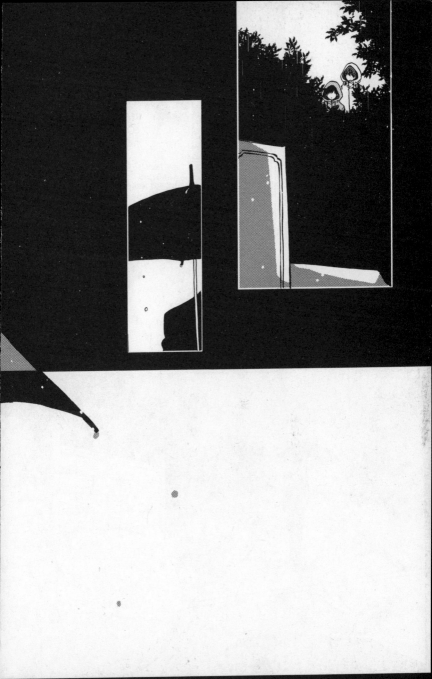

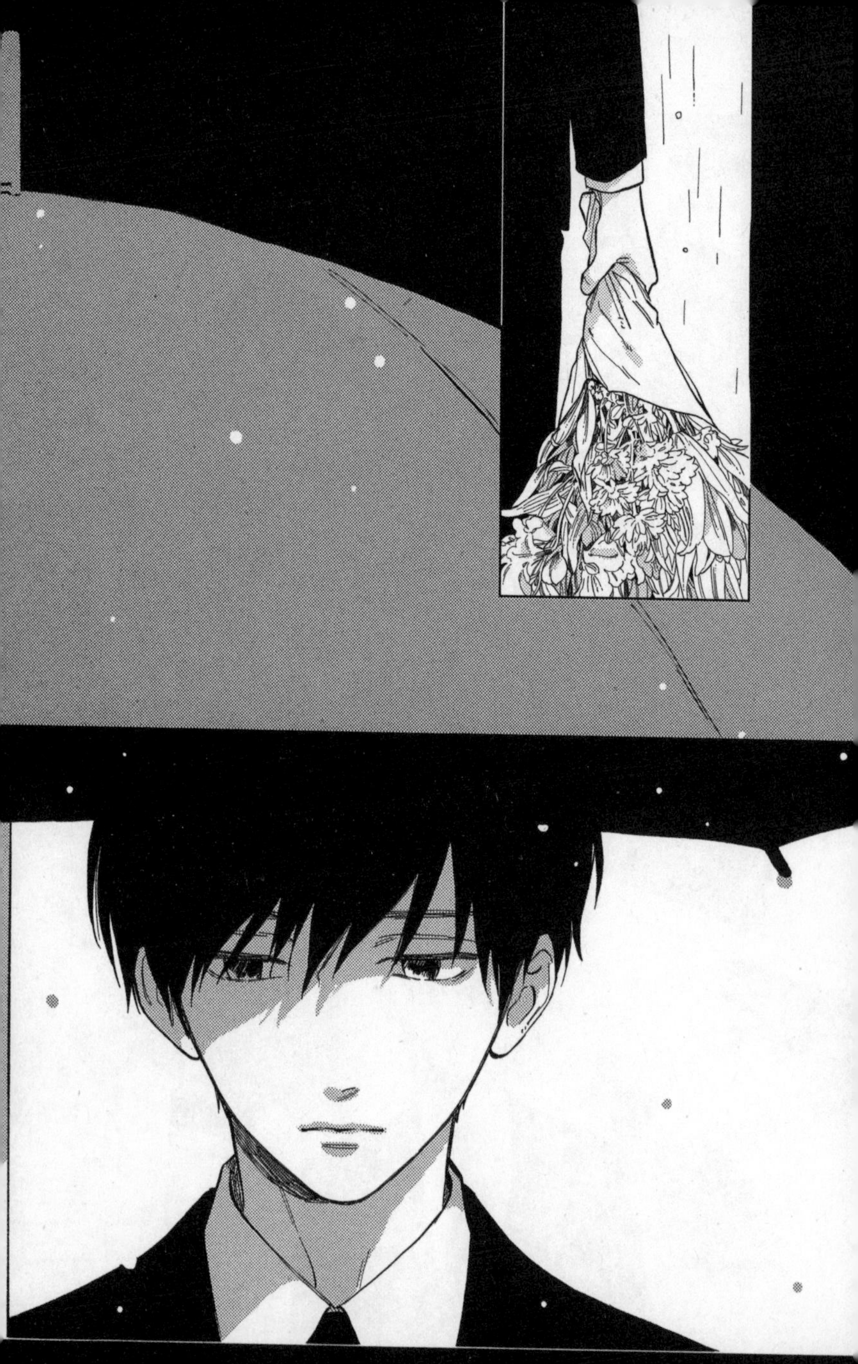

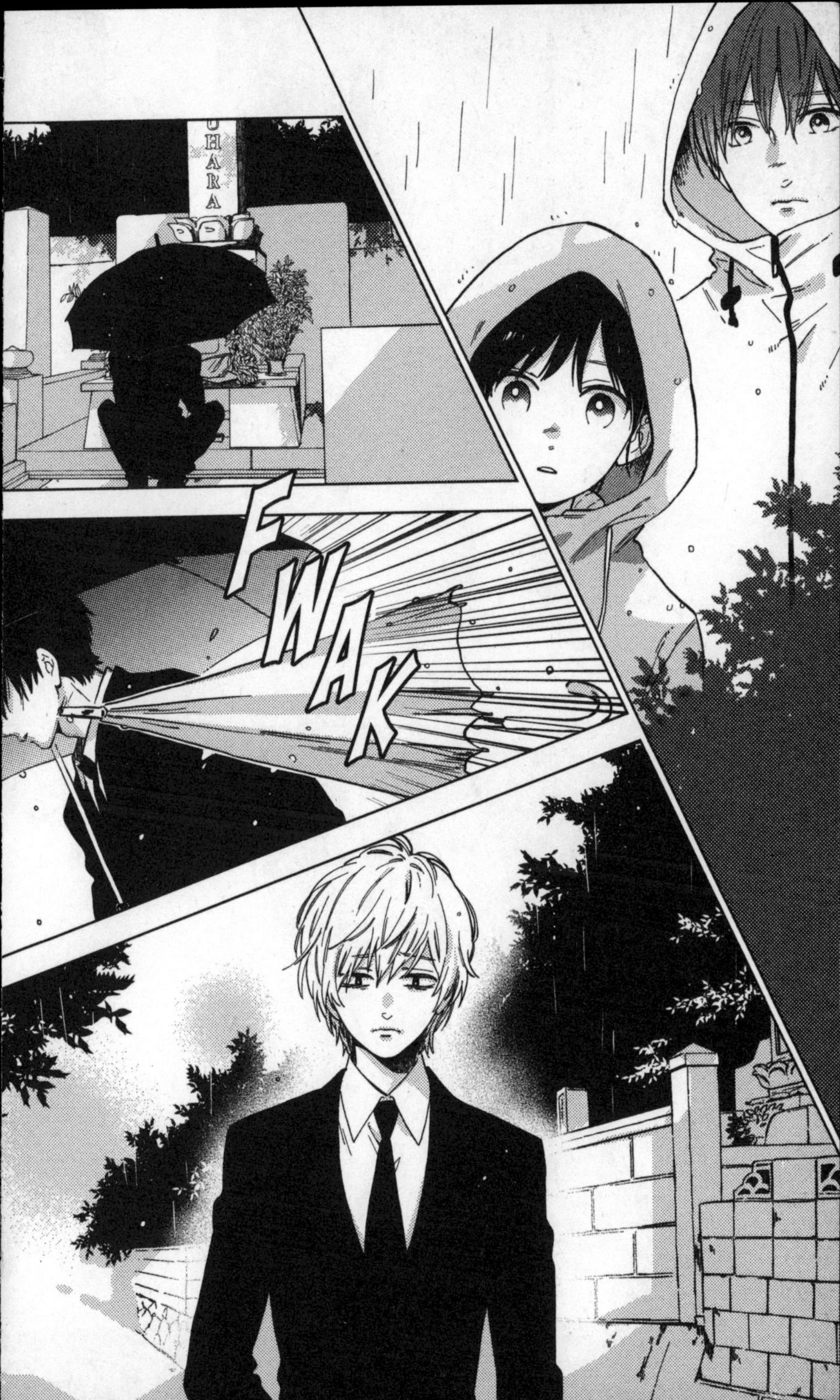
UHARA
FWAK

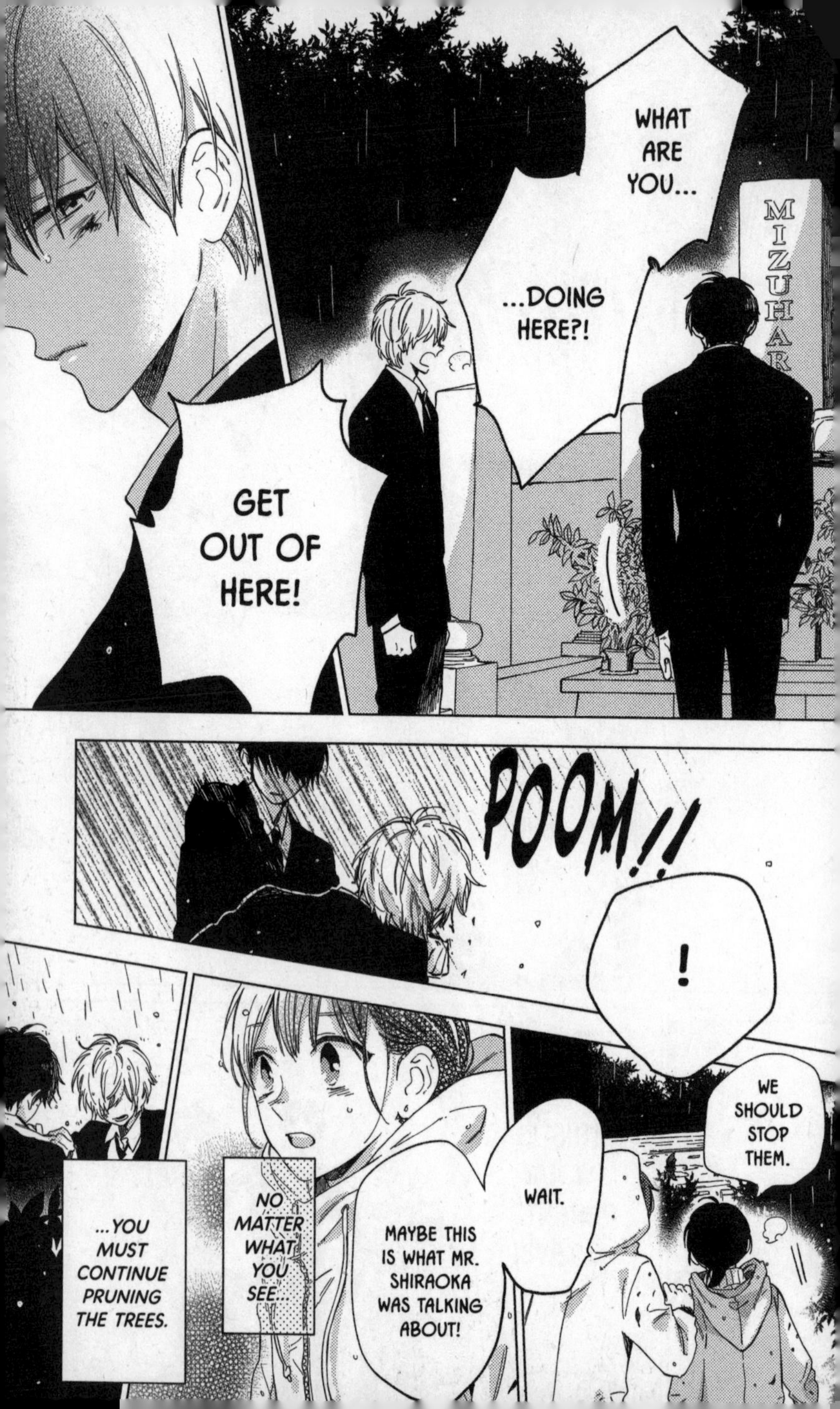
WHAT ARE YOU...
...DOING HERE?!
GET OUT OF HERE!
POOM!!
!
WE SHOULD STOP THEM.
WAIT.
MAYBE THIS IS WHAT MR. SHIRAOKA WAS TALKING ABOUT!
NO MATTER WHAT YOU SEE...
...YOU MUST CONTINUE PRUNING THE TREES.
MIZUHARA

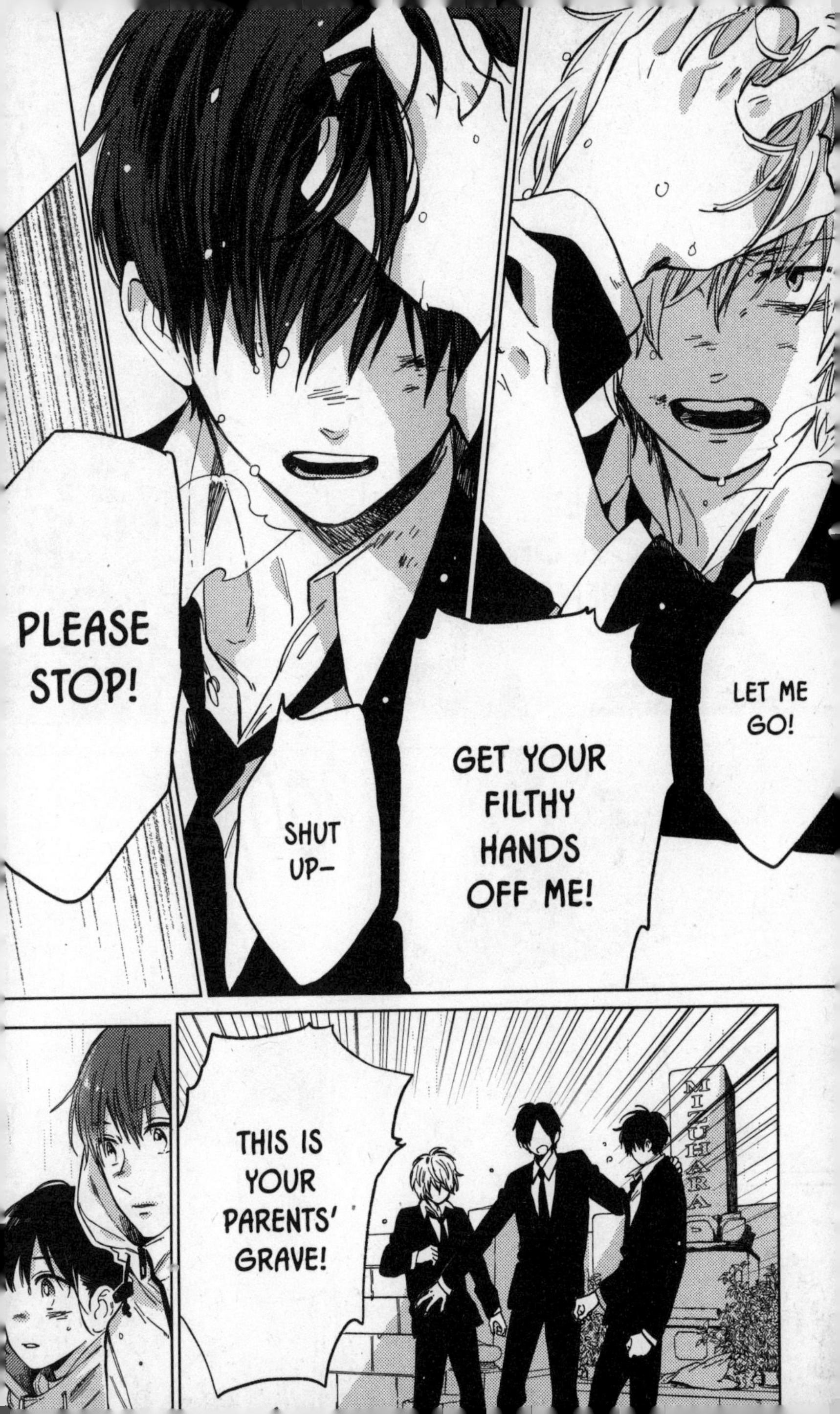
LET ME GO!
GET YOUR FILTHY HANDS OFF ME!
SHUT UP-
PLEASE STOP!
MIZUHARA
THIS IS YOUR PARENTS' GRAVE!

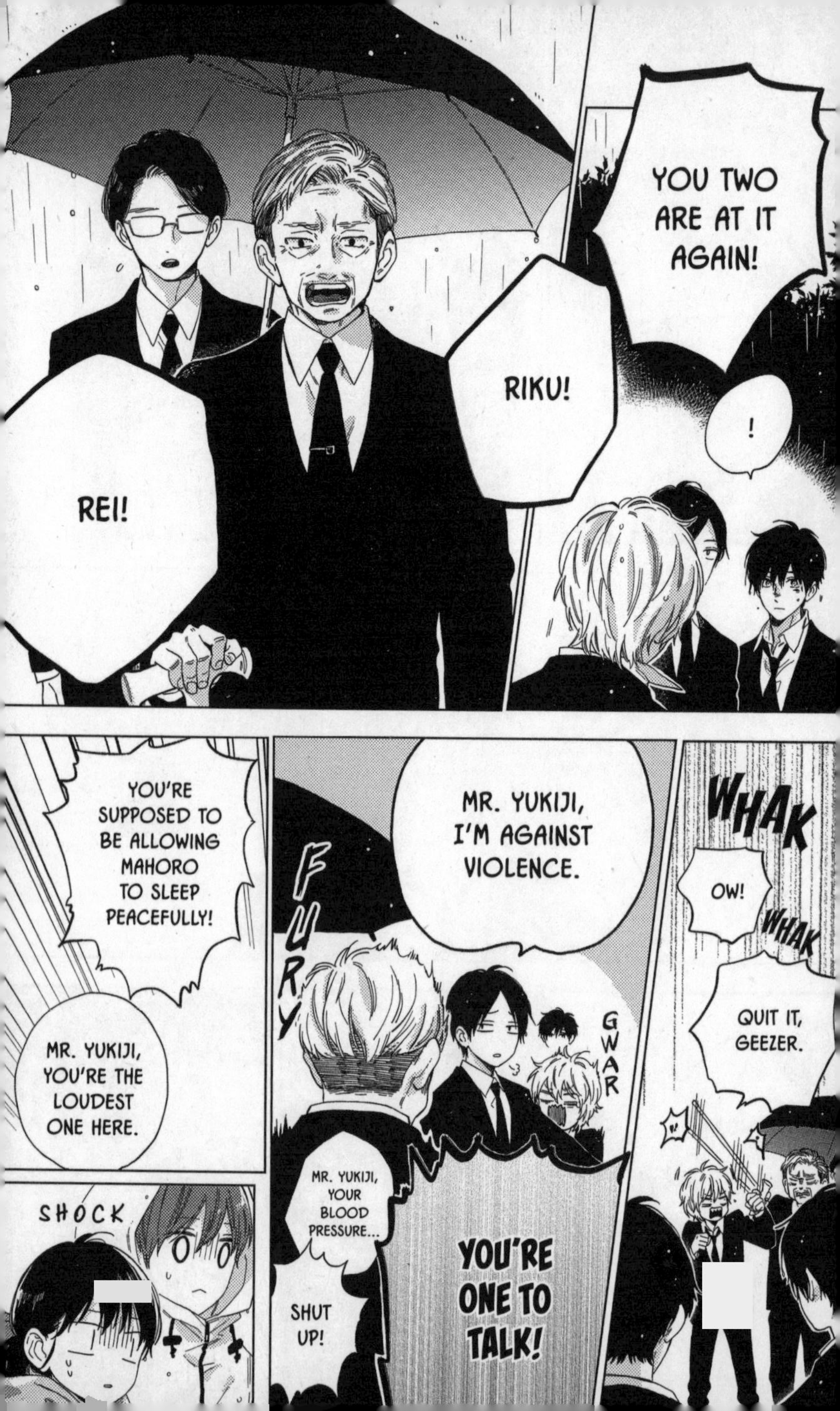
YOU TWO ARE AT IT AGAIN!
!
RIKU!
REI!
WHAK
OW!
WHAK
QUIT IT, GEEZER.
MR. YUKIJI, I'M AGAINST VIOLENCE.
FURY
GWAR
MR. YUKIJI, YOUR BLOOD PRESSURE...
YOU'RE ONE TO TALK!
SHUT UP!
YOU'RE SUPPOSED TO BE ALLOWING MAHORO TO SLEEP PEACEFULLY!
MR. YUKIJI, YOU'RE THE LOUDEST ONE HERE.
SHOCK

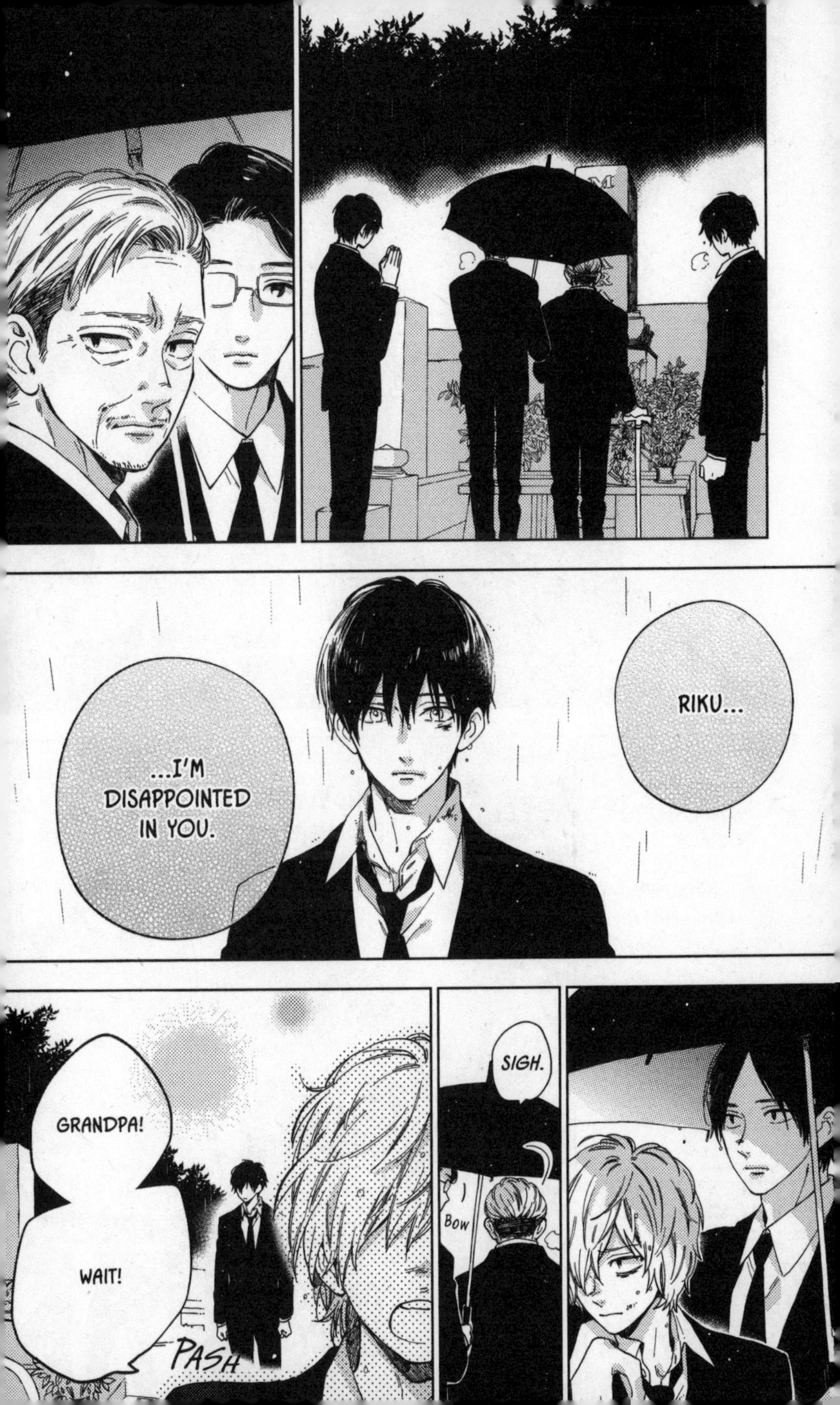
RIKU...
...I'M DISAPPOINTED IN YOU.
SIGH.
Bow
GRANDPA!
WAIT!
PASH

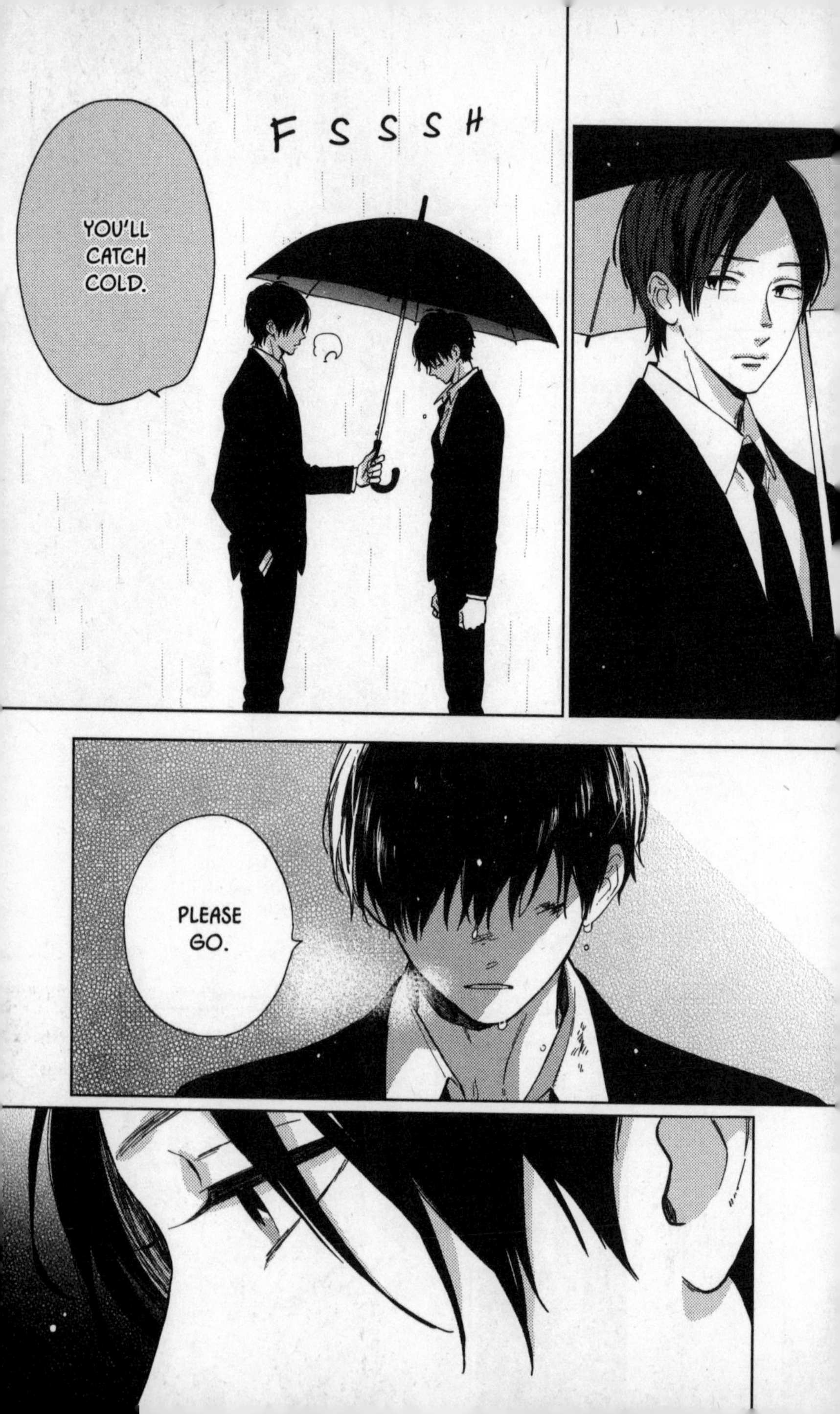
FSSSH
YOU'LL CATCH COLD.
PLEASE GO.

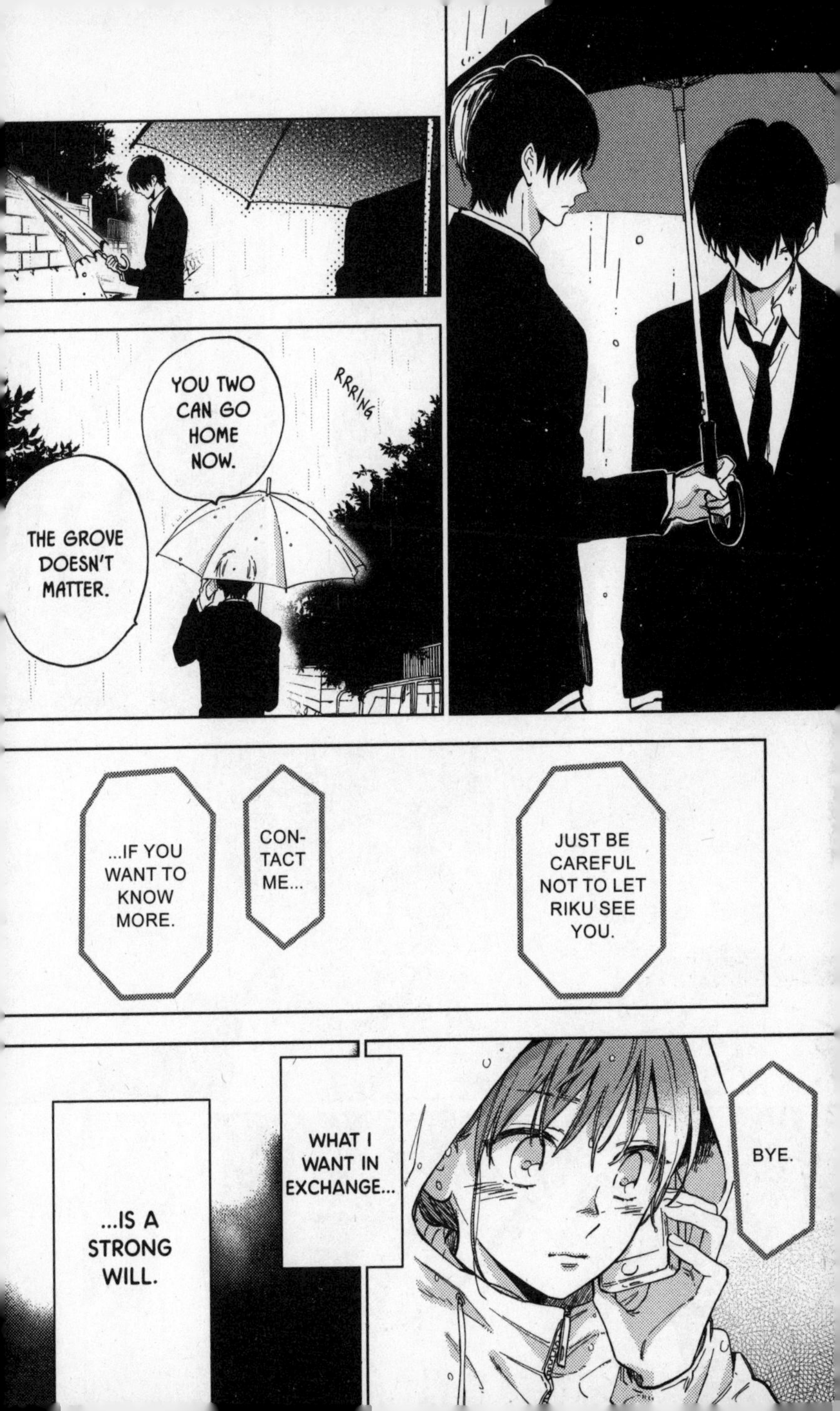
RRRING
YOU TWO CAN GO HOME NOW.
THE GROVE DOESN'T MATTER.
JUST BE CAREFUL NOT TO LET RIKU SEE YOU.
CON-TACT ME...
...IF YOU WANT TO KNOW MORE.
BYE.
WHAT I WANT IN EXCHANGE...
...IS A STRONG WILL.

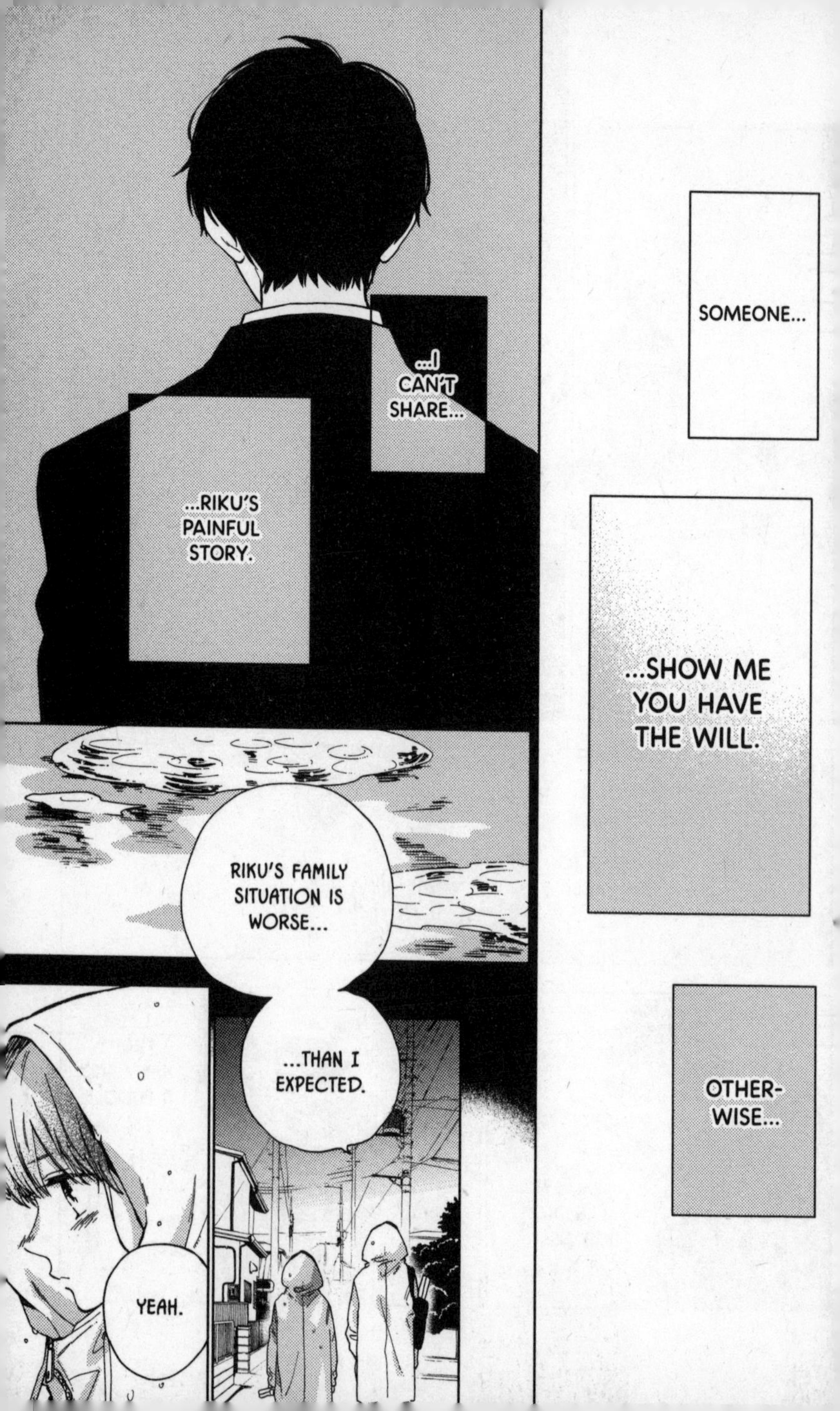
SOMEONE...
...SHOW ME YOU HAVE THE WILL.
OTHER-WISE...
...I CAN'T SHARE...
...RIKU'S PAINFUL STORY.
RIKU'S FAMILY SITUATION IS WORSE...
...THAN I EXPECTED.
YEAH.

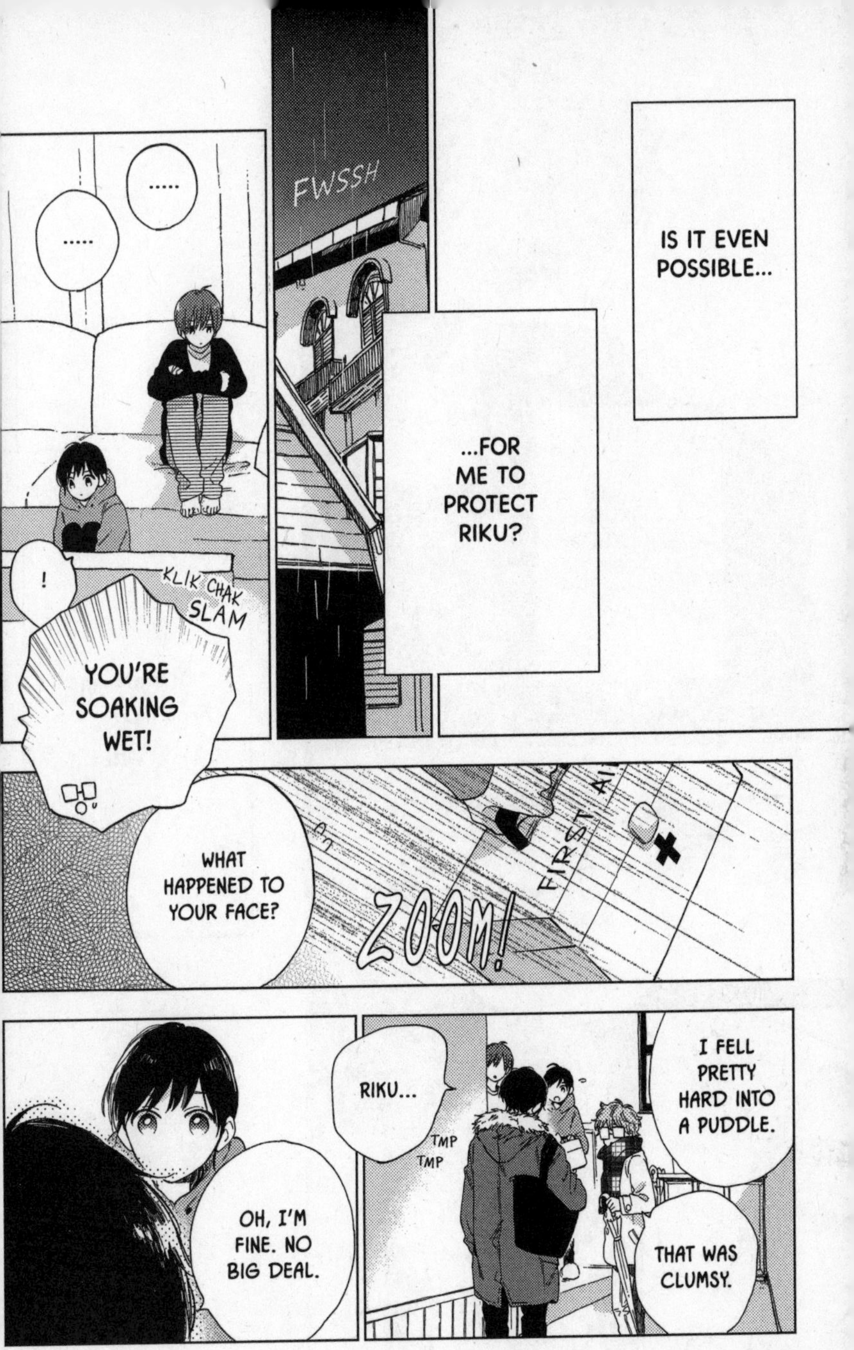
IS IT EVEN POSSIBLE...
FWSSH
...FOR ME TO PROTECT RIKU?
......
......
!
KLIK CHAK
SLAM
YOU'RE SOAKING WET!
WHAT HAPPENED TO YOUR FACE?
ZOOM!
FIRST
I FELL PRETTY HARD INTO A PUDDLE.
THAT WAS CLUMSY.
RIKU...
TMP
TMP
OH, I'M FINE. NO BIG DEAL.

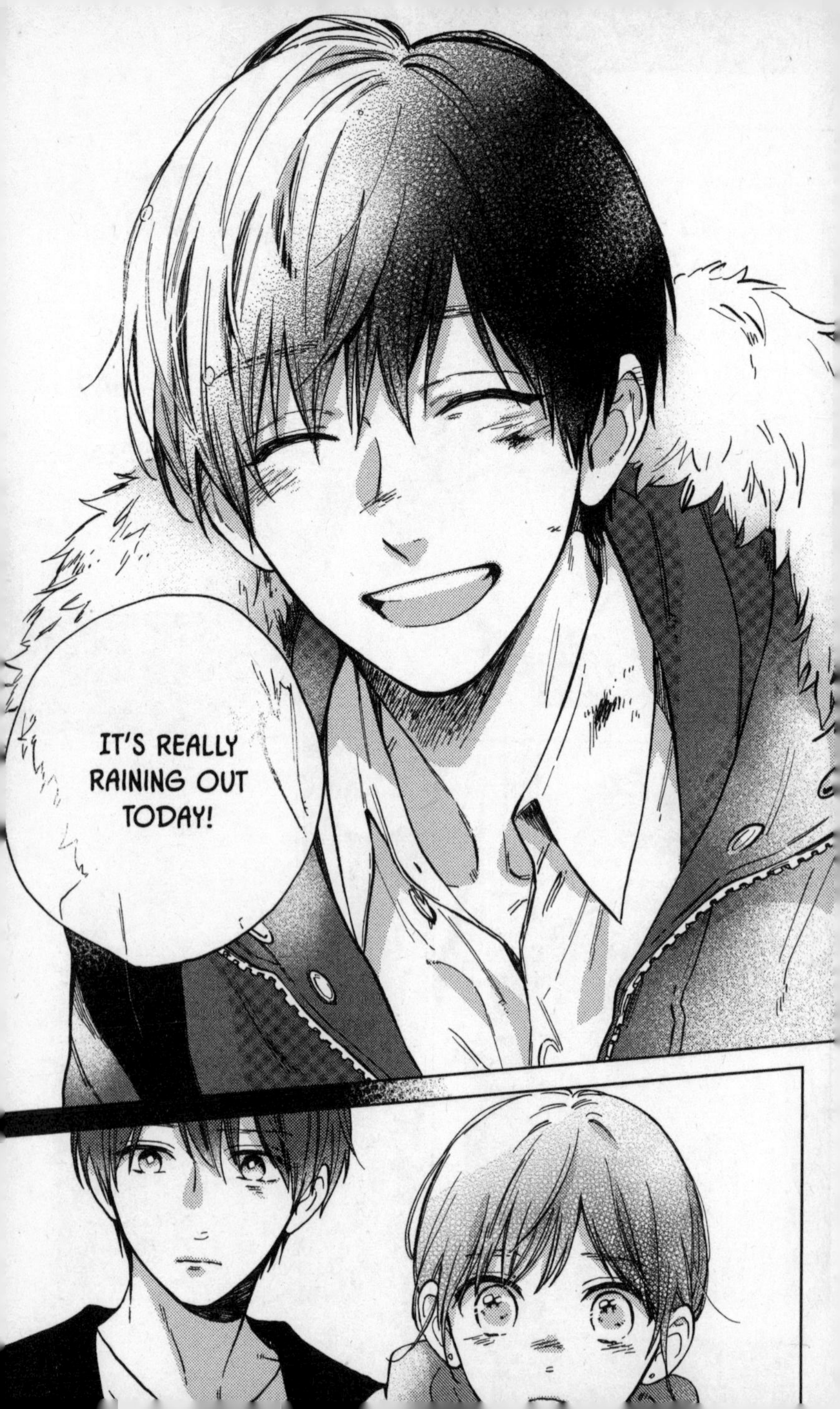
IT'S REALLY RAINING OUT TODAY!

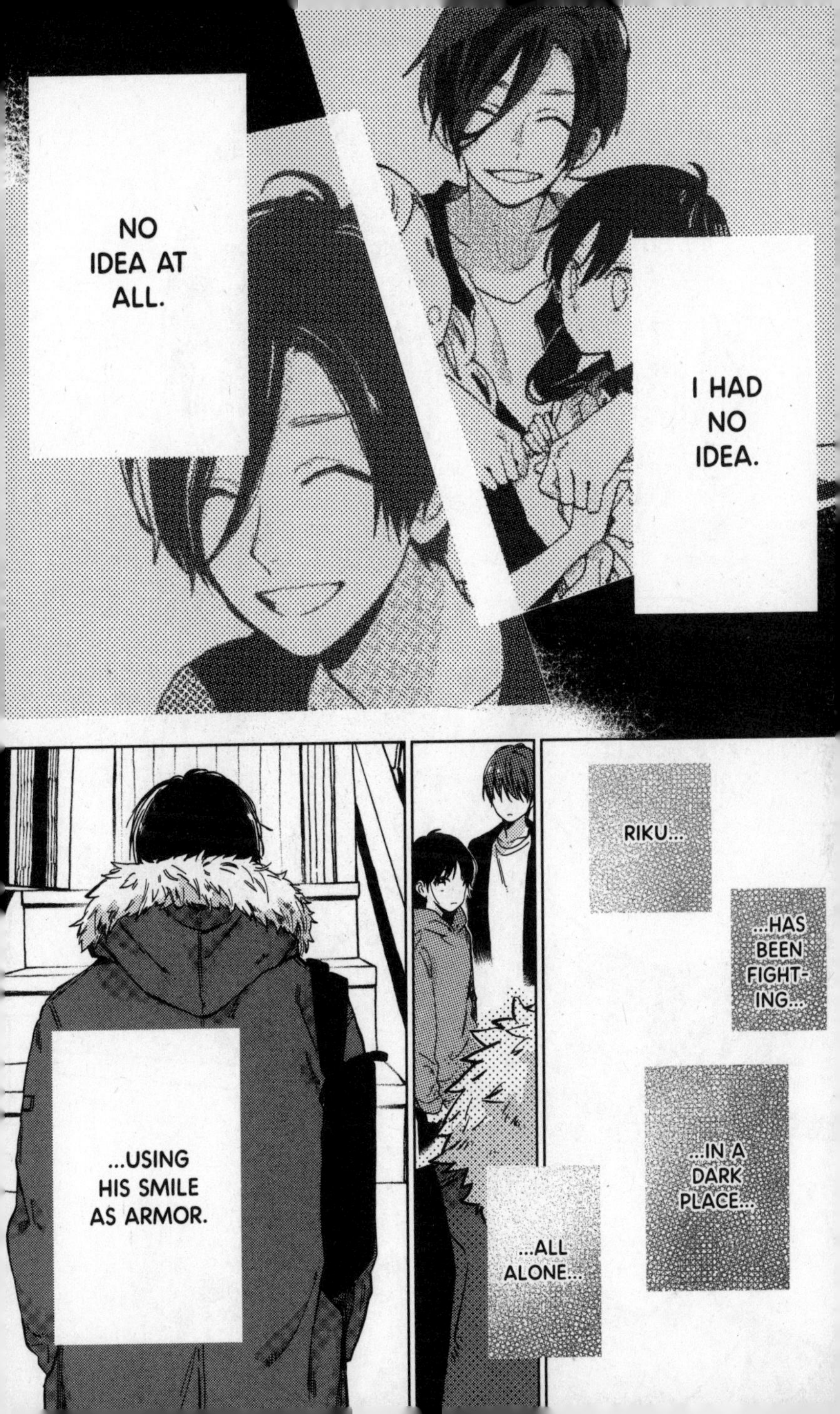
I HAD NO IDEA.
NO IDEA AT ALL.
RIKU...
...HAS BEEN FIGHT-ING...
...IN A DARK PLACE...
...ALL ALONE...
...USING HIS SMILE AS ARMOR.

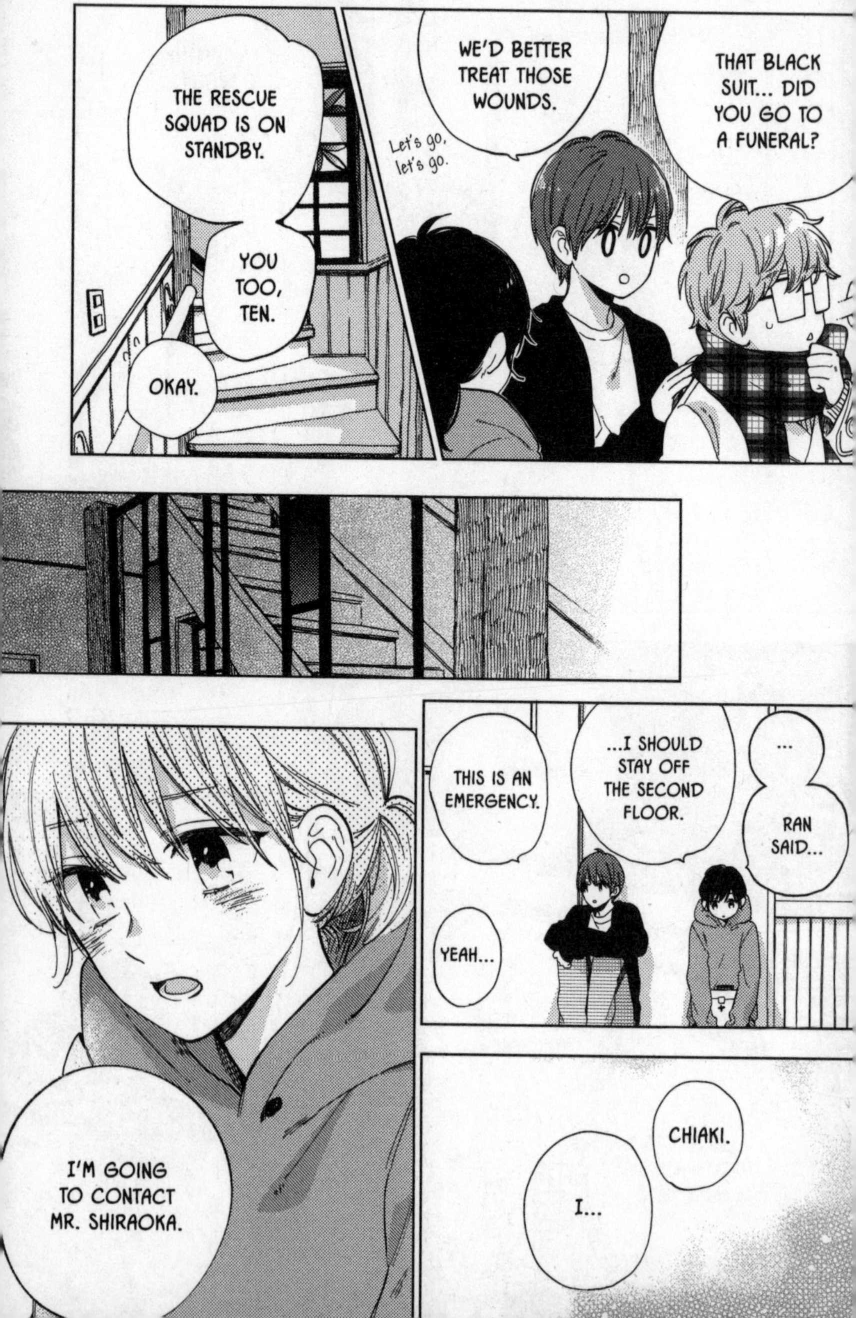
THAT BLACK SUIT... DID YOU GO TO A FUNERAL?
WE'D BETTER TREAT THOSE WOUNDS.
Let's go, let's go.
THE RESCUE SQUAD IS ON STANDBY.
YOU TOO, TEN.
OKAY.
...
RAN SAID...
...I SHOULD STAY OFF THE SECOND FLOOR.
THIS IS AN EMERGENCY.
YEAH...
CHIAKI.
I...
I'M GOING TO CONTACT MR. SHIRAOKA.

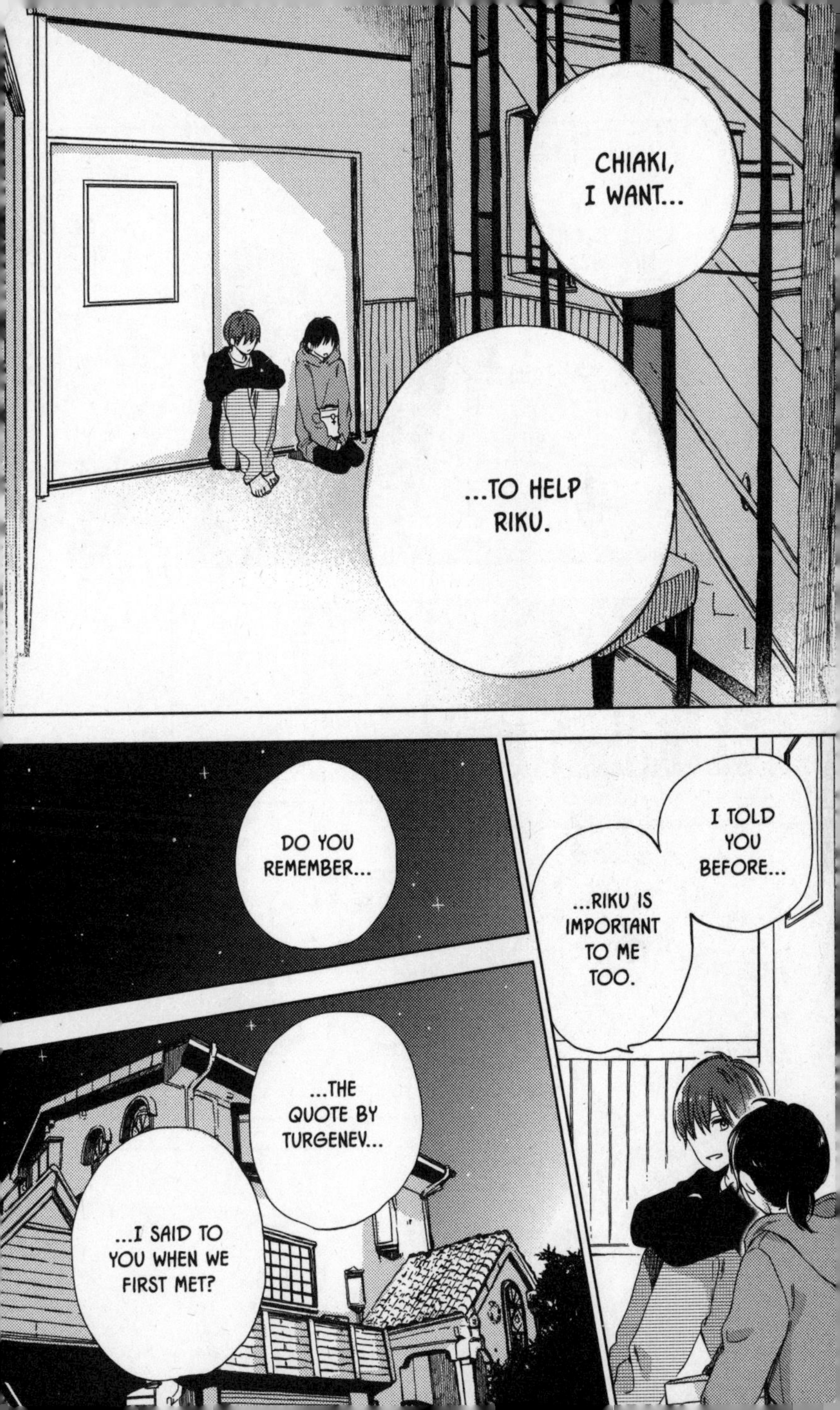
CHIAKI, I WANT...
...TO HELP RIKU.
I TOLD YOU BEFORE...
...RIKU IS IMPORTANT TO ME TOO.
DO YOU REMEMBER...
...THE QUOTE BY TURGENEV...
...I SAID TO YOU WHEN WE FIRST MET?

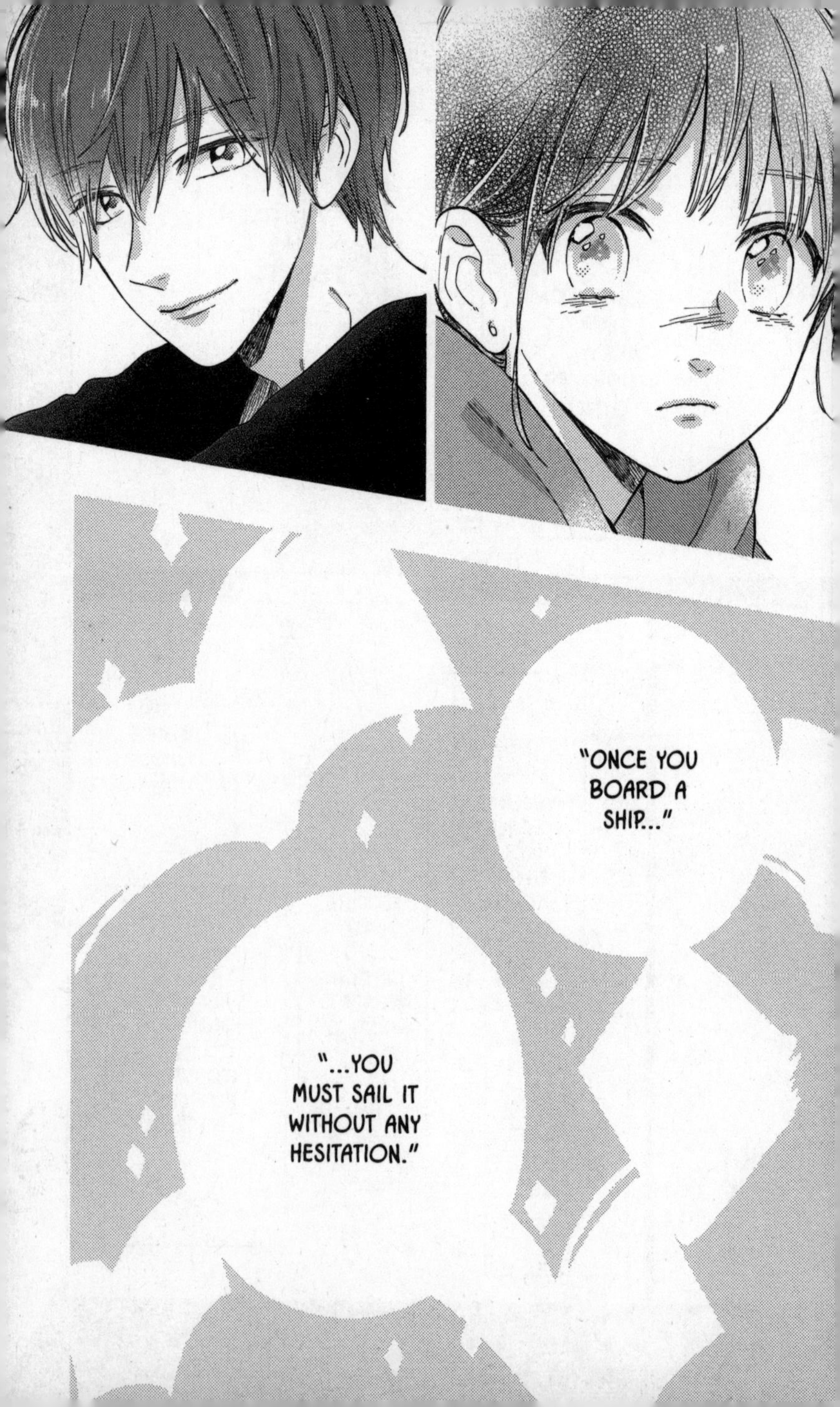
"ONCE YOU BOARD A SHIP..."
"...YOU MUST SAIL IT WITHOUT ANY HESITATION."

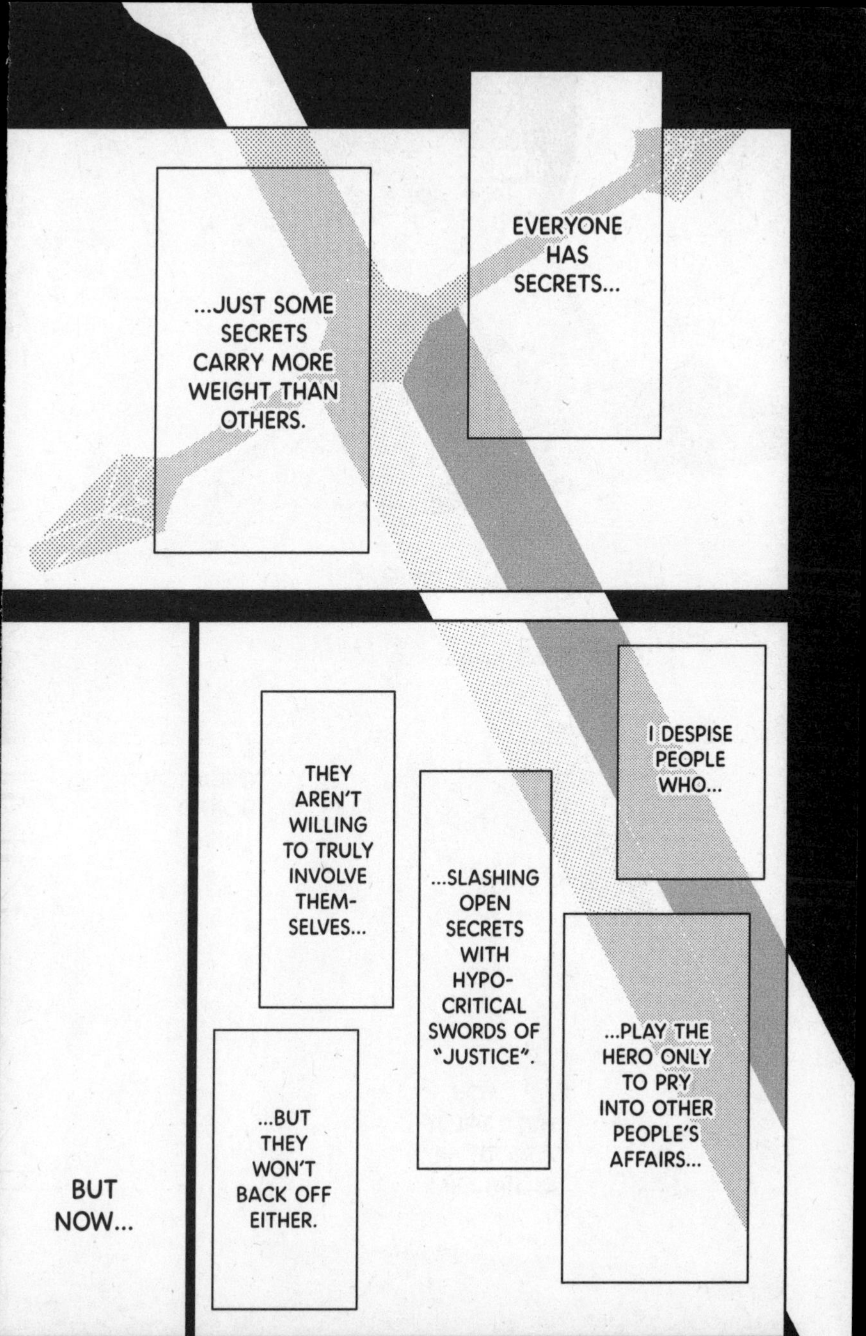

EVERYONE HAS SECRETS...
...JUST SOME SECRETS CARRY MORE WEIGHT THAN OTHERS.
I DESPISE PEOPLE WHO...
...PLAY THE HERO ONLY TO PRY INTO OTHER PEOPLE'S AFFAIRS...
...SLASHING OPEN SECRETS WITH HYPOCRITICAL SWORDS OF "JUSTICE".
THEY AREN'T WILLING TO TRULY INVOLVE THEMSELVES...
...BUT THEY WON'T BACK OFF EITHER.
BUT NOW...

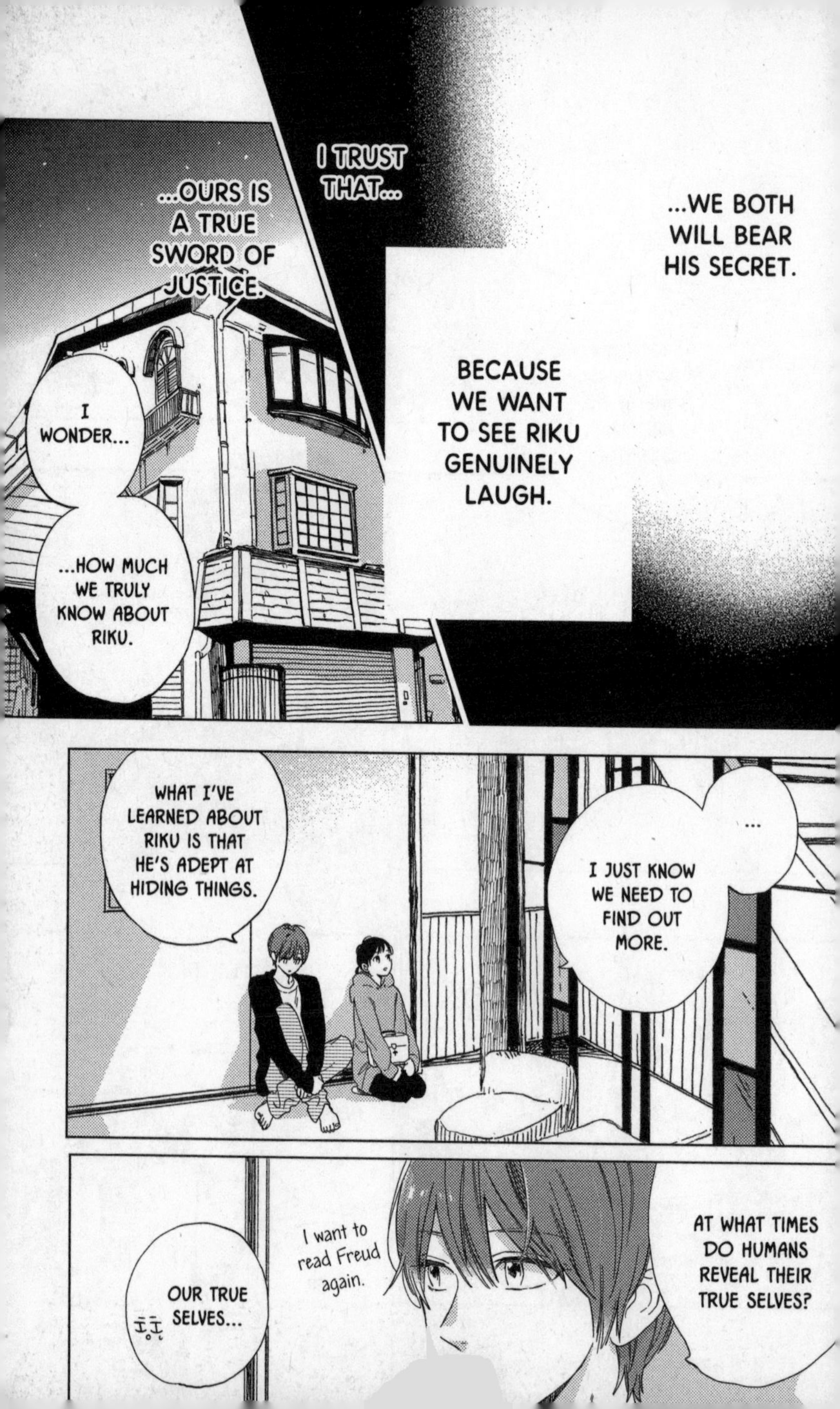
...WE BOTH WILL BEAR HIS SECRET.
BECAUSE WE WANT TO SEE RIKU GENUINELY LAUGH.
I TRUST THAT...
...OURS IS A TRUE SWORD OF JUSTICE.
I WONDER...
...HOW MUCH WE TRULY KNOW ABOUT RIKU.
...
I JUST KNOW WE NEED TO FIND OUT MORE.
WHAT I'VE LEARNED ABOUT RIKU IS THAT HE'S ADEPT AT HIDING THINGS.
AT WHAT TIMES DO HUMANS REVEAL THEIR TRUE SELVES?
I want to read Freud again.
OUR TRUE SELVES...

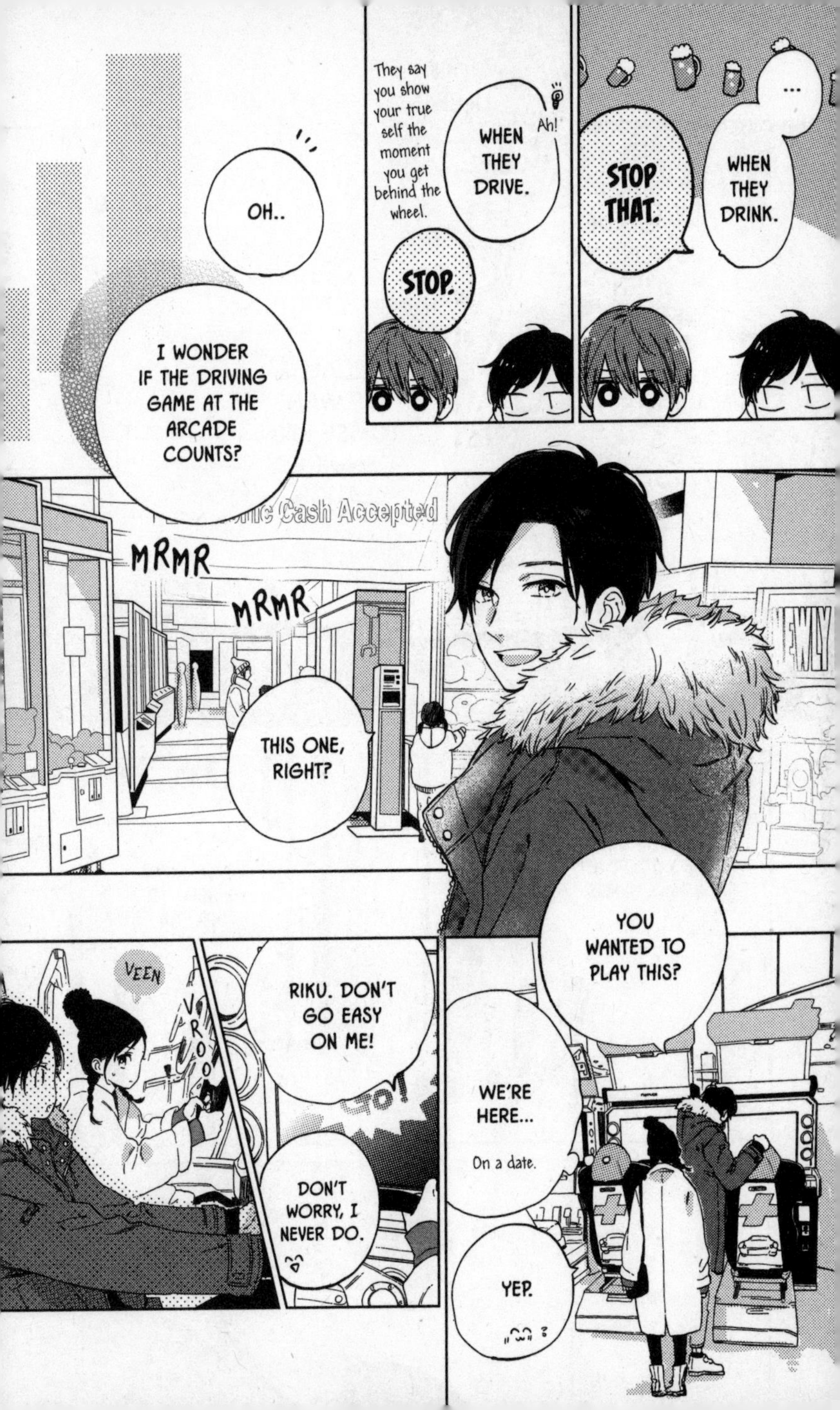
WHEN THEY DRINK.
...
STOP THAT.
WHEN THEY DRIVE.
Ah!
They say you show your true self the moment you get behind the wheel.
STOP.
OH..
I WONDER IF THE DRIVING GAME AT THE ARCADE COUNTS?
Cash Accepted
MRMR
MRMR
THIS ONE, RIGHT?
YOU WANTED TO PLAY THIS?
WE'RE HERE...
On a date.
YEP.
RIKU. DON'T GO EASY ON ME!
GO!
DON'T WORRY, I NEVER DO.
VEEN
VROOO

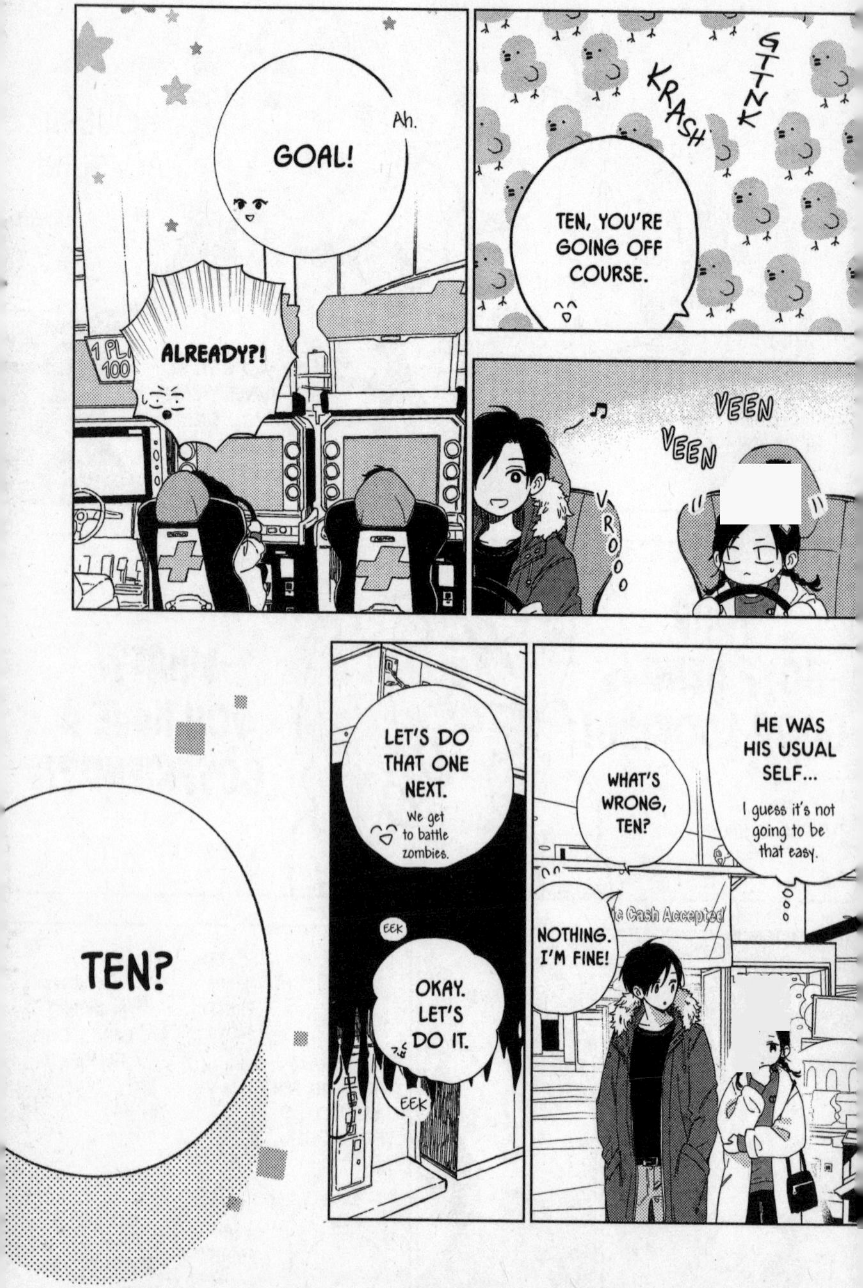
GTTNK
KRASH
TEN, YOU'RE GOING OFF COURSE.
VEEN
VEEN
VROOO
Ah.
GOAL!
ALREADY?!
HE WAS HIS USUAL SELF...
I guess it's not going to be that easy.
WHAT'S WRONG, TEN?
NOTHING. I'M FINE!
LET'S DO THAT ONE NEXT.
We get to battle zombies.
EEK
OKAY. LET'S DO IT.
EEK
TEN?

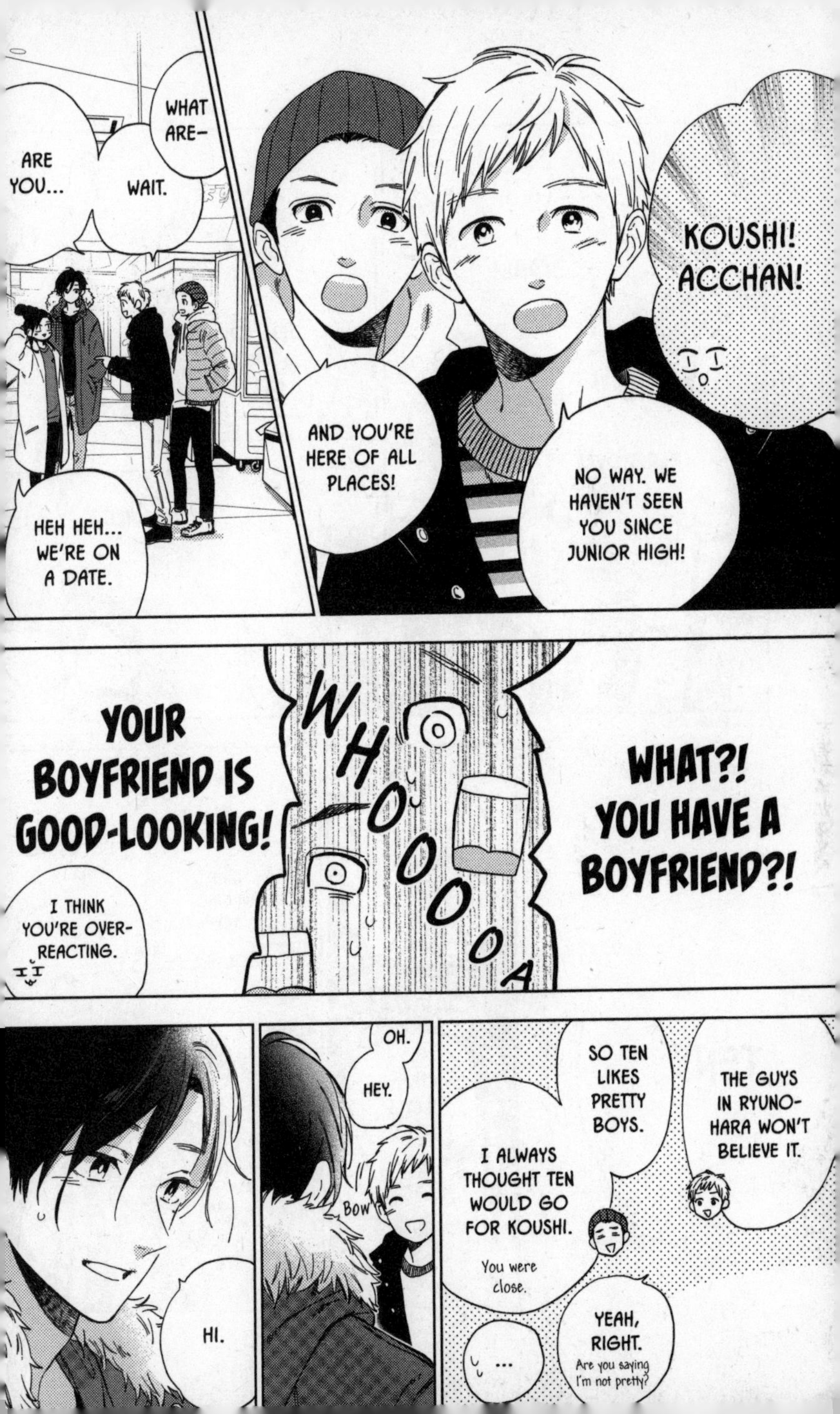
KOUSHI! ACCHAN!
NO WAY. WE HAVEN'T SEEN YOU SINCE JUNIOR HIGH!
AND YOU'RE HERE OF ALL PLACES!
WHAT ARE—
WAIT.
ARE YOU...
HEH HEH... WE'RE ON A DATE.
WHAT?! YOU HAVE A BOYFRIEND?!
WHOOOOOA
YOUR BOYFRIEND IS GOOD-LOOKING!
I THINK YOU'RE OVER-REACTING.
THE GUYS IN RYUNO-HARA WON'T BELIEVE IT.
SO TEN LIKES PRETTY BOYS.
I ALWAYS THOUGHT TEN WOULD GO FOR KOUSHI.
You were close.
YEAH, RIGHT.
Are you saying I'm not pretty?
...
OH.
HEY.
BOW
HI.

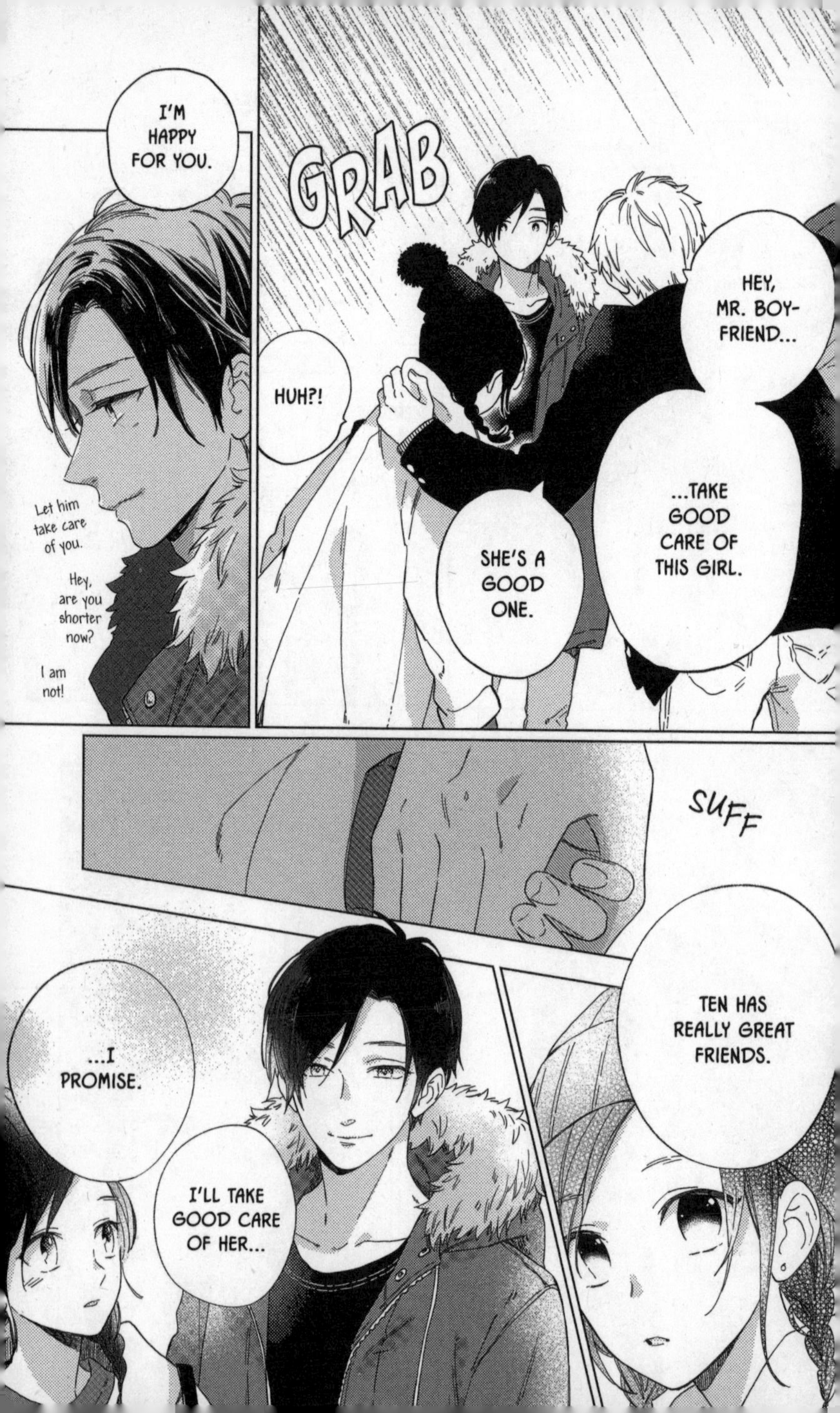
GRAB
HUH?!
HEY, MR. BOY-FRIEND...
...TAKE GOOD CARE OF THIS GIRL.
SHE'S A GOOD ONE.
I'M HAPPY FOR YOU.
Let him take care of you.
Hey, are you shorter now?
I am not!
SUFF
TEN HAS REALLY GREAT FRIENDS.
I'LL TAKE GOOD CARE OF HER...
...I PROMISE.

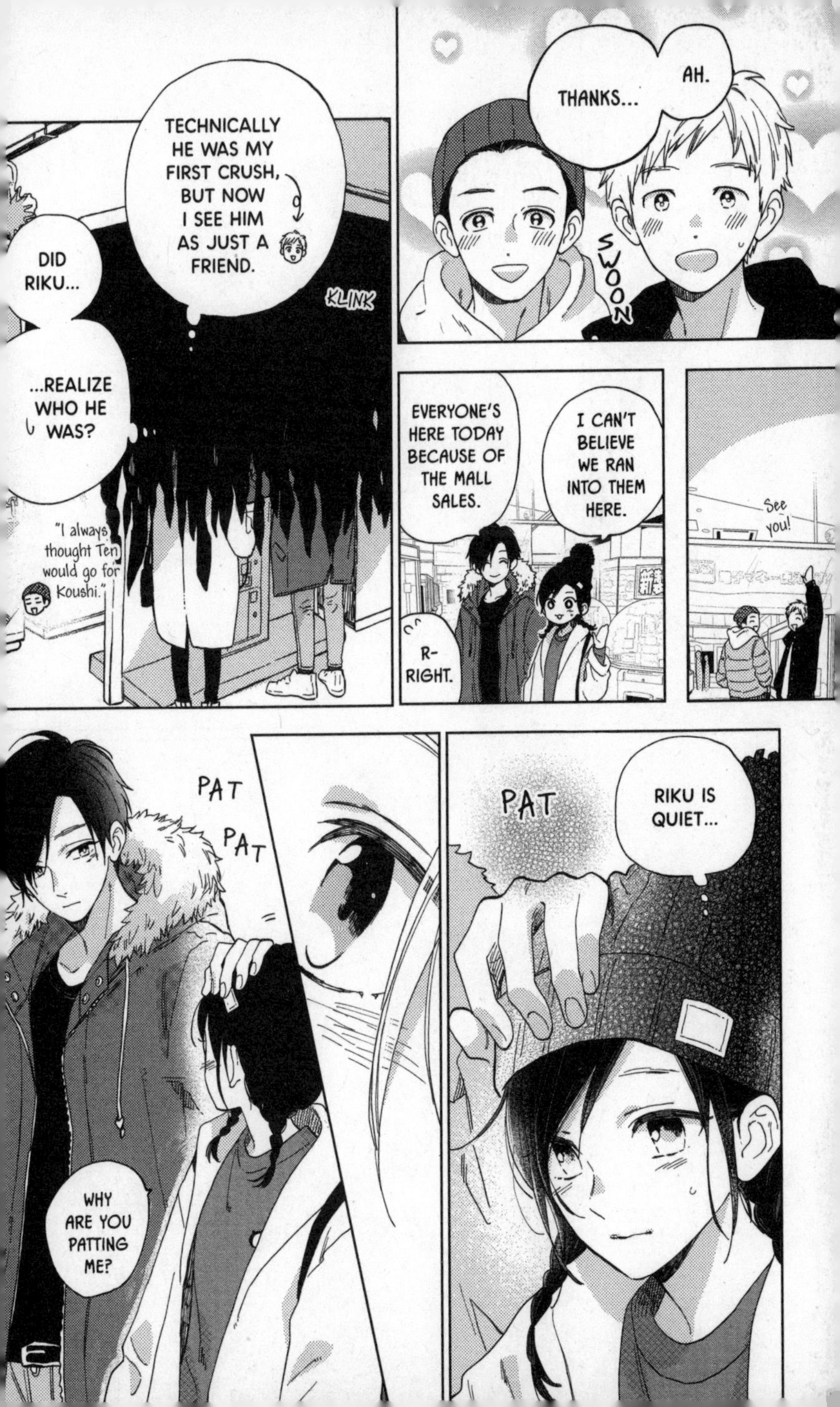
AH.
THANKS...
SWOON
See you!
I CAN'T BELIEVE WE RAN INTO THEM HERE.
EVERYONE'S HERE TODAY BECAUSE OF THE MALL SALES.
R-RIGHT.
TECHNICALLY HE WAS MY FIRST CRUSH, BUT NOW I SEE HIM AS JUST A FRIEND.
KLINK
DID RIKU...
...REALIZE WHO HE WAS?
"I always thought Ten would go for Koushi."
RIKU IS QUIET...
PAT
PAT
PAT
WHY ARE YOU PATTING ME?

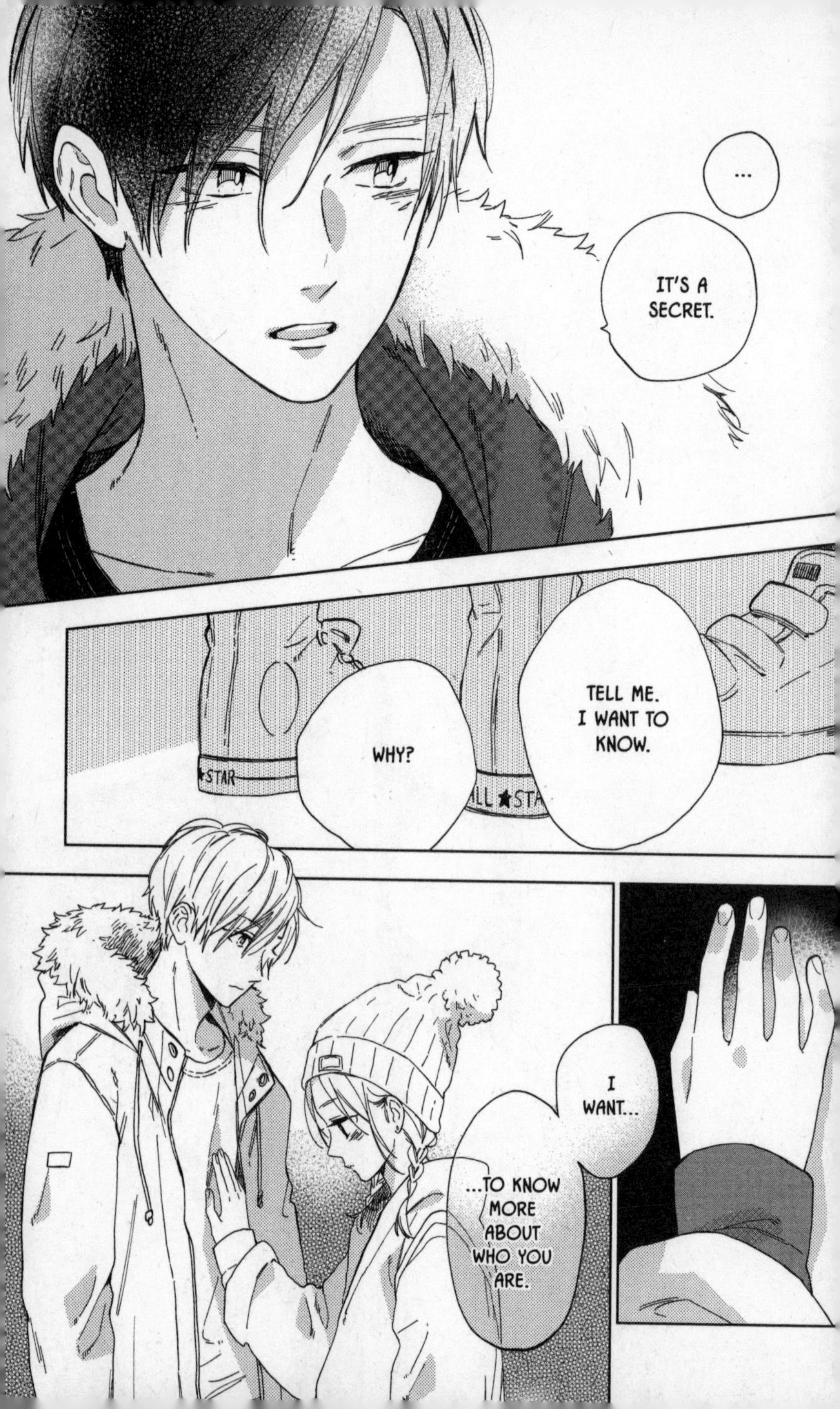
...
IT'S A SECRET.
TELL ME. I WANT TO KNOW.
WHY?
I WANT...
...TO KNOW MORE ABOUT WHO YOU ARE.

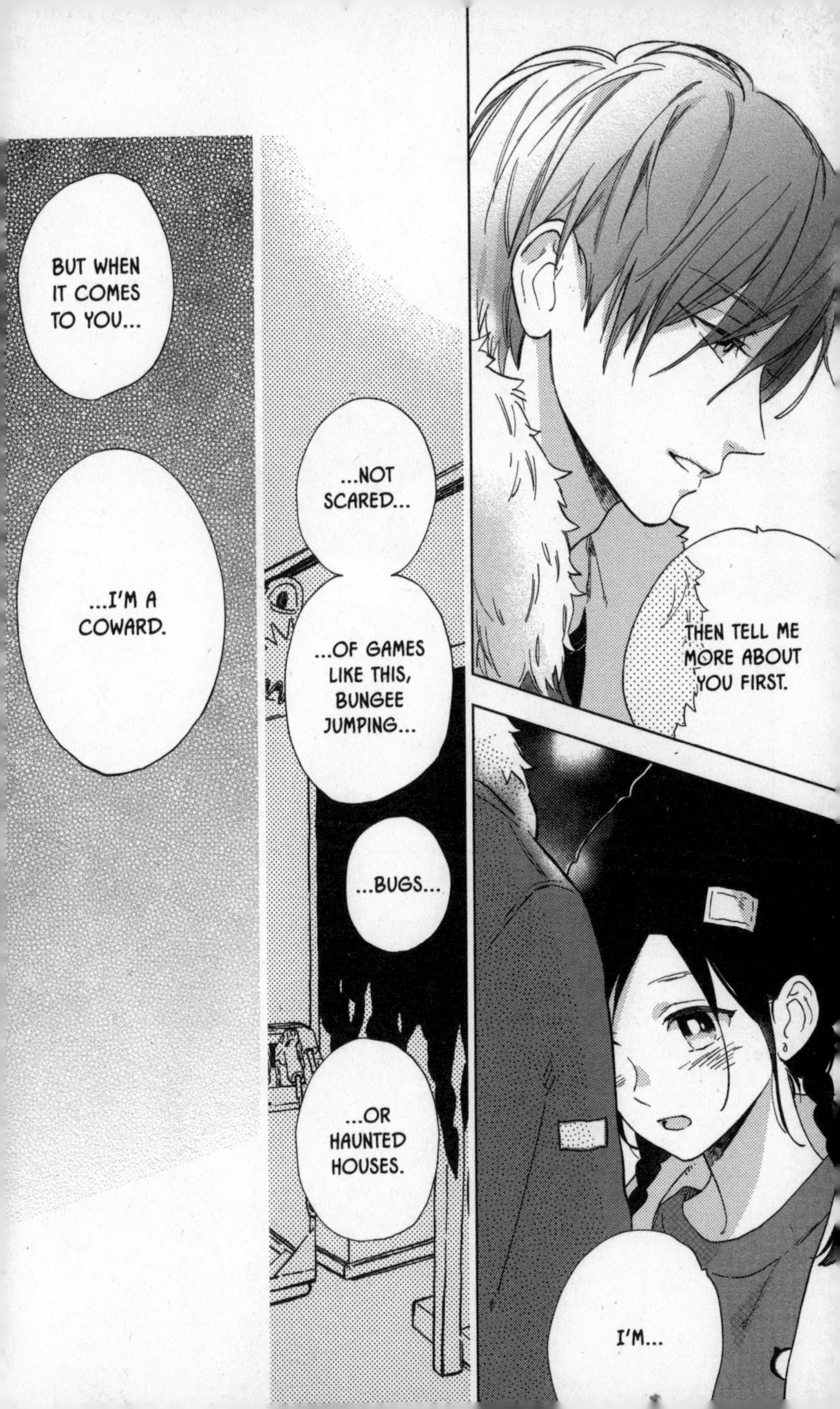
THEN TELL ME MORE ABOUT YOU FIRST.
I'M...
...NOT SCARED...
...OF GAMES LIKE THIS, BUNGEE JUMPING...
...BUGS...
...OR HAUNTED HOUSES.
BUT WHEN IT COMES TO YOU...
...I'M A COWARD.

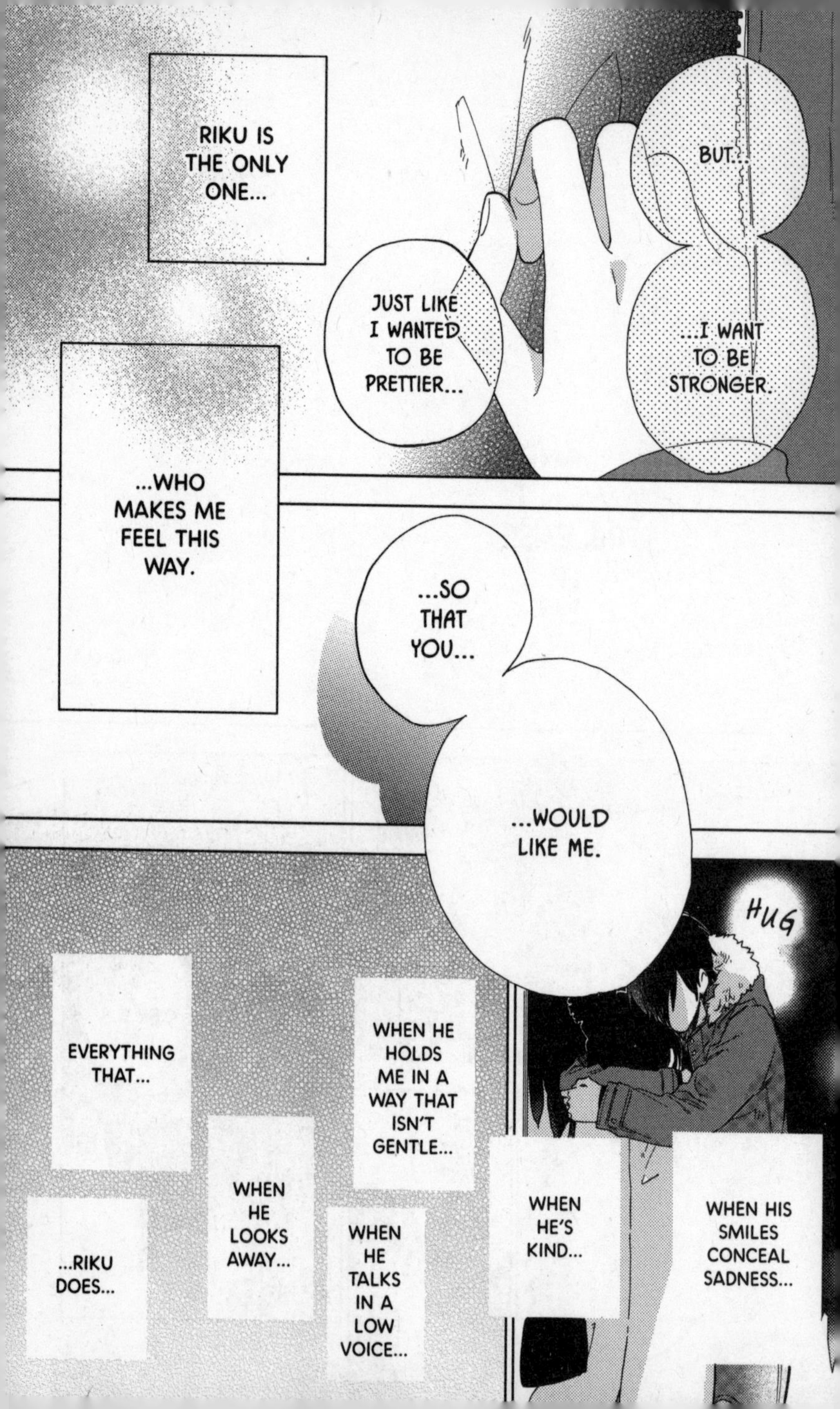
BUT...
...I WANT TO BE STRONGER.
JUST LIKE I WANTED TO BE PRETTIER...
...SO THAT YOU...
...WOULD LIKE ME.
RIKU IS THE ONLY ONE...
...WHO MAKES ME FEEL THIS WAY.
HUG
WHEN HIS SMILES CONCEAL SADNESS...
WHEN HE'S KIND...
WHEN HE HOLDS ME IN A WAY THAT ISN'T GENTLE...
WHEN HE TALKS IN A LOW VOICE...
WHEN HE LOOKS AWAY...
EVERYTHING THAT...
...RIKU DOES...

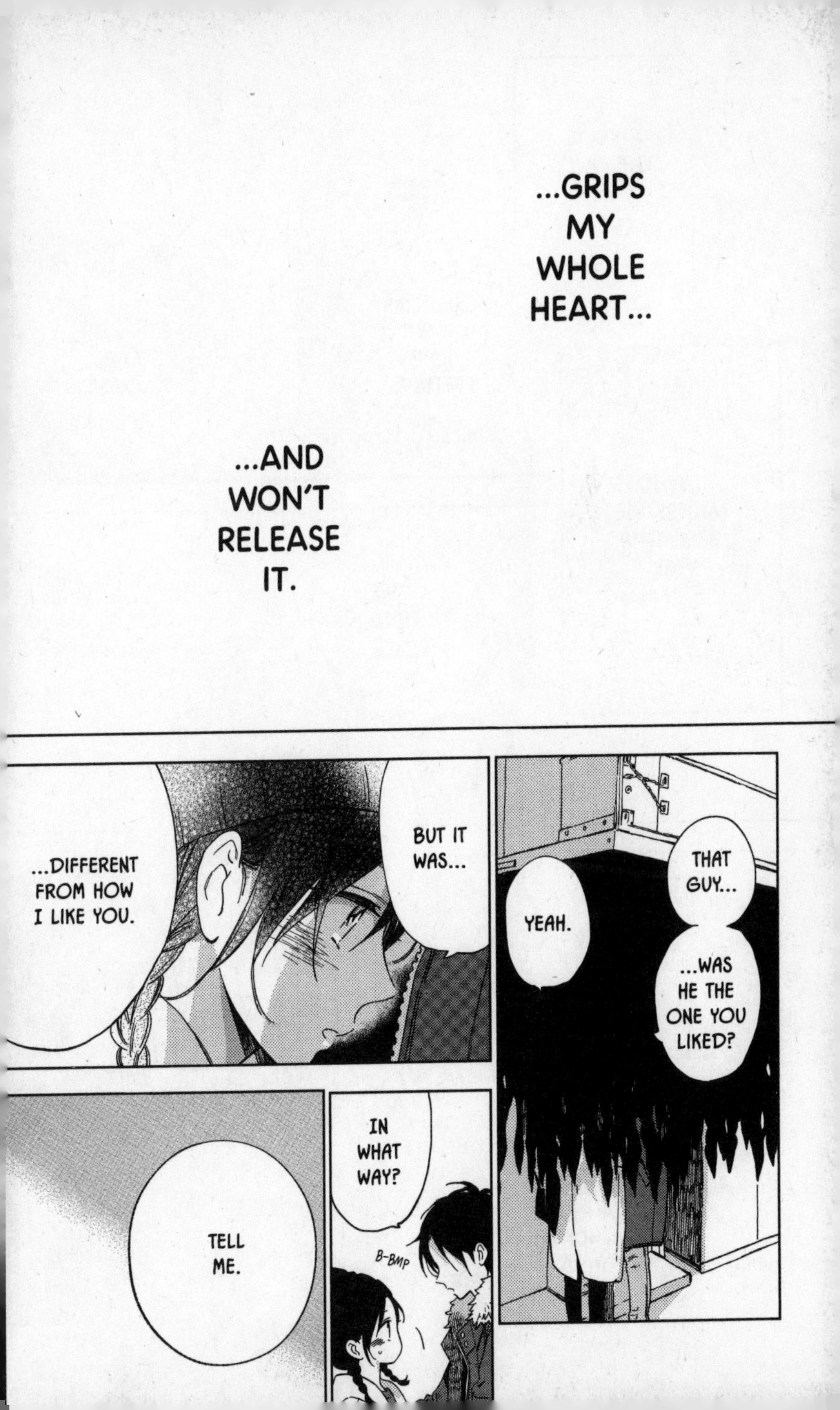
...GRIPS MY WHOLE HEART...
...AND WON'T RELEASE IT.
THAT GUY...
...WAS HE THE ONE YOU LIKED?
YEAH.
BUT IT WAS...
...DIFFERENT FROM HOW I LIKE YOU.
IN WHAT WAY?
B-BMP
TELL ME.

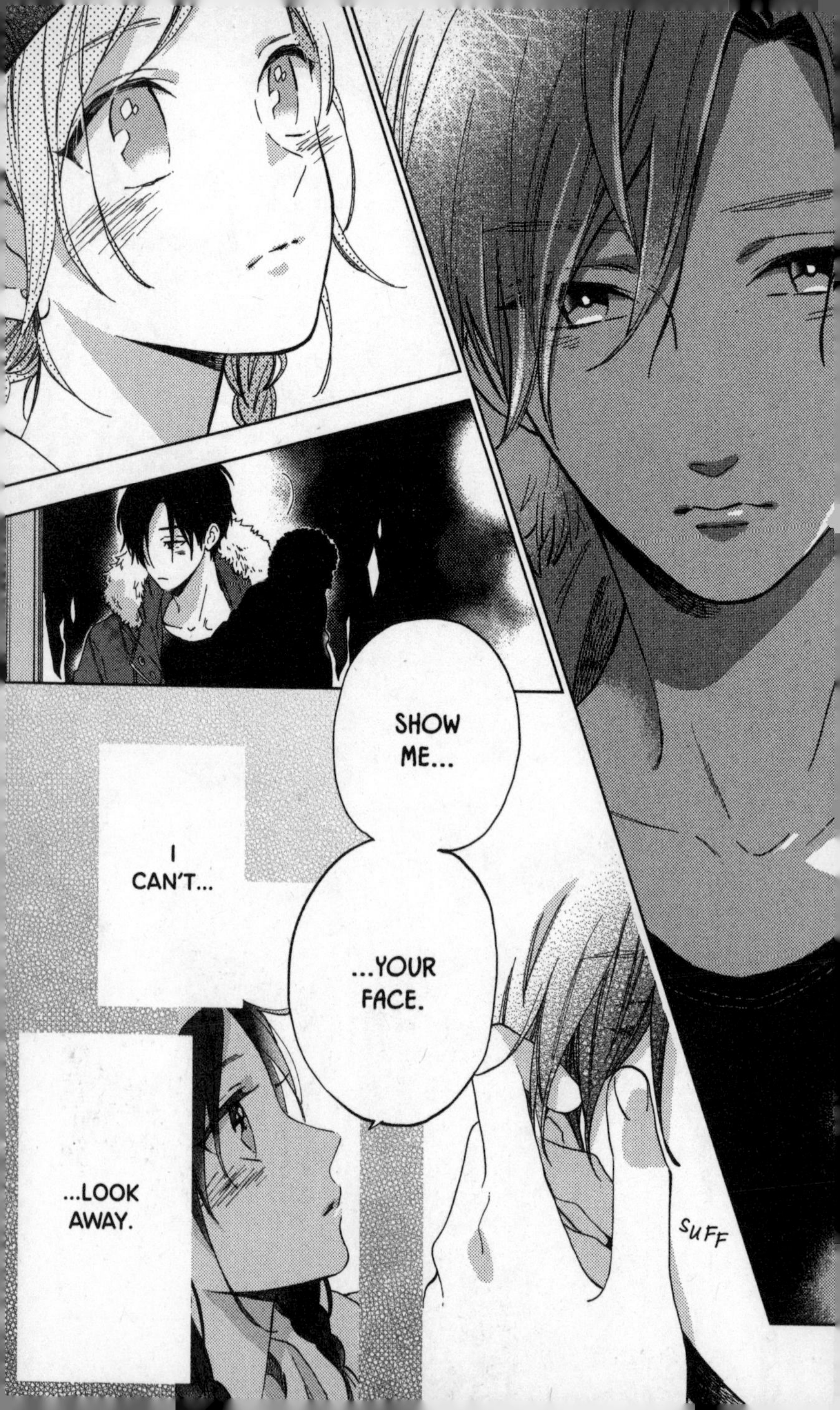
SHOW ME...
...YOUR FACE.
I CAN'T...
...LOOK AWAY.
SUFF

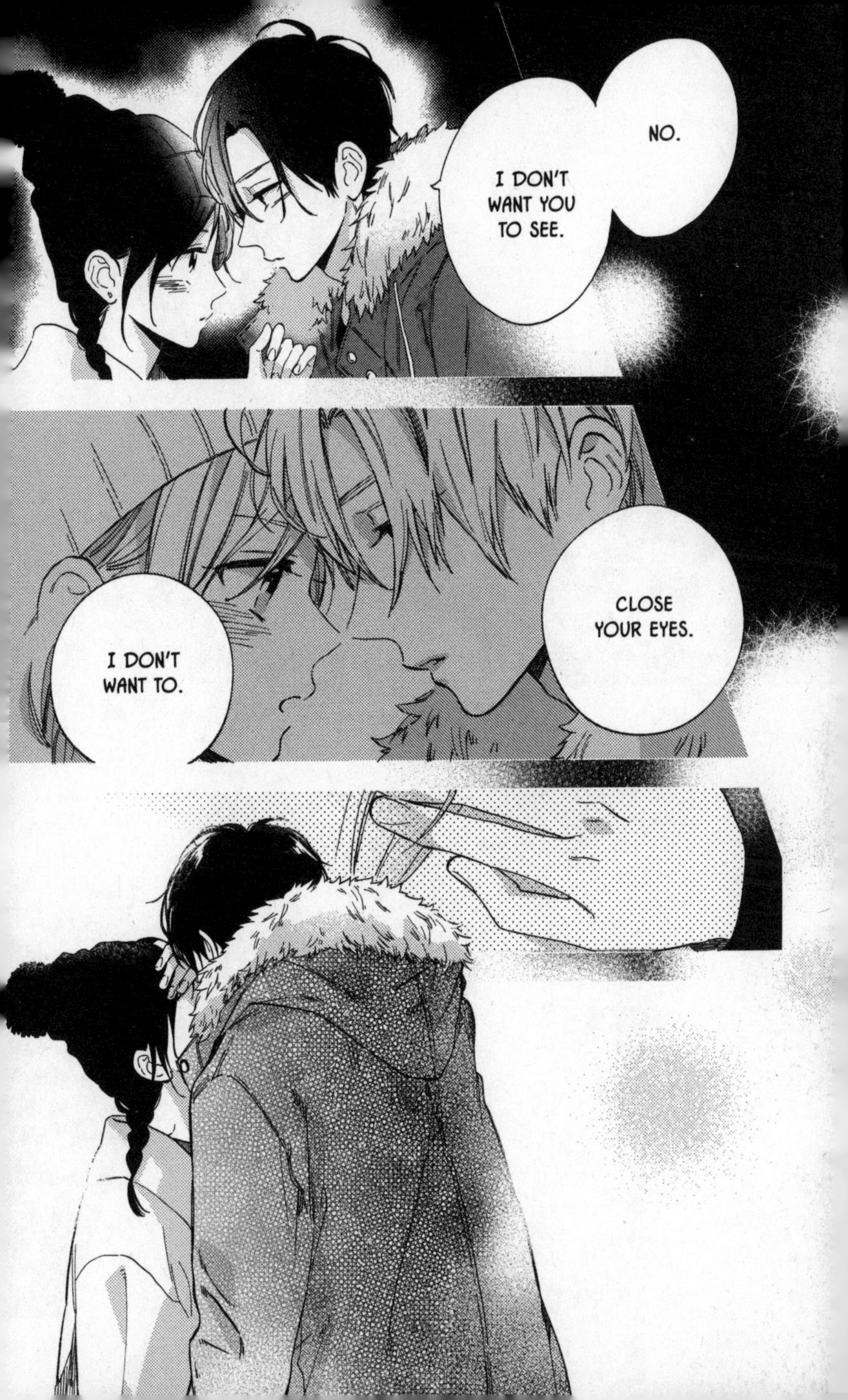
NO.
I DON'T WANT YOU TO SEE.
CLOSE YOUR EYES.
I DON'T WANT TO.

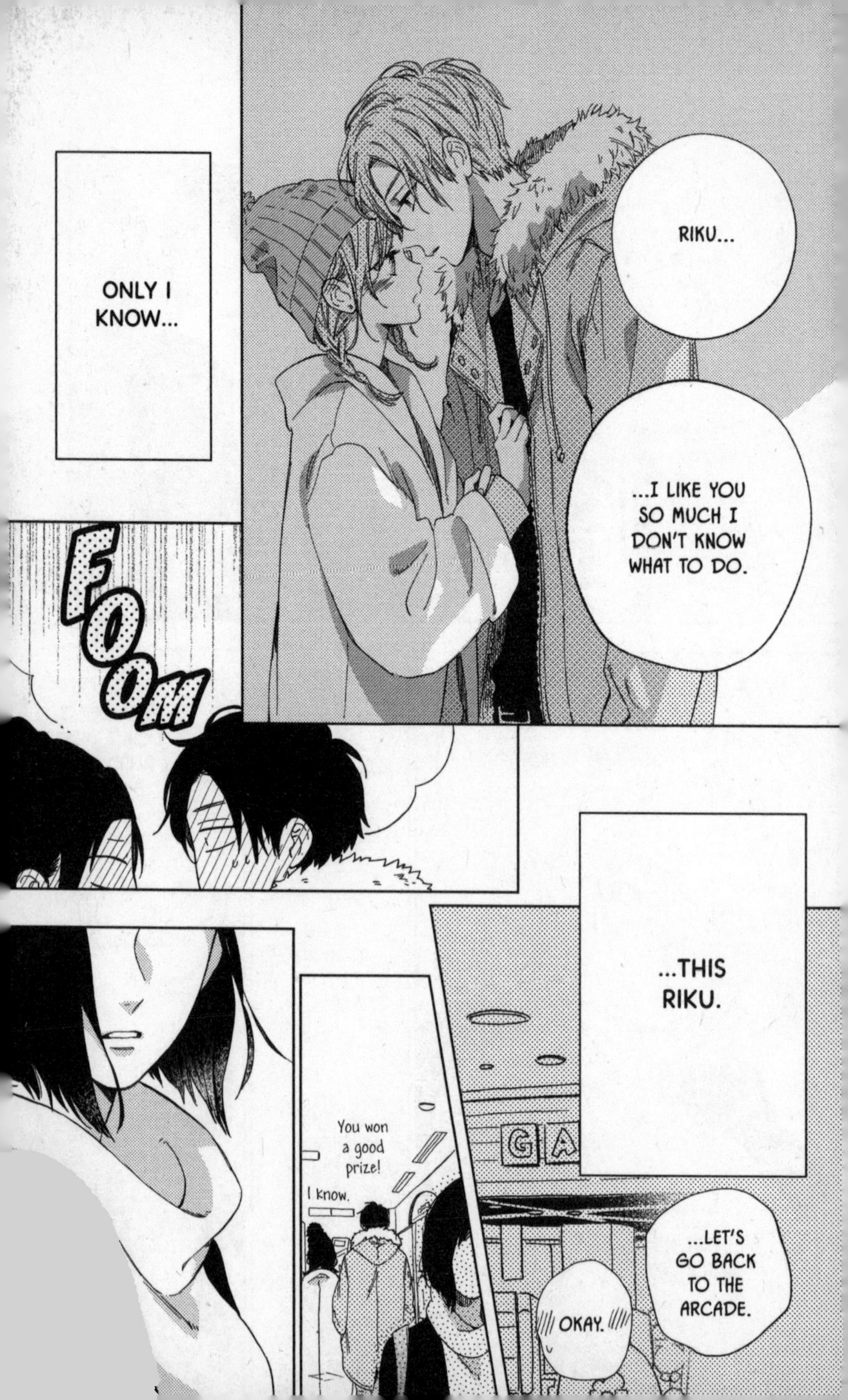
RIKU...
...I LIKE YOU SO MUCH I DON'T KNOW WHAT TO DO.
ONLY I KNOW...
...THIS RIKU.
FOOM
...LET'S GO BACK TO THE ARCADE.
OKAY.
You won a good prize!
I know.

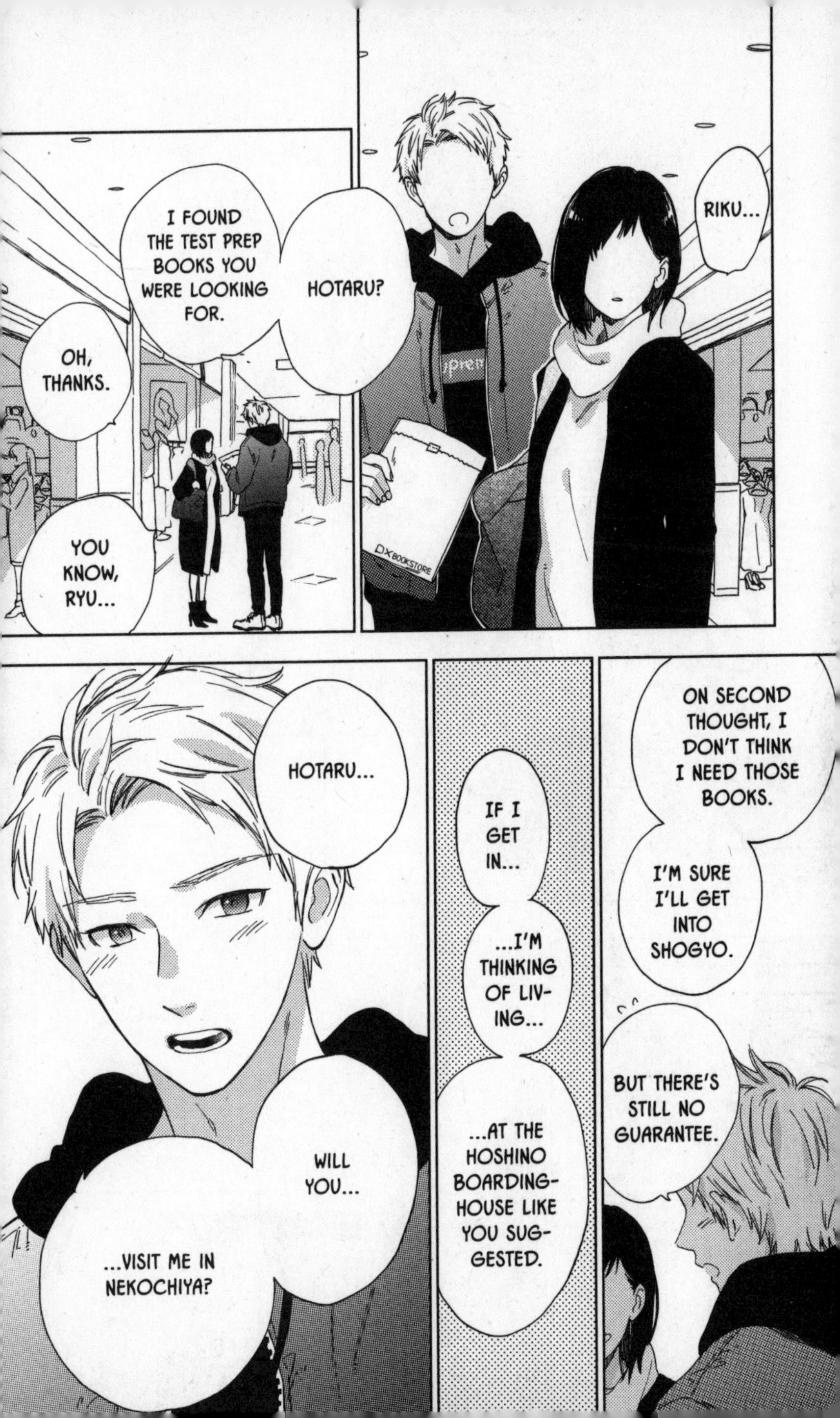
RIKU...
HOTARU?
I FOUND THE TEST PREP BOOKS YOU WERE LOOKING FOR.
OH, THANKS.
YOU KNOW, RYU...
DX BOOKSTORE
ON SECOND THOUGHT, I DON'T THINK I NEED THOSE BOOKS.
I'M SURE I'LL GET INTO SHOGYO.
BUT THERE'S STILL NO GUARANTEE.
IF I GET IN...
...I'M THINKING OF LIV-ING...
...AT THE HOSHINO BOARDING-HOUSE LIKE YOU SUG-GESTED.
HOTARU...
WILL YOU...
...VISIT ME IN NEKOCHIYA?

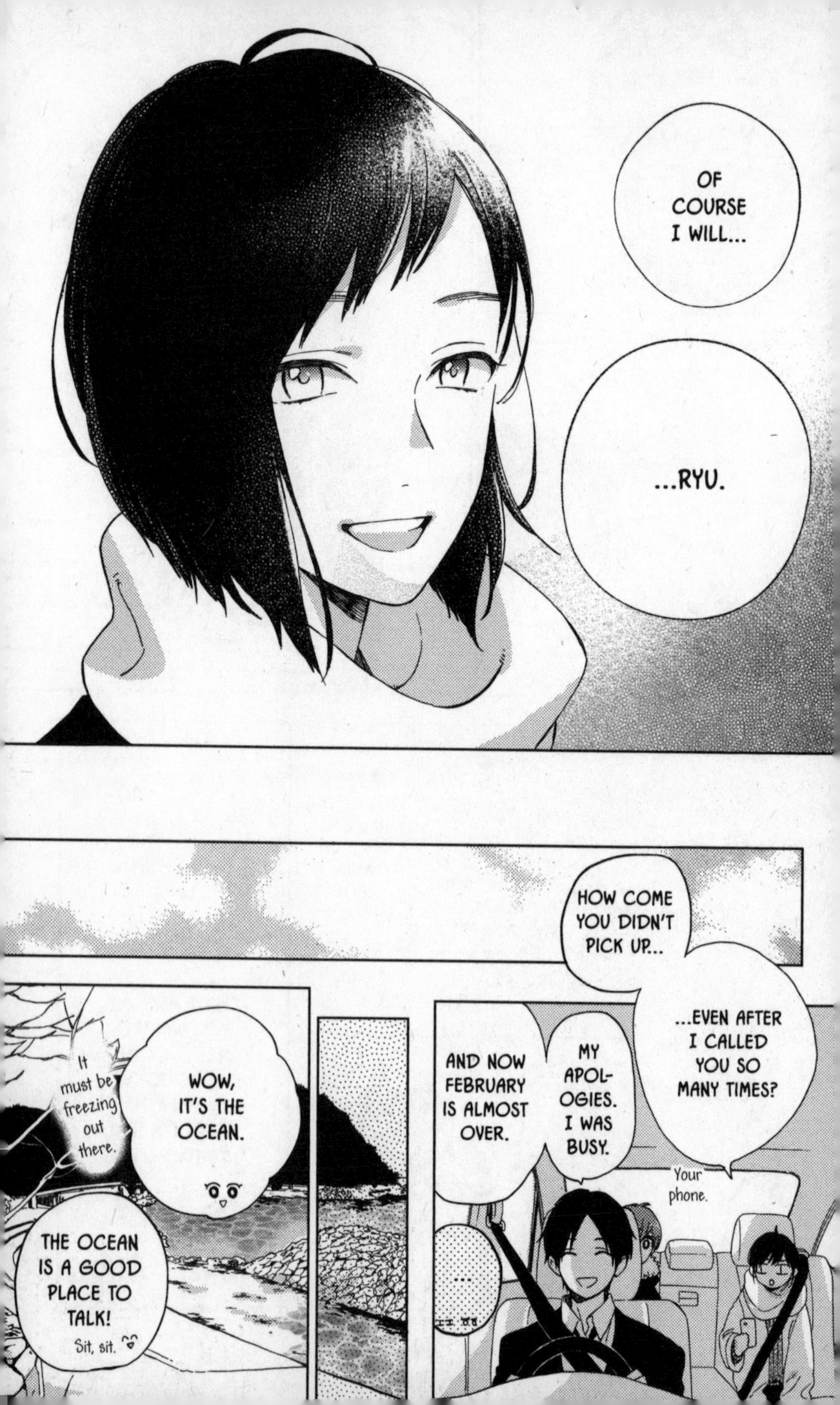

OF COURSE I WILL...
...RYU.
HOW COME YOU DIDN'T PICK UP...
...EVEN AFTER I CALLED YOU SO MANY TIMES?
Your phone.
MY APOLOGIES. I WAS BUSY.
AND NOW FEBRUARY IS ALMOST OVER.
...
WOW, IT'S THE OCEAN.
It must be freezing out there.
THE OCEAN IS A GOOD PLACE TO TALK!
Sit, sit.

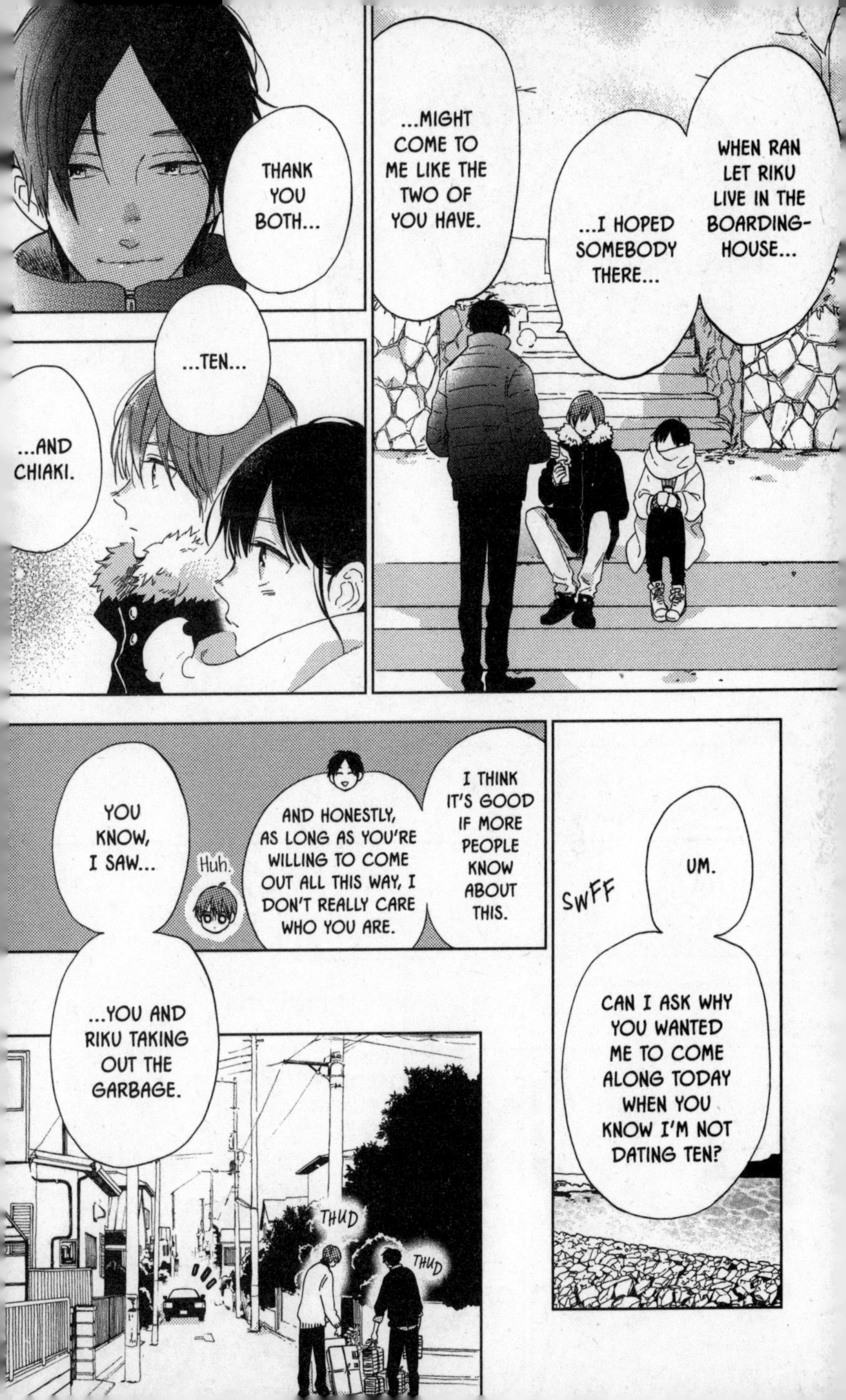
WHEN RAN LET RIKU LIVE IN THE BOARDING-HOUSE...
...I HOPED SOMEBODY THERE...
...MIGHT COME TO ME LIKE THE TWO OF YOU HAVE.
THANK YOU BOTH...
...TEN...
...AND CHIAKI.
UM.
SWFF
CAN I ASK WHY YOU WANTED ME TO COME ALONG TODAY WHEN YOU KNOW I'M NOT DATING TEN?
I THINK IT'S GOOD IF MORE PEOPLE KNOW ABOUT THIS.
AND HONESTLY, AS LONG AS YOU'RE WILLING TO COME OUT ALL THIS WAY, I DON'T REALLY CARE WHO YOU ARE.
Huh.
YOU KNOW, I SAW...
...YOU AND RIKU TAKING OUT THE GARBAGE.
THUD
THUD

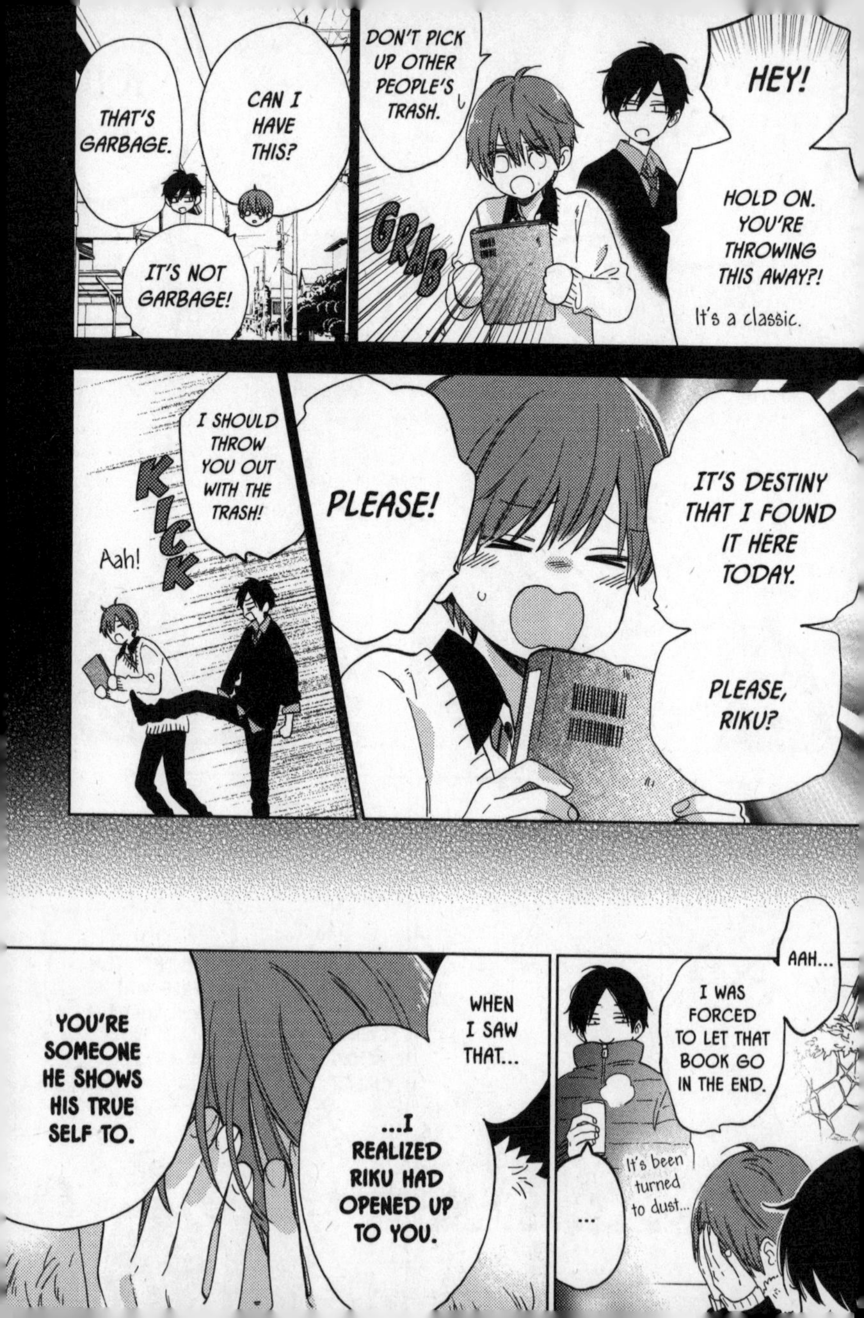
HEY!
HOLD ON. YOU'RE THROWING THIS AWAY?!
It's a classic.
DON'T PICK UP OTHER PEOPLE'S TRASH.
GRAB
CAN I HAVE THIS?
THAT'S GARBAGE.
IT'S NOT GARBAGE!
IT'S DESTINY THAT I FOUND IT HERE TODAY.
PLEASE, RIKU?
PLEASE!
I SHOULD THROW YOU OUT WITH THE TRASH!
KICK
Aah!
AAH...
I WAS FORCED TO LET THAT BOOK GO IN THE END.
It's been turned to dust...
...
WHEN I SAW THAT...
...I REALIZED RIKU HAD OPENED UP TO YOU.
YOU'RE SOMEONE HE SHOWS HIS TRUE SELF TO.

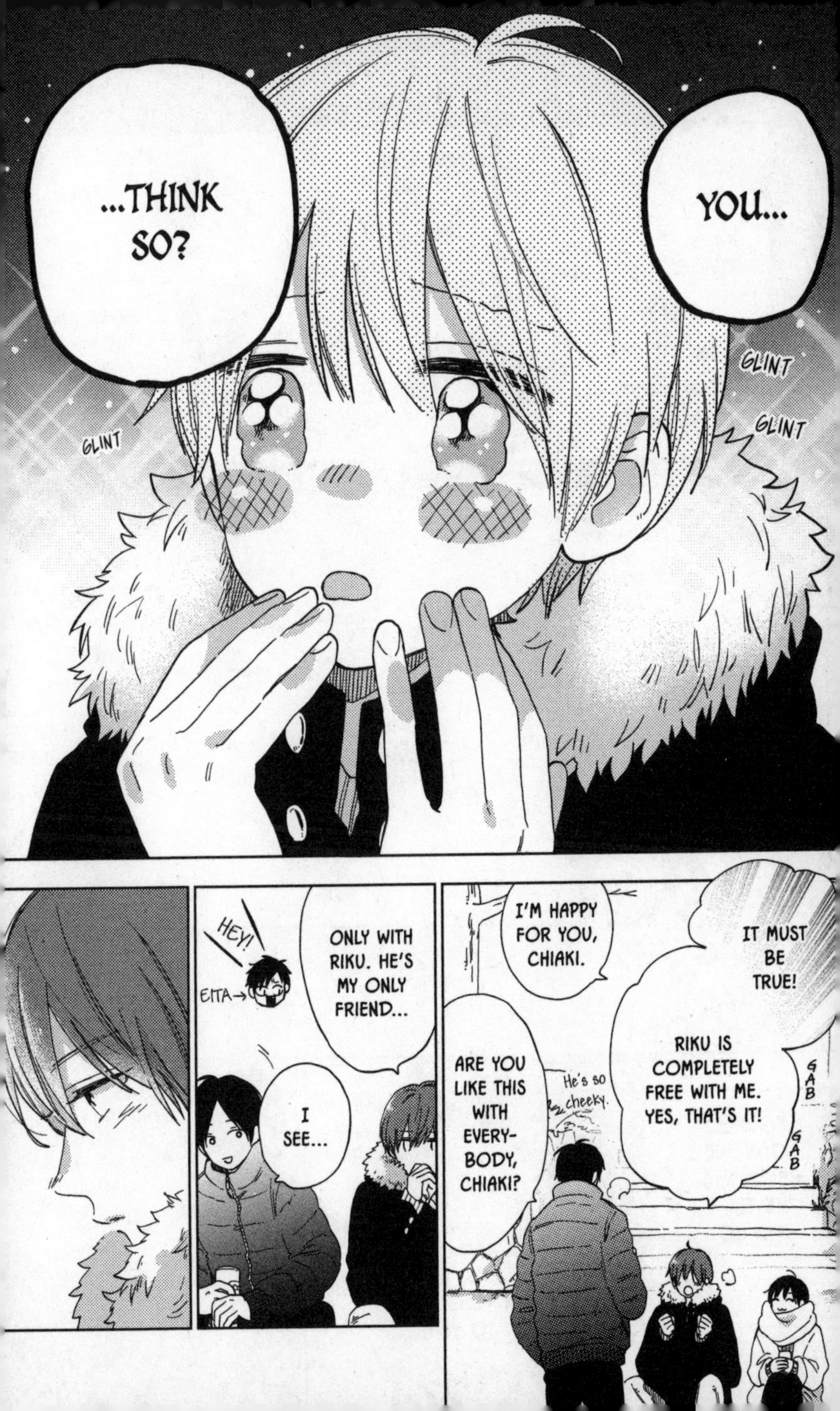
YOU...
...THINK SO?
GLINT
GLINT
GLINT
IT MUST BE TRUE!
I'M HAPPY FOR YOU, CHIAKI.
RIKU IS COMPLETELY FREE WITH ME. YES, THAT'S IT!
GAB
GAB
ARE YOU LIKE THIS WITH EVERY-BODY, CHIAKI?
He's so cheeky.
ONLY WITH RIKU. HE'S MY ONLY FRIEND...
HEY!
EITA→
I SEE...

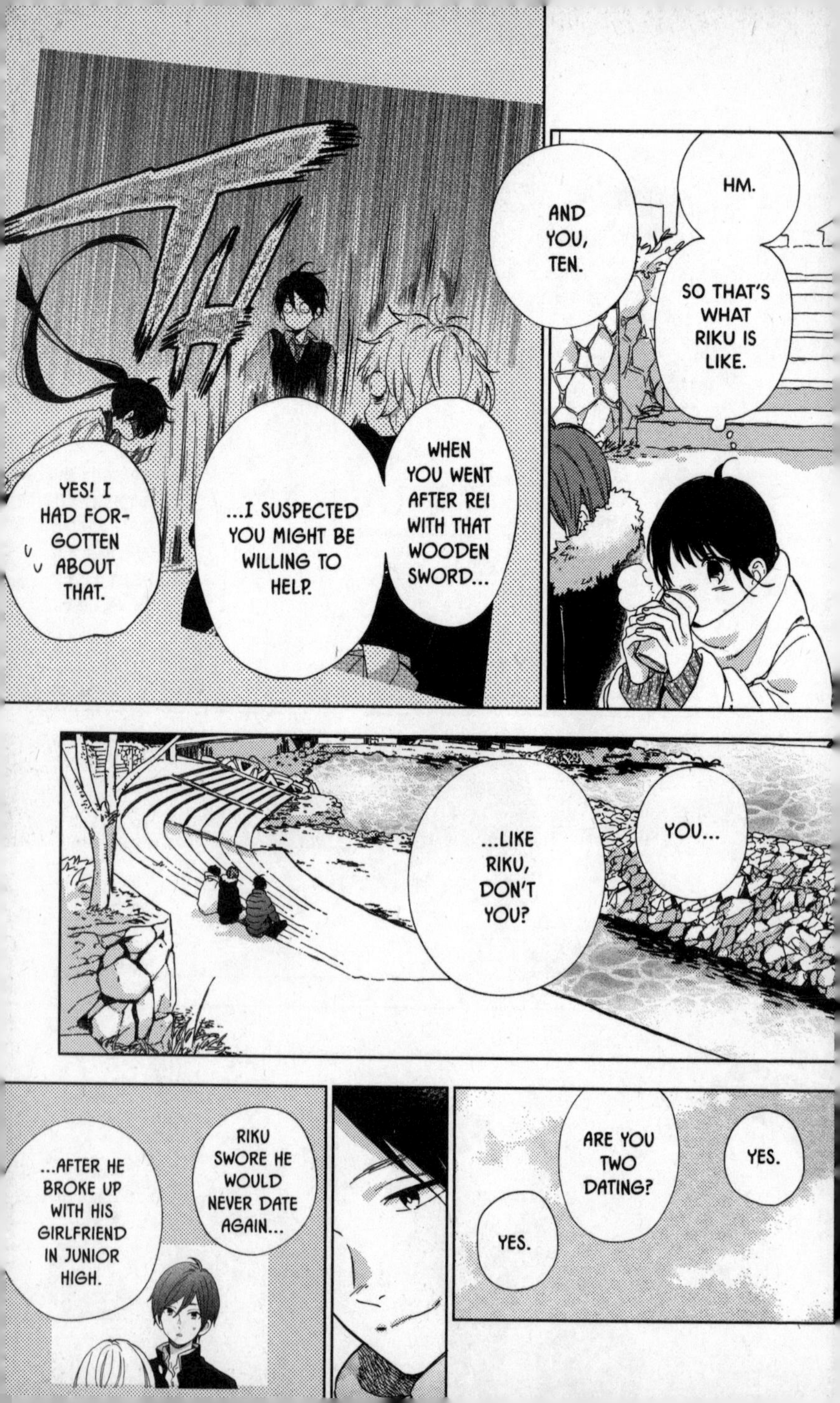
HM.
SO THAT'S WHAT RIKU IS LIKE.
AND YOU, TEN.
WHEN YOU WENT AFTER REI WITH THAT WOODEN SWORD...
...I SUSPECTED YOU MIGHT BE WILLING TO HELP.
YES! I HAD FOR-GOTTEN ABOUT THAT.
YOU...
...LIKE RIKU, DON'T YOU?
ARE YOU TWO DATING?
YES.
YES.
RIKU SWORE HE WOULD NEVER DATE AGAIN...
...AFTER HE BROKE UP WITH HIS GIRLFRIEND IN JUNIOR HIGH.

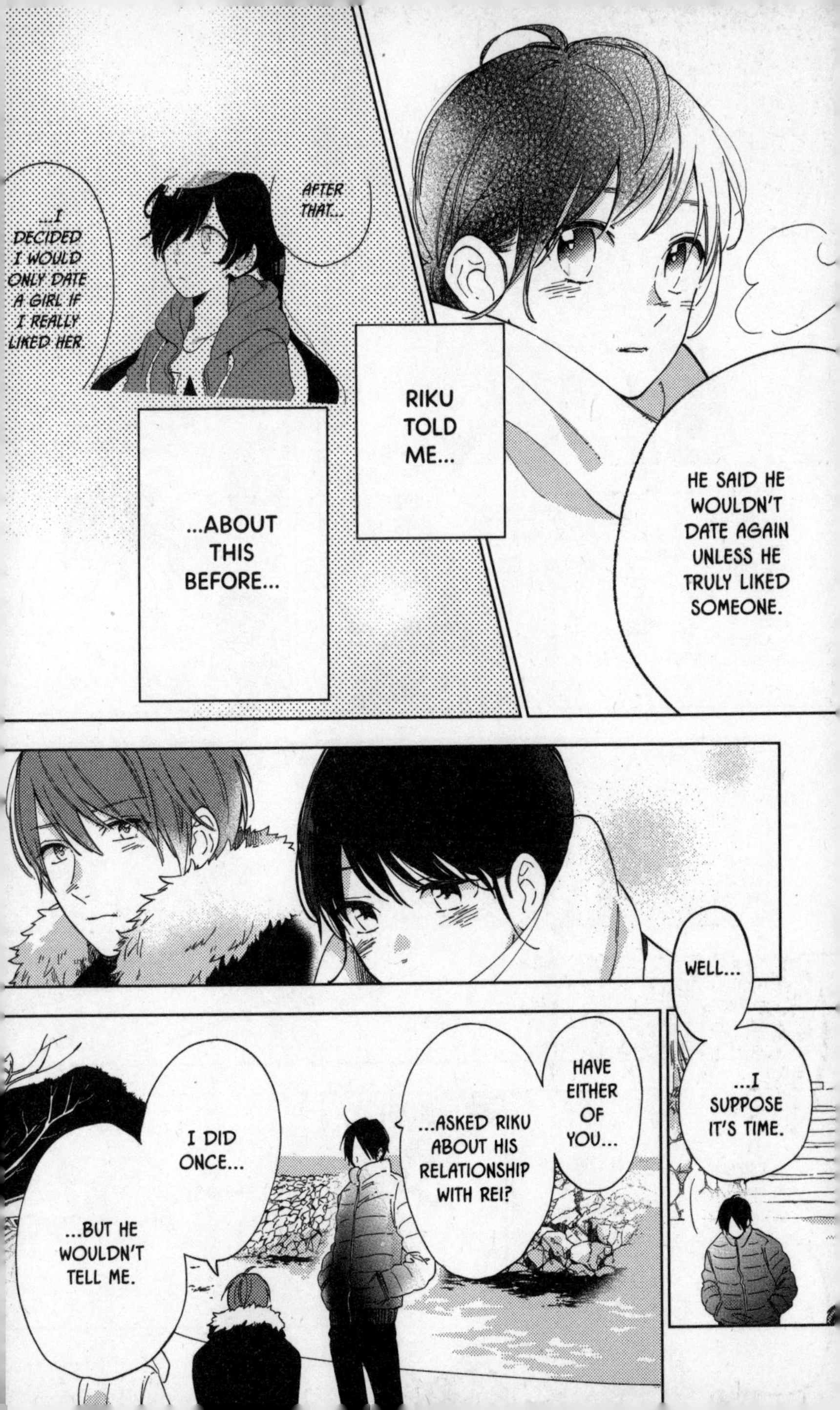
RIKU TOLD ME...
HE SAID HE WOULDN'T DATE AGAIN UNLESS HE TRULY LIKED SOMEONE.
AFTER THAT...
...I DECIDED I WOULD ONLY DATE A GIRL IF I REALLY LIKED HER.
...ABOUT THIS BEFORE...
WELL...
...I SUPPOSE IT'S TIME.
HAVE EITHER OF YOU...
...ASKED RIKU ABOUT HIS RELATIONSHIP WITH REI?
I DID ONCE...
...BUT HE WOULDN'T TELL ME.

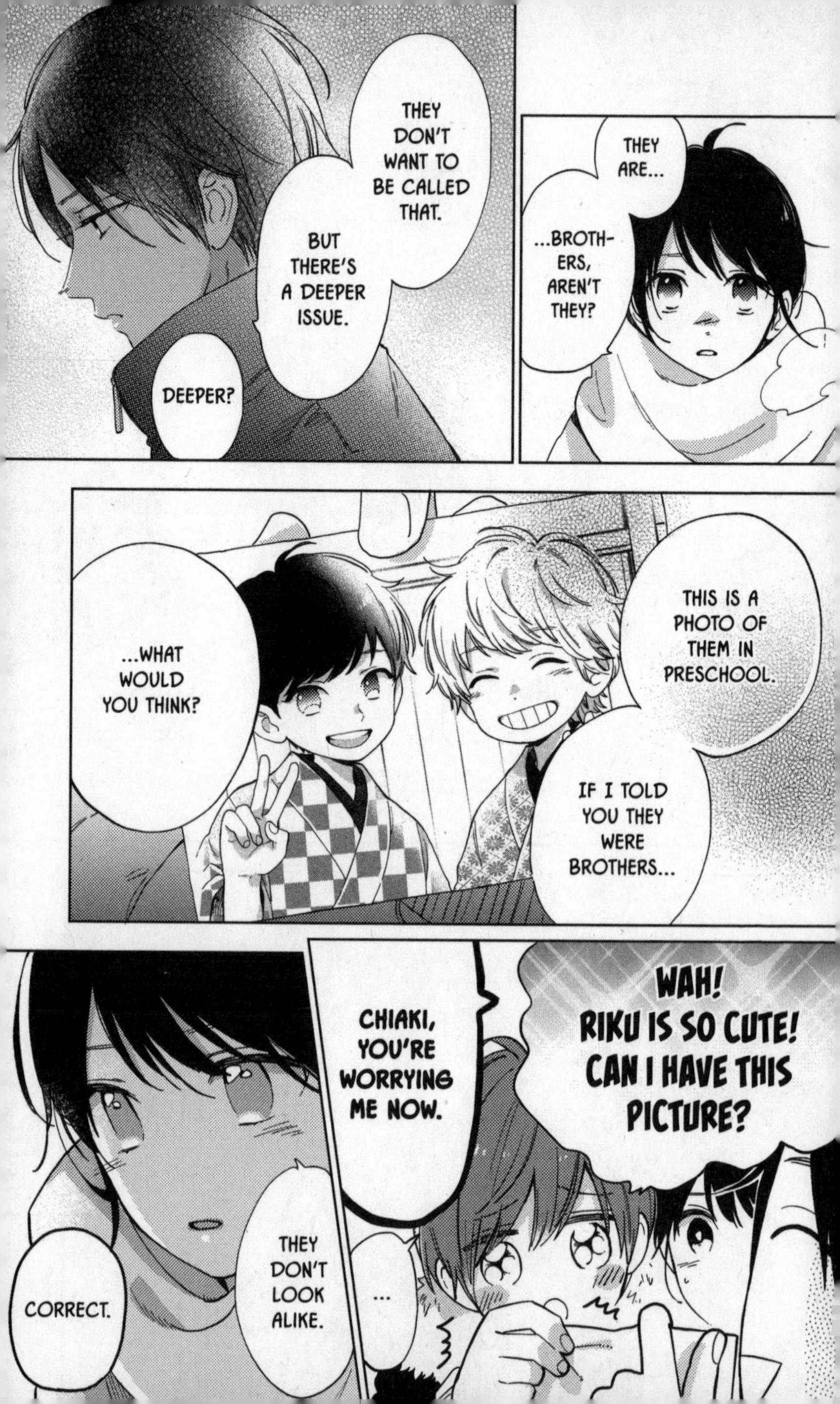
THEY ARE...
...BROTH-ERS, AREN'T THEY?
THEY DON'T WANT TO BE CALLED THAT.
BUT THERE'S A DEEPER ISSUE.
DEEPER?
THIS IS A PHOTO OF THEM IN PRESCHOOL.
IF I TOLD YOU THEY WERE BROTHERS...
...WHAT WOULD YOU THINK?
WAH! RIKU IS SO CUTE! CAN I HAVE THIS PICTURE?
CHIAKI, YOU'RE WORRYING ME NOW.
...
THEY DON'T LOOK ALIKE.
CORRECT.

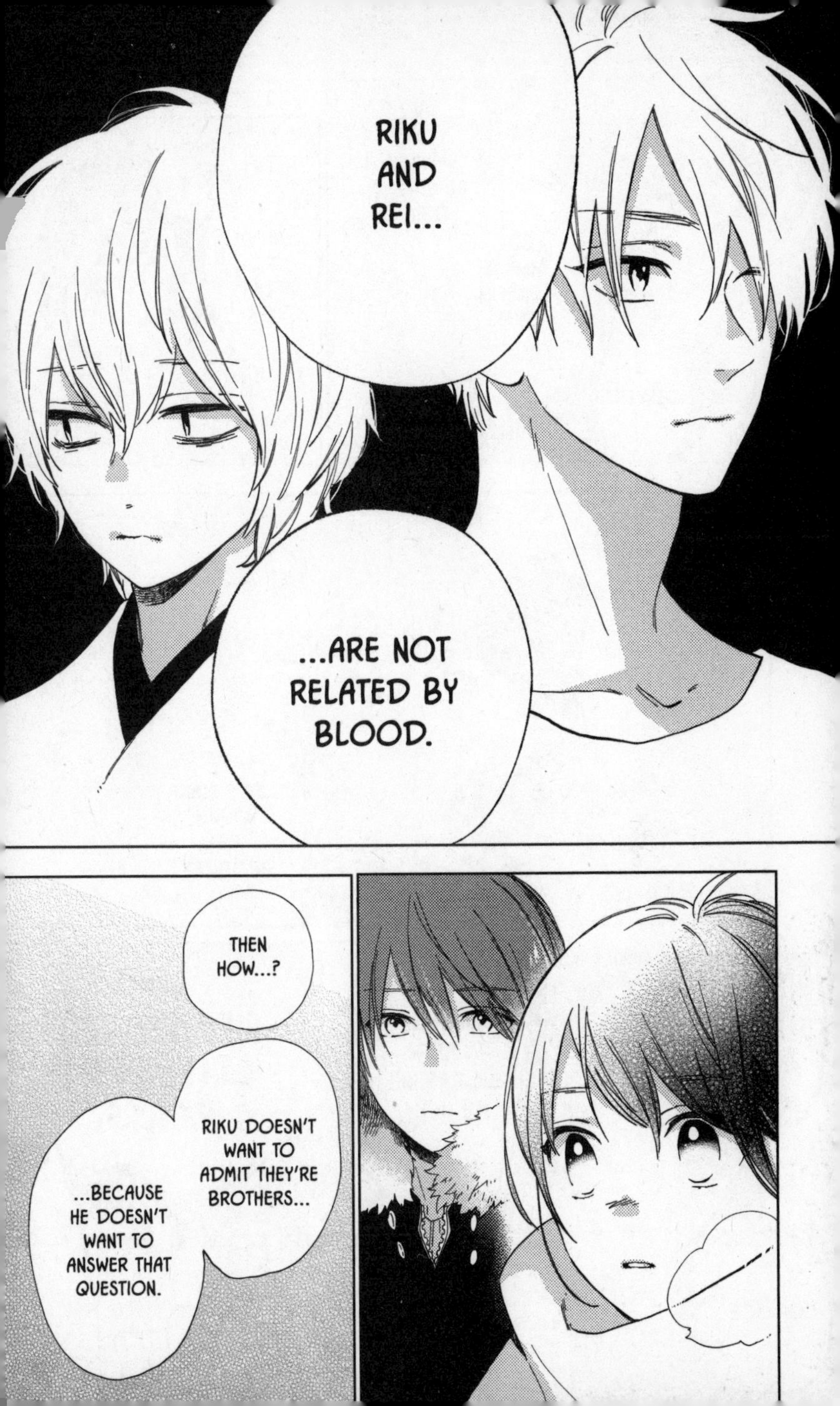
RIKU AND REI...
...ARE NOT RELATED BY BLOOD.
THEN HOW...?
RIKU DOESN'T WANT TO ADMIT THEY'RE BROTHERS...
...BECAUSE HE DOESN'T WANT TO ANSWER THAT QUESTION.

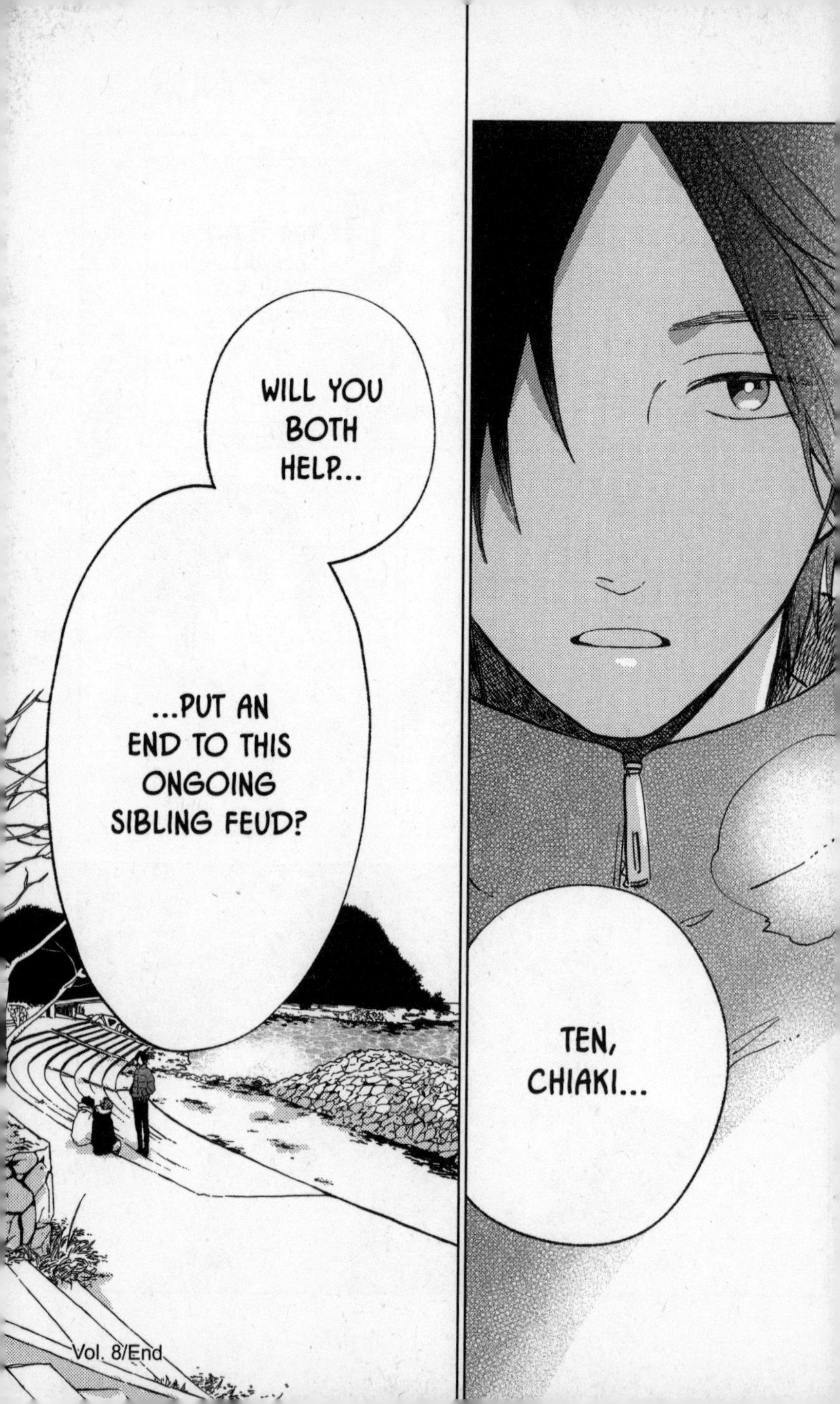
TEN, CHIAKI...
WILL YOU BOTH HELP...
...PUT AN END TO THIS ONGOING SIBLING FEUD?
Vol. 8/End

# BONUS

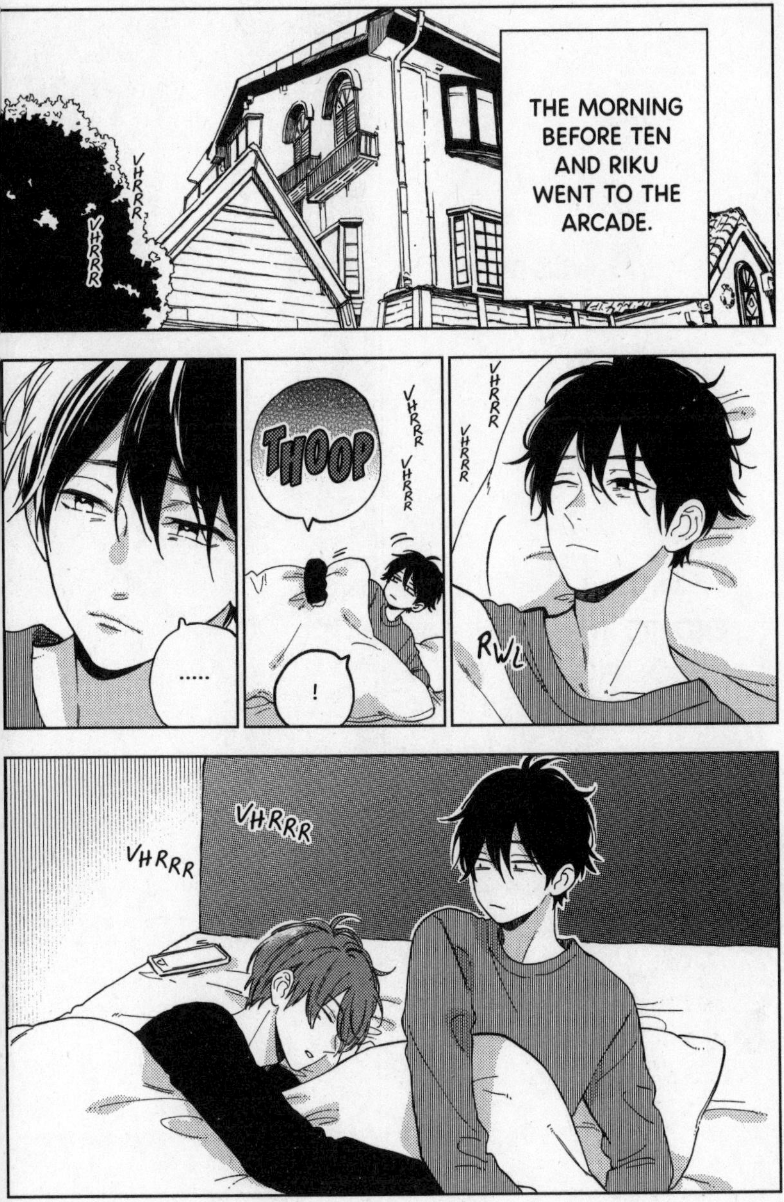

THE MORNING BEFORE TEN AND RIKU WENT TO THE ARCADE.
VHRRR
VHRRR
VHRRR
VHRRR
RWL
VHRRR
VHRRR
THOOP
!
.....
VHRRR
VHRRR

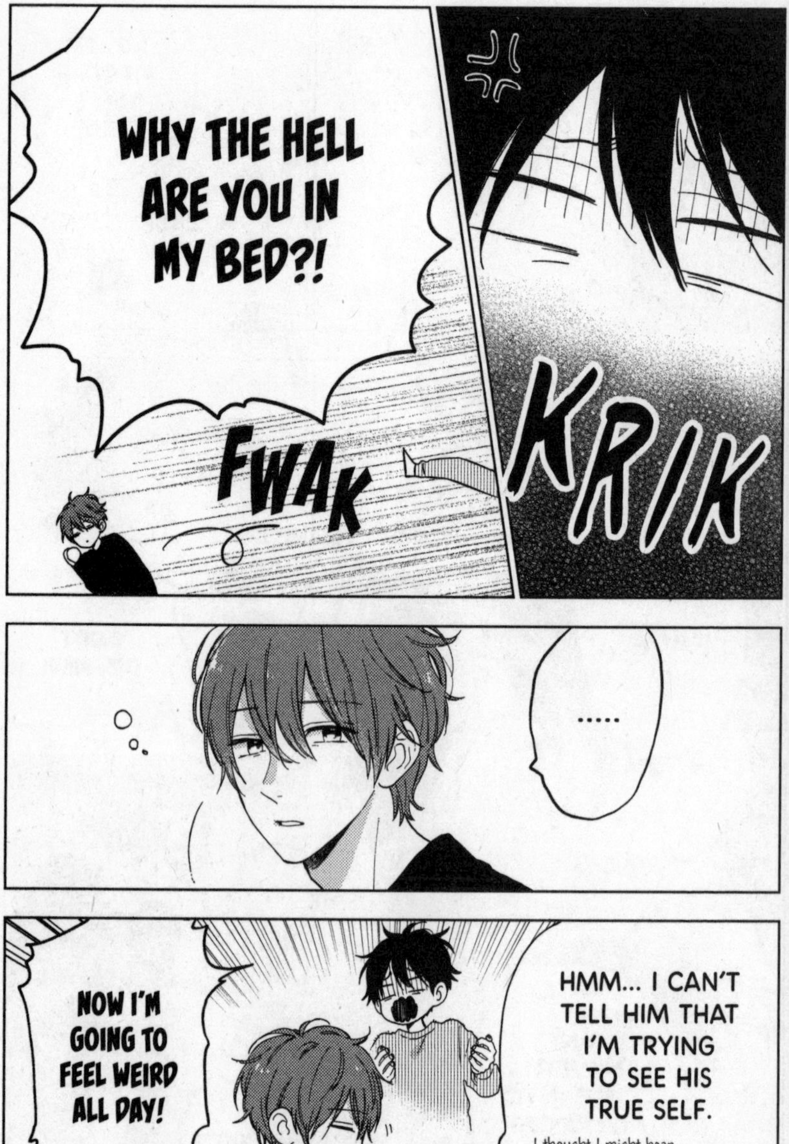
KRIK
WHY THE HELL ARE YOU IN MY BED?!
FWAK
.....
HMM... I CAN'T TELL HIM THAT I'M TRYING TO SEE HIS TRUE SELF.
I thought I might hear him talk in his sleep.
DROWSY
NOW I'M GOING TO FEEL WEIRD ALL DAY!

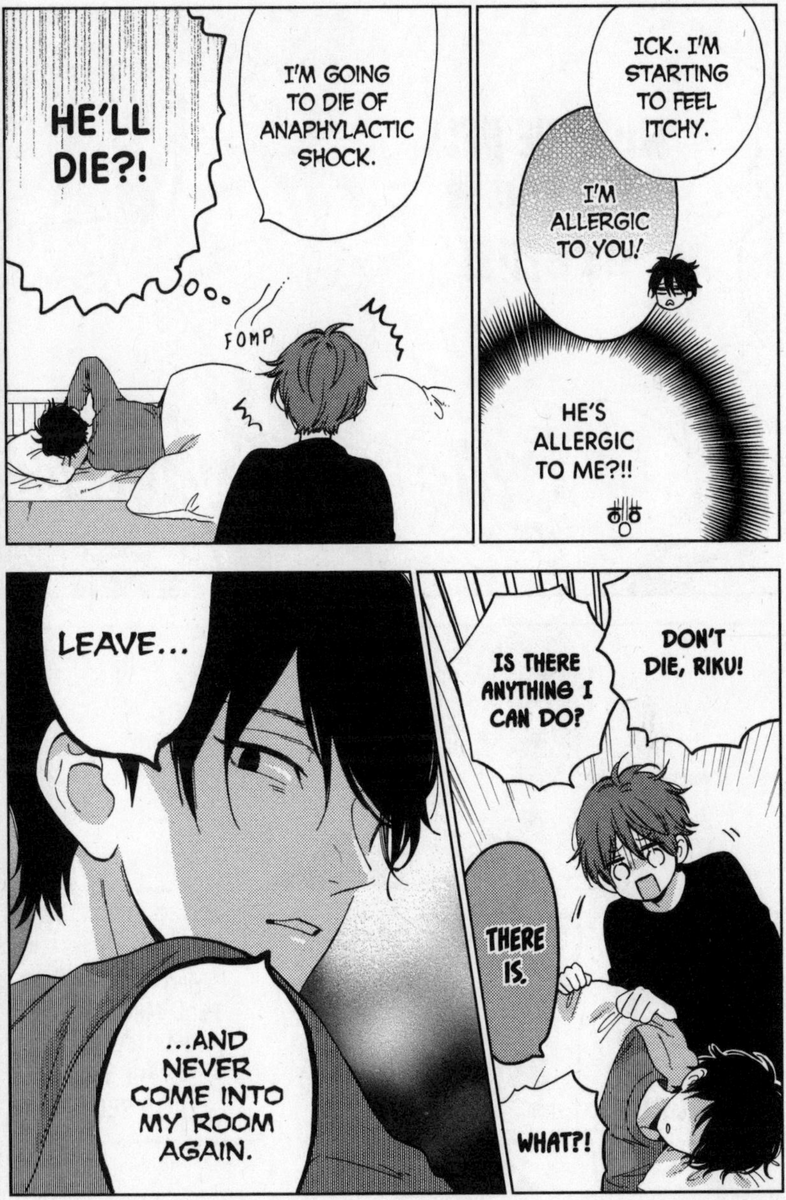
ICK. I'M STARTING TO FEEL ITCHY.
I'M ALLERGIC TO YOU!
HE'S ALLERGIC TO ME?!!
I'M GOING TO DIE OF ANAPHYLACTIC SHOCK.
HE'LL DIE?!
FOMP
DON'T DIE, RIKU!
IS THERE ANYTHING I CAN DO?
THERE IS.
WHAT?!
LEAVE...
...AND NEVER COME INTO MY ROOM AGAIN.

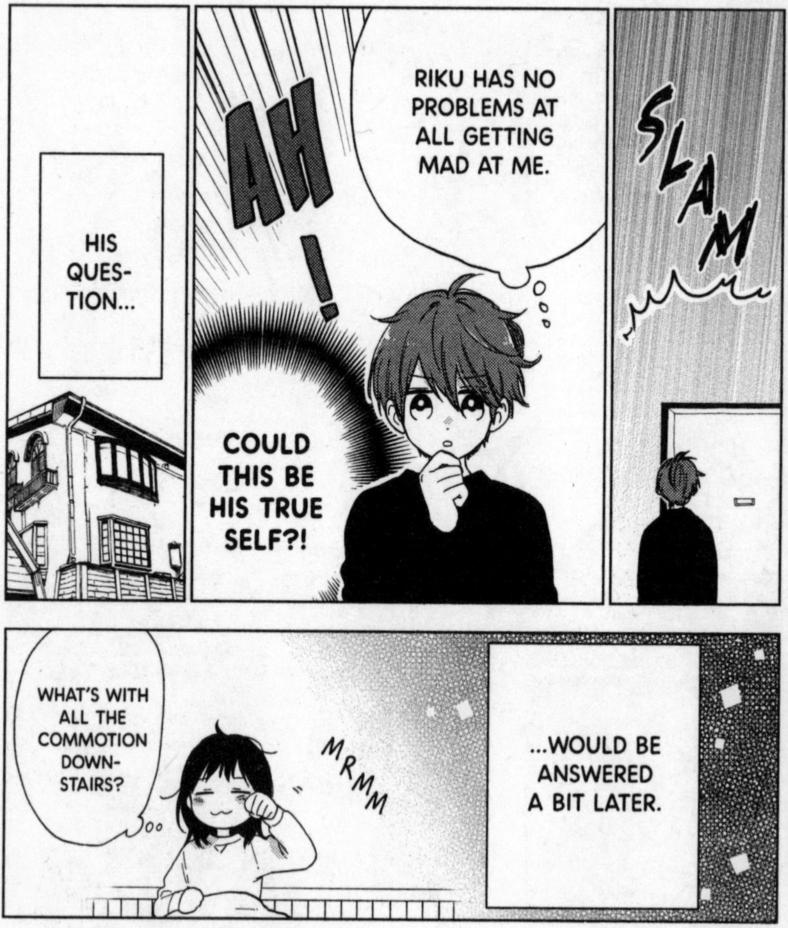
SLAM
RIKU HAS NO PROBLEMS AT ALL GETTING MAD AT ME.
AH!
COULD THIS BE HIS TRUE SELF?!
HIS QUES-TION...
...WOULD BE ANSWERED A BIT LATER.
MRMM
WHAT'S WITH ALL THE COMMOTION DOWN-STAIRS?

## ♥ Special Thanks ♥

- Editor J
- Yasuhisa Kawatani (designer)
- Nao Hamaguchi (assistant)
- Kame-chimu (assistant's helper)
- Everyone involved in producing this work

& all of our readers!!
We hope you will enjoy volume 9!

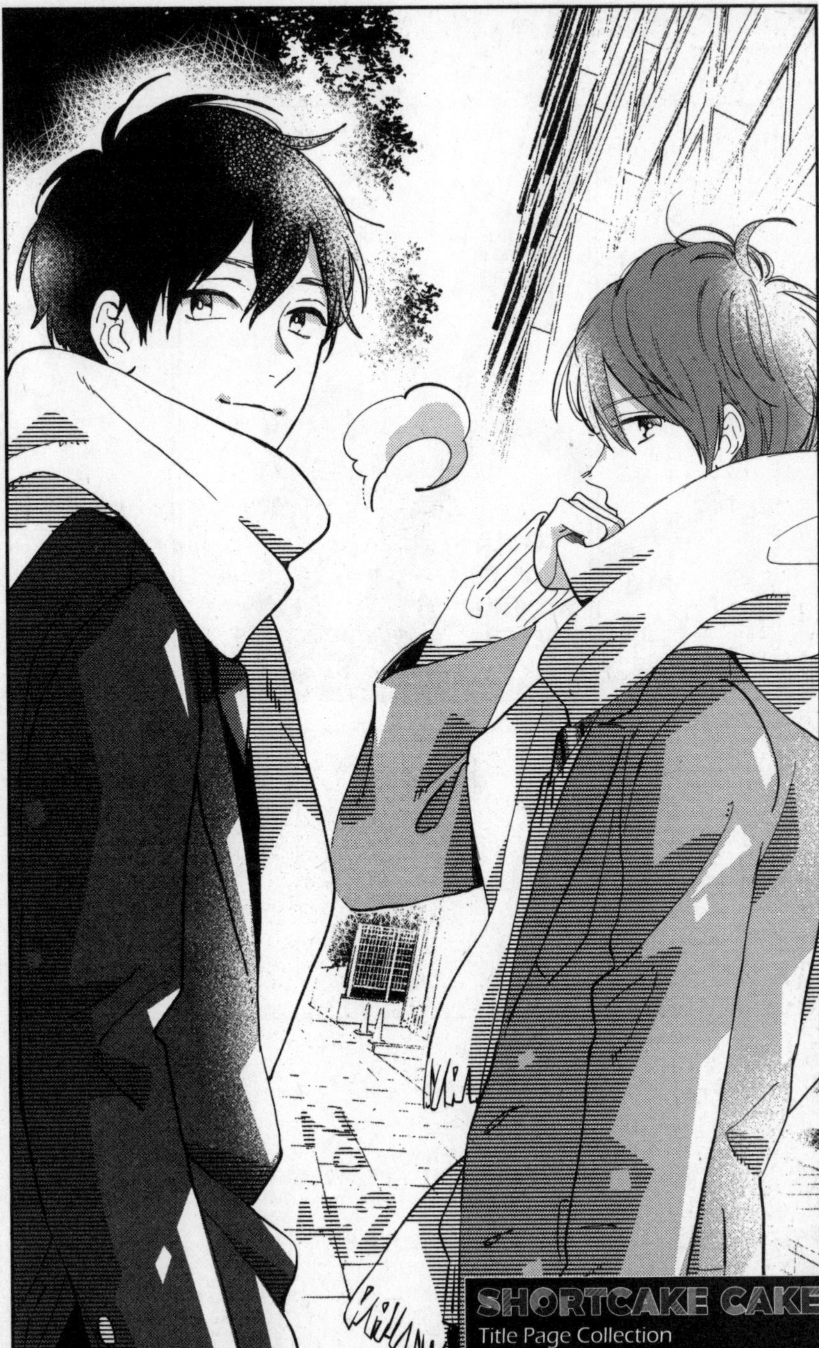
SHORTCAKE CAKE
Title Page Collection
Chapter 42

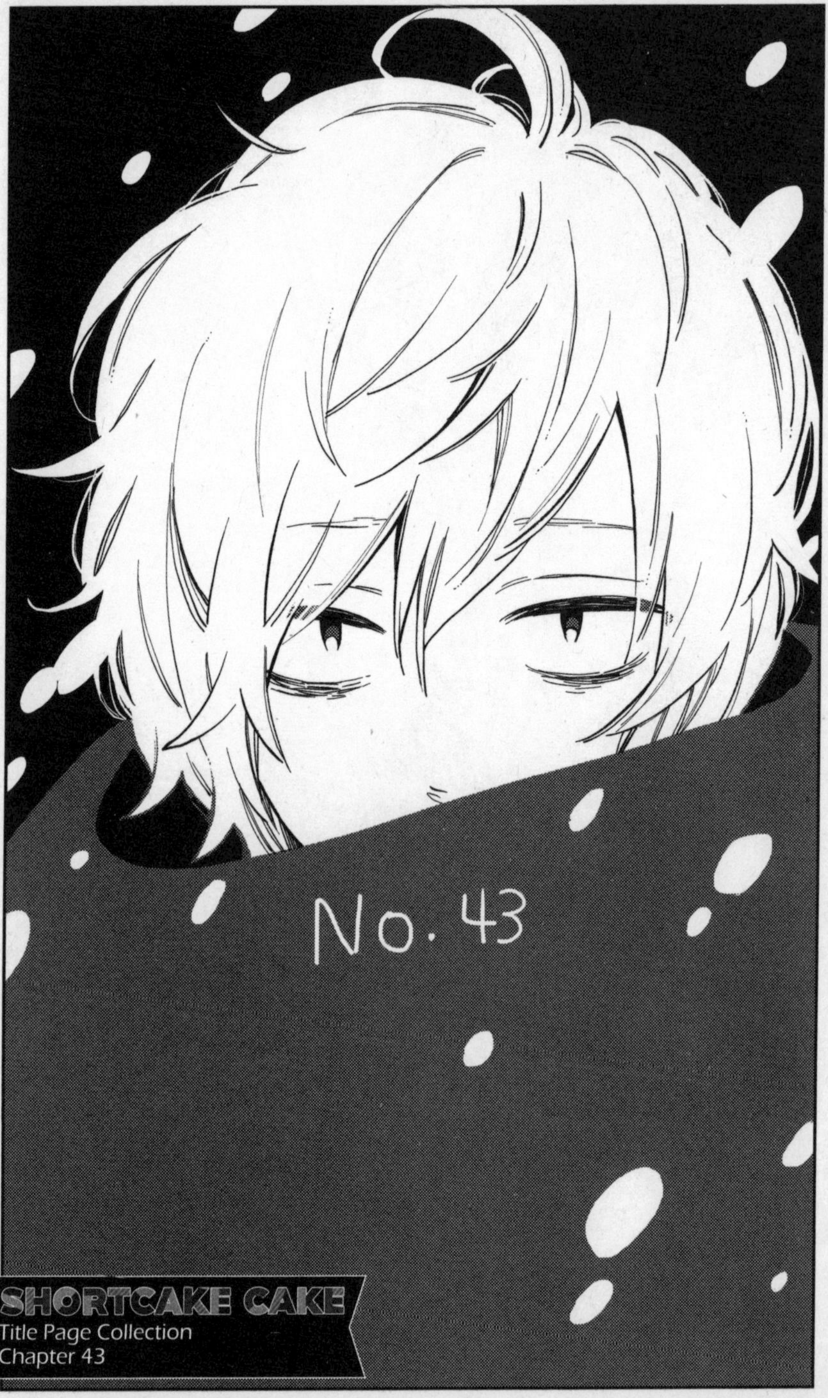
No. 43

SHORTCAKE CAKE
Title Page Collection
Chapter 43

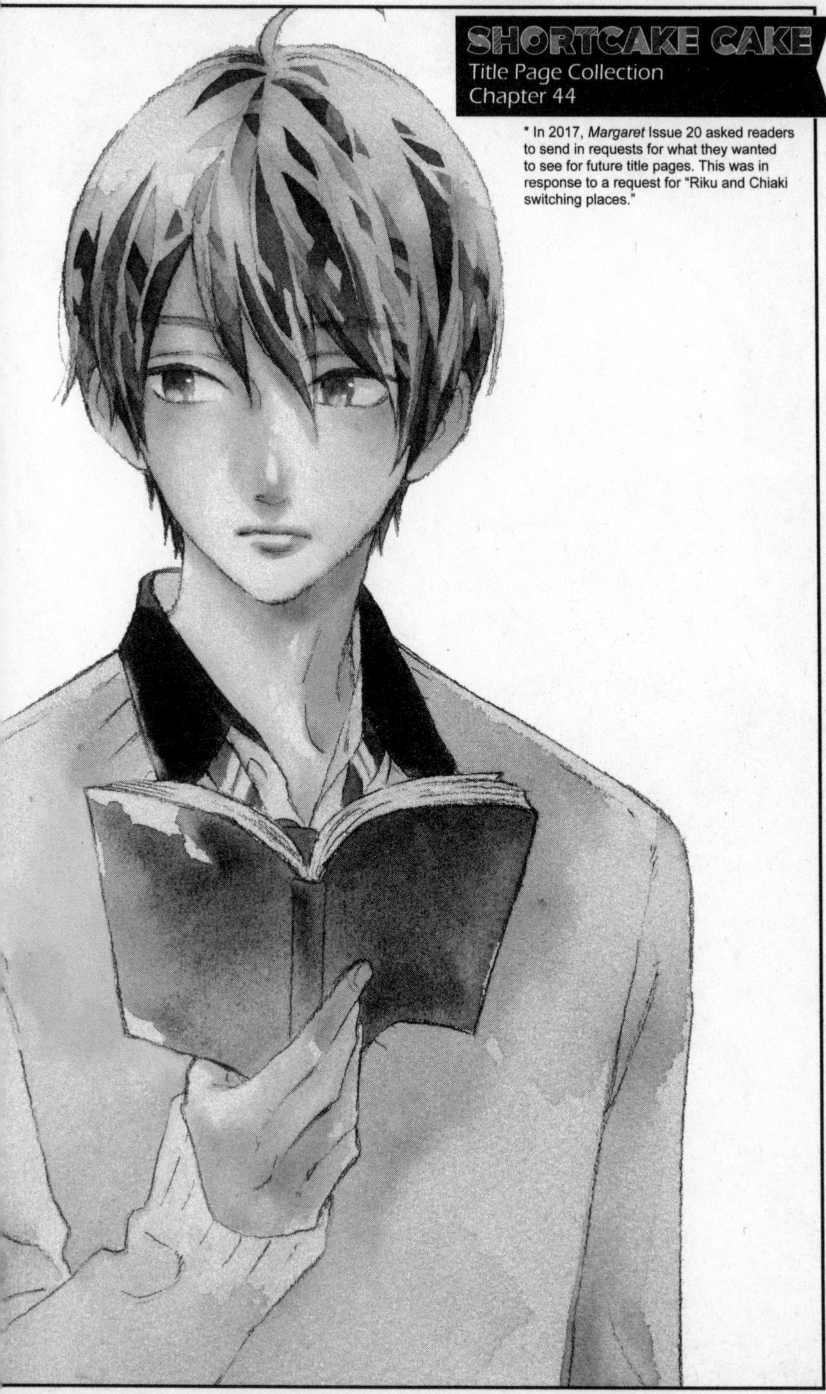

# SHORTCAKE CAKE

Title Page Collection
Chapter 44

* In 2017, *Margaret* Issue 20 asked readers to send in requests for what they wanted to see for future title pages. This was in response to a request for "Riku and Chiaki switching places."

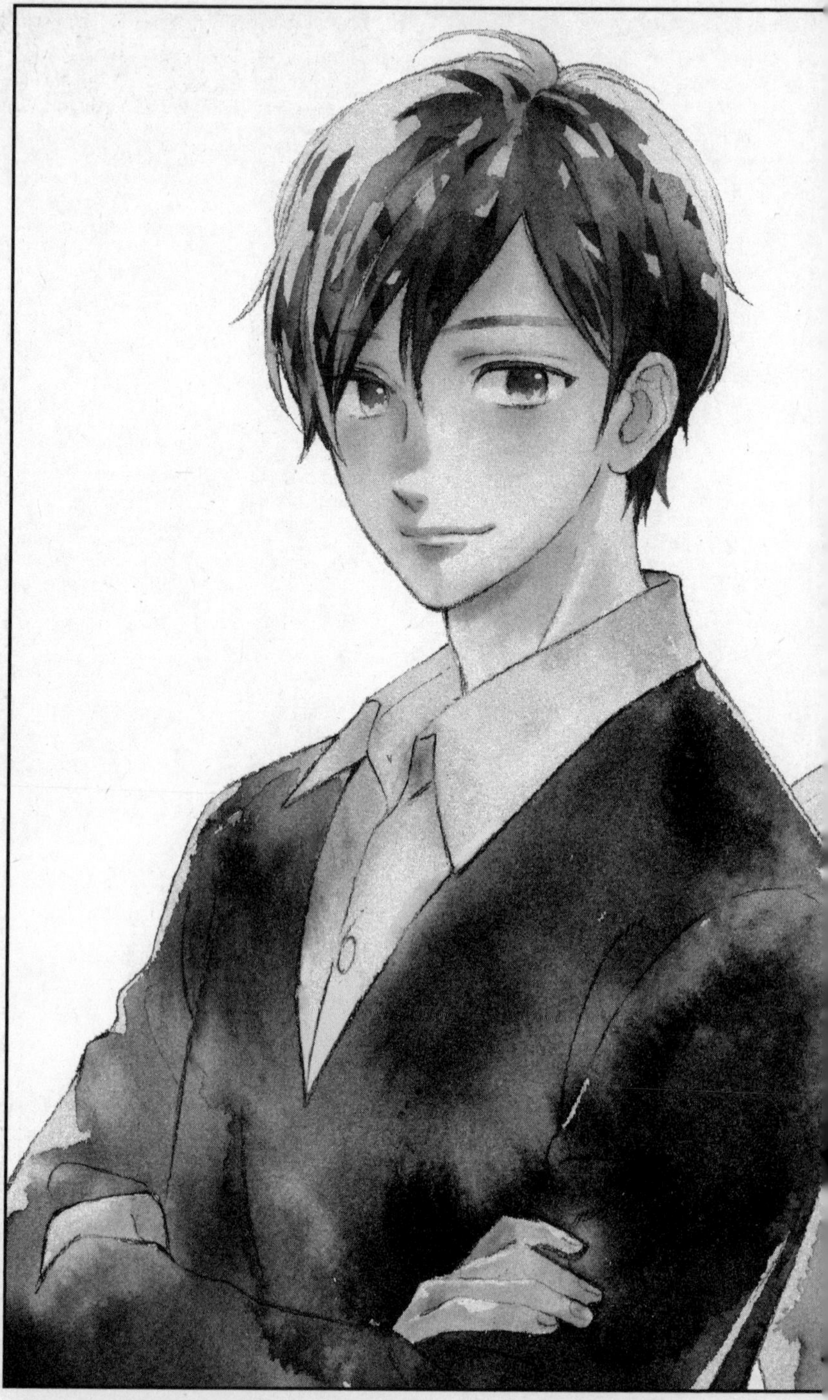

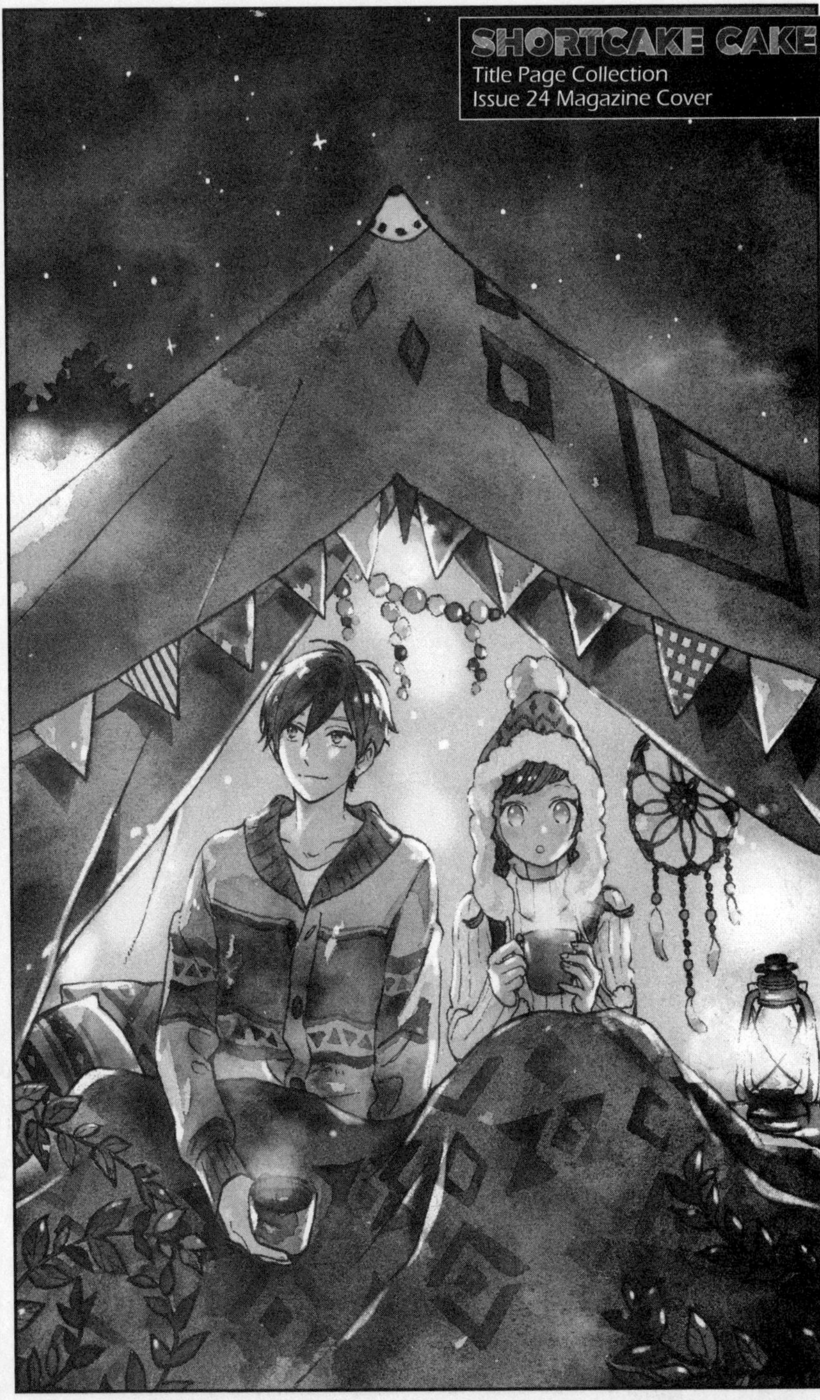

**SHORTCAKE CAKE**
Title Page Collection
Issue 24 Magazine Cover

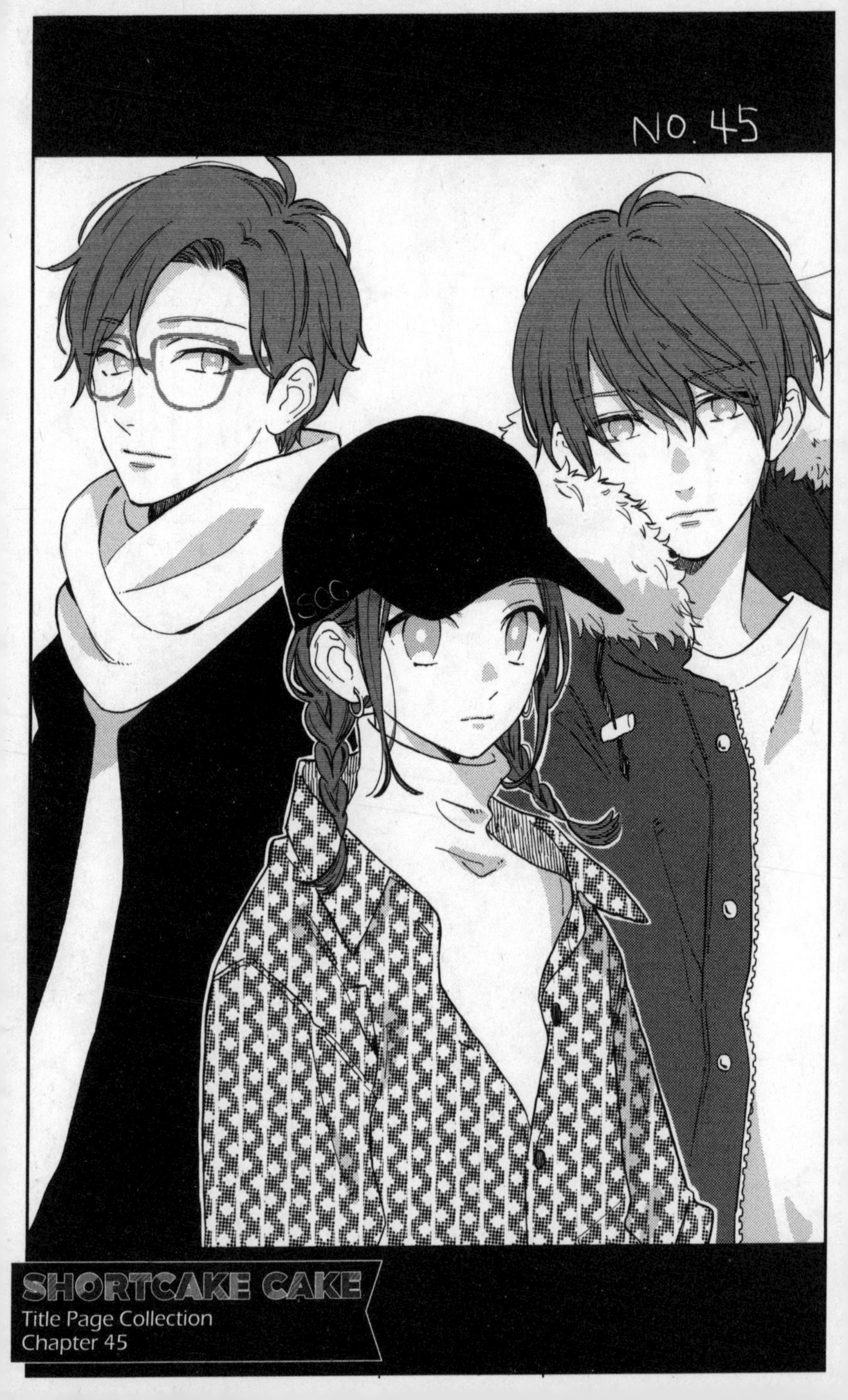
NO. 45

**SHORTCAKE CAKE**
Title Page Collection
Chapter 45

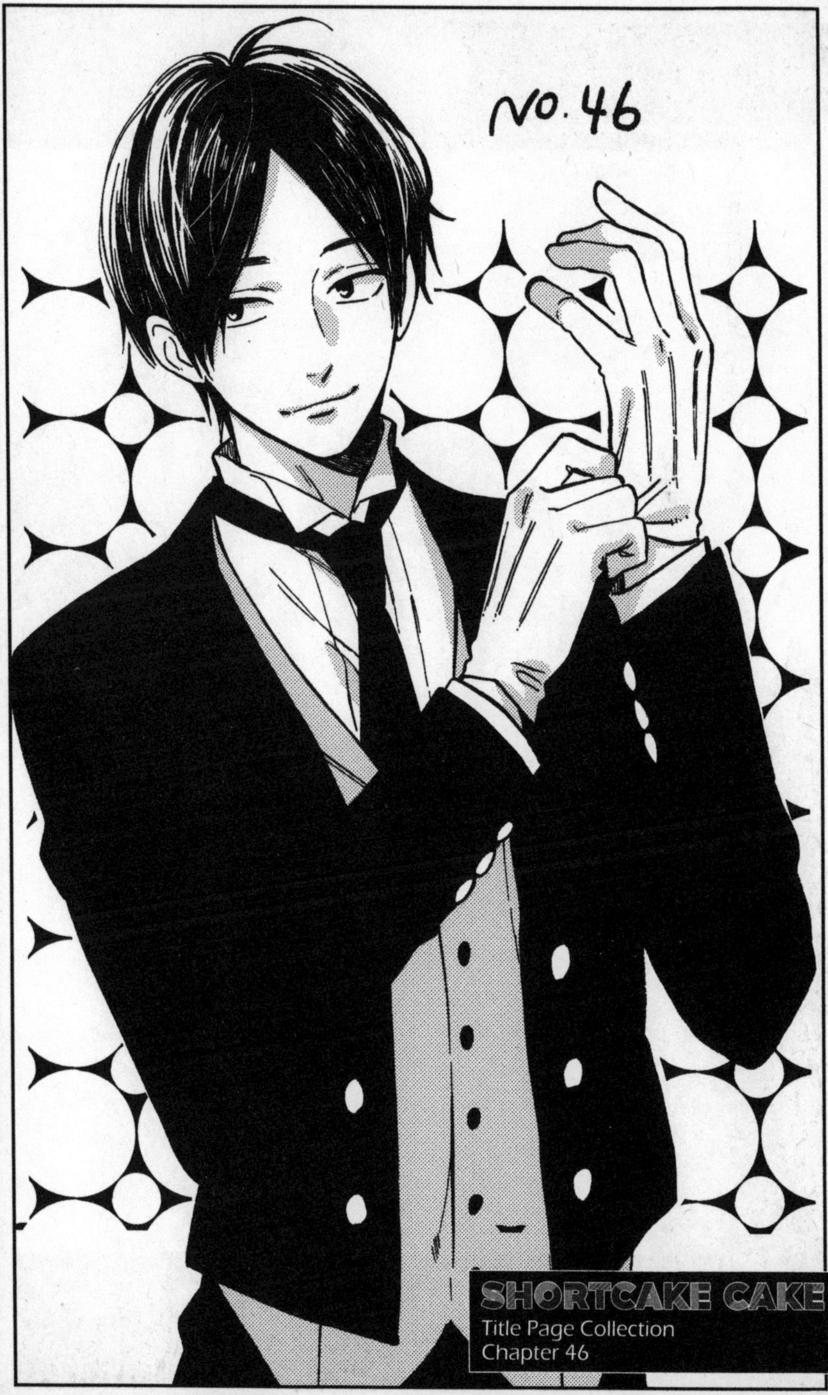
No.46
SHORTCAKE CAKE
Title Page Collection
Chapter 46

**SHORTCAKE CAKE**
Title Page Collection
Chapter 47

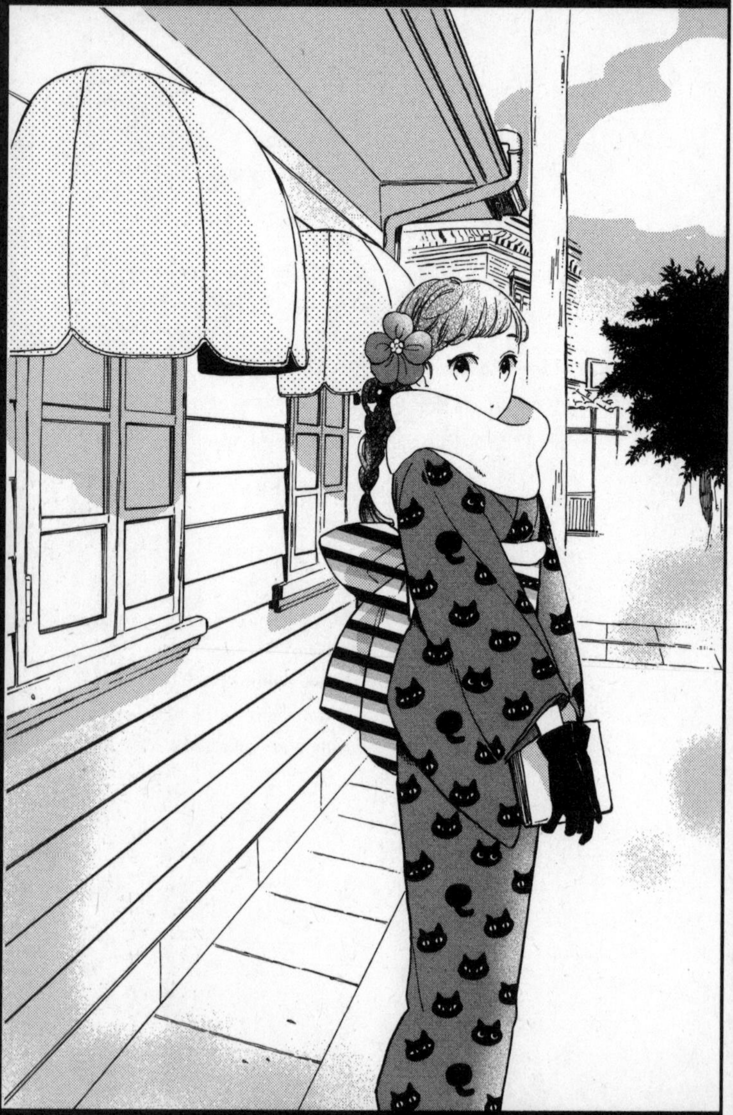

I tried to draw the spread on pages 114 and 115 as if it were Riku's first appearance. I'm excited to finally be able to tell this part of the story. I hope you enjoy it.

**—suu Morishita**

suu Morishita is a creator duo.
The story is by Makiro, and the art is by
Nachiyan. In 2010 they debuted with the
one-shot "Anote Konote." Their works include
*Hibi Chouchou* and *Shortcake Cake*.

VOLUME 8
SHOJO BEAT EDITION

STORY + ART BY **suu Morishita**

TRANSLATION **Emi Louie-Nishikawa**
TOUCH-UP ART + LETTERING **Inori Fukuda Trant**
DESIGN **Shawn Carrico**
EDITOR **Nancy Thistlethwaite**

SHORTCAKE CAKE © 2015 by Suu Morishita
All rights reserved.
First published in Japan in 2015 by SHUEISHA Inc., Tokyo.
English translation rights arranged by SHUEISHA Inc.

The stories, characters and incidents mentioned
in this publication are entirely fictional.

Printed in the U.S.A.

Published by VIZ Media, LLC
P.O. Box 77010
San Francisco, CA 94107

10 9 8 7 6 5 4 3 2 1
First printing, May 2020

viz.com          shojobeat.com

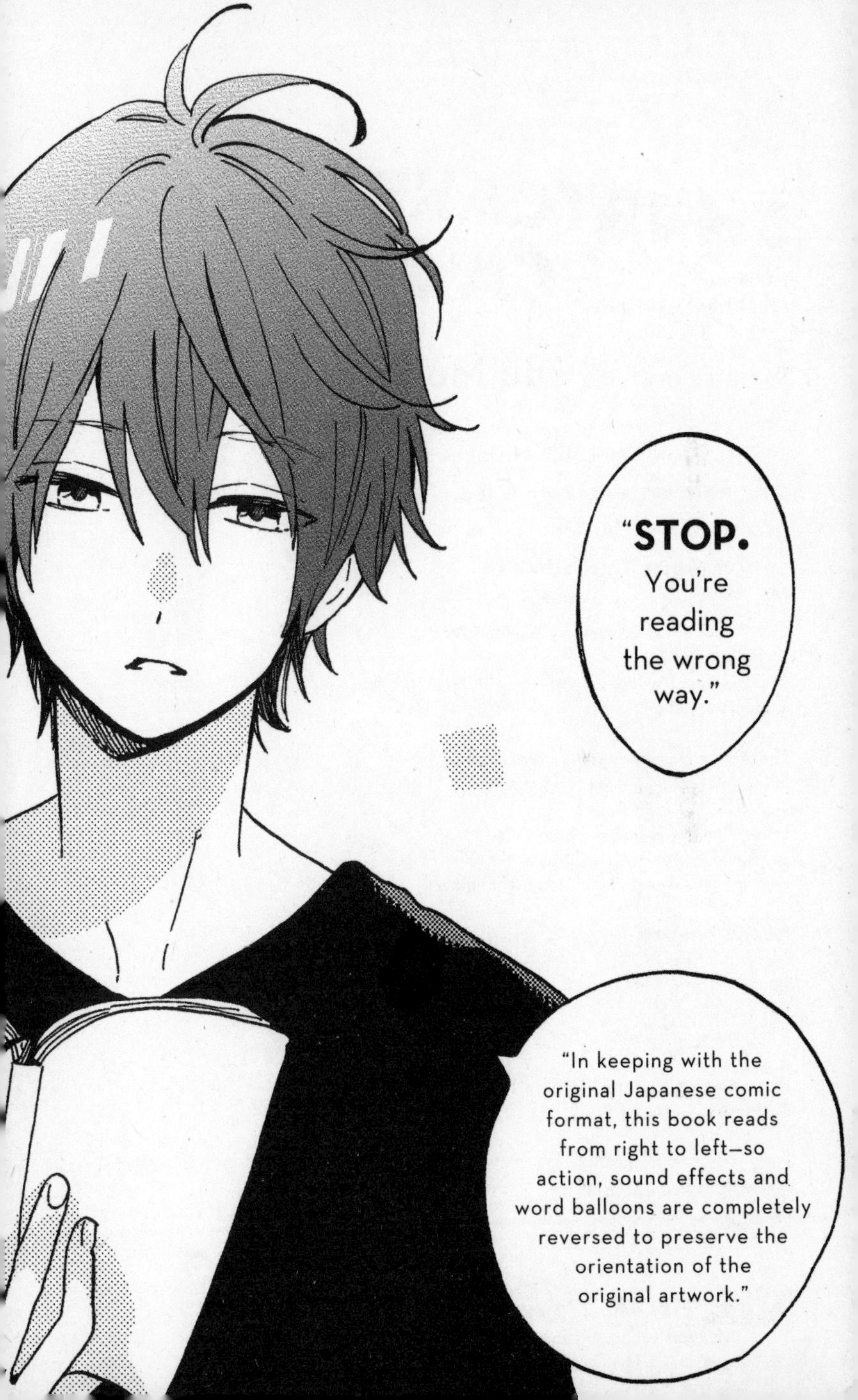
"STOP. You're reading the wrong way."
"In keeping with the original Japanese comic format, this book reads from right to left—so action, sound effects and word balloons are completely reversed to preserve the orientation of the original artwork."